BASIC INCOME PROPERTY APPRAISAL

DONALD R. EPLEY
University of Arkansas

JAMES H. BOYKIN
Virginia Commonwealth University

Addison-Wesley Publishing Company

Reading, Massachusetts • Menlo Park, California
London • Amsterdam • Don Mills, Ontario • Sydney

To Amy, Sara, and Sue;
and Donald P. Chamblee, Sr.

Library of Congress Cataloging in Publication Data

Epley, Donald R., 1942–
Basic income property appraisal.

Includes bibliographical references and index.
1. Real property—Valuation. 2. Real estate investment. 3. Income. I. Boykin, James H., 1936– . II. Title.
HD1387.E6 333.33′2 81-14929
ISBN 0-201-03206-6 AACR2

ISBN 0-201-03206-6
ABCDEFGHIJ-MA-898765432

PREFACE

The purpose of this text is to describe the concepts and techniques that are the basic tools of income-property appraisal. This volume contains several unique features.

Approximately one-half of the material is a discussion of concepts and procedures, and the remaining one-half is worked problems based on many different property types and applications. Thus the book provides material for the instructor and/or student who favors discussion, solved problems, or both.

We have attempted to offer something for all levels of users. This balance between the written material and the solved problems makes the book suitable for several levels of users and can be used in a graduate seminar, an undergraduate course, or a professional development-continuing education course.

An effort was made to require a level of understanding of the concepts and techniques that is consistent with the material presented in the current professional literature. Professional journals that are read by practitioners such as *The Appraisal Journal, The Real Estate Appraiser and Analyst, The Assessor's Journal,* and *The Appraisal Review Journal* are used as references.

Assumptions, tools, and derivations, not covered in other appraisal texts, are explained here. This material has been integrated into several chapters and appropriate appendices.

The symbols used are largely consistent with those used by the American Institute of Real Estate Appraisers and the Society of Real Estate Appraisers. Although some differences do exist between the sets of symbols adopted by the two groups, we think that we have selected an appropriate compromise set from the two that will not confuse the reader. In addition, definitions of terms and concepts were checked whenever appropriate with the recommended guide titled *Real Estate Appraisal Terminology* by Byrl Boyce.

A fully developed illustrative narrative appraisal covering an office building in San Antonio, Texas, was included as a capstone for many of the techniques described earlier. This report was written and provided by Mr. Scruggs Love, Jr., MAI, SRPA, San Antonio, Texas. We are indebted to Mr. Love and his client, Mr. William B. Stevenson, Sierra Real Estate Equity Trust, for giving their permission to publish a well-prepared example of an actual appraisal.

Selected keystroke examples are included in certain chapters using the HP 38 series calculator as opposed to a lengthy computer program simulating cash flows and expenses that produce after-tax cash flows and an internal rate of return. Our rationale for this choice covers several points. First, many practicing appraisers have already committed to electronic equipment in their offices that includes a program for real estate analysis. Second, there are several good real estate analysis programs that have been published in inexpensive documents from different sources that can be purchased and adapted to fit equipment already being used. Third, our objective is to instruct the reader on the basic concepts and techniques as opposed to a lengthy discussion of market or project analysis, which would involve a computer program and simulation of income levels, expenses, and resulting rates of return.

In selected areas, we have illustrated important concepts in the literature and documents published by the professional appraisal organizations. For example, Chapter 5 on the cost approach illustrates a difference in the measuring tools recommended by the AIREA and the SREA for estimating accrued depreciation through the breakdown approach. Our purpose in these situations is to inform.

The text is organized around a theme of presenting the material in a "need-to-know" order as the practitioner would encounter a need for it in an appraisal assignment. To accomplish this objective, the material is organized and presented in the following eleven modules:

Module I:	Basis of Value
Module II:	Market Analysis
Module III:	Valuation Process and Reports
Module IV:	Direct Sales Comparison Approach to Value
Module V:	Cost Approach to Value
Module VI:	Tools for Income Valuation
Module VII:	Income Approach to Value
Module VIII:	Renovation Analysis
Module IX:	Final Review and Reconciliation
Module X:	Special Cases
Module XI:	Illustrated Narrative Appraisal

For an undergraduate level course on income-property appraising, the book can be used as the sole text in combination with a set of tables, such as the *Ellwood Tables* (Ballinger Press). For a course at the graduate level, the book could be used with the *Ellwood Tables,* a readings book such as *Readings in Income Property Appraising* (AIREA), and a short reading list emphasizing the instructor's preferences, which could be readily compiled from the Additional Readings at the end of each chapter. A professional development course could use the *Ellwood Tables* and probably would cover only selected portions of the text. Some instructors may want to utilize the *American Institute of Real Estate Appraisers Financial Tables* published by the Financial Publishing Company. A hand calculator could be required for all levels of instruction.

A number of people have provided helpful comments. These include Frank Faulkner and Karen Trisko of the Society of Real Estate Appraisers; Terrell Oetzel, MAI, of the American Institute of Real Estate Appraisers; Douglas Bible, Old Dominion University; Robert Kelley, CPA, University of Arkansas; Scruggs Love, Jr., MAI, SRPA, San Antonio, Texas; Kenneth Lusht, SRPA, Pennsylvania State University; Felica Rocca, MAI, SREA, Philadelphia; Anthony Sanders, Ohio State University; and Robert Zerbst, MAI, SRPA, Southern Methodist University.

A number of organizations and journals gave permission to reprint their material. These include *The Appraiser* and *The Appraisal Journal* of the American Institute of Real Estate Appraisers; *Farm and Land REALTOR;* Federal Home Loan Mortgage Corporation; Federal National Mortgage Association; Hewlett-Packard Company; Marshall-Swift Publication Company; and *The Real Estate Appraiser and Analyst* of the Society of Real Estate Appraisers.

We feel that this text has three major strengths. First, it is pedagogically sound. Second, it is teachable because of its organization and many problems covering various properties, and the inclusion of Learning Objectives, Questions for Review, Additional Readings, and Important Terms and Phrases within each chapter. Third, it is readable.

Our intention in writing this text is to inform the reader. It should be viewed as a document for study, review, source of helpful information, and critical thought that collectively will expand the reader's frontier of knowledge. It should not be viewed as a substitute for sound professional advice covering a specific market situation.

The usual caveat applies concerning the accuracy of the material and responsibility of the authors.

March 1982

D.R.E.
J.H.B.

SIX FUNCTIONS OF $1

Present Value (PV)	current dollar investment; sometimes called *present worth.*
$V^n = 1/S^n$	*present value of $1* that is collected at a future date and discounted at an interest rate for *n* periods.
$a_{\overline{n}\vert} = (1 - V^n)/i$	*present value of $1 per period paid* in *n* equal installments over *n* equal periods and discounted at the rate *i*.
$1/a_{\overline{n}\vert} = i/(i - V^n)$	present value of *the installment that will repay a future sum of $1 with interest* in a given number of equal periods *n* at the interest rate *i*.
Future Value (FV)	future dollar investment; sometimes called the *compound amount.*
$S^n = (1 + i)^n$	*the future value to which $1* will grow over *n* equal periods at the interest rate *i*.
$S_{\overline{n}\vert} = (S^n - 1)/i$	*the future value of $1* per period with interest over *n* equal periods at the interest rate *i*.
$1/S_{\overline{n}\vert} = i/(S^n - 1)$	the future value of $1 that will result from equal periodic payments over *n* equal periods at the interest rate *i*. Called the *sinking fund factor.*

SYMBOLS

a = An annualizer or conversion factor such as a sinking fund factor

ADS = Annual Debt Service

app = Appreciation as a fraction of original price

ATCF = After-Tax Cash Flow

B = Bldg. %

BOP = Payments made at the *beginning of the period*

C = Mortgage coefficient

CTO = Cash Throw Off (before-tax cash flow)

DB = Declining Balance depreciation

dep = Depreciation as a fraction of original price

DSCR = Debt Service Coverage Ratio

EOP = Payments made at the *end of the period*

f = Mortgage constant (R_M)

FMRR = Financial Management Rate of Return

f_p = Annual constant that is required to amortize the entire loan within the projection period p

G = Income adjustment factor

g = Compound growth rate

GIM = Gross Income Multiplier (GRM)

I = Income (in the basic equation)

i = Effective interest per dollar per period; mortgage interest rate

i_L = Used with the FMRR, represents the after-tax sale investment rate that may be earned on the relatively riskless investments

i_R = Used with the FMRR, represents the after-tax risk rate that may be earned on competitive investments

IRR = Internal Rate of Return
I_S = Stabilized income
J = Income adjustment factor
M = Loan to value ratio
$1 - M$ = Equity to value ratio
n = Number of compounding periods; term of the mortgage
NOI = Net Operating Income
P = Percentage of mortgage paid off in projection period
p = Projection period or contemplated period of ownership
pay = A series of equal dollar payments over n equals periods
R = Capitalization rate (general)
r = Basic rate (weighted average of two rates adjusted for equity build-up)
R_B = Building capitalization rate
R_E = Equity capitalization rate (equity dividend)
Rev = Reversion (proceeds of resale)
R_L = Land capitalization rate
R_M = Mortgage capitalization rate (mortgage constant) (f)
R_{M_p} = Mortgage cap rate for the projection period p (Same as f_p)
R_0 = Overall capitalization rate
SL = Straight-Line depreciation
SOYD = Sum of Years Digits Depreciation
t = Tax rate
t_g = Capital gain tax rate
Δ = Change in value
V = Value
V_B = Building value
V_E = Equity value
V_L = Land value
V_M = Mortgage value
V_0 = Property value
Y = Yield (discount) rate
Y_E = Equity yield rate
Y_0 = Property yield rate
Y_t = After-tax equity yield

CONTENTS

MODULE I
Basis of Value

Any appraisal student must learn early the basics of market demand and supply relationships. Value in use and value in exchange should be explained within this context and related to the market demand concept. The differences among market price, market value, most probable selling price, and going concern value should be explained here also. Many of these concepts are used to dispel common myths and cliches concerning income-producing properties. Once completed, the student has a rudimentary knowledge of market forces and can fit concepts like market value and most probable selling price within these forces.

CHAPTER 1

LEARNING OBJECTIVES

When a student finishes this chapter, he or she should be able to:

- Explain the relationship between value in use and value in exchange and evaluate their role in estimating the value of property.
- Explain the role of highest and best use, anticipation, and substitution.
- Explain and give examples of demand stock, demand flow, supply stock, and supply flow.
- Use the demand and supply graphs to explain how a specific type of property within a specific geographical area and during a predetermined time period possesses a certain value.
- Discuss the concepts of market price, market value, most probable selling price, and going concern value.
- Explain the role of the professional appraisal organizations.
- Discuss several cliches and myths that exist about income-producing property and appraisers.

Why Property Is Valuable

IMPORTANT TERMS AND PHRASES

anticipation: The value or worth of property is the present value of all future benefits.

appraiser: One who estimates value; specifically, one who possesses the necessary qualifications, ability, and experience to execute or direct the appraisal of real or personal property.

demand flows: The value in use and value in exchange motives to purchase property in the current market.

demand stocks: The summation of the buyers' desires to buy and hold property.

going concern value: An intangible asset caused by the presence (in a profitable firm) of marketing efficiencies, operating efficiencies, avoidance of start-up costs, and administrative efficiencies.

highest and best use: That reasonable and probable use that will support the highest present value as defined as of the effective date of the appraisal.

market demand: The relationship between the market price and the quantity demanded.

market price: The transaction price actually observed in the market.

market supply: The relationship between price and the quantity offered for sale.

market value: The highest price in terms of money that a property will bring in a competitive and open market under all conditions requisite to a fair sale, the buyer and seller, each acting prudently, knowledgeably, and assuming the price is not affected by undue stimulus.

most probable selling price: The price for which a property would most probably sell if exposed to the market for a reasonable time under market conditions prevailing as of the date of the appraisal.

substitution: A rational prudent buyer will pay no more for property than the cost of acquiring an equally desirable substitute on the open market.

supply flows: The sellers' desires to offer for sale on the current market some portion of the total amount in existence.

supply stock: The total amount of the property type in question within a predetermined location and during a predetermined time period.

value in exchange: The amount of goods and services or purchasing power which an informed purchaser would offer in exchange for an economic good under given market conditions.

value in use: The value of an economic good to its owner-user which is based upon productivity (income, utility, or amenity form) of the economic good to a specific individual.

The purpose of this chapter is to introduce the reader to the basic market factors that influence and determine value. In addition, common cliches concerning income-producing properties are discussed and evaluated. The professional appraisal organizations that designate members who have completed a prescribed course of education, passed a series of examinations, and demonstrated various terms and forms of field experience are discussed.

VALUE IN USE AND VALUE IN EXCHANGE

The demand for property may be thought to be composed of two elements: value in use and value in exchange.

Value in Use

Value in use, defined by Byrl Boyce, is "the value of an economic good to its owner-user which is based upon productivity (privacies in income, utility, or amenity form) of the economic good to a specific individual."[1] The owner of the property wants to hold the property for some future benefit in the form of income, tax deductions, or intangible benefits such as recreation. In addition, there may be a lack of data to support an income or market data approach in estimating value.[2]

Value in use is a *utility for a particular owner*. It is usually measured by some type of cost such as book cost, original cost, or replacement cost.[3] An example of value in use might be a 1945 structure that can produce a specific product at a profit for the owner. If the building were placed for sale on the open market, it might have no utility for any potential buyers. The use value exists for a particular owner who can make a profit by producing a specific product in that building.

Value in Exchange

Value in exchange is one component of demand for the purchase of property, which is defined as "the amount of goods and services or purchasing power which an informed purchaser would offer in exchange for an economic good under given market conditions."[4] Value in exchange represents the utility that the product has to a potential buyer in the market. It may be estimated by deriving the market value[5] or the most probable selling price.[6] Each is discussed later.

HIGHEST AND BEST USE, ANTICIPATION, AND SUBSTITUTION

Highest and Best Use

Any purchaser of property wants to buy or create the highest income stream possible for the property. The owner wants to find the income stream among all alternative uses that will create the most income. Thus highest and best use can be defined as "that reasonable and probable use that will support the highest present value as defined as of the effective date of the appraisal. . . ."[7] A later chapter explains that highest and best use can be divided into two parts: the site and the improvement. The highest and best use for the site ignores any improvements that exist and examines alternative income flows that could exist under local zoning ordinances, building codes, and physical restrictions such as water and natural gas availability. Highest and best use for the improvement examines the alternative income flows that can be created for the existing improvement. The two analyses can and often do give different results.

The conclusion here is that the purchaser and owner always maintains some concept covering the highest present value that can be realized for property. Since this idea is always carried with the investor, it serves as a motivating force behind purchases.

Anticipation

The principle of anticipation has long been used to determine the value of stocks, bonds, and real estate. It means that the value or worth of property is the present value of all future benefits.[8] In real estate, those benefits are typically four types: periodic income usually called rent, income in the form of capital gains that is sometimes called net sale proceeds, income from a tax deduction, and psychic income that can arise from the ownership of recreational, leisure, and residential property.

Substitution

A rational prudent buyer will pay no more for property than the cost of acquiring an equally desirable substitute on the open market. This purchaser will act prudently with the information available to him or her and will shop around among the alternatives available.[9]

Combining these Principles

These four concepts may be combined to interpret critical motivating forces in the market that cause purchasers to buy property and hold it.

1. Anticipation means that a buyer will view the future income stream to be very important in determining the value of the property.
2. Highest and best use means that the purchaser-owner-investor will always be interested in the highest present value.
3. Substitution means that the potential purchaser will use this information to set a price once he or she has spent sufficient time in shopping among the alternatives.

MARKET DEMAND AND SUPPLY

Interpreting the forces of market demand and supply are basic to the appraisal. This section identifies and discusses the demand and supply conditions that underlie the appraisal.

Market Demand

Market demand is the relationship between the market price and the quantity demanded, other things being equal. "Other things being equal" means that income, tastes, preferences, population, and expectations of future price changes should be held reasonably constant. To construct a meaningful demand relationship, the analyst should initially define the (1) type of land use, (2) location, and (3) time period. Thus the demand relationship may be estimated for a twelve-unit apartment complex within the city limits over the next twelve months.

Once these assumptions have been made, the typical demand relationship between price and quantity is downward sloping, as shown in Fig. 1.1. The relationship shown is that the quantity demanded will increase if the price should be lowered, and vice-versa.

Demand stocks Market demand may be divided into parts: demand stocks and demand flows.[10] Demand stocks represent the summation of the buyers' two desires to buy and hold property discussed earlier—value in use and value in exchange. The summation of these two reflect the general overall well-being of the community's economy. For example, the appraiser will most likely examine trends on population, employment, migration, income, retail sales, and industrial location to estimate the public's desire to buy and hold both sites and structures under consideration in the appraisal.

Industrial expansion, for example, could cause value in use and exchange for a particular property type to be strong. The resulting demand stock line would lie in a position that would cause a relatively high market price.

Demand stock is shown by the first graph in Fig. 1.2.

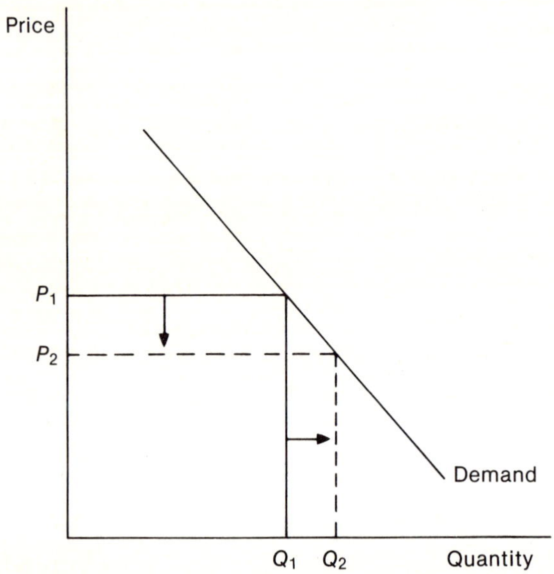

Fig. 1.1 Market demand for a specific property use (12-unit apartment complex) for a specific location (within the city limits) for a particular time (12 months)

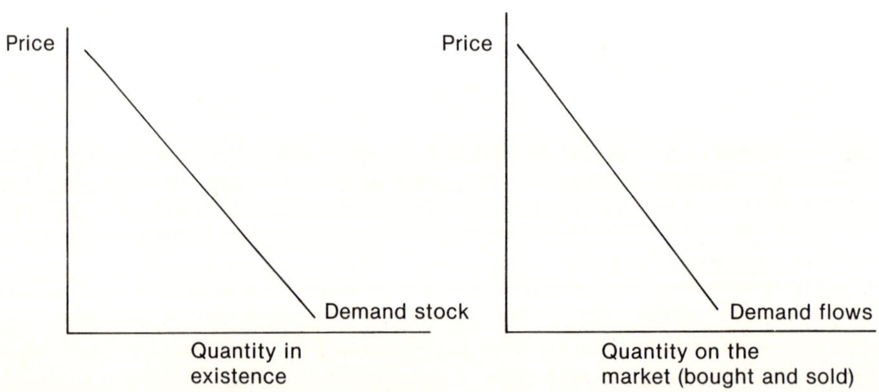

Fig. 1.2 Demand stock and demand flow

Demand flow Demand flow represents the value in use and value in exchange to buy property on the current market. It represents the demand for the day-to-day transactions. Consequently, the demand flow is part of the demand stock.

For example, the demand stock or total available supply within the next twelve months within the city limits of Anywhere, USA, has been estimated to be 32,500 parcels. The number of those parcels actually demanded by prospective buyers (called demand flow) within the next month might be 365. Thus the flow represents the daily, weekly, or monthly (or some appropriate time period) demand to purchase from the demand stock in existence.

Market Supply

Market supply is the relationship between price and the quantity offered by sale, other things being equal. "Other things being equal" refers to the costs of the factors of production. This relationship is usually thought to be upward sloping, as shown in Fig. 1.3. This relationship shows that the higher the price, the greater the quantity supplied, and vice-versa.

Supply stock The supply stock is a vertical or near-vertical line representing the total amount of the property type in question within the location confinement and during the time period.[11] Thus once all the available twelve-unit

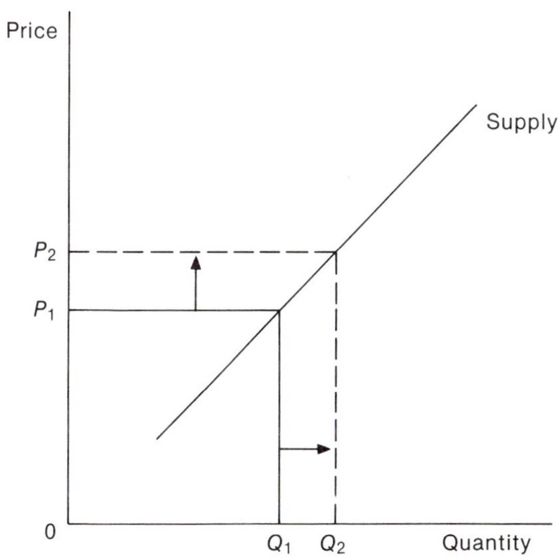

Fig. 1.3 Market supply for a specific property use (12-unit apartment complex) for a specific location (within the city limits) for a particular time (12 months)

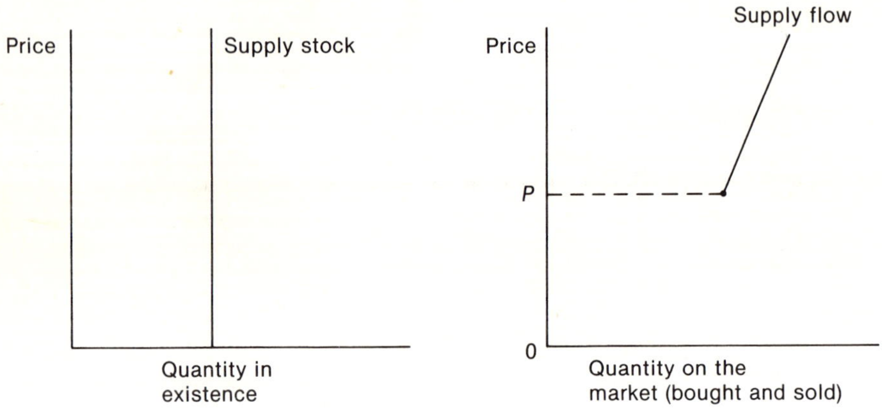

Fig. 1.4 Supply stock and supply flow

apartment complexes have been counted within the city limits for the next twelve months, their number cannot be changed readily. The price is irrelevant since the quantity cannot be altered significantly within the next twelve-month period, as shown in the first graph in Fig. 1.4.

Supply flow Supply flow represents the sellers' desire to offer for sale on the current market some portion of the total amount in existence. Supply flow is part of the supply stock. The price OP represents the capital requirement that a new buyer will need to meet to purchase any of the supply offered for sale. No supply or sales will occur below this price.

Market Demand and Market Supply

The demand stock can be put together with the supply stock, and the demand flow can be put together with the supply flow. The result is shown in Fig. 1.5. Since the demand and supply flow are part of the demand and supply stock, the stock graphs determine the magnitude of the flow graphs. *Specifically, the price set by the intersection of the demand and supply stocks determines the price set in the current demand and supply flow market.* Since the supply stock graph cannot change readily in the time period defined, the most important component of determining value is the demand stock line. In other words, the community's desire to hold the property in existence because of future value in use and exchange motives determines the market price of the property in existence and the market price of the property selling in the current market (flows).

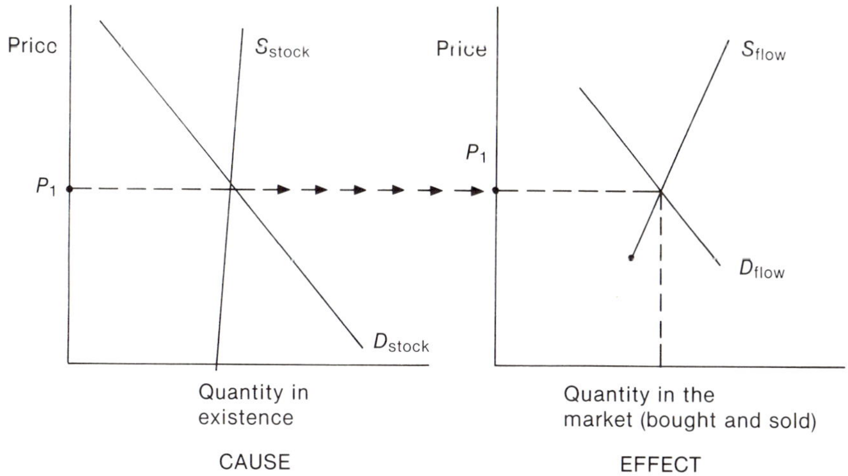

Fig. 1.5 Demand and supply stock with demand and supply flow

Use of These Concepts in an Appraisal

The logic of these graphs reflecting market demand and supply is used within an appraisal. Every market analyst should remember:

1. An appraisal is a study of the local market demand and supply conditions since the objective is, in most cases, to estimate what a willing and knowledgeable buyer will pay a willing and knowledgeable seller, given other limiting conditions.

2. The demand to hold the quantity in existence within the time period defined determines the quantity being demanded on the daily market. Thus the general economic well-being of the community determines the market prices of the property bought and sold daily. An analyst must be sure that sample prices taken from the daily market adequately reflect the community's economic health.

3. Within a given time period, movements in the demand to hold line (stock) will change market prices. Thus the appraiser can watch factors influencing thc location of this line such as population, employment, income, and the level of retail sales.

4. These graphs have applications in studies related to appraisal and often can be completed by an appraiser. For example, a feasibility study typically involves the estimation of the demand for a product, which could involve both the demand to hold (stock) and the demand flow.

MARKET PRICE, MARKET VALUE, MOST PROBABLE SELLING PRICE, AND GOING CONCERN VALUE

Market Price

Market price is the transaction price actually observed in the market. Any transaction price along the vertical price-axis in Fig. 1.4 represents a market price. It may or may not be the value of the property. Market prices are one set of market observations that are inserted into the valuation process (discussed in Chapter 3) to estimate a market value.

Market Value

Market value may be defined to be "the highest price in terms of money which a property will bring in a competitive and open market under all conditions requisite to a fair sale, the buyer and seller, each acting prudently, knowledgeably and assuming the price is not affected by undue stimulus."[12] Implicit in this definition is the consummation of a sale as of a specified date and the passing of title from seller to buyer under conditions whereby:

1. Buyer and seller are typically motivated.
2. Both parties are well informed or well advised and each acting in what he or she considers one's own best interest.
3. A reasonable time is allowed for exposure in the open market.
4. Payment is made in cash or its equivalent.
5. Financing, if any, is on terms generally available in the community at the specified date and typical for the property type in its locale.
6. The price represents a normal consideration for the property sold unaffected by special financing amounts and/or terms, services, fees, costs, or credits incurred in the transaction.

If all of the conditions in this definition hold, the market prices represented by P_1 in Fig. 1.5 is market value.

The valuation process discussed in Chapter 3 attempts to produce an estimate of some type of value. Market value is the most common estimate. One of the major problems with this definition is that the actual market and its observed market prices suffer from many imperfections that do not conform with the assumptions in the definitions. Thus some authors argue that the valuation process should attempt to estimate the most probable selling price.

One corrected definition of market value One author has suggested several minor changes to the definition of market value given earlier that would make it usable in all market situations (changes underlined): "The *estimated* price, in terms of money which a property *should bring* in a competitive and open market under all conditions requisite to a fair sale, with the buyer and seller each acting prudently and knowledgeably and presuming the price is not affected by undue influence.''[13] Implicit in this definition is the consummation of a sale as of a specified date and the passing of title from seller to buyer under conditions whereby:

1. Both buyer and seller are typically motivated.
2. Both parties are well informed or well advised, acting in what they consider their own best interests.
3. A reasonable time is allowed for exposure in the open market.
4. *Equity* payment is made in cash or its equivalent.
5. Financing, if any, is on terms generally available in the community at the specified date and typical for the property type in its locale.
6. The price represents a normal consideration for the property sold, unaffected by special financing amounts and/or terms, fees, costs, or credits incurred in the transaction.

According to this author, these changes in the definition permit the appraiser to estimate market value where the market is limited or nonexistent.

Statistical definitions One author has attempted to define several appraisal concepts in statistical terms. His question is, ''Is market value the expected selling price, the median selling price, or the most probable selling price?''[14] The expected selling price is the sample mean (average) of market prices of competitive properties that have recently sold. The median selling price is the price that causes 50 percent of the transactions to fall below and 50 percent to lie above. The most probable selling price is the mode, which is the market price that appears the most frequently. According to this author, the expected selling price (sample mean) is the most statistically correct definition of market value.

Most Probable Selling Price

Most probable selling price is defined to be ''the price that a property would most probably sell if exposed to the market for a reasonable time under market conditions prevailing as of the date of the appraisal.''[15] This concept of value imposes no constraints on any of the participants. If one of the parties is poorly informed and pays an uninformed price that is too high or too low, that price represents the property's market value. Economic conditions, financial considerations, or undue stimuli may influence the magnitude of the price paid, and the result will still be the property's market value.[16]

Going Concern Value

Going concern value is defined to be:

1. The value existing in a proven property operation considered as an entity with a business established, as distinct from the value of real estate only, ready to operate but without a going business.
2. Includes consideration of the efficiency of plant, the know-how of management, and the sufficiency of capital.
3. An excess of value over cost, which arises as a consequence of a complete and well-assembled operation production mechanism; it is the value of an efficient layout and operational control system resulting in the most desirable synchronization of the merchandising, production, or distribution activities of the enterprise, and includes goodwill.[17]

Going concern value is typically viewed as similar to value in use. It is an intangible asset caused by the presence (in a profitable firm) of marketing efficiencies, operating efficiencies, avoidance of startup costs, and administrative efficiencies.[18] The rate of return on these items is higher than for a newly established firm. Recent court decisions have viewed going concern value as a nondepreciable intangible asset distinct from goodwill.[19]

PROFESSIONAL APPRAISAL GROUPS

Several professional groups have been formed which award designations to members who have completed a prescribed course of study and demonstrated satisfactory experience. These groups are identified and discussed briefly with several facts about the appraisal profession in general.

An Appraiser

An appraiser is defined as "one who estimates value; specifically, one who possesses the necessary qualifications, ability, and experience to execute or direct the appraisal of real or personal property."[20] No national license exists to certify the qualifications of an individual who advertises to be an appraiser. Several states do require appraisers to be licensed by the state, which typically means that at least one elementary exam has been passed and, in some cases, minimal experience requirements have been met. The majority of states have no state regulations placed on individuals who appraise property, except those who are influenced indirectly since they have a real estate license and are covered by the state licensing law.

To assist the public in identifying those appraisers who have completed a prescribed course of study and demonstrated minimal experience requirements from those who have not, several professional appraisal organizations have been organized to designate members. Several of these groups and the designations given by each are discussed briefly:

> American Institute of Real Estate Appraisers (AIREA)
> Sometimes called "the Institute," this group designates members in the area of real property appraisal only. They award the RM (Residential Member) for those members concentrating on residential properties, and the MAI (Member of the Appraisal Institute) for residential and all other properties.
>
> Society of Real Estate Appraisers (SREA)
> Sometimes called "the Society," this group designates members in the area of real property appraisal only. They award the SRA (Senior Residential Appraiser) for members concentrating on residential properties only, and the SRPA (Senior Real Property Appraiser) for those members concentrating on residential and income properties. A sister organization, the Society of Real Estate Analysts, awards the SREA (Senior Real Estate Analyst) for those members concentrating on residential, income, and market analytical problems.
>
> International Association of Assessing Officers (IAAO)
> This group awards designations to members who are setting value on property for taxation purposes. They award the CAE (Certified Assessment Evaluator) to real property appraisers employed by a governmental agency, the CPE (Certified Personal Evaluator) to members who are personal property appraisers employed by a government agency, and the AAE (Accredited Assessment Evaluator) for real personal property appraisers who are not employed by an assessment agency.
>
> American Society of Appraisers (ASA)
> This group awards a designation to members for demonstrating appraisal competence in estimating value of real or various types of personal property. Their designation is the ASA (senior member of the American Society of Appraisers).
>
> National Association of Review Appraisers (NARA)
> The NARA awards the CRA (Certified Review Appraiser) to its members who have demonstrated appropriate education and experience in the field of review appraising.
>
> National Association of Independent Fee Appraisers (NAIFA)
> The NAIFA awards the IFA (member), IFAS (senior member), and the IFAC (appraiser-counselor) designations to members who have demonstrated appropriate education and experience.

A recent article attempted to identify all of the real estate groups and the designation each awarded:[21]

AAE	Accredited Assessment Educator	— International Association of Assessing Officers
AFLB	Accredited Farm and Land Broker	— Farm and Land Institute
AFLM	Accredited Farm and Land Member	— Farm and Land Institute
AFM	Accredited Farm Manager	— American Society of Farm Managers and Rural Appraisers
AMO	Accredited Management Organization	— Institute of Real Estate Management
ARA	Accredited Rural Appraiser	— American Society of Farm Managers and Rural Appraisers
ARM	Accredited Resident Manager	— Institute of Real Estate Management
ASA	Senior Member	— American Society of Appraisers
CAE	Certified Assessment Evaluator	— International Association of Assessing Officers
CCIM	Certified Commercial Investment Member	— REALTORS® National Marketing Institute
CPM	Certified Property Manager	— Institute of Real Estate Management
CRA	Certified Review Appraiser	— National Association of Review Appraisers
CRB	Certified Residential Broker	— National Institute of Real Estate Brokers
CRE	Counselor of Real Estate	— American Society of Real Estate Counselors
CRS	Certified Residential Specialist	— REALTORS® National Marketing Institute
CRSM	Certified Real Estate Securities Marketer	— Real Estate Securities and Syndication Institute

CRSS	Certified Real Estate Securities Sponsor	— Real Estate Securities and Syndication Institute
CSM	Certified Shopping Center Manager	— International Council of Shopping Centers
GRI	Graduate, REALTOR® Institute	— State Associations related to NATIONAL ASSOCIATION OF REALTORS®
MAI	Member, Appraisal Institute	— American Institute of Real Estate Appraisers
NAR	Abbreviation	— NATIONAL ASSOCIATION OF REALTORS®
REALTOR®	Member	— Local real estate board affiliated with NATIONAL ASSOCIATION OF REALTORS®
RM	Residential Member	— American Institute of Real Estate Appraisers
SIR	Member	— Society of Industrial REALTORS®
SCV	Senior Certified Valuer	— International Institute of Valuers
SRA	Senior Residential Appraiser	— Society of Real Estate Appraisers
SREA	Senior Real Estate Analyst	— Society of Real Estate Appraisers
SRPA	Senior Real Property Appraiser	— Society of Real Estate Appraisers
SR/WA	Senior Member	— American Right of Way Association

Obviously, an individual appraiser may hold several designations simultaneously from several organizations. The designations held will often correspond with the type of business in which the individual wishes to specialize. For example, a fee appraiser doing only appraisals on real property may hold an MAI, SREA, and ASA. An individual wishing to specialize only in personal property such as coins, stamps, and antiques will probably hold only an ASA. These designations assist the public and the client in selecting those appraisers who should have the education and experience necessary to perform a competent appraisal. In addition, the AIREA and the SREA have mandatory continuing education requirements to renew their designations, and the AIREA has a required appraisal review program.

COMMON MYTHS AND CLICHES ABOUT INCOME-PRODUCING PROPERTIES

Several common cliches and myths about income-producing properties exist. They are discussed here briefly and will be answered in more detail over the balance of the book.

"Buy land because they ain't making it no more." (Will Rogers)

Since value is created by future value in use and value in exchange, a potential future stream of benefits arising from one or both of these must exist for a potential buyer to want the property. If these two do not exist, no market for the property exists. Land is valuable only for a particular use at a given time and location.

"All property increases in value."

Not all property increases in value. Again, a future value in use and a value in exchange must exist for a number of buyers to want to purchase the property.

"The price of wheat is high because the price of farmland is high."

The previous demand and supply graphs have shown the underlying market forces that cause a buyer to purchase property. The value in use and value in exchange motives are based upon a future stream of benefits, usually income. The conclusion here is that the sale of the product from the site (in some cases the sale of the site such as condominiums) generates income to the owner. Thus the motive for ownership is to collect the future income stream. The cliche should read that the price of wheat generates an income stream to the owner of the site, or the price of farmland is high because the high price of wheat generates a high income stream to the site owner.

"Value is found by dividing the income stream by a discount rate."[22]

This statement is only true under very limited conditions, which are discussed in later chapters. It assumes that the discount rate never changes and the income flow is constant and continues to infinity.

"The cost approach always sets the upper limit to value."[23]

This statement ignores the market supply and demand conditions. For example, the reproduction cost of a structure might be $500,000, but the buyers are willing to pay $550,000 because of a shortage of available similar structures. In addition, the statement confuses "cost new" with "depreciable cost."

"Appraisers determine value."[24]

Appraisers interpret market trends. If they report these trends and facts accurately, they do not influence the forces of demand and supply.

"Investment value and market value are the same."

Investment value is the value that a property has to an individual investor taking into consideration debt service (amortization and interest payments), depreciation deductions, and income taxes. Thus an investment value is estimated for an individual client. Market value is not unique to one individual, but is related to the market. The after-tax rate-of-return to an individual could create a higher (lower) investment value than the market value.

SUMMARY

The demand for property is composed of the value in use and value in exchange. Potential buyers must see a future income stream to justify its purchase. Value in use represents the utility of the property to an individual owner, while the value in exchange represents the utility of the property's most probable use.

Market demand and market supply can be divided into demand stock and flow and supply stock and flow. The stock concept reflects the community's desire to hold the total amount of the supply stock that exists. The demand flow reflects the current buyers' desire to buy, and the supply flow represents the current sellers' desire to sell. The market factor that is the primary force in determining the value of the property is the demand stock, which is the community's desire to hold the property in existence.

Market price is the transaction price. Market value is determined by the intersection of demand and supply. It represents the price that a willing, knowledgeable buyer will pay a willing, knowledgeable seller under certain limiting conditions. Most probable selling price is the price that the property will bring regardless of the market conditions. Going concern value is a nondepreciable intangible asset that represents the efficiencies of the firm originating in operations, marketing, administration.

No national licensing exists for real estate appraisers. Several states do require an appraiser to complete an educational requirement and satisfy minimum experience requirements prior to accepting employment. To assist in differentiating among those who are qualified and those who may not be, several professional organizations have given designations to those members who have predetermined educational and experience requirements.

REVIEW QUESTIONS

1. Define value in use and value in exchange. Contrast the two.
2. Explain the role of the following:

highest and best use	substitution
anticipation	

3. Define and discuss each of the following:

market demand	market supply
demand stock	supply stock
demand flow	supply flow

   Are these definitions related to the specific land use? Location? Time period? Explain.
4. Once demand stock is placed together with supply stock, what do the graphs represent, in general? What is the price that reflects their intersection?
5. What is the prime factor determining value? Why?
6. How do these concepts of demand and supply relate to the appraiser?
7. Define and contrast the following:

market price	going concern value
market value	

8. Identify the professional appraisal organizations and the designations awarded by each.
9. Explain several common myths and cliches about income-producing property and discuss their merits.

ENDNOTES

1. Byrl Boyce, *Real Estate Appraisal Terminology* (Cambridge, Mass.: Ballinger Publishing Co., 1975), p. 214.
2. Donald H. Treadwell, "Value in Use in Perspective," *The Appraisal Journal* 46 (April 1978): 228.
3. William M. Shenkel, "Value in Use, Value in Exchange, and Investment Value," *Real Estate Appraiser and Analyst* 46 (May-June 1980): 28-29.
4. Boyce, *Real Estate Appraisal Terminology,* pp. 81, 215-216.
5. American Institute of Real Estate Appraisers, *The Appraisal of Real Estate* (Chicago: AIREA, 1978), p. 23.
6. Shenkel, "Value in Use," p. 31.
7. Boyce, *Real Estate Appraisal Terminology,* p. 107.
8. Ibid., p. 11.
9. Ibid., p. 201.
10. D. R. Epley, "A Further Note on the Theory of Value," *The Real Estate Appraiser* 42 (January-February 1976): 13-16.
11. Ibid.
12. Boyce, *Real Estate Appraisal Terminology,* p. 137.
13. Harold D. Albritton, "A Critique of the Prevailing Definitions of Market Value," *The Appraisal Journal* 48 (April 1980): 205.
14. Peter F. Colwell, "A Statistically Oriented Definition of Market Value," *The Appraisal Journal* 47 (January 1979): 53-58.
15. Boyce, *Real Estate Appraisal Terminology,* p. 145.
16. Halbert C. Smith, "Value Concepts as a Source of Disparity Among Appraisals," *The Appraisal Journal* 45 (April 1977): 208-209.
17. Boyce, *Real Estate Appraisal Terminology,* p. 101.
18. Jon Paulsen and Larry Sherman, "The Problem of Going Concern Value: The Relationship Between Cost and Income Approach," *The Real Estate Appraiser and Analyst* 45 (September-October 1979): 16-19.
19. Ibid., p. 16.
20. Boyce, *Real Estate Appraisal Terminology,* p. 13.
21. William B. Knipe, Jr., "Your Best Investment in Real Estate," *Farm and Land REALTOR®* 33 (May 1981): 10-11. This material originally appeared in the *Farm and Land REALTOR®* and is reprinted by permission of the Farm and Land Institute of the National Association of REALTORS.®
22. Austin Jaffe and C. F. Sirmans, "Some Myths About Real Estate," *Real Estate Review* 8 (Spring 1978): 40.
23. Ibid., p. 41.
24. Ibid.

ADDITIONAL READINGS

Adams, John. "Analysis of Factors Influencing Value." *The Appraisal Journal* 37 (April 1969): 239–242.

Barrett, G. Vincent. "Appraisal Should be Market Study: Techniques of Analysis." *The Appraisal Journal* 47 (October 1979): 538–555.

Case, Fred E. "The Value of a Thing is the Price It will Bring." *American Real Estate and Urban Economics Association Journal* 7 (Summer 1979): 265–268.

Church, Byron. "What are We Talking About?" *The Appraisal Journal* 38 (July 1970): 418–423.

Entreken, Henry C. "Are We Really Seeking Market Value?" *The Appraisal Journal* 48 (July 1980): 428–431.

Epley, Donald R., and Millar, James A. *Basic Real Estate Finance and Investments* (New York: John Wiley & Sons, Inc., 1980), Chapter 1.

Featherson, J. B. "Historical Influences on Development of the Theory of Value." *The Appraisal Journal* 43 (April 1975): 165–182.

Hall, Thomas. "Market Value vs. Equity Price." *The Appraisal Journal* 44 (January 1976): 118–119.

Hartman, Donald J. "Industrial Real Estate: Estimating Value in Use." *The Appraisal Journal* 47 (July 1979): 340–350.

Howcroft, Paul. "A Rational Expectation Approach to Concepts of Value." *The Appraisal Journal* 48 (July 1980): 402–413.

Neilsen, Donald A. "Certification of Appraisers: Issues, Dilemmas, and Prospects." *The Appraisal Journal* 49 (April 1981): 259–270.

Ratcliff, Richard. "Capitalized Income is Not Market Value." *The Appraisal Journal* 36 (January 1968): 33–41.

White, John Robert. "Values and Valuation Techniques in the Seventies." *The Appraisal Journal* 40 (October 1972): 545–555.

MODULE II
Market Analysis

The concepts in this chapter are used to elaborate further on other principles of value such as anticipation, substitution, and highest and best use. The role of elasticity in demand and supply is explained in order that the appraiser can better estimate the market's responsiveness to changes. Feasibility studies are explained and their components outlined since many of these studies involve demand and supply applications. When finished with this chapter and the first one, the student has learned the basics of demand and supply with common definitions and concepts that originate from demand and supply or are used to help interpret them, and has examined applications of these concepts such as in highest and best use and feasibility analysis.

CHAPTER 2

LEARNING OBJECTIVES

When a student finishes this chapter, he or she should be able to:

- Explain the relationship among demand, supply, market value, and market price.
- Explain the role of elasticity.
- Outline the types of feasibility studies.
- Discuss the components of feasibility studies.
- Explain the concept of highest and best use and the methods for typically measuring it.

Market Analysis, Property Trends, and Highest and Best Use

IMPORTANT TERMS AND PHRASES

demand elasticity: The percentage change in the quantity demanded over the percentage change in the price.

feasibility study: A market analysis undertaken to determine whether the client's objectives can be achieved within the constraints imposed by the client. Examples of these studies include market demand, financial analysis, location, cost, and a combination.

highest and best use of the improvement: The highest present value of the existing improvement.

highest and best use of the site: The highest present value of the site as though it were vacant.

inelasticity: An elasticity less than one.

reservation demand: A capital requirement that is necessary for a buyer to overcome to purchase the property from the owner.

supply elasticity: The percentage change in the quantity supplied over the percentage change in the price.

unit elasticity: An elasticity equal to one.

The purpose of this chapter is to discuss the relationship among demand, supply, market value, market price, feasibility studies, and highest and best use. When finished with the chapter, the reader should have knowledge of how these are related, their definitions, and in some cases, typical measuring tools.

DEMAND AND SUPPLY ANALYSIS

An estimate of value is an analysis of market trends. Consequently, any appraiser must have an introductory knowledge of supply and demand analysis to understand how the market functions and what interrelationships among the market forces are involved. This section gives an introductory discussion of demand, supply, and the relationship among the three.

Market Demand

Market demand is composed of two forces motivating buyers to buy: value in use and value in exchange (explained in Chapter 1). Briefly, value in use represents the purchaser's desire to purchase property and hold it. The buyer typically wants to hold the property because it will generate a future stream of benefits, either in dollars or psychic income such as leisure and recreational property. Included here also is the motivation to hold the property because it will generate a tax deduction. Value in exchange refers to the purchaser's desire to purchase the property because it can be resold in the market at a future date—hopefully, a capital gain. *Both motivations reflect the buyer's desire to collect future income in the form of a regular stream through the sale of a product, income for a tax shelter, or a capital gain.*

Typically, the relationships between the amount paid for the product and the amount demanded is thought to be inverse, meaning that the lower the price, the greater the amount demanded, and vice-versa. This assumes that during the measurement period, incomes do not change, tastes and preferences remain constant, population remains constant, and the purchaser does not expect future prices to change. This relationship is shown in Fig. 2.1 by a demand curve.

Demand elasticity One feature of the demand line that is important is the amount of change in the quantity caused by a change in the price. The question to be answered is, "How responsive is the quantity demanded to a change in the price?"

The *elasticity* is defined as the percentage change in the quantity demanded over the percentage change in the price. If this figure is greater than one, the demand line is said to be *elastic*. If this figure is less than one, it is said to be *inelastic*. If it is equal to one, it is called *unit elasticity*.

Each type of elasticity is shown in Fig. 2.2 by different slopes of the demand line. For example, D_{elastic} reveals that the line is elastic and will be somewhat flatter than the other two lines. The line that is $D_{\text{inelastic}}$ will be somewhat

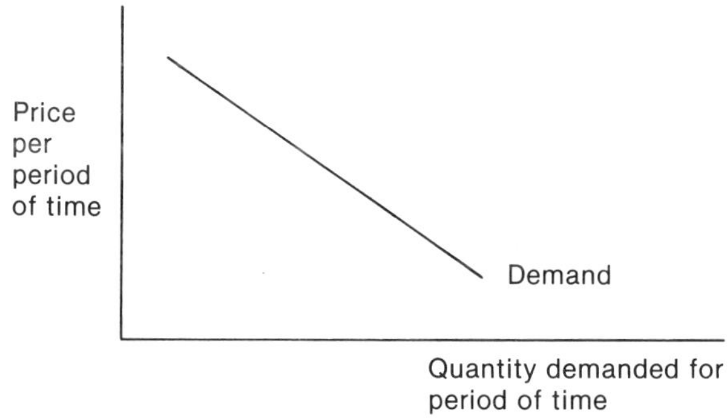

Fig. 2.1 Demand

more vertical than the other two. The line that is D_{unit} will reflect equal percent changes in the price and the quantity demanded.

For example, the $D_{inelastic}$ line could refer to the demand for housing within a specific time period and location. Few, if any, substitutes exist for the category of goods called housing. The $D_{elastic}$ line could refer to the type of housing called duplexes. Substitutes do exist within the market in the form, perhaps, of single-family housing, fourplexes, and mobile homes. Thus, the quantity on the x-axis is much more sensitive to changes in the price. The D_{unit} curve might represent another type of housing where equal percent changes in the price cause equal changes in the quantity.

A demand curve that is strongly inelastic means that the inventory holder of the property type in question could most likely (within limits) obtain a higher price for the site. A demand curve that is strongly elastic means that the pricing of the site in question is critical since a slight alteration of the price will mean a greater percentage change in the quantity. Both bits of information will be influential in determining the rate of return on any investments involving either site.

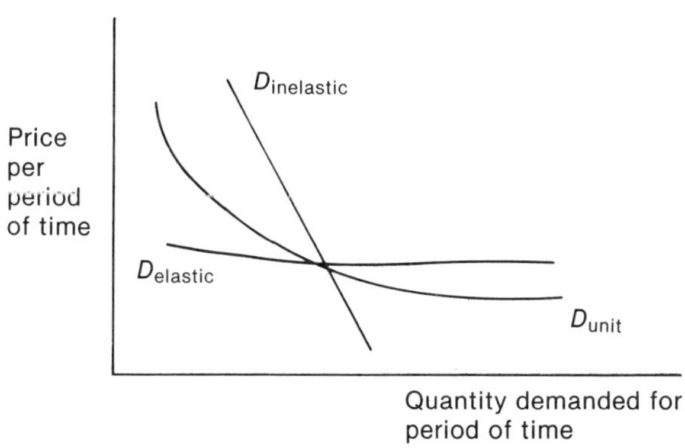

Fig. 2.2 Types of elasticity

The strength of the elasticity is directly dependent upon the number of substitutes for the product in question. In general, the fewer the number of substitutes, the stronger the inelasticity, and the greater the number of substitutes, the stronger the elasticity.

Number of Substitutes	*Type of Elasticity*	*Degree of Strength*
few substitutes	inelastic or < 1	strong inelasticity
several substitutes	inelastic or < 1	weak inelasticity
perfect substitutability	unit elasticity or 1	equal change
many substitutes	elastic or > 1	weak elasticity
numerous substitutes	elastic or > 1	strong elasticity

The classification of the demand line as inelastic, elastic, or unit elasticity and the estimation of the approximate strength of the elasticity can be useful information to the market analyst. For example, the estimation that the demand line for eight-unit apartments within a city over the next twelve months is inelastic, and the conclusion that the strength of the inelasticity is very strong means that the line is somewhat vertical. This tells the owner that very few products in the market are considered by the purchasers to be substitutes for eight-unit apartments and, consequently, a price increase (decrease) may not cause the buyer's motivations to buy to significantly decrease (increase).

A conclusion that the demand line for duplexes within the city over the next twelve months is elastic, and the estimation that the purchasers consider many types of housing to be substitutes means to an owner that a price increase (decrease) will cause a much larger decrease (increase) in the duplexes demanded. Any owner, potential buyer, or mortgagee would like to possess this information.

Market Supply

The supply line reflects the relationship between the price paid to the supplier-owner of the product and the number of units supplied to the market. This relationship is thought to be direct in that the higher the price, the higher the number of units supplied, and vice-versa.

The supply lines may be described as inelastic, unit, or elastic. The definitions are identical to the ones used for demand elasticity, except the quantity now refers to the quantity supplied. Figure 2.3 shows the $S_{\text{inelastic}}$ and S_{elastic} lines.

The $S_{inelastic}$ line means that few substitutes can be brought onto the market within the time period because of zoning requirements, building code requirements, and perhaps a high urban density. Consequently, what exists in inventory is most likely all that will be seen on the market during this time period. A supply line that is relatively elastic means that the zoning, building code, and urban density restrictions can be overcome within the time period to bring additional properties onto the market within the time period.

Reservation demand[1] The price OP_1 is the minimum price that a potential buyer must pay the owner to obtain the minimum quantity, OQ_1. The price OP_1 may be viewed as a capital requirement that is necessary for the buyer to pay the owner to overcome the owner's reservation demand to hold this product in inventory for his or her own use.

The price OP_1 is the minimum capital requirement among all potential suppliers. The minimum capital requirement for the remaining suppliers on this supply line must be higher than OP_1. Thus every supplier's reservation demand is going to influence the position and shape of this supply line through all prices.

Reservation demand exists typically for any product that is not reproducible, such as antiques, coins, stamps, and art. It exists also for certain types of real estate that are difficult to bring onto the market within the time period being considered because of institutional barriers or simply that this type of land use is finite in number. Any purchase must be made from the owner who holds this product in inventory, and the purchaser must buy it from inventory as opposed to buying it from a producer who can produce a new unit. Rare coins, antiques, and art are not produced but purchased from an owner who holds an

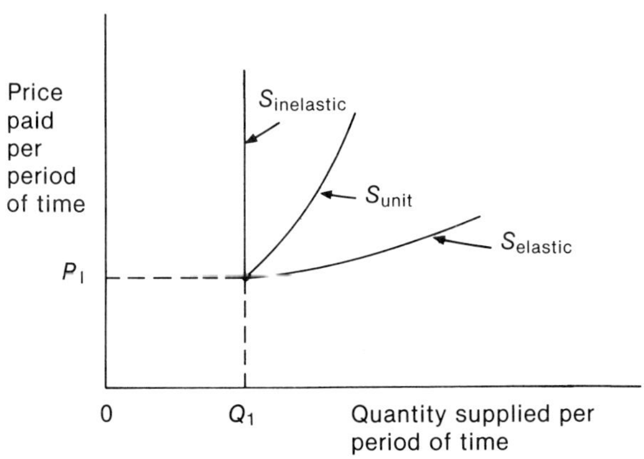

Fig. 2.3 Types of elasticity

inventory. The same is true, say, for a site ready for construction within the city limits of Anywhere, USA, and suitable for a twenty-four-unit apartment complex over the next twelve months. If no new sites can be brought onto the market during that period, the buyer must buy an existing site from an owner's inventory.

Market Demand and Market Supply Together[2]

Once the proper demand line is selected and its elasticity estimated, and once the proper supply line is estimated and its elasticity approximated, the two may be placed together. An example shown in Fig. 2.4 reflects the demand line for a twelve-unit apartment complex within the city limits of a midwestern city with a population of about 50,000. The town has restrictive zoning, restrictive building regulations, strong demand for rentals originating from the local university enrollment, and a good industrial base. Many available parcels have already been purchased and committed to other uses. The conclusion reached by the analysis of demand and supply trends indicated that the demand line should be inelastic and the degree of inelasticity was strong. No new lots are expected to be brought onto the market during this time period.

The minimum price that any owner will accept for a suitable lot is $43,000, which brings one lot into the market. At a price of $45,000, the buyer

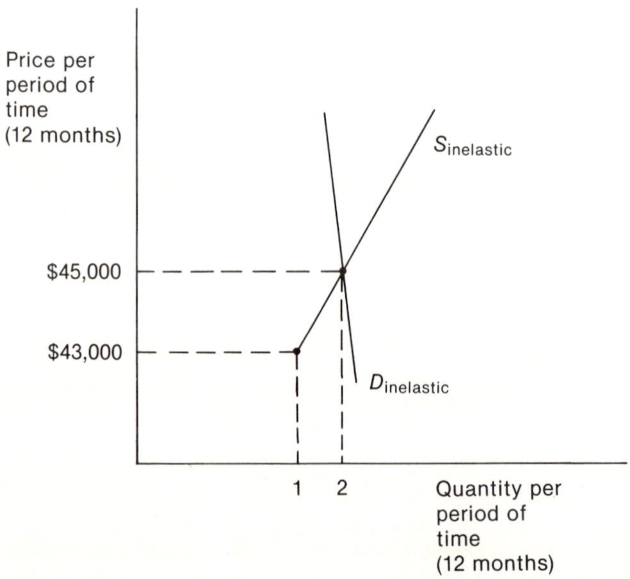

Fig. 2.4 Demand and supply of 12-unit apartment complexes within the city limits for the next 12 months

can purchase the first lot or a second offered by a competitive seller. The demand and supply intersection shows that the equilibrium market price where the forces of demand and supply are equal is $45, 000. Two lots are demanded and two are offered for sale at this price.

Market Value vs. Market Price

The *equilibrium price* where the demand line intersects the supply line is the *market value* of the property. If the market is allowed to function according to the conditions within the definition of market value, the forces of demand and supply should create the market value and property then sells for that price.

Market price is the *selling price,* which is often called the transaction or purchase price. It is the price that is observed in the market. The critical question that the appraiser must ask is, "Does the market price equal the market value?" The appraisal process described in the next chapter is a logical procedure for answering this question numerically.

The concept to remember in answering this question is that the two *may* be equal. The buyer and seller *may* agree to a price that has been caused by the forces of demand and supply. The appraisal process attempts to locate those market prices that have occurred and uses them to derive as estimate of market value. *Thus market value is often considered to be an abstract concept which may or may not appear in the market, depending upon things such as knowledge, duress, time, and financial conditions. The appraiser uses observed market prices to estimate market value.* Market value, by definition, is always determined by the forces of demand and supply. Market price *may* be determined by demand and supply, as shown in Figure 2.5.

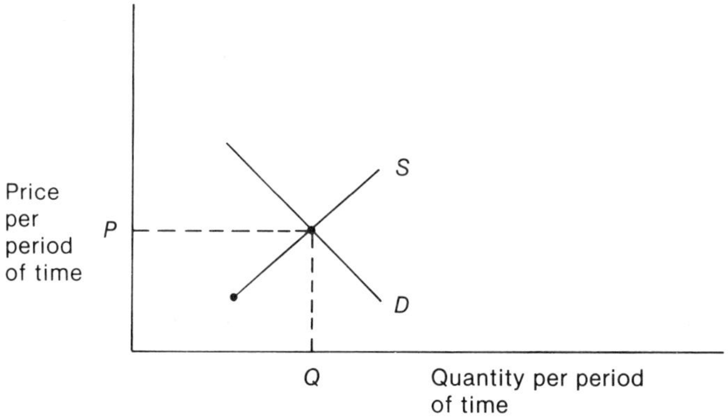

P = equilibrium price = market value, which may or may not be the observed *market price.*

Fig. 2.5 Market demand and supply for a site

FEASIBILITY STUDIES

Feasibility studies are often utilized to estimate market demand and supply conditions, or some specific component of each. Their purpose and components are discussed in this section. A definition of feasible can be given as "... reasonable likelihood of satisfying explicit objectives and when a selected course of action is tested for fit to a context of a specific constraint and limited resources. The context defines the problem. Feasibility of a real estate project is normally related to its probable economic potential."[3] A feasibility study is a market analysis undertaken to determine whether the client's objectives can be achieved within the constraints imposed by the client.

Types of Feasibility Studies

Feasibility studies typically fall into several categories, although a specific client can ask for any combination. First, a client may want to determine whether the market is sufficiently large and composed of the type of clientele that would purchase or use the product. This study is called a *market demand* study and is mostly market research into all of the variables that can influence the demand for the product produced from the site. Trends are examined in population, employment, retail sales, income, and the existing competition. Other items can be added as needed. Second, a client may want to know if the income flow from the market demand will produce a rate of return that is sufficient to warrant the investment. In this type of *financial analysis* study, the analyst typically reviews the quantity, quality, and duration of the projected income stream, scrutinizes the expenses, and may examine depreciation, debt service, and tax rates. The result typically gives the client an estimated rate of return before and/or after taxes. Third is the *location study,* which attempts to find an appropriate site for a business that has specific needs for labor, transportation and accessibility, market, and utilities. Fourth, a *composite study* combines all or several of these categories into one comprehensive review of the market. In addition, any combination of these may be used to satisfy the client's needs.

James Graaskamp[4] has set forth that feasibility studies are basically one of three types: a business looking for a site, a site owner looking for a business, or an investor who wants a piece of the action from the two points above. This view of feasibility conforms with the first three types previously described.

Examples

The components of several composite feasibility studies are described as examples of the preceding points.

Composite One author[5] holds in a recent article that a feasibility study should have five components. His components were:

1. The identification of alternative uses:
   All alternative uses of the property should be considered within local zoning and building codes. Use should be related to the type of property in the neighborhood and trends for development.

2. The cost to develop each alternative:
   The client should be given an estimate of developing each alternative use.

3. The market demand for each alternative:
   The demand for each alternative should be estimated and shown.

4. The identification of the competition:
   Every effort should be made to identify the plans of the competition. In addition, the competition should be surveyed to show the client.

5. The optimum alternative:
   The analyst should make a definite recommendation concerning the optimum use tying all of the above information together.

Composite One set of authors[6] has explained in a recent article that a feasibility study consists of two components: a market study and a financial analysis. The components of each are:

- Market Demand

  Market Demand and Supply: A land use study may be needed to provide a current pattern and trends. This can include a definition of the market area, analysis of housing demand and supply, and analysis of the physical factors required by the project and offered by the available sites. Specific factors can include the following:
  primary market area
  secondary market area
  demographic characteristics of housing demand
  economic characteristics of housing demand
  household size characteristics
  age mix of households by income class
  year households moved into the present housing
  vacancy rates
  absorption rates of competitive units
  detailed list of current stock
  resale units and frequency
  competitive developments
  absorption rates of the competition
  amenities of the competition
  competitive developments being planned

  Site Analysis: The authors recommend that this part of the study include a description of the available transportation to and near the site, availability of sewer and water, zoning and building code requirements, location of services that are used by the site, and the adjacent land use.

Marketing Recommendations and Conclusions: This part of the study gives a recommendation on marketing from the preceding data. It includes a development schedule, an absorption rate, and specific recommendations on the type of development.

- Financial Analysis
  Pre-Tax Cash flow: The income is reviewed for quality, quantity, and duration. All expenses are considered. An appropriate pre-tax rate of return is calculated.

  After-Tax Cash flow: The client's income taxes are considered and an appropriate rate of return is calculated.

In sum, the authors recommend that the following components be included in a market study: (1) type of product most marketable; (2) number and size of units and mix, if applicable; (3) the quality of the units; (4) pricing structure; (5) absorption rate; and (6) marketing recommendations.

In a financial analysis study, the components should include: (1) summary of expected revenues; (2) analysis of construction budget, if applicable; (3) year-by-year pre-tax cash flow; and (4) year-by-year after-tax cash flow.

Composite James Graaskamp[7] argues that a feasibility study should contain the following components:

1. Objectives:
   This includes the objectives of the client, alternatives that are acceptable, and decision rules.

2. Market trends that identify opportunities consistent with the objectives:
   This includes data on population, employment, public attitudes, and political factors.

3. Market segmentation for merchandising:
   Specialized markets should be identified, consumer profiles generated, and absorption rates estimated.

4. Legal-political factors:
   All regulatory controls are identified.

5. Environmental factors:
   This category includes information such as environmental impacts on the land and neighborhood, obligations to future users, and ethical considerations of the developer.

6. Physical constraints:
All engineering considerations are considered here with appropriate alternatives.

7. Financial analysis:
Appropriate flows of income and rates of return are estimated. Strategies for future operations may be proposed.

Criticism of Feasibility Studies

The biggest criticism of feasibility studies is that they often are compilations of data with no conclusions. The reader is left to his or her own conclusions concerning the worthiness of the project.

The client is attempting to minimize the risk by using the results of the study to provide additional information. Thus the analyst should reach conclusions and make recommendations to assist in mitigating the risk. The client must overcome the *equity risk* that the upfront equity cash will not be returned, and the *marginal product risk* that the income flow will not be sufficiently large or not exist once the intended project is completed.[8]

Bailey, Spies, and Weitzman[9] recommend that the study include: (1) the product type describing what to build; (2) the mix, size, amenities, etc., of how to build; (3) the construction and production and sales schedule; and (4) the range of profitability. All studies may not need these points, but the conclusion is still valid—make sure that the feasibility study includes definite recommendations based upon the data.

HIGHEST AND BEST USE

An estimate of highest and best use (HBU) in some form should be made in every appraisal assignment. The purpose of this section is to examine the HBU concept and alternative measurements.

Rationale for Estimating HBU

Land is an immobile factor of production among land, labor, capital, and entrepreneurship ability. Capital and labor must be moved to the site to produce a product. The rate of return received on capital and labor from the sale of a product from the site must be sufficient to attract these two factors of production away from competing uses. Consequently, the site is paid any surplus productivity that remains after capital and labor have been paid. This residual income historically is called rent and represents a return to the land that is used to estimate its value. Naturally, any owner or potential owner of the site in question wants the potential residual income left over for the site to be as large as possible. Thus the definition of HBU includes only the use that maximizes this residual income.[10] HBU may be remembered as the use that generates the highest residual income to the site while concurrently paying a competitive rate of return to capital, labor, and entrepreneurship ability that is necessary to produce a product from the site.

HBU is defined to be "that reasonable and probable use that will support the highest present value, as defined, as of the effective date of the appraisal."[11] Boyce's definition continues to state that the phrase "most probable use" is used within the context of investment value. Since the emphasis in this chapter is estimating market value, the phrase "highest and best use" is used.

HBU of the Site

The teachings of the AIREA and the SREA emphasize that two types of HBU be estimated. The first is the *HBU of the site,* and the second is the *HBU of the existing combination of land and improvements.*[12] The two may differ.

The HBU of the site assumes that the site is vacant. Any existing structure is not given significant weight in estimating the HBU of the vacant site. In fact, this concept could consider a different structure from what exists on the site.

The appraiser typically answers several initial questions in helping to estimate HBU. These are:

1. What is the highest use allowed under local zoning laws and/or building codes (the legal use)?
2. What type of buildings will fit in the space available (the physical use)? Construction on the site may be limited by ingress and egress, the supply of natural gas and electricity, transportation availability, topography, and other physical factors. This question attempts to identify all physical limitations that control and limit potential construction.
3. What alternative use generates the highest present value (the financial feasibility use)? All alternative uses of the property are examined to estimate the use that provides the highest present value. Is the potential income stream sufficiently large to make the possible use financially worthwhile?
4. What type of use is "logical" in that (a) the potential construction conforms to the neighborhood, and (b) the market demand exists for the type of land use? The intended use should fit the market demand. Two additional criteria that can be used to help judge are *use intensity* and *use density*. Use intensity[13] is defined as the reflection of capital and labor use per unit of land area to indicate physical development. Use density[14] is defined as the number of buildings of a particular use per unit of area, which is sometimes measured by the floor area of the building divided by the square feet of its plot. Both can be used to estimate whether the structure conforms to the neighborhood. Another important point is the type

of market demand. The market demand must be "logical" in that the potential buyers and users must exist for the product.

Once the appraiser has answered these four questions, the answers may then be used to develop an estimate of the value. The five traditional techniques used for site analysis are the direct sales comparison approach, the land residual technique, the extraction (allocation) approach, the capitalized ground rent method, and the anticipated use (development) method. All five of these are shown and explained in Chapter 5.

Site HBU and obsolescence The existing structure, if one exists, is not ignored, but it is not given significant weight in estimating the HBU of the site as though it was vacant. In addition, any alternative structure considered as a possible HBU of the site is always a new structure without any obsolescence.[15] An existing structure may not be qualified to be the HBU of the site if the building exhibits some type of obsolescence that is eliminated in the newer alternative uses. If the building continues to contribute to site value and provides a return that justifies its retention, the existing structure can constitute the HBU.

Uses of the site value The HBU for the site is estimated for several purposes. First, it may be needed in that the client may be interested in the site purchase only. Second, it may be used in calculating a property tax bill that could be levied on the site only. Third, it is required as the first step of the cost approach. Fourth, it is needed in the physical residual techniques, as explained in Chapters 13–15. Fifth, in estimating ground rental for insurance purposes, some courts may require a separate estimate of site and improvement value.

HBU and the Improvement

The HBU of the improvement must be estimated in addition to the HBU of the site. The HBU of the improved property estimates the HBU of the property as a whole, given that a structure exists.[16] Demolition is typically not considered as an alternative unless the structure has reached the end of its economic life and the property value can be increased by tearing down the structure.

The appraiser first answers the same four questions presented earlier for estimating the HBU of the site. Special emphasis must be placed on the last question, which includes an estimate of market demand. A use must be found in the market that will create the best income flow possible within physical and legal constraints to make the property financially feasible.

Once the HBU has been estimated, the existing improvement can be compared to a "perfect" improvement at its HBU as a basis for estimating the functional obsolescence. This estimate of obsolescence can be used later in the cost approach as one part of accrued obsolescence.

Limitations to the Estimation of HBU

One author[17] gives several reasons in a recent article that explain why a detailed analysis of HBU is often not found in many appraisal reports. These reasons are:

1. HBU analysis often requires an extensive review of demand and supply conditions of potential uses of the site or improved property. This type of market review may be more extensive than the analysis desired by the client. Consequently, the fee for the assignment may not justify the time invested.
2. The local zoning laws and building codes may greatly restrict the alternative building types and uses on a specific site. Consequently, the alternative uses may be somewhat obvious and do not require extensive analysis.
3. A specific client may have a specific objective for the site and does not want alternative uses investigated.
4. The property is already improved with a relatively new building that obviously conforms with the surrounding neighborhood. Typically, no additional analysis is warranted.

An Alternative View of HBU

Paul Wendt[18] published an alternative view of HBU which stated that "...'highest and best use' is not a fact to be found, but rather an opinion which can be expected to vary widely among investors and appraisers."[19] He goes on to state that the HBU decision will be determined by the individual's judgments and view of market conditions. His alternative definition of HBU is "the use which maximizes the difference between the discounted after-tax cash flows and the equity investments for alternative uses."[20] This definition accounts for a wide range of judgments covering types of uses, timing, scale, and risks. It also states that the HBU is the maximum difference between the cash flows (including resale proceeds) from a projected use and the equity investment required to enter an alternative use. For example, a potential use may be a pizza parlor if the capital requirement to convert to another use such as apartments is prohibitive.

Justification and Documentation

A recent article[21] contains suggestions for AIREA candidates covering the HBU section of their demonstration reports. Although these suggestions may not be included in every income property appraisal, they provide a good insight into what should be included in this section and how it should be presented to the client. The author states that the HBU section of the report is the "pivital point" of the appraisal. All of the earlier data on market trends lead to a conclusion reached in this section concerning the property's HBU. The HBU should be a logical conclusion after considering and weighing all of the previous material on neighborhoods, the economy, assessed values, zoning, and the relevant principles of value.

All applicable principles of value that have been considered in previous sections should be considered and brought together into one conclusion. Other principles of value such as anticipation, change, competition, and balance may be summarized since they typically appear in other sections. HBU should be demonstrated for (1) the site as though vacant, and (2) the improvement. Income, expenses, and construction costs may be used.

Care should be taken to document the existence of any obsolescence. The type and amount shown here become the basis for justifying deductions later in the cost and income approaches.

In conclusion, the HBU section of the appraisal report typically consists of several parts:

1. An outline of the conclusions from previous sections of the report
2. A discussion of the principles of value not included in previous sections but which apply here
3. An analysis of construction costs, expenses, and income that leads to the HBU.

A definite conclusion about the type of use should be reached for the site *and* the improvement, which may differ. For example, the HBU for the site may be a retail store, while the HBU for the improvement may be a type of office building.

PROBLEMS

All of the topics discussed in this chapter require extensive amounts of data and analysis to derive meaningful conclusions. The data requirements are too large to be described adequately in sample problems. Consequently, none are presented. Our recommendation is that the student read several of the references on each topic that are listed under "Additional Readings" at the end of the chapter. One or two references should be read in each of the following categories: Supply and Demand; Feasibility Studies; and Highest and Best Use.

USE OF THESE CONCEPTS

The previous two chapters have discussed concepts that are the basis of many things in the appraisal process. Appraisal is said to be an interpretation of the market, and certainly the analyst must understand the basic demand and supply relationships before an accurate interpretation can be rendered. In addition, an understanding of these concepts gives the appraiser/analyst a sense of direction and a grasp of "what it's all about." This becomes even more important as the novice moves into more complex problems where judgment and opinion play an important role in assisting the client in correctly evaluating the risk of investment in a particular project.

SUMMARY

The relationship between the price of real estate and the demand is generally thought to be inverse. The relationship between the price of real estate and its supply is generally thought to be direct. The elasticity of demand is determined by the number of substitutes for the type of real estate in question. The elasticity of the supply line is determined by the number of barriers the owner has to overcome to bring the real estate onto the market. The concept of elasticity is important because it tells the amount of change that will occur in the quantity from a change in the price.

The intersection of the demand and the supply line gives the market value. Market value is an abstract concept that a knowledgeable seller will accept and a knowledgeable buyer will pay if the forces of supply and demand are allowed to function. Market price is the transaction price that the appraiser may use to estimate the market value. The market price may or may not be equal to the market value.

Feasibility studies are conducted to determine whether the client's objectives can be accomplished within his or her constraints. Feasibility studies can include a market study, a financial analysis, a location study, a composite study, or some appropriate combination. The analyst must be sure in each study to assist the client in estimating the risks from the venture and to reach definite conclusions.

Highest and best use is one principle of value stating that the property should always be utilized in the use that gives the highest present value within the existing legal and physical constraints. One highest and best use exists for the site and another may exist for the site plus improvement. Both should be estimated.

ENDNOTES

1. George Stigler, *Theory of Price, 3rd ed.* (New York: Macmillan Co., 1966), pp. 96–98.
2. D. R. Epley, "A Further Note on the Theory of Value," *The Real Estate Appraiser* 42 (January–February 1976): 13–16.
3. Byrl Boyce, *Real Estate Appraisal Terminology* (Cambridge, Mass.: Ballinger Publishing Co., 1975), p. 86.

4. James Graaskamp, "Rational Approach to Feasibility Analysis," *The Appraisal Journal* 40 (October 1972): 513–521.
5. Tan Tek Lum, "Feasibility Analysis of Condominiums," *The Appraisal Journal* 40 (April 1972): 246–252.
6. John B. Bailey, Peter F. Spies, and Marlyn Kramer Weitzman, "Market Study + Financial Analysis = Feasibility," *The Appraisal Journal* 45 (October 1977): 550–577.
7. Graaskamp, *"Rational Approach to Feasibility Analysis."*
8. Lum, *"Feasibility Analysis of Condominiums."*
9. Bailey, Spies, and Weitzman, *"Market Study + Financial Analysis = Feasibility."*
10. G. Vincent Barrett, "A Restatement of Highest and Best Use," *The Real Estate Appraiser and Analyst* 45 (November–December 1979): 4–9.
11. Boyce, *Real Estate Appraisal Terminology,* p. 107.
12. Halbert C. Smith and Mark R. Maurais, "Highest and Best Use in the Appraisal Profession," *The Real Estate Appraiser and Analyst* 46 (March–April 1980): 27–37.
13. Boyce, *Real Estate Appraisal Terminology,* p. 116.
14. Ibid., p. 214.
15. Smith and Maurais, "Highest and Best Use in the Appraisal Profession."
16. Society of Real Estate Appraisers, *A Guide to Narrative Demonstration Appraisal Reporting* (Chicago: SREA, 1976).
17. Barrett, *"A Restatement of Highest and Best Use."*
18. Paul Wendt, "Highest and Best Use—Fact or Fancy," *The Appraisal Journal* 40 (April 1972): 165–174.
19. Ibid.
20. Ibid.
21. Robert J. Heinrich, "A Candidate's Guide to Writing a Passing MAI Demonstration Appraisal Report," *The Appraisal Journal* 47 (October 1979): 565–566.

REVIEW QUESTIONS

1. Explain the relationship among demand, supply, market price, and market value. Why are these concepts important to the appraiser?
2. Explain the role of elasticity in market analysis. What is the difference between elasticity and inelasticity?
3. Why is the concept of highest and best use important in appraisal? What is the difference between HBU for the site and HBU for the improvement?
4. How important is HBU analysis to the appraisal?

ADDITIONAL READINGS

Albritton, Harold. "Testing Highest and Best Use." *The Appraisal Journal* 47 (July 1979): 406–411.

Crouch, William H. "A Prospective Look at Highest and Best Use." *The Appraisal Journal* 34 (April 1966): 166–176.

Derbes, Max J. "Highest and Best Use—What is It?" *The Appraisal Journal* 49 (April 1981): 166–178.

Dolman, John. "Real Estate Counseling: Some Distinction from and Relationships with Real Estate Valuation." *The Appraisal Journal* 41 (October 1973): 453–463.

Graybeal, Ronald. "Condominium Computerized Feasibility Analysis." *The Appraisal Journal* 41 (October 1973): 526–534.

Hanford, Lloyd. *Feasibility Study Guidelines* (Chicago: Institute of Real Estate Management).

Kahn, Sanders A. "Real Estate Value: Its Genesis and Demise." *The Real Estate Appraiser and Analyst* 45 (January–February 1979): 13–20.

Ordway, Nicholas, and Harris, Jack. "The Dynamic Nature of Highest and Best Use." *The Appraisal Journal* 49 (July 1981): 325–334.

Ross, Thurston. "The Counselor and Investment Feasibility." *The Appraisal Journal* 44 (January 1976): 44–45.

Rowlson, John. "The Feasibility and Appraisal of Garden-Type Condominiums." *The Appraisal Journal* 41 (July 1973): 338–349.

Scribner, David Jr. "Highest and Best Use or Most Probable Use." *The Real Estate Appraiser and Analyst* 44 (May–June 1978): 23–28.

Shales, Jared. "The Counseling Process." *The Appraisal Journal* 43 (January 1975): 62–70.

Woodward, F. O., and Epley, D. R. "Feasibility Study of Richmond Coliseum: A Comment." *The Appraisal Journal* 39 (April 1971): 285–292.

MODULE III
Valuation Process and Reports

The purpose of this section is to introduce the reader to the valuation process used in the income approach and to explain and contrast the various types of reports that are used to communicate this information to the client. This material is covered early in the book to provide a framework for determining the proper location within the appraisal report of concepts that appear later. For example, an early task in the valuation process is to estimate potential income for the subject. The location of this information in several appraisal reports is shown to the reader, and a later chapter discusses the concept of income in more detail. In addition, the student can see firsthand how the demand and supply concepts discussed in the first two chapters are communicated to the client and what information the client wants.

CHAPTER 3

LEARNING OBJECTIVES

When a student finishes this chapter, he or she should be able to:

- Outline and discuss the steps followed to derive an estimate of value from the income approach.
- Contrast the letter report, letter of opinion, form report, narrative, and the demonstration report.
- Explain the recommended contents of a good appraisal.

The Valuation Process and Reports

IMPORTANT TERMS AND PHRASES

appraisal process: A procedure designed to produce an estimate of value in a logical series of steps.

demonstration report: A written report considered an examination that is submitted to a professional association for designation credit.

form report: A report given to a client on a preprinted standardized form that requests certain types of data be reported in a format required by the client.

letter of opinion: Based on a preliminary study, a statement of what, within a range, a final opinion probably would be if an appraisal were made.

letter report: A letter that summarizes the results of an appraisal.

narrative report: A report explaining what the appraiser did, how it was done, and why it was done.

valuation process for income-producing properties: One part of the appraisal process that produces an estimate of value.

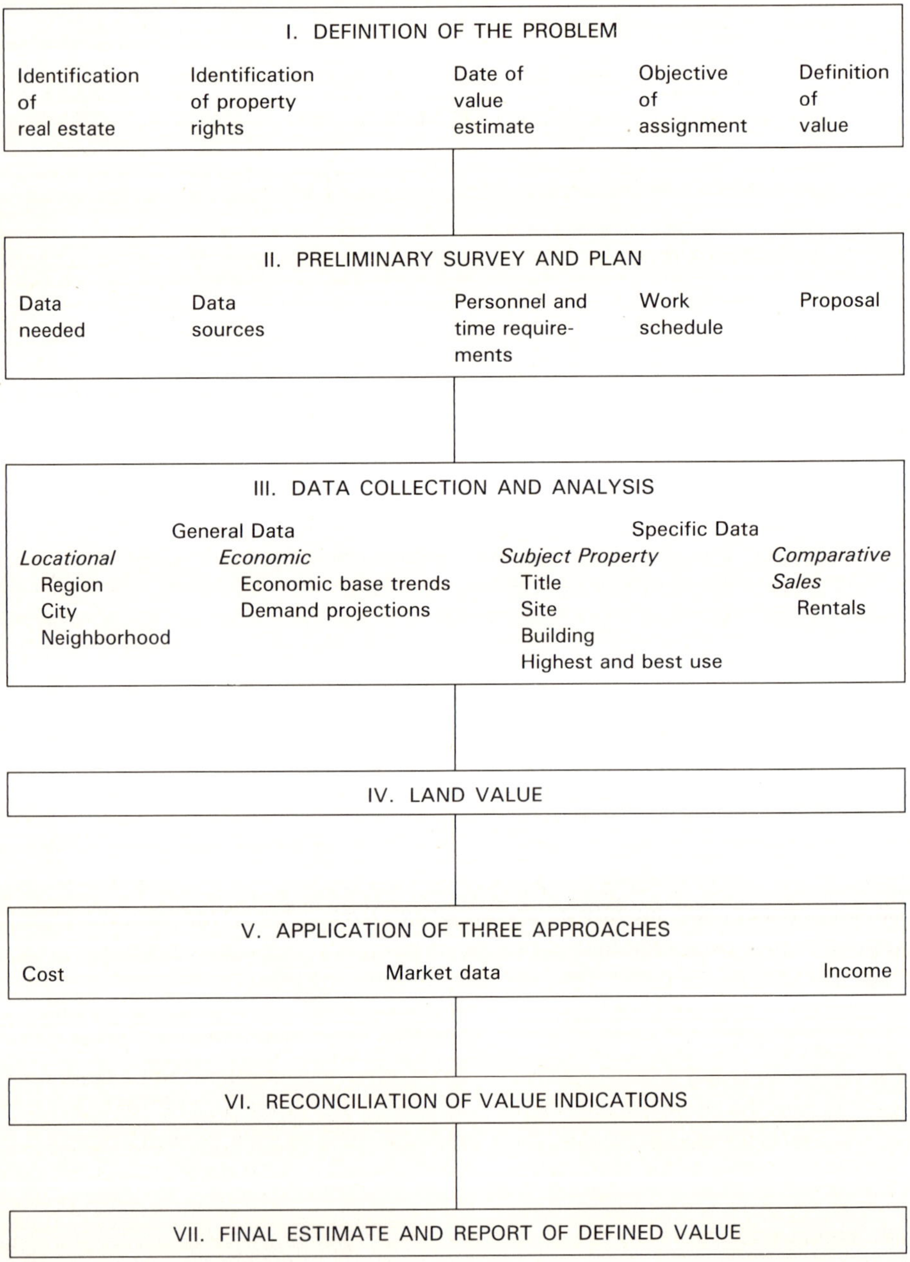

Fig. 3.1 The valuation process

Source: American Institute of Real Estate Appraisers, *The Appraisal of Real Estate* (Chicago: AIREA, 1978), p. 52. Reprinted with permission.

The purpose of this chapter is to illustrate and discuss the steps that are followed in deriving an estimate of value from income, and to illustrate the various types of appraisal reports that may be given to a client to communicate information on all or selected parts of these steps. Also, Chapter 20 contains an example of the valuation process and a report that may be used to communicate these steps to the client to satisfy his or her needs.

THE VALUATION PROCESS

The *valuation process for income-producing properties* (called the "income approach") is one part within the larger valuation or appraisal process. The valuation process is shown in Fig. 3.1. These seven steps are applied to all properties of any type to estimate value. The valuation process for income-producing properties is contained under the heading marked "Income" in step V. Once an estimate of value for the income-producing property is derived, it is used as one of three estimates in step V. The estimates of value derived from the cost approach, the market data approach, and the income approach are then reconciled into one final estimate of value. The seven steps in Fig. 3.1 are not explained in detail since one of the purposes of this chapter is to concentrate on the income approach.

THE VALUATION PROCESS FOR INCOME-PRODUCING PROPERTIES

Income-Producing Property

Income property is defined by Byrl Boyce as "a type of property the primary purpose of which is to produce monetary income."[1] The income approach may be applied to any property where the investor(s) purchased the property for the purpose of receiving money or other benefits periodically.[2] If the property is residential rental, the SREA requires at least five units[3] before it is classified as "income producing." Apartments containing four or fewer units are classified as "residential." These criteria are not universal.

Certain types of land uses do not typically generate a monetary income stream and are not good examples of the income approach. Single-family residential, recreational, and leisure property are illustrations where the stream of benefits may be more psychic than monetary. Ranch and pasture land may have no periodic income stream. In these cases, the income approach may not provide a good estimate of value.

The Valuation Process

Exhibit 3.1 shows the seven steps taught by the AIREA for estimating value from the income approach. Exhibit 3.2 shows the nine steps taught by the SREA for deriving the same result. In the opinion of the authors, either method can be used since both derive the same result. The nine steps used by

Exhibit 3.1
AIREA steps to translate income into value

Priority	Steps
1.	Estimate potential gross income. This step involves estimating income from all sources to the subject property.
2.	Estimate and deduce a vacancy and collection loss allowance to derive effective gross income. The income loss from bad debts and vacancies is estimated.
3.	Estimate and deduct expenses of operation to derive net operating income (net income before recapture). All appropriate expenses are estimated and subtracted.
4.	Estimate remaining economic life for the duration and pattern of the projected income stream. The remaining years for income to be generated is estimated; income may be projected.
5.	Select an applicable capitalization method and technique. A method of transforming income into value is selected.
6.	Develop the appropriate rate or rates. The rates of return to be used in the capitalization technique selected in Priority 5 are developed.
7.	Complete the necessary computations to derive an economic valuation by the income approach. The last step is to derive a final estimate of market value.

Source: American Institute of Real Estate Appraisers, *The Appraisal of Real Estate* (Chicago: AIREA, 1978), pp. 320–321.

the SREA are more detailed, but the differences are not critical. Either approach is acceptable.

Both exhibits can be reduced to a shortened version:

1. Estimate the future income flow and expenses
   a. the reversion is future income and must be estimated
   b. the remaining economic life must be estimated.
2. Select an appropriate capitalization technique that matches the characteristics of the property.
3. Estimate the rate or rates needed by the technique in step 2.
4. Derive the estimate of value.

Exhibit 3.2
SREA outline of income Capitalization methodology

Priority	Steps
1.	Estimate future annual income flow. Estimates of net operating income, before-tax income, or after-tax income are derived here.
2.	Estimate necessary rate of return on investment. This step derives an appropriate rate of return on the investment in the subject.
3.	Estimate type and amount of reversion. This step identifies the form, source, and type of additional income that the investor may receive at a time in the future.
4.	Estimate the capital recovery period. This step estimates the economic life of the improvements, the investment holding period, the mortgage amortization period, or the lease term, whichever is appropriate.
5.	Estimate the method of capital recovery. This step estimates the method capital recovery and can use techniques such as straight line, sinking fund, annuity, mortgage amortization, resale, or refinancing.
6.	Estimate the capitalization technique to employ: Identify the residual. This step selects a technique to fit the property which may value one part of the property independently. Examples include direct capitalization, building residual, land residual, property residual, and mortgage equity.
7.	Estimate present worth of anticipated annual-income flow. This step derives the present value of the future income flow from the operation of the property.
8.	Estimate present worth of anticipated future reversion. This step estimates the present value of any future reversion.
9.	Estimate value (present worth) of the property. The results of steps 7 and 8 are summed.

Source: William N. Kinnard, Jr., *Income Property Valuation* (Lexington, Mass.: D. C. Heath & Co., 1971), pp. 69–76.

Recommendation to the Reader

The steps contained in Exhibits 3.1 and 3.2 should be learned. They are not explained in detail since the remainder of the book concentrates on the techniques that can be used for each step. For example,

In this text	Steps
Chapters 8, 12	1. Estimate potential gross income (AIREA).
	1. Estimate future annual income flow (SREA).
	3. Estimate the type and amount of reversion (SREA).
Chapters 8, 12	2. Estimate the vacancy and collection loss (AIREA).
	1. Estimate future annual income flow (SREA).
Chapters 8, 12	3. Estimate expenses and derive NOI (AIREA).
	1. Estimate future annual income flow (SREA).
Chapters 8, 12	4. Estimate remaining economic life or the pattern of projected income (AIREA).
	4. Estimate the capital recovery period (SREA).
Chapters 9, 10, 11, 12, 13, 14, 15	5. Select the appropriate capitalization technique (AIREA).
	6. Estimate the capitalization technique (SREA).
	5. Estimate method of capital recovery (SREA).
Chapters 9, 10, 11, 12, 13, 14, 15	6. Develop the appropriate rate or rates (AIREA).
	2. Estimate the necessary rate of return on investment (SREA).
Chapters 9, 10, 11, 12, 13, 14, 15, 16	7. Complete the necessary calculations (AIREA).
	7., 8., 9. Estimate present worth of annual income flow, estimate present worth of future reversion, estimate value of the property (SREA).

TYPES OF APPRAISAL REPORTS

Four types of appraisal reports are in general use: *the letter of opinion, the letter report, the form report, and the narrative report*. A *demonstration report* is prepared by candidates for an appraisal designation and is considered as an examination where the candidate demonstrates acceptable appraisal techniques. Since the latter is not used with the public, it is not covered in this chapter. References are made throughout the text to techniques within a demonstration report since these provide a useful guide to acceptable principles and the preparation of the other reports.

Minimum Standards of Any Appraisal Report

SREA As an illustration of the minimum contents for an appraisal report, Exhibit 3.3 shows the recommendation of the SREA Standards of Professional Practice.

North American Conference of Appraisal Organizations In March 1981, representatives of this group met and issued a report containing minimum standards for an appraisal report. The following are reported in the April 1981 issue of *The Appraiser:*

- Purpose and/or objectives (with value defined)

Exhibit 3.3
SREA minimum requirements for an appraisal report

1. An adequate and definite description of the property being appraised.
2. The purpose of the appraisal and a definition of the value estimated.
3. The effective date of the appraisal.
4. The data and reasoning supporting the value conclusion which may include the direct sales comparison approach, the income approach and the cost approach. The exclusions of any of the usual three approaches must be explained and supported.
5. The final estimate of value.
6. Assumptions and limiting conditions.
7. The appraiser's certification and signature.
8. It is unethical for a member to omit any of the above minimum requirements from his appraisal report transmitted to the client without good cause. If, with good cause, any of the above minimum requirements are not included in the appraisal report transmitted to the client, the appraiser shall clearly set forth within the appraisal report transmitted to the client a statement to the effect that the portions excluded (named specifically) are included in the appraiser's written appraisal which has been prepared and retained in the appraiser's file for this assignment, and that said written appraisal is incorporated herein by reference and is an integral part hereof.

Source: Section III-A-8, Standards of Professional Practice, Society of Real Estate Appraisers, Chicago, Illinois.

- Legal description and/or adequate identification of the property
- Date(s) of value estimate
- Physical property description
- Known and/or observed encumbrances
- Statement of highest and best use and analysis, if appropriate
- Property rights appraised
- Direct sales comparison approach
- Cost approach
- Income approach
- Conclusion
- Reports (the appraiser must have the minimum data requirements on file to properly support the final estimate of value)
- Assumptions and limiting conditions
- Signature of appraiser
- Confidentiality

Letter of Opinion

One type of service the appraiser may perform for the client is to give a *letter of opinion.* The letter of opinion is defined as a statement of what, within a range, a final opinion would probably be if an appraisal were made, which is based upon a preliminary study.[4]

This type of report has two essential characteristics. First, it is *not* an appraisal, and the letter must clearly state this fact. Second, the appraiser must have sound support in his or her files for the range of value. This file should be maintained for at least five years since the client may ask for a detailed appraisal at a future date.

Exhibit 3.4 illustrates the recommended format for a letter of opinion given by the SREA Professional Practice Committee. Exhibit 3.5 is a letter of opinion published recently by an appraiser who uses this type of report.

Letter Report

A *letter report* is a letter that summarizes the results of an appraisal.[5] Consequently, the letter report may be viewed as an appraisal. All of the requirements for a complete appraisal must be within the appraiser's supporting file. The letter gives a specific value and a summary of the pertinent data needed to explain the value.

Exhibit 3.4
SREA recommended format for a letter of opinion

For: ____________________ Date: ____________________
____
____

Re: Property located at ____

Dear____________________:

In accordance with your request, I have made a preliminary study of the above referenced property as of ____(date)____. This preliminary study consisted of (state specifically what steps the appraiser performed in his study, and what analysis, if any, he made). It should be clearly understood that an appraisal has not been made of the above referenced property, and that this letter does not constitute an appraisal report, nor should it in any way be construed as same.

Based upon this preliminary study, it is the appraiser's belief that if an appraisal were made, the final __________ estimate would probably be in the range of approximately $________ to $________ (See Note A).

It should be clearly understood that the range of value approximated herein is subject to adjustment upon completion of an appraisal.

____
(Signature)

Note A: The letter of opinion never refers to a specific value.

Source: Society of Real Estate Appraisers Professional Practice Committee, Chicago, Illinois.

Exhibit 3.5
Sample letter of opinion

RE: Preliminary Opinion of
Value of Property
Located at: (Address)

Dear Mr., Mrs., or Ms. ______________

In accordance with your request, I have made a preliminary study and analysis of the above referenced property. The purpose of the study is to indicate a range in value, for sale purposes, as of (Date). It should be clearly understood that this letter constitutes only a preliminary opinion and should not be construed as an appraisal.

Fair Market Value is defined to mean:
The highest price in terms of money which a property will bring in a competitive and open market under all conditions requisite to a fair sale, the buyer and seller, each acting prudently, knowledgeably and assuming the price is not affected by undue stimulus. (SREA-AIREA, 1975: *Real Estate Appraisal Terminology*.)

Implicit in this definition is the consummation of a sale as of a specified date and the passing of title from seller to buyer under conditions whereby:

1. Buyer and seller are typically motivated.
2. Both parties are well informed or well advised, and each acting in what he considers his own best interest.
3. A reasonable time is allowed for exposure in the open market.
4. Payment is made in cash or its equivalent.
5. Financing, if any, is on terms generally available in the community at the specified date and typical for the property type in its locale.
6. The price represents a normal consideration for the property sold unaffected by special financing amounts and/or terms, services, fees, costs, or credits incurred in the transaction.

Optional Section

The study consisted of personal inspection of the property on (Date) as well as preliminary study of the general area. In addition the county assessor's office, title company office records and our own office files were researched for data (sales and cost data), which were used to arrive at the indicated range in value.

Considering this study as a preliminary analysis, only two of the three approaches to value were used. One of these methods was the Cost Approach to value. In this method a national cost service is used to estimate what it would cost to replace the building and improvements today.

Replacement Cost is defined as:

The cost of construction at current prices of a building having utility equivalent to the building being appraised but built with modern materials and according to current standards, design and layout. The use of the replacement cost concept presumably eliminates all functional obsolescence, and only depreciation to be measured is physical deterioration and economic obsolescence. (SREA-AIREA, 1975: *Real Estate Appraisal Terminology.*) } Optional Section

This method indicated a range in value of between $__________ and $__________.

The second method which was considered was the Market Approach to value which is defined as:

The Market Approach is the process of analyzing sales of similar recently sold properties in order to derive an indication of the most probable sales price of the property being appraised. (SREA-AIREA, 1975: *Real Estate Appraisal Terminology.*) } Optional Section

Because of the dissimilarities of homes in the area it is difficult to find sales which are truly comparable. Over the last year, however, there have been several sales which do give an indication as to the value of the subject property. The sales which were considered in this approach sold from $__________ to $__________. After considering the differences between the sale properties and the subject, the indicated range in value was between $__________ to $__________.

An investigation was then made of properties currently listed for sale. This was done to determine alternative purchases a prospective buyer might have to the subject. In other words, what would a prospective buyer have to pay for a home offering the same utility and similar amenities as the subject. This was done on the premise that no prudent purchaser will pay more for a property than what it would be necessary to spend for a reasonable substitute. Listing prices also tend to set an upper limit of value.

(continued)

Exhibit 3.5 (continued)

Based upon the information gathered in the analysis of the subject property, it is my opinion that if an appraisal were made, the Final Fair Market Value estimate would most probably be in a range from $__________ to $__________, depending on the marketing of the home and how well the subject property fills the purchaser-user's need. This would also be the range of the property's most probable selling price which is defined as:

> That price at which a property would most probably sell if exposed to the market for a reasonable time, under market conditions prevailing as of the date of the appraisal. (SREA-AIREA, 1975: *Real Estate Appraisal Terminology*.) } Optional Section

It should be clearly understood that an appraisal was not made and that this letter is a preliminary opinion/study of the above referenced property.

Should you have any questions regarding this letter, please do not hesitate to contact me.

Very truly yours,

____

(Name)

Source: Reprinted with permission from the July–August, 1979, issue of *The Real Estate Appraiser and Analyst*, published by the Society of Real Estate Appraisers, Chicago, Illinois. No further reproduction is authorized.

Letter reports are typically used in very specific situations where the summary serves the client's needs more than the appraisal report. In these cases, the user is probably knowledgeable about appraisal practices and terminology and can interpret accurately the contents of the letter. Exhibit 3.6 shows the format recommended by the SREA for a letter report.

Form Report

The *form report* (sometimes called the short form or the checksheet) is a report given to a client on a preprinted standardized form that requests certain types of data be reported in a format required by the client.[6] The preprinted form requires the appraiser to report only the type and amount of information that the user considers important. Typically, the form is designed to include many boxes that may be checked and blanks that may be filled in.

The appraiser should always remember two points in using the form report. Any report given to the client must include all of the minimum requirements shown earlier in Exhibit 3.3. Any report that does not include these seven points must comply with step eight that requires the appraiser to include a letter with the report stating that the portion of the report excluded (specifically named) has been included in the analysis and is in the appraiser's file.

Exhibit 3.7 shows a form report used by the Federal Home Loan Mortgage Corporation for residential income property of two to twelve units.

Narrative Report

The *narrative appraisal report* reflects what the appraiser did, how he or she did it, and why it was done.[7] This type of report should stand on its own content since the appraiser has ample opportunity to justify and document conclusions. References to additional information maintained in a file are not typically necessary since the conclusions from the data can be shown and explained. This type of report is the most preferable since the complete appraisal process can be shown and explained.

Exhibit 3.8 contains the suggested guidelines published by the AIREA for a candidate to follow in preparing a demonstration report for MAI credit. Since the demonstration report is a longer and more detailed appraisal completed for the purpose of an examination grade, the time and data requirements that are necessary to complete it are longer than the narrative report done for the client. However, these recommendations can successfully be applied to the completion of a professional narrative report. In addition, a sample narrative report is shown in Module 11.

Exhibit 3.6
SREA recommended format for a letter report

For: ______________________ Date: ______________________

____

____

Re: Property located at ____ (*See Note A*)

Dear______________________:

In accordance with your request, I have personally made a complete inspection of the above referenced property for the purpose of estimating its ____________ value, which is defined to mean: ____

____

It is my opinion that the estimated ________________ value as of the _______ day of _______ A.D. is $______________________.

It should be clearly understood that this letter constitutes only a statement of the final value estimate, but that said value has been based upon a complete written appraisal. The written appraisal, although in rough form, has been prepared and retained in my files, and is available to you for review should you desire. Should you require a more formal typed report, the same is available to you upon request. My fee for this service would be $____________. The written appraisal retained in my files is incorporated herein by reference and is an integral part hereof. (*See Note B*).

The written appraisal, retained in my file, includes a complete description of the property appraised (*See Note A and Note D*), and it includes developed indications of value employing direct sales comparison, cost and income data and analysis (*See Note C and Note D*).

I hereby certify that I have no present or contemplated future interest in the real estate that is the subject of this report and that I have no personal interest or bias with respect to the subject matter of this report or the parties involved and that the amount of the fee is not contingent upon reporting a predetermined value or upon the amount of the value estimate. I certify that, to the best of my knowledge and belief the statements of fact contained in the written appraisal, upon which the analysis, opinions and conclusions are based, are true and correct subject to the special and limiting conditions contained therein (or attached hereto), that this report has been made in conformity with, and is subject to, the requirements of the Code of Ethics and the Standards of Professional Practice and Conduct of the Society of Real Estate Appraisers and that no one other than the undersigned prepared the analyses, conclusions and opinions concerning real estate that are set forth in the written appraisal.

....SEAL
(Signature)

Note A: A complete description of the property being appraised must be included in the written appraisal in the appraiser's file for the assignment, *i.e.*, description of the subject property (land and improvements) and identification of the location of subject (preferably a legal description); matters relating to title (nature of ownership, easements, restrictions, etc.); highest and best use identification and support; political, social and economic factors affecting the property; and physical, functional and economic factors affecting the value conclusion.

Note B: When the letter report is preliminary to the transmission of a full narrative report, this paragraphy might read as follows: "It should be clearly understood that this letter constitutes only a statement of the final value estimate, but that said value has been based upon a complete appraisal, and that a full report will follow, which is incorporated herein by reference and is an integral part hereof."

Note C: The exclusion of any of the usual three approaches must be explained and supported (Section III-A-4 of the Standards of Professional Practice).

Note D: If, with good cause, any of the minimum requirements of an appraisal are omitted in the appraisal report transmitted to the client, then the appraiser must clearly set forth within the appraisal report transmitted to the client a statement to the effect that the portions excluded (named specifically) are included in the appraiser's written appraisal which has been prepared and retained in the appraiser's file for the assignment, and that said written appraisal is incorporated herein by reference and is an integral part hereof (Section III-A-8 of the Standards of Professional Practice).

Source: Society of Real Estate Appraisers Professional Practice Committee, Chicago, Illinois.

Exhibit 3.7
Appraisal Report—Small Residential Income Property

To be completed by Lender

Borrower ______ Census Tract ______ Map Reference ______

Property Address ______

City ______ County ______ State ______ Zip Code ______

Legal Description ______

Sale Price $ ______ Date of Sale ______ Loan Term ______ yrs. Property Rights Appraised: ☐ Fee ☐ Leasehold ☐ Other ______

Actual Real Estate Taxes $ ______ (yr) Loan charges to be paid by seller $ ______ Other sales concessions ______

Lender/Client ______ Address ______

Occupant ______ Appraiser ______ Instructions to Appraiser ______

NEIGHBORHOOD

Location . . . . . . ☐ Urban . . . . ☐ Suburban . . . . ☐ Rural

Built-up . . . . . . ☐ Over 75% . . . . ☐ 25% to 75% . . ☐ Under 25%

Present land use . . . . ___% Condominiums ___% 1-Family ___% 2-4 Family

___% Apartments ___% Commercial ___% Vacant ___%

Change in present land use . . ☐ Not likely . . . . ☐ Likely (*) . . . . ☐ Taking Place(*)

(*) From ______ To ______

Property values . . . . ☐ Increasing . . . . ☐ Stable . . . . ☐ Declining

Housing demand/supply . . . ☐ In balance . . . . ☐ Shortage . . . . ☐ Oversupply

Predominant occupancy . . . ☐ Owner . . . . ☐ Tenant . . . . ___% Vacant

Single Family: Price range $ ______ to $ ______ Predominant $ ______

Age ______ yrs. to ______ yrs. Predominant ______ yrs

Typical multifamily bldg. Type ______ No. Stories ______ No. Units ______

Age ______ yrs. Condition ______

Typical rents $ ______ to $ ______ ☐ Increasing ☐ Stable ☐ Declining

Est. neighborhood apt. vacancy ___% ☐ Decreasing ☐ Stable ☐ Increasing

Rent controls ☐ No ☐ Yes ☐ Not likely ☐ Likely

OVERALL RATING	Good	Avg.	Fair	Poor
Adequacy of Shopping				
Adequacy of Utilities				
Employment Opportunities				
Police and Fire Protection				
Recreational Facilities				
Property Compatibility				
Protection from Detrimental Conditions				
General Appearance of Properties				
Appeal to Market				

	Distance	Access or Convenience
Public Transportation		
Employment Centers		
Shopping Facilities		
Grammar Schools		
Freeway Access		

Note: FHLMC/FNMA do not consider race or the racial composition of the neighborhood to be reliable appraisal factors.

Describe those factors, favorable or unfavorable, affecting marketability (incl. mkt. area population size & financial ability). ______

SITE

Dimensions ______ = ______ Sq. Ft. or Acres ☐ Corner Lot

Zoning classification ______ Present improvements ☐ do ☐ do not conform to zoning regulations

Highest and best use: ☐ Present use ☐ Other (specify)

	Public	Other (Describe)
Elec.	☐	______
Gas	☐	______
Water	☐	______
San.Sewer	☐	______
	☐ Underground Elec. & Tel.	

OFF-SITE IMPROVEMENTS

Street Access: ☐ Public ☐ Private

Surface ______

Maintenance ☐ Public ☐ Private

☐ Storm Sewer ☐ Curb/Gutter

☐ Sidewalk ☐ Street Lights

Topo ______

Size ______

Shape ______

View ______

Drainage ______

Is the property located in a HUD Identified Special Flood Hazard Area? ☐ No ☐ Yes

Comments (favorable or unfavorable conditions including any apparent adverse easements or encroachments) ______

DESCRIPTION OF IMPROVEMENTS

☐ Existing ☐ Proposed ☐ Under Construction Type: ☐ Elevator ☐ Walk-up ☐ Det. ☐ Semi-Det. ☐ Row No. Stories ______

No. Bldgs. ______ No. Units ______ No. Rooms ______ No. Baths ______ Parking Spaces: No. ______ Type ______

Basic Structural System ______ Exterior Walls ______ Roof Covering ______

Foundation Walls ______ Basement ___% Finished ___% Describe use ______

Interior Walls ______ Floors ______ Bath Floor and Walls ______

Insulation ______ Adequacy ______ Adequacy of Soundproofing ______

Heating: ☐ Central ☐ Individual Type ______ Fuel ______ Adequacy & Condition ______

Air Conditioning: ☐ Central ☐ Individual Fuel ______ Make ______ Adequacy & Condition ______

Kitchen Cabinets, Drawers and Counter space ☐ Adequate ☐ Inadequate

Total No. Appliances: ______ Range/Oven ______ Fan/Hood ______ Dishwasher

______ Disposal ______ Refrigerator ______ Washer ______ Dryer ______ Compactor

Water Heater(s) (make, capacity, fuel) ______

Plumbing Fixtures (make) ______

Electrical Service (amps per unit) ______

Security Features ______

Special Features (including energy efficient items) ______

OVERALL PROPERTY RATING	Good	Avg.	Fair	Poor
Quality of construction (materials and finish)				
Condition of improvements				
Room sizes and layout				
Closets and storage				
Plumbing—adequacy and condition				
Electrical—adequacy and condition				
Kitchen equipment—adequacy and condition				
Amenities and parking facilities				
Overall livability				
Appeal to market				

Age: Actual ______ yrs., Effective ______ yrs. to ______ yrs. Est. Remaining Economic Life ______ yrs. to ______ yrs. Explain if less than Loan Term

COMMENTS: (including functional or physical inadequacies, repairs needed, modernization, etc.) ______

COST APPROACH

ESTIMATED REPRODUCTION COST NEW

______ x ______ = ______ sq. ft. x ______ (Stories) = ______ sq. ft. x $ ______ $ ______

______ x ______ = ______ sq. ft. x ______ (Stories) = ______ sq. ft. x $ ______

______ x ______ = ______ sq. ft. x ______ (Stories) = ______ sq. ft. x $ ______

OTHER IMPROVEMENTS (Including special energy efficient items) ______

SITE IMPROVEMENTS ______

TOTAL ESTIMATED COST NEW OF IMPROVEMENTS . . . . . . $ ______

LESS DEPRECIATION Physical $ ______ Functional $ ______ Economic $ ______ ( )

DEPRECIATED VALUE OF IMPROVEMENTS . . . . . . $ ______

ADD-ESTIMATED LAND VALUE (If leasehold, show only leasehold value — attach calculations) . . . . $ ______

INDICATED VALUE BY THE COST APPROACH ☐ FEE SIMPLE ☐ LEASEHOLD . . . . $ ______

FHLMC Form 72 7/79 2-12 Units

ATTACH LAYOUT SKETCHES SHOWING UNIT ENTRIES, LOCATION MAP AND DESCRIPTIVE PHOTOGRAPHS OF SUBJECT PROPERTY AND STREET SCENE

FNMA Form 1025 7/79 2-4 Units

Source: Reprinted with permission of the Federal National Mortgage Association.

Exhibit 3.7 (continued)

COMPARABLE RENTAL DATA

ITEM	COMPARABLE No. 1	COMPARABLE No. 2	COMPARABLE No. 3
Address			
Proximity to subject			
Rent survey date			
Description of property and conditions	No. Units ___ No. Vac. ___ Yr. Blt. 19___	No. Units ___ No. Vac. ___ Yr. Blt. 19___	No. Units ___ No. Vac. ___ Yr. Blt. 19___
Individual unit breakdown	Rm. Count Tot BR b / Size Sq. Ft. / Monthly Rent $ / ¢ / Rm	Rm. Count Tot BR b / Size Sq. Ft. / Monthly Rent $ / ¢ / Rm	Rm. Count Tot BR b / Size Sq. Ft. / Monthly Rent $ / ¢ / Rm
Utilities, furniture and amenities incl. in rent			
Compare comps to subj.			

RENT SCHEDULE

Utilities included in actual rents: ☐ Water ☐ Gas ☐ Heat ☐ Electric ☐ Air Conditioning ☐ ______

Utilities included in forecasted rents: ☐ Water ☐ Gas ☐ Heat ☐ Electric ☐ Air Conditioning ☐ ______

No. of Units	Individual Unit Rm. Count Tot. BR b	Total Rooms	Sq. Ft. Area Per Unit	No. Units Vacant	ACTUAL RENTS Per Unit Unfurnished	ACTUAL RENTS Per Unit Furnished	ACTUAL RENTS Total Rents	FORECASTED RENTS Per Unit Unfurnished	FORECASTED RENTS Per Unit Furnished	FORECASTED RENTS Per Sq. Ft. or Room	FORECASTED RENTS Total Rents
					$	$	$	$	$	$	$
	TOTAL						$				$

Other Monthly Income (Itemize) ______ $ ______

Vacancy: Actual last yr. ___% Prev. yr. ___% Forecasted: ___% $ ______ Total Gross Monthly Forecasted Rent $ ______

Discuss rental concessions, forecasted rents: ______

MARKET DATA ANALYSIS

ITEM	SUBJECT	COMPARABLE No. 1	COMPARABLE No. 2	COMPARABLE No. 3
Address				
Proximity to subject				
Price	$ ☐ Unf. ☐ F	$ ☐ Unf. ☐ F.	$ ☐ Unf. ☐ F.	$ ☐ Unf. ☐ F.
Date of sale				
Individual unit breakdown	Yr. Blt. 19___ No. Vac. ___ / No. of Units / Individual Unit Room Count Tot. BR b	Yr. Blt. 19___ No. Vac. ___ / No. of Units / Individual Unit Room Count Tot. BR b	Yr. Blt. 19___ No. Vac. ___ / No. of Units / Individual Unit Room Count Tot. BR b	Yr. Blt. 19___ No. Vac. ___ / No. of Units / Individual Unit Room Count Tot. BR b
Compare to subject, including condition, terms of sale/financing				
Gross Bldg. Area (GBA)	sq. ft.	sq. ft.	sq. ft.	sq. ft.
Gross Monthly Rent	$	$	$	$
Gross Mo. Rent Mult. (1)				
Price Per Unit	$	$	$	$
Price Per Room	$	$	$	$
Price Per S.F. GBA	$ /sq. ft. GBA	$ /sq. ft. GBA	$ /sq. ft. GBA	$ /sq. ft. GBA

(1) Sale Price ÷ Gross Monthly Rent — Value Indication for Subject

Val. Per Unit $ ______ X ______ Units = $ ______. Val. Per S.F. G.B.A. $ ______ X ______ S.F. Bldg. Area = $ ______

Val. Per Rm $ ______ X ______ Rms = $ ______ G.R.M. ______ X ______ Total Monthly Rent = $ ______

Reconciliation: ______

INDICATED VALUE BY MARKET DATA APPROACH $ ______

EXPENSE ANALYSIS

ANNUAL EXPENSE SUMMARY - (If for FNMA - Lender must prepare operating data on sep. form for appraiser to review, comment on & attach to appraisal)

	ACTUAL	FORECAST	CALCULATIONS OR COMMENTS
1. Utilities: ☐ Heat $ ______ ☐ Electric $ ______			
☐ Gas $ ______ ☐ Water & Sewer $ ______ Total:	$	$	
2. Real Estate Taxes $ ______ 3. Insurance $ ______ Total:			
4. Management $ ______ Salaries $ ______ Total:			
5. Maint. & Decor. $ ______ Repairs $ ______ Reserves $ ______ Total:			
6. Other ______ Total:			
TOTAL EXPENSES & REPLACEMENT RESERVES	$	$	

This appraisal is made ☐ "as is" ☐ subject to the repairs, alterations, or conditions listed below ☐ completion per plans and specifications.

Comments, Conditions and Final Reconciliation ______

This appraisal is based upon the above requirements, the certification, contingent and limiting conditions, and Market Value definition that are stated in ☐ FHLMC Form 439 (Rev. 10/78)/FNMA Form 1004B (Rev. 10/78) filed with client ______ 19___ ☐ attached.

I ESTIMATE THE MARKET VALUE, AS DEFINED, OF SUBJECT PROPERTY AS OF ______ 19___ to be $ ______

Appraiser(s) ______ Review Appraiser (If applicable) ______

☐ Did ☐ Did Not Physically Inspect Property

FHLMC Form 72 7/79
2-12 Units

FNMA Form 1025 7/79
2-4 Units

Exhibit 3.8
AIREA recommendations for the preparation of a demonstration report for M.A.I. credit (Form A-20) (paraphrased by authors)

A. The title page
B. Letter of transmittal
C. Table of contents
D. Photo of subject property
E. Necessary items such as:
   - Assumptions and limiting conditions
   - Qualifications of the appraiser
   - Employment in chronological order
   - Education
   - Real estate experience
   - Professional and trade affiliations
   - Important appraisal assignments

F. Body of report
   1. Identification of the property
   2. Objective of the appraisal
   3. Definition of market value
   4. Property rights appraised
   5. Function of the appraisal
   6. Statement of ownership
   7. Date
   8. Region or city data
   9. Neighborhood data
   10. Land or site data
   11. Zoning
   12. Assessment and taxes
   13. Description of improvements
   14. History
   15. Highest and best use and improvement analysis
   16. Land valuation
   17. Cost approach
   18. Market data approach
   19. Income approach
   20. Reconciliation
   21. Certificate of appraisal
   22. Addendum

SUMMARY

Five types of appraisal reports have been used to communicate the results of a market investigation to the reader. The letter of opinion, letter report, form report, and the narrative have been used with the public. The demonstration report is used to demonstrate knowledge of appraisal practices and principles for receiving credit toward a designation in appraisal.

The letter of opinion is a preliminary study that states a range that most likely contains the final estimate of value. It is used when the client does not want a complete appraisal, and is not considered to be an appraisal. The letter report is a summary of an actual appraisal, and contains an estimate of the market value. It must be substantiated by an actual appraisal, and is considered to be an appraisal. The form report is a report given to a client on a preprinted standardized form. It contains an estimate of market value and is considered to be an appraisal. Any parts of the appraisal that have been omitted on the form should be carefully documented and communicated. The narrative report is a written description of what the appraiser did, how it was done, and why it was done. The appraiser can take whatever space is needed to justify and document the final estimate.

The income approach is one estimate of the value of property that must then be reconciled with the cost and direct sales comparison estimates. The income approach to estimating value contains a series of steps recommended by the AIREA and the SREA.

Any appraisal report should contain an adequate and definite description of the subject; the purpose and definition of value; effective date of the appraisal; the data and reasoning for the direct sales, income, and cost approaches; final estimate of value; assumptions and limiting conditions; the appraiser's certification signature; and an explanation if any of the above are omitted. The complete appraisal report may be written according to the guidelines recommended by the AIREA and/or the SREA.

REVIEW QUESTIONS

1. Contrast and explain the following:

   letter report
   letter of opinion
   form report
   narrative report
   demonstration report

2. Outline the steps that are recommended by the AIREA and the SREA to derive an estimate of value under the income approach.

3. Explain the contents of any appraisal as contained in the Standards of Professional Practice published by the SREA.

4. Discuss, in general, the recommended contents of a demonstration report.

ENDNOTES

1. Byrl N. Boyce, *Real Estate Appraisal Terminology* (Cambridge, Mass: Ballinger Publishing Co., 1975), p. 113.
2. Ibid.

3. SRA/SRPA Admissions Committee, *A Guide to Narrative Demonstration Appraisal Reporting* (Chicago: SREA, 1976), p. 9.
4. Professional Practices Committee, *Interpretation of Types of Appraisal Reports and Letters of Opinion* (Chicago: SREA); see also, Chester R. Pyle, "Letters of Opinion: Should We or Shouldn't We?" *Real Estate Appraiser and Analyst* 45 (July-August, 1979): 4-12.
5. Pyle, "Letters of Opinion."
6. Ibid.
7. Ibid.

ADDITIONAL READINGS

American Institute of Real Estate Appraisers. *Preparation of Form Demonstration Report for R.M. Credit, Form A-20B* (Chicago: AIREA, May 1978).

American Institute of Real Estate Appraisers. *Preparation of Demonstration Appraisal Reports for M.A.I. Credit, Form A-20* (Chicago: AIREA, May 1979).

Burton, James C. "The Real Estate Professor as a Review Appraiser." *Appraisal Review Journal* 3 (Spring-Summer, 1980): 16-25.

Drennan, R. Peter. "The Appraiser's Responsibility to the Reviewer and to Market Value." *Appraisal Review Journal* 3 (Spring-Summer 1980): 56-67.

Hanford, Lloyd. "Mortgage Loan Appraisal or Rubber Stamp?" *The Appraisal Journal* 40 (July 1972): 325-331.

Hart, William S., Jr. "Review from the Income Side." *Appraisal Review Journal* 3 (Winter 1980): 30-37.

Heinrich, Robert J. "A Candidate's Guide to Writing a Passing MAI Demonstration Appraisal Report." *The Appraisal Journal* 47 (October 1979): 561-573.

Kahn, Sanders. "Review Appraising—Professionally." *Appraisal Review Journal* 3 (Winter 1980): 64-73.

Nielsen, Donald A. "Certification of Appraisers: Issues, Dilemmas, and Prospects." *The Appraisal Journal* 49 (April 1981): 259-270.

O'Flaherty, John D. *Candidate's Checklist for Writing a Narrative Demonstration Report on a Single-Family Residential Property* (Chicago: AIREA, March 1978).

Pyle, Chester. "Letters of Opinion: Should We or Shouldn't We?" *Real Estate Appraiser and Analyst* 45 (July-August 1979): 4-12.

Seymour, Charles. "Responsibilities of the Review Appraiser." *The Appraisal Journal* 39 (October 1971): 508-513.

Tronowsky, Otto. "A Lenders View of Good and Bad Markets." *Appraisal Review Journal* 2 (Fall 1979): 26-31.

MODULE IV
Direct Sales Comparison Approach to Value

The purpose of this module is to explain the technique for estimating market value using the sales comparison approach. The chapter repeats definitions of market price and market value and includes a discussion of the elements of comparison and their use, the types of units of comparison, data sources, methods for selecting comparable properties, methods of documenting and justifying adjustments, uses of regression analysis, the steps in the sales comparison approach, and the common errors often found in demonstration reports written by MAI candidates. When finished with the chapter, a student should have an understanding of the nature and purpose of this approach in estimating market value.

In the first two chapters, the student learns the basics of demand and supply and applications of these in the appraisal. In Chapter 3, the reader can read and see the manner in which this information is communicated to the client through various reports. The next step is to start the valuation process. The direct sales comparison approach is reviewed first.

CHAPTER 4

LEARNING OBJECTIVES

When a student finishes this chapter, he or she should be able to:

- Explain, in general, how the appraiser uses the direct sales comparison approach to estimate market value.
- Identify and discuss the elements of comparison.
- Discuss the units of comparison.
- Explain how comparable properties can be selected.
- Explain the concept involved in the adjustment process.
- Illustrate the methods of determining the adjustment for time.
- Illustrate the methods of determining the adjustment for location.
- Illustrate the methods of determining the adjustment for physical characteristics including the matched pair technique.
- Discuss the need to identify adjustments for financial arrangements.
- Explain the role of multiple regression and statistical analysis to appraisal.
- Explain the steps in the direct sales comparison approach.
- Outline common errors in the direct sales comparison approach section of demonstration reports.

Estimate of Value by Direct Sales Comparison

IMPORTANT TERMS AND PHRASES

adjustment process: The selling price of the comparable property is transformed into an estimate of market value for the subject.

direct sales comparison approach: One procedure for estimating value by using the selling price of recently sold similar properties.

elements of comparison: Criteria that are used to select recently sold similar properties from the market.

matched pairs: A procedure for comparing similar properties to derive a market justified dollar figure for a specific property feature.

units of comparison: A common denominator of measurement that can be used to compare properties.

The purpose of this chapter is to discuss and illustrate the direct sales comparison approach to estimating market value. A problem at the end of the chapter illustrates many of the concepts within the chapter.

MARKET PRICE AND MARKET VALUE

Market price has been defined in several locations in this book to be the transaction price that is the selling (buying) price that is actually observed in the market. *Market value* has been defined to be an abstract concept that represents an ideal price negotiated between a knowledgeable, willing buyer and a knowledgeable, willing seller. Market value may or may not be equal to market price. If the transaction in the market that resulted in a market price has satisfied all of the assumptions that are included within the definition of market value, the market price that is observed is most likely very close to the market value of the property.[1]

Consequently, the direct sales comparison approach to estimating market value revolves around locating a sufficient number of recently sold comparable or similar properties to the subject property being appraised. This approach argues, using the rationale above, that the selling prices of these comparable properties can be processed through a series of adjustments and the result could provide a good approximation of market value for the subject being appraised.

Since this approach relies upon prices set by the market between a willing buyer and a willing seller, this estimate of market value is given considerable weight. If the comparable properties are very similar, the other estimates of market value—reproduction cost-new and income—could conceivably be used as only a check on the "reasonableness" of the market value estimate derived by this approach. In addition, the direct sales comparison approach may be given total weight if a sufficient number of comparables exist to justify the estimate of market value. For example, good recent sales of comparable properties may indicate to the appraiser a value of $600,000. The reproduction cost-new estimate is $650,000 to build an exact replica of the structure at current prices. The direct sales comparison approach should be given priority since the objective of estimating market value is to determine what a willing, knowledgeable buyer and a willing, knowledgeable seller would negotiate as a price.

ELEMENTS OF COMPARISON

Two important steps in applying the direct sales comparison approach are the selection of the comparable properties and the adjustments that are performed to the comparables. In both steps, the *elements of comparison* are used, which consist of four criteria that serve as a basis for categorizing the similar characteristics among properties. Each of the criteria are discussed below.

Time of sale The comparable properties should have sold as recently to the date of the appraisal as possible. No criteria exists for using or eliminating sales that happened one year, three years, six years, or ten years ago. The answer depends on the number of comparable properties that have sold in the past and the other elements of comparison considered as a group.

Physical features The comparable should be as similar to the subject as possible in terms of physical features. No two properties are exactly the same since differences arise in areas such as physical and functional depreciation.

Location Ideally, the recently sold comparables should be adjacent to the subject property being appraised. Since this does not often occur, the application of this element of comparison is as follows:

1. Select a comparable on the same block if possible.
2. Select a comparable on the same street if possible.
3. Select a comparable in the same neighborhood if possible.
4. Select a comparable in the same community if possible.
5. Select a comparable from the same region if possible.

The reasons for these rules are not as simple as they may appear on the surface. Two properties located in different neighborhoods may bring different prices for no reason other than the location. Neighborhood A may be characterized by higher-priced properties than neighborhood B, even though the two properties in question are quite similar in appearance. Anytime the appraiser selects a comparable from another block, neighborhood, community, city, or region, he or she must be able to prove that the two locations and their influence on the value of the property are the same. This task becomes more difficult the further removed the comparable is from the location of the subject being appraised. If comparables are difficult to find, using one from a location that is subject to market forces that are not quite the same as the subject may be more acceptable if the supply and demand factors between the two properties can be adequately compared and analyzed.

Statistical procedures may be useful in selecting locations that are subject to the same market forces. In this manner, property X in neighborhood A may be comparable to property Y in neighborhood B.

Financial Arrangements Ideally, the financial arrangements (conditions of sale) for the subject and the comparable should be similar. Since they are not always the same, the analyst typically looks at the data to determine whether the financial arrangements have influenced the transaction price. Have any "deals" been arranged that might influence the price? For example, could the buyer have arranged with the seller to pay an artificially higher price in return for a lower than usual mortgage rate or down payment?

Adjustments to the selling price of the comparable property when a lower than market interest rate is involved is found in Chapter 7 under Cash Equivalency.

UNITS OF COMPARISON

A *unit of comparison* is a common denominator upon which all properties analyzed for the appraisal may be compared. Examples include items such as the following *physical units:*

- rent per square foot
- price per square foot
- rent or price per cubic foot
- rent or price per rentable area
- credit rating of the tenants
- square feet of parking area
- square feet of office area
- square feet of common maintenance area
- price per square foot of the site area
- square feet of docking area
- square feet of storage
- number of rental units by type of unit
- price per apartment of condominum unit
- price per acre
- building area per acre

A number of financial ratios may be used as a basis of comparison.[2] The following *financial units* could be appropriate for some types of properties:

gross income multiplier (gross rent multiplier):
GIM: sales price/annual rental income

operating ratio: annual operating expenses/gross income

breakeven point: (operating expenses + debt service)/gross income

loan-to-value ratio: mortgage value/property value

debt service coverage ratio: net operating income/debt service

payback period: equity capital/cash flow before income taxes

cash-on-cash return before taxes: annual cash flow before income taxes/equity investment

equity build-up rate: (annual cash flow before taxes + amortization)/equity investment

cash-on-cash return after income taxes: cash flow after taxes/equity investment

after-tax buildup rate: (cash flow after taxes + amortization)/equity investment

Selection of the Units of Comparison

The units of comparison that should be used are the ones that are the most appropriate to compare the relevant features of the property with the subject. For example, a warehouse could use cubic feet as a unit of comparison. An apartment building might not have a use for cubic feet since square footage is typically more valid.

One recommendation sometimes used in connection with the selection of units of comparison and the comparables is to "use the appropriate units that adequately describe the buying trend." This is saying that the buying public will establish a buying trend, assuming that the demand exists for the property, and the appraiser's job is to find that trend. For example, the public could be buying frontage feet that might be spotted by using total price paid per frontage foot. The buying trend could be square feet of living area, which could be located by examining the total price per square foot of living area.

In sum, the units that are selected are those that are appropriate to describe the major characteristics of the property and, hopefully, identify the buying trend.

SELECTION OF THE COMPARABLES

A question that arises early in using this approach is, "Which of the recently sold properties that are comparable to the subject should be used, or which of the comparable properties are the most comparable?" This section investigates this question.

Editing the Sales of Comparable Properties

All recent sales of comparable properties should be edited to eliminate all transactions that were not between a willing, knowledgeable buyer and a willing, knowledgeable seller. Typically, sales in the following classes are eliminated:

1. *Sales resulting from a legal process.* This includes sales such as those resulting from divorce, bankruptcy, a judgment, mortgage default, or condemnation proceedings.
2. *Sales that were "love and affection" transactions.* This class includes those transactions where the last names of the grantor and the grantee are the same. In addition, the consideration on the deed could be written something like "$10 and love and affection."
3. *Sales where the owner was suffering financial duress.* The property may have been on the market for a period of time that was longer than average for the type of property. The owners may have vacated and moved to another city and simply given the agent instructions to "move the property at any reasonable price to eliminate my financial burden." Also, transactions involving a buyer who has a compelling need to buy rapidly can be eliminated.
4. *Sales resulting from a special need.* This type of transfer includes sales where either the buyer or seller has paid or received an unusually high or low price for the property. For example, the owner of a growing business may pay a premium to acquire an adjoining property in order to expand the business. The same buyer would pay far more for this particular property than for a similar parcel a block away.

Number of Comparables

From all of the recently sold comparables available, the analyst has typically narrowed the list to the best or most comparable to be used in the adjustment process described in the following section.[3] The analyst may use all comparable properties to assure that market trends are spotted accurately. Several techniques for selecting the best comparables have appeared in the literature.

Major value factors One source[4] reported in a recent illustration of the direct sales comparison approach that the most important factors in the sample neighborhood influencing rentals and sales prices of the type of property under question were quality of location, air-conditioning, a modern kitchen, and a two-car garage. Since market research over time had derived these conclusions, the illustration concentrated on these factors only in selecting the comparables. Thus the objective was to locate recent sales of comparable properties that were the most similar to the subject in these attributes.

Statistical procedures Statistical procedures employing t-scores may be used, if available, to select comparables from a data file.[5] The computer is told to search the data file using predetermined criteria, find the comparable using these criteria, and run the t-scores to determine whether the comparable and the subject are statistically acceptable.

Trial and error This technique allows the analyst to select a comparable by whatever criteria appear appropriate and place it into the adjustment process described in the next section. The selling price of the comparable property is adjusted up or down according to any differences between it and the subject. If the final adjusted selling price is more than approximately 10% of the original selling price, the comparable could be discarded in lieu of a new one.

Data sources The data source of each comparable should always be identified. Possible data sources have been identified by Henry Harrison[6] to include the following:

- Appraiser's own files
- Multiple listing services
- Deed records
- Title companies
- Assessment records
- Mortgage loan records
- Real estate brokers' files
- Government and private mortgage insurers
- Atlases and survey maps
- Other appraisers
- Real estate newspapers
- Special publications
- General circulation newspapers
- SREA Market Data Center
- Miscellaneous sources.

THE ADJUSTMENT PROCESS

The *adjustment process* covers the steps where the selling price of the comparable property is transformed into an estimate of market value for the subject. This section discusses the procedure involved in this transformation.

Important Concepts

Several important concepts must be discussed early to assure that the nature of the adjustment process is understood.

1. *Place the features of the subject property into the comparable property.* A grid is prepared containing all of the important features of the subject and the comparable properties. On paper, all of the important features of the subject are placed into the comparable property. The selling price of the comparable is then adjusted up or down. An upward adjustment means that the feature in the subject was better (superior) to the comparable and would bring more money in the market. A downward adjustment means that the feature in the subject was worse (inferior) to the comparable and would not bring as much money as the comparable.

2. *Adjustments are made for the differences.* Once the features of the subject are compared to the comparable property, *adjustments are made upward or downward to the comparable's selling price for the differences, not the similarities.* Similarities do not cause changes in the selling price.

3. *The amount of the adjustment should be market derived.* The amount of the adjustment in the selling price of the comparable should be derived from the market. The correct interpretation of the adjustment is the additional (or lower) amount that a buyer would pay because of the difference in question between the subject and the comparable. The cost of adding (deleting) an item that represents the difference between the subject and the comparable is not typically used since the cost may not be equal to value. The amount that a buyer would pay may or may not be equal to the cost.

4. *The method of adjustment can be a dollar amount, percent amount, or whole amount.* The methods of performing the adjustment can be in terms of the dollar amount derived from the market, the percent change in the selling price of the comparable, or the whole selling price. *Whichever is used, all adjustments for the same property feature throughout the report should be made using the same method.*

5. *For convenience, the adjustments are done by element of comparison and/or distinct property features under an element of comparison.* Comparisons and adjustments are done by the four elements of comparison of time, location, physical features, and financial arrangements. Property differences spotted by the appraiser or of interest to the client should be identified separately. However, no property feature can be identified that does not fit under one of the preceding four elements.

Since the comparisons and adjustments are done by the elements of comparison or by using some division of the property features under the elements, the adjustments under each element should be discussed separately.

Time

The sale of the comparable property should be as recent as possible. The most common situation is to locate good comparable properties that have sold within the immediate past. The analyst must consider adjusting the selling price of the comparable upward or downward (or no change), depending upon his or her research of market trends. The key question here is, "By what procedure do I determine the amount of the time adjustment, if any?"

Two methods have been suggested for estimating the amount of the time adjustment by analyzing the resales of the same property over time.

Simple difference in resale prices Perhaps the oldest method for estimating the time adjustment is a simple adjusted difference between the new price and the old price. Henry S. Harrison recently described this method by the following, which describes the use of this adjustment for houses but applies to income-producing property:

> *The best way to obtain a time adjustment is by finding some houses in the neighborhood that have been sold and resold within the recent past. After adjustments are made for any improvements between the sales and for any change in depreciation, the difference between the sale prices can be attributed to the time differential.*[7]

Assessed value-to-sales price The same author illustrated recently a technique for deriving a time adjustment using a ratio calculated by dividing the assessed value by the sale price of the property. Exhibit 4.1 shows a sample of recent sales in a neighborhood and the corresponding assessed values. The last column shows the division of the two figures. The bottom half of the table shows a sample of six-month-old sales taken from the same neighborhood. The same assessment value-to-sales ratios are calculated. The average ratio for the recent sales was 40.95%, and the same figure for the sample in a previous time period was 36.66%. Harrison argues that the difference of 4.29% is an indication of how values have changed between the two time periods. If the 4.29% is divided by the average ratio for the previous period of 36.66%, the result of 11.7% is the adjustment. This adjustment is used by multiplying it by the sale price of a comparable that occurred in the time period shown in the second part of the table. For example, a property that sold six months ago for $60,000 would be multiplied by .117 to receive the adjustment of $7020.

Exhibit 4.1
Estimating the time adjustment using assessed values

Sample of recent sales

Sale no.	Sale price	Assessed value	Percentage assessment is of sale price
1	$60,000	$24,000	40
2	72,000	31,700	44
3	40,000	15,200	38
4	42,500	16,600	39
5	55,000	24,800	45
6	50,000	18,000	36
7	51,250	21,000	41
8	56,000	22,400	40
9	43,000	16,800	39
10	49,000	22,000	45
11	46,300	18,300	39.5
12	63,000	25,200	40
13	41,000	15,400	37.5
14	45,000	17,500	39
15	49,900	21,000	42
16	51,900	23,400	45
17	64,000	28,100	44
18	44,000	20,200	46
19	44,600	18,300	41
20	55,600	21,100	38

The mean (average) the percentage the assessment is of the sale price is 40.95 percent. The standard deviation is 2.94 percent.

Source: Reprinted, with permission, from the November–December, 1978, issue of *The Real Estate Appraiser and Analyst,* published by the Society of Real Estate Appraisers, Chicago, Illinois. No further reproduction is authorized.

Sample of sales 6 months ago			
Sale no.	Sale price	Assessed value	Percentage assessment is of sale price
1	$60,600	$20,600	34
2	51,600	19,100	37
3	51,000	21,400	42
4	69,000	27,600	40
5	56,000	23,000	41
6	54,900	20,900	38
7	50,000	17,500	35
8	46,000	15,400	33.5
9	67,000	23,450	35
10	51,600	18,800	36.5
11	53,500	21,950	41
12	48,000	16,800	35
13	61,000	21,350	35
14	56,000	20,150	36
15	55,000	17,600	32
16	47,300	19,400	41
17	45,000	15,750	35
18	41,300	14,050	34
19	76,000	29,650	39
20	63,000	22,700	36
21	42,000	15,550	37
22	51,300	17,450	34

The mean (average) the assessment is of the sale price is 36.66 percent. The standard deviation is 2.86 percent.

Another method for deriving a time adjustment is from matched pairs, which is described in the next section.

Location

The adjustment for location differences in the selling price is best justified by using matched pairs. Consider two small residential rental properties that are being compared on five major value factors of location, air-conditioning, modern kitchen, size, and a two-car garage. The appraiser concludes that the two should be compared as follows:

Major Value Factors

Property	*Selling Price*	*Location*	*Air Cond.*	*Modern Kit.*	*Garage*	*Time*	*Size*
#1	$140,000	superior	same	same	same	current	same
#2	$135,000	-----	same	same	same	current	same
	$5,000	difference					

The two properties are the same except for location. Thus the $5000 difference in price may be attributed to the superiority in the location of comparable 1 and is market derived. The $5000 is not an opinion of the analyst, but determined by the forces of supply and demand. The $5000 is the location adjustment that may be applied to the comparable, if needed, when giving the comparable all of the characteristics of the subject and adjusting the selling price of the comparable property.

Physical Characteristics

The oldest and most common technique for deriving an adjustment for physical characteristics is to use the matched pairs procedure under location. Carrying the matched pair example further, assume that two additional recent sales of comparables could be located that were the same except for a difference in the kitchen appliances:

Property	*Selling Price*	*Location*	*Air Cond.*	*Modern Kit.*	*Garage*	*Time*	*Size*
#4	$138,000	same	same	superior	same	current	same
#5	136,000	same	same	-----	same	current	same
	$2,000			difference			

The difference of $2000 in the price could be attributed to the difference in the kitchen appliances. The adjustment of $2000 may be applied to the subject, if needed, when comparing the kitchen in the subject to the comparables selected for the appraisal. This adjustment has been market derived and justified.

This procedure can be repeated for any number and type of value factors. Any time two similar properties are seen in the market which have one major difference that influences the selling or rental price, the transaction and adjustment should be entered into the appraiser's card file to be used on a later appraisal assignment.

Financial Arrangements (Conditions of the Sale)

This element of comparison has been the most ignored. No standard procedure exists for developing the amount of the adjustment if differences exist in the financing arrangements. In the past, the financial arrangements of the comparables were examined to see if they had financing that contained "payment and financing (that) are consistent with the current market."[8] Cash equivalency analysis from Chapter 7 could be useful if lower than market interest rates exist.

A number of appraisal questions remain unsolved with respect to the financing. For example, how does a property with a fixed rate mortgage compare with property financed with a variable rate mortgage (VRM) that has not been adjusted upward? Does the probability of a later adjustment cause the VRM property to sell for less?[9] What is the influence of an attractive assumable loan on the selling price? How does the variety of new mortgage types influence the selling price?

One author[10] recently argued that a single-family home in a southern county in the $15,000 to $42,000 price range with an assumable loan is worth about $1000 more to the seller. Another study[11] concluded that, on average, within the sample studied, buyers taking FHA or VA insured or guaranteed loans paid the sellers a higher selling price than buyers using conventional loans. The higher prices for FHA and VA mortgages were the result of sellers passing 39 percent of the points charged by the lender to the buyer through the selling price.

PERCENTAGE ADJUSTMENTS

Percent adjustments are the appraiser's estimate of the difference between the subject and the comparable in percent terms rather than dollar amounts. Applied correctly, percent adjustments should give the same answer and adjustment as compared to dollar values.

Percent adjustments are determined by matched pairs also. The dollar amount justified by the comparison is expressed as a percent of a base price. For example, in the previous two examples for location and physical characteristics:

Location:
$5,000/$135,000 = 3.7%.

Physical Characteristics:
$2,000/$136,000 = 1.5%.

In addition, the matched pair analysis for the time adjustment revealed that the selling price of the comparable properties should be adjusted upward by 8.2 percent.

The selling prices of the comparable properties should be made current prior to any adjustments for other dissimilarities.[12] Thus the time adjustment would be applied first, then the other adjustments. Percent adjustments should always be compared with dollar adjustments to assure that the magnitude is accurate. For example, a 1.5 percent adjustment on a $2 million property could be justifiable, but a 1.5 percent adjustment on a $1 million property could be inaccurate.

MULTIPLE REGRESSION AND STATISTICAL ANALYSIS

The importance of multiple regression and statistical analysis to an appraisal cannot be over emphasized. Certainly every appraiser should have a rudimentary knowledge covering the application and interpretation of a multiple regression equation. A number of good calculators exist which may be purchased or rented that provide the necessary software programs to develop a regression equation from the appraiser's data. The cost can be small and the benefits tremendous.

This section will not cover the concepts of regression and statistical analysis. Our discussion will be devoted to the *application* of regression and statistical techniques to the direct sales comparison approach. Essentially four areas of application have been developed.

Selecting the Major Value Factors

Regression methods can be used to select the major value factors from a large group of data. Applied mostly to large quantities of data, these regression efforts have shown what the buyer considers to be important within each local predefined market. For example, three applications in different markets have

Exhibit 4.2
Major value factors selected by regression techniques

Study	Major value factors
1. Kamath and Yantek Revindra Kamath and Kenneth Yantek, "Linear Multiple Regression Analysis Applied to the Valuation of Single Family Homes," *The Real Estate Appraiser and Analyst* 45 (September-October 1979): 36–41.	living area number of rooms 1976 land assessment number of bathrooms building cost index physical condition
2. Miles W. Porcher Miles, "Applied Multiple Regression Analysis," *The Real Estate Appraiser* 41 (October 1975): 32.	living area sale date site area car spaces half baths age condition full baths central air-conditioning
3. Gloudemans and Miller Robert J. Gloudemans and Dennis W. Miller, "Multiple Regression Analysis Applied to Residential Properties: A Study of Structural Relationships Over Time," *Decision Sciences* 7 (April 1976): 294–304.	living area physical condition dishwasher construction quality fireplaces baseboard and heating other improvements hip roof shake roof

derived the major value factors shown in Exhibit 4.2 to be the factors the buyer considers the most important. Once these value factors are determined, the analyst can use these in a search for comparables and in making adjustments.

Exhibit 4.3 shows two sets of value factors in a study done for apartments. The first part of the table shows those value factors that were statistically significant using regression analysis. The second part of the table shows those value factors that were found to be related to market value using various types of ratios such as valuation ratios, income and expense ratios, and property tax assessment ratios.

Exhibit 4.3
Multiple regression coefficients relating apartment sales prices with property characteristics (12 units or over)

Item number	Property characteristic	Multiplier (coefficient)	Unit value (Yes = 1; No = 0)
	(Add constant value of $18,624)		
1	Elevator	270,996.0	1 or 0
2	12–24 units	–25,982.0	1 or 0
3	Number of buildings	8,210.0	Actual Number
4	Land area	–.91.0	Square Feet
5	Total floor area	3.2	Square Feet
6	Number of efficiencies	6,620.0	Actual Number
7	Number of 1 bedroom	689.0	Actual Number
8	Number of 3 bedroom	920.0	Actual Number
9	Annual gross possible income	4.2	In Dollars
10	Utilities included	–76,340.0	1 or 0
11	Laundry room	31,712.0	1 or 0
12	Maid service	15,073.0	1 or 0
13	Other services included	–41,466.0	1 or 0
14	Other recreational services	24,682.0	1 or 0
15	Distance to beach	–1,433.0	In ¼ Mile Units
16	Distance to airport	–27,041.0	In ¼ Mile Units

Financial ratios derived from the income appraisal of 170 apartment buildings (Ft. Lauderdale, Florida*)

Valuation ratios	
Land value per square foot	$ 1.80
Building value per square foot	12.49
Market value per room	5,660.90
Market value per apartment	18,948.29
Gross rate of return	17.70
Gross income multiplier	5.65
Overall capitalization rate (includes property tax levy of $.0244)	12.04
Income and expense ratios	
Gross possible income per apartment	$ 3,354.17
Gross possible income per room	1,002.07
Gross possible income per square foot	2.34
Expenses per apartment	77.28
Expenses per unit	1,073.33
Expenses per room	320.66
Expenses per square foot	0.75
Expenses as a percent of gross possible income	32.00
Property tax assessment ratio	
Property tax as a percent of gross income	$ 13.91
Property tax per square foot of building	0.32
Property tax paid per room	139.35
Property tax paid per apartment	466.44

*Data are taken from a seven-page computer analysis applied to each building prepared for William Markham, Broward County Assessor, Fort Lauderdale, Florida.

Source: Reprinted, with permission, from the July–August, 1973, issue of *The Real Estate Appraiser and Analyst*, published by the Society of Real Estate Appraisers, Chicago, Illinois. No further reproduction is authorized.

Selecting the Comparable Properties

A computer program can be developed to select comparables from a large body of data using predetermined criteria. The SREA Data Center has programs and an information network system that can be used,[13] and Tchira[14] has demonstrated recently the use of t-scores in determining if a selected value feature is statistically significant.

Estimating the Dollar Value of the Major Value Factor

If the regression equation is structured carefully, the coefficients calculated for the independent variables may be used as the amount of the adjustment, if needed. For example, consider the regression equation developed for farmland values:[15]

$$\begin{aligned} P = {} & \underset{(.60)}{6.32(1A)} + \underset{(.96)}{5.77(1B)} + \underset{(2.34)}{5.38(1C)} + \underset{(.45)}{3.46(W1 \text{ and } W2)} + \\ & \underset{(1.25)}{2.40(W3)} + \underset{(101)}{264.(RF)} + \underset{(104)}{206(I\text{-}16)} \end{aligned}$$

where

P = average 1975 price per acre of agricultural land,

1A, 1B, 1C, W1, W2, W3 = land classes,

RF = dummy variable,

I-16 = dummy variable for land located adjacent to an interstate highway.

The researcher's interpretation of the coefficients are that the average price per acre will change if the particular land class is increased. "For example, if 1 percent more of the land is in class 1B, the per-acre price would increase by $5.77, other things being equal. . . . Land with river frontage is worth an additional $264 per acre. Land adjacent to I-16 is worth an additional $206 per acre."[16] Similar applications can be completed for the major value factors of any type of property.

Estimating the Selling Price of the Property

The regression equation can be used to derive an estimate of the selling price of the property. The reader should remember that the purpose of the equation is to derive the best fitting equation on the minimum number of major value factors using the sales of recently sold comparable properties. Once this equation is derived, it is then applied to all similar properties being appraised, whether they have been recently sold or not. Thus the coefficients in the equation are derived from the sold properties and applied to all similar properties being appraised. The equation represents a market derived and documented approach.

With experimentation among major value factors and statistical techniques, the estimates of selling price can be quite accurate. These estimates provide one more tool in the appraiser's kit that can be used to verify the accuracy of market value estimates derived from the other approaches.

STEPS IN THE MARKET DATA APPROACH

The market data approach is applied by following five steps:[17]

1. Find recent sales of comparable properties.
2. Analyze the data for the purpose of eliminating any sales that are not valid transactions between the buyer and the seller.
3. Using the elements of comparison, compare the major value factors of the comparable property with the subject to assure that the properties are similar.
4. Using the elements of comparison, compare and adjust for dissimilarities between the subject and the comparable.
5. Reach an opinion of value from this approach.

All of these steps have been discussed in the aggregate in earlier sections of this chapter.

Advantages of this Approach

The objective of the appraiser that has an assignment to estimate market value or one of the similar values such as investment value is to interpret market trends. This interpretation and analysis should result in the "worth" of the property as determined by the forces of demand and supply. Thus, the principal advantage of this approach is that it produces a market-derived estimate of value. This approach typically is regarded as the most important of the three and should be given significant weight if sufficient data and conditions exist to apply it accurately.

Disadvantages of this Approach

The direct sales comparison approach does not produce good estimates[18] of market value when (1) no comparables exist, and (2) the adjustments between the comparable and the subject are too large. Obviously, the application of this approach relies on the ability of the analyst to locate recent sales of comparable properties. In addition, those located must be reasonably comparable to the subject.

COMMON ERRORS IN APPLYING THE DIRECT SALES COMPARISON APPROACH

One author[19] has recently summarized his experiences from observing frequent errors in the direct sales comparison approach that are committed by candidates writing a demonstration report for an MAI designation. Also, this source gives recommendations covering the necessary content that should be shown by the appraiser. Although not every appraisal produced by the appraiser for a client is a demonstration report, the conclusions give a good guide. His recommendations for correcting these errors follow. The overall summary of the direct sales comparison approach is that it

> . . . *must consider all the subject property's major value characteristics, compare each comparable property to the subject property, reconcile each comparable sale, apply the selected market data approach completely, and justify the common denominators and sales price adjustments.*[20]

In addition, many candidates present too many generalities and unsupported opinions. Each of these points is discussed:

1. *Consider all the subject property's major value characteristics.* All of the major value factors should be identified and thoroughly described for the subject and the comparable.
2. *Compare each comparable property to the subject property.* For each comparable selected, the candidate must always answer the question, "What would the comparable's sale price have been had it possessed the subject property's value characteristics at the time of valuation?"[21] All features identified in previous report sections such as site analysis and depreciation must be identified and evaluated.
3. *Reconcile each comparable sale.* A discussion should be included identifying the reasons why the comparable is a good indication of the market value of the subject. The result should be explained any time an estimate of market value is derived that is significantly different from the others.
4. *Apply the selected direct sales comparison approach completely.* The analyst must explain thoroughly why the direct sales comparison approach is the best estimate of market value for this specific application. This discussion should attempt to tie in the estimate of value under the site analysis and the property's highest and best use.
5. *Justify common denominator and sales price adjustments.* The candidate must derive a market supported estimate of the adjustments used. Good application of concepts and principles should be demonstrated even though the conclusion is not perfect.

Exhibit 4.4
Units of comparison and major value factors

Major value factor	Subject	Comparable 1	Comparable 2	Comparable 3
A. Square footage	14,400	14,400	14,450	14,350
B. Sales price per square foot	—	$43.40	$42.21	$43.21
C. Gross Rent Multiplier	—	12.02	11.96	11.85
D. 2-car parking	yes	yes	yes	yes
E. Mechanical equip. Unit: brand name	superior	average	average	superior
F. Pool	yes	yes	yes	yes
G. Arch. design Unit: colonial, western, rambler, rustic, Spanish	colonial	colonial	colonial	colonial
H. Siding Unit: shingle, aluminum, brick venerr, cedar and stone, stucco, plywood	aluminum	plywood	plywood	shingle
I. Lot size	large corner lot	same	same	same

ILLUSTRATION NUMBER 1

The purpose of this illustration is to show how the various parts of the direct sales comparison approach fit together. The subject is a twenty-one-unit apartment complex. You determine from your own files and market research that the major value factors are those shown in Exhibit 4.4:

square footage
sales price per square foot
gross income multiplier
2-car parking
mechanical equip.
pool
arch. design
siding
lot size

Exhibit 4.5
Grid analysis with adjustments (Date of appraisal: August 1, 1981)

Elements of comparison	Subject Description	Subject Adj.	Comparable 1 Description	Comparable 1 Adj.	Comparable 2 Description	Comparable 2 Adj.	Comparable 3 Description	Comparable 3 Adj.
Selling Price	------	------	$625,000.	------	$610,000	------	$620,000	------
1. Time of sale	------	------	8/1/81	0	10/1/80	+12,200	5/1/81	+3,720
2. Location	adjacent to 6-lane thoroughfare	------	same type location	0	(inferior) residential light commercial	+2,500	(inferior) residential light commercial	+2,500
3. Physical characteristics								
a. square feet	14,400	------	14,400	0	(superior) 14,450	–2,100	(inferior) 14,350	+2,100
b. mech. equip.	superior	------	average	+1000	average	+1,000	superior	0
c. pool	yes	------	yes	0	yes	0	yes	0
d. 2-car parking	yes	------	yes	0	yes	0	yes	0
e. arch, design	colonial	------	colonial	0	colonial	0	colonial	0
f. lot size	large corner lot	------	large corner lot	0	large corner lot	0	large corner lot	0
g. siding	aluminum	------	(inferior) plywood	+1200	(inferior) plywood	+1,200	(inferior) shingle	+1,200
4. Financial arrangements	75% mortgage at a market rate	------	similar 70% financing at mkt. rate	0	similar 75% financing at mkt. rate	0	similar 75% financing at mkt. rate	0
Total adjustments				+2200		+14,800		+9,520
Adjusted sales price				$627,200		$624,800		$629,520

The appropriate unit of comparison for the mechanical equipment is the brand name, the style for the architectural design, and the type of exterior. You examine the six recently sold properties that are reasonably comparable and select three since the major value factors are the most similar to the subject.

Next, you search for the dissimilarities among the comparables when contrasted to the subject to determine which items should be adjusted. Those items that have been adjusted for property differences are shown in Exhibit 4–5. You determine the time adjustment by using the resales of property that are comparable to the subject. Your estimate shows that the property value is increasing by 2.5% per year over the last two years.

The adjustments for all of the other elements of comparisons (except financial arrangements) are made on the basis of matched pairs. Your office maintains a matched pair file that records market justification for each adjustment for square footage, location, mechanical equipment, pool, architectural design, two-car parking, lot size, and siding. In addition, your office has a memory calculator that verifies these major value factors using statistical procedures. The same program that performs these statistical tests also runs a multiple regression analysis on the data to estimate the market adjustments for each major value factor. In this manner, the major value factors and the market adjustments are crosschecked.

The exact amount of the adjustments is shown in Exhibit 4–5. The adjustment for time is:

.025 per year/12 months = .002 per month.

Comparable 2:
10/1/80 − 8/1/81 = 10 months
10 months × .002 per month = .02
.02 × $610,000 = $12,200.

Comparable 3:
3 months × .002 per month = .006
.006 × $620,000 = $3,720.

The total net adjustments for comparable 1 is $2200, which creates an adjusted sales price of $627,200; for comparable 2, the net adjustment is $14,800, which gives an adjusted selling price of $624,800; and the net adjustment for comparable 3 is $9,520, which gives a net adjusted selling price of $629,520. Comparable 1 was thought to be the most similar to the subject because this comparable showed the smallest amount of adjustments—$2200, contrasted to $14,800 for comparable 2, and $9,520 for comparable 3.

These three estimates were *correlated* into one estimate by using weights. The comparable that was considered to be the most similar was assigned a weight of 70%, the second most comparable was weighted 25%, and the third was weighted 5 percent. Thus the final estimate was derived as follows:

Comparable 1: \$627,200 × .70 = \$439,040
Comparable 3: \$629,520 × .25 = \$157,380
Comparable 2: \$624,800 × .05 = \$ 31,240

1.00
Total: \$627,660
rounded to \$627,700.

The weights were based upon the appraiser's experience with similar properties in the area.

ILLUSTRATION NUMBER 2

You are given an assignment to estimate the market value of a twenty-four-unit apartment complex in a southwestern city. Your knowledge of market trends and your view of the highest and best use leads you to the conclusion that for units this size, three units of comparison are valid: the value per square foot, the value per unit, and the GRM. You have located four comparables that you feel are similar to the subject, and the relevant data for each follows:

	C1	*C2*	*C3*	*C4*
Value per sq. ft.	\$24.88	\$18.00	\$17.68	\$19.97
Value per unit	\$20,584	\$18,000	\$15,371	\$17,208
GRM	7.61	6.94	5.57	4.89
Sale price	\$800,000	\$376,000	\$1,149,000	\$464,000

Comparable 1 You feel that a 3% downward adjustment for age and lack of maintenance is justifiable. A good location merits a 2% upward adjustment, causing a net adjustment of −1%.

Value per sq. ft. : \$ 24.88 × .99 = \$ 24.63
Value per unit : \$20,584 × .99 = \$20,378
GRM : 7.61 (unadjusted)

Comparable 2 You estimate that a 5% increase is appropriate from age and condition. No adjustment for date of sale is necessary. A good location merits another 5% increase, causing a net adjustment of +10 percent.

Value per sq. ft.	:	$18.00 × 1.10	= $19.80
Value per unit	:	$18,000 × 1.10	= $19,800
GRM	:	6.94	(unadjusted)

Comparable 3 You believe that no adjustment is warranted from age and condition. A 10% increase is appropriate from the date of sale. Location appears to require a 2% decrease. The net adjustment is +8%.

Value per sq. ft.	:	$ 17.68 × 1.08	= $19.09
Value per unit	:	$15,371 × 1.08	= $16,601
GRM	:	5.57	(unadjusted)

Comparable 4 A decrease of 8.5% is warranted from age and maintenance. An increase of 5% is required from the date of sale, and an increase of 22% is appropriate for location. The net adjustment is +18.5%.

Value per sq. ft.	:	$ 19.97 × 1.185	= $23.66
Value per unit	:	$17,208 × 1.185	= $20,391
GRM	:	4.89	(unadjusted)

Correlation Your opinion is that the comparables with the least adjustment are the most comparable, which means that C1 and C3 are the main value indicators. The value per square foot for these two ranges from $24.63 to $19.09. In your judgment, a value per square foot of $22.50 is warranted.

19,400 square feet
for the subject × $22.50 = $436,500.
+50,000 site value
$486,500

In your judgment, C1 and C3 are also the main value indicators of the value per unit, which ranges from $20,378 to $16,601. Your best estimate is that $19,000 is the value per unit.

24 units for the subject × $19,000 = $456,000

The GRM for C1 and C3 range from 7.61 to 5.57. Your best judgment gives a GRM of 6.80.

$70,000 gross annual
income × 6.8 = $476,000

The three units of comparison gave:

Value per sq. ft	:	$486,000
Value per unit	:	$456,000
GRM	:	$476,000

In your opinion, the local investors use the GRM more than the other two value indicators in estimating value. Consequently, you conclude that the subject's value is $476,000.

SUMMARY

Recent sales of properties that are comparable to the subject can serve as a good indication of the market value of the subject. These properties can be given the characteristics of the subject on paper, and the selling price of the comparable can be adjusted upward or downward accordingly.

The subject and comparable properties can be compared on the basis of predetermined units of comparison. They can be analyzed on the basis of the elements of comparison categorized for convenience on the basis of time, location, physical characteristics, and financial arrangements.

All sales of comparable properties must be edited to assure that only bona fide transactions exist. The comparables can be selected on the basis of major value factors, statistical procedures, and/or trial and error.

The adjustment process attempts to place all the characteristics of the subject into the comparable and adjust the comparable's recent selling price upward or downward respectively. The resulting price is an estimate of the market value. Percent adjustments can be used, but this method suffers from inherent difficulties with subjectivity.

Multiple regression and statistical techniques can be used to select the major value factors, select the comparable properties, and estimate the selling price of the property.

Common errors reported in demonstration reports are based mainly on overgeneralization and unsupported opinions. This part of the report should consider all of the subject property's major value characteristics, compare each comparable property to the subject property, reconcile each comparable sale, apply the selected direct sales comparison approach completely, and justify common denominators and sales price adjustments.

REVIEW QUESTIONS

1. Explain, in general, the purpose of the direct sales comparison approach.
2. Discuss the elements of comparison.
3. Outline the purpose of the units of comparison and give examples.

4. Outline the techniques for selecting comparables.
5. Discuss the concept of the adjustment process.
6. Explain the techniques for determining the adjustment for time.
7. Explain the method for estimating the adjustment for location.
8. Explain the method for estimating the adjustment for physical characteristics.
9. Explain the need for estimating the adjustment for financial arrangements.
10. What is the purpose of the percent adjustment?
11. What role can multiple regression play in appraisal?
12. What role can statistical techniques play in appraisal?
13. Outline the steps in the direct sales comparison approach. When is it not meaningful?
14. What are the common errors committed by candidates in their demonstration reports?

ENDNOTES

1. D. R. Epley, "A Further Note on the Theory of Value," *The Real Estate Appraiser* 42 (January–February 1967): 13–16; also William M. Shenkel, "Value in Use, Value in Exchange, and Investment Value," *The Real Estate Appraiser and Analyst* 46 (May–June 1980): 27–38.
2. John L. Hysom, "Financial Feasibility of Income Properties: Borrowers' and Lenders' Views," *Appraisal Review Journal* 3 (Spring–Summer 1980): 26–43.
3. For a discussion of the number of comparables to be selected, see Robert H. Zerbst, "A Caution on the Adjustment of Comparable Sales," *The Real Estate Appraiser* 43 (November–December 1977): 28–29.
4. J. R. Kimball, "How to Document, Justify, and Support," *The Real Estate Appraiser* 43 (November–December 1977): 25–27.
5. Karel J. Clettenberg, "Statistical Applications of the SREA Market Data Center, Inc.," *The Real Estate Appraiser* 39 (September–October 1973): 43–49; John E. Shannon, "Statistical Applications for the SREA Market Data Center, Inc.," *The Real Estate Appraiser* 39 (November–December 1973): 48–51; and Arnold Tchira, "Comparable Sales Selection—A Computer Approach," *The Appraisal Journal* 47 (January 1979): 86–98.
6. Henry Harrison, "Direct Sales Comparison Approach Part II," *The Real Estate Appraiser and Analyst* 44 (November–December 1978): 72.
7. Ibid., p. 73.

8. Society of Real Estate Appraisers, *An Introduction to Appraising Real Property,* (Chicago: SREA, 1977), pp. 10–11.

9. Donald R. Epley, ''Variable Mortgage Plans and Their Unsolved Issues,'' *The Appraisal Journal* 45 (April 1977): 242–248.

10. Douglas Bible, ''Financial Conditions as Related to Residential Value,'' *The Real Estate Appraiser and Analyst* 46 (May–June 1980): 39–41.

11. Robert H. Zerbst and William Brueggeman, ''Adjusting Comparable Sales for FHA and VA Financing,'' *The Appraisal Journal* 47 (July 1979): 374–380.

12. For additional reading on percent adjustments and their use, see Normand Terry, ''Support and Justify: An Associate's Problem,'' *The Real Estate Appraiser and Analyst* 44 (September–October 1978): 28–31; Jay S. Berger, ''Resolving Confusion in Percentage Adjustment Techniques,'' *The Appraisal Journal* 39 (April 1971): 272–276; and Richard Ratcliff and Dennis Swan, ''Getting More From Comparables by Rating and Regression,'' *The Appraisal Journal* 40 (January 1972): 68–75.

13. Clettenberg, ''Statistical Applications,'' and Shanahan, ''Statistical Applications.''

14. Tchira ''Comparable Sales Selection.''

15. L. Reid Schott and Fred C. White, ''Multiple Regression Analysis of Farmland Values by Land Classes,'' *The Appraisal Journal* 45 (July 1977): 427–434.

16. Ibid., p. 433.

17. American Institute of Real Estate Appraisers, *The Appraisal of Real Estate* (Chicago: AIREA, 1978), pp. 68–69.

18. Ibid., p. 569.

19. Robert J. Heinrich, ''A Candidate's Guide to Writing a Passing MAI Demonstration Appraisal Report,'' *The Appraisal Journal* 47 (October 1979): 569.

20. Ibid., p. 569.

21. Ibid., p. 569.

ADDITIONAL READINGS

Berger, Jay S. ''Resolving Confusion in Percentage Adjustment Techniques.'' *The Appraisal Journal* 39 (April 1971): 272–276.

Bible, Douglas S. ''Measuring Dwelling Unit and Neighborhood Attribute Importance,'' *The Real Estate Appraiser and Analyst* 45 (January–February 1979): 32–34.

Christensen, Barbara. ''Take the Guesstimating out of Adjustments.'' *The Appraisal Journal* 48 (April 1980): 255–260.

Dickerson, Frederick. ''A Technique for the Analysis of Owner-Financed Sales.'' *The Appraisal Journal* 44 (January 1976): 55–59.

Guntermann, Karl L. ''The Corner Influence on Value: Some Empirical Results.'' *The Real Estate Appraiser and Analyst* 45 (January–February 1979): 32–34.

Kimball, J. R. ''How to Document, Justify, and Support.'' *The Real Estate Appraiser* 43 (November–December 1977): 25–27.

Kruggel, Arthur, Jr. "A Simplified Formula for Appraising the Single-Family Residence in Today's Confusing Market." *The Appraisal Journal* 48 (April 1980): 194–198.

Lane, Donald E. "Comparable Sales on Trial." *The Appraisal Journal* 45 (July 1977): 435–441.

Shanahan, John E. "Statistical Applications for the SREA Market Data Center, Inc." *The Real Estate Appraiser* 39 (November–December 1973): 48–51.

Smith, Theodore R. "Adjusting Land Comparables for Size Variation: Another EDUCARE Application." *The Appraisal Journal* 42 (July 1974): 346–357.

White, Wilbert. "Price Indexing for Time Adjustments." *The Appraisal Journal* 48 (January 1980): 15–23.

MODULE V
Cost Approach to Value

The direct sales comparison approach to value can be cross-checked by the cost approach to value. When the student finishes with this chapter, he or she should possess a basic knowledge of how to estimate reproduction and replacement cost for income-producing property using any of three methods to estimate cost. Accrued depreciation and the differences in measurement concepts taught by the AIREA and the SREA are also shown.

CHAPTER 5

LEARNING OBJECTIVES

When a student finishes this chapter, he or she should be able to:

- Explain the difference between reproduction cost new and replacement cost.
- Outline the steps in estimating cost and the disadvantages of this approach.
- Contrast the methods of measuring cost.
- Contrast the indirect, age-life, and the breakdown methods of estimating accrued depreciation.
- Discuss the concept of accrued depreciation.
- Outline several characteristics of the cost approach.
- Explain the common mistakes made in demonstration reports (submitted for designation credit) concerning the cost approach.

Estimate of Value by the Cost Approach

IMPORTANT TERMS AND PHRASES

accrued depreciation: A loss in value at the date of the appraisal caused by physical, functional, and environmental factors.

age-life method: One method of estimating accrued depreciation by a percent found by dividing an estimate of the property's effective age by its economic life.

capitalized ground rent: A valuation technique that is based upon the premise that the present value of a site equals the capitalized value of the lease payments plus the present value of the reversion.

component effective age: One method of estimating accrued depreciation which applies an effective age percent to the building's major components.

curable deterioration or obsolescence: The cost to cure is less than or equal to the increase in benefits or utility created by correcting this item.

deficiency: Comparable structures reveal that this item is deficient.

development method: One valuation technique that is based on the premise that the present value of a site is the discounted sum of future income benefits.

direct costs: Costs of construction covering labor and materials.

economic life: The period over which the improvements contribute to the value of the property.

effective age-life: One method of estimating accrued depreciation using a percent found by dividing an estimate of the property's age in comparison with similar properties by its economic life.

environmental obsolescence (economic, location): Diminished utility originating from neighborhood influences that are external to the site.

incurable deterioration or obsolescence: The cost to cure is greater than the increase in benefits or utility created by correcting this item.

indirect costs: Costs of construction covering items such as taxes, sales commissions, engineering fees, permits, legal fees, points, insurance, and profit.

indirect method: One method of estimating accrued depreciation by subtracting the value derived from the income approach from the estimate of cost.

land residual technique: A valuation technique that is based on the premise that the total income may be divided between the improvement and the site, and the residual for the site may be capitalized to estimate its value.

modernization: Comparable structures reveal that this item is out-of-date.

obsolescence: A decline in market value caused by diminished utility and benefits.

physical deterioration: An adverse effect on value caused by physical wear-and-tear.

replacement cost: The cost of building a structure that possesses the same functional utility at current prices.

reproduction cost: The cost of constructing an exact replica at current prices.

segregated cost: A method that measures the cost of the major components in the structure.

site: A parcel of land which is improved to the extent that it is ready for use for the purpose for which it is intended.

site analysis: The identification and analysis of the characteristics that create, enhance, or detract from the utility and marketability of a site.

superadequate (excess): Comparable structures reveal that this item is excessive.

trade breakdown method: A method of estimating total cost by summarizing each item according to the trade group that supplies it.

unit-in-place: Similar to segregated cost, it contains more detailed cost information on a building's structure.

The purpose of this chapter is to cover the methods of estimating value from the cost approach. The phrase *cost approach* is used in a broad sense to cover both the reproduction cost-new and replacement cost methods. In general, the steps involved in deriving an indicator of market value involve the following: (1) an estimate of the site value, (2) an estimate of the cost-new of the improvements and any supplemental improvements, and (3) an estimate of accrued depreciation. Each is discussed individually and then collectively.

SITE ANALYSIS

The purpose of this section is to discuss the techniques that have been used to estimate a value for the site. These include the market sales technique, the development method, the capitalized ground rent method, the land residual technique, and the extraction/allocation approach. Site valuation is located at this point in the text since it is the first step of the cost approach.

A site may be defined as ". . . a parcel of land which is improved to the extent that it is ready for use for the purpose for which it is intended."[1] Site analysis is the ". . . identification and analysis of the characteristics that create, enhance, or detract from the utility and marketability of a site."[2]

Direct Sales Comparison

The direct sales comparison technique involves selecting similar properties using the elements of comparison discussed in Chapter 4. Adjustments are made to the selling prices of the properties using the adjustment procedures illustrated in Chapter 4.

Consider the example in Exhibit 5.1. The subject site is a vacant lot that contains 37,500 square feet that will sell for cash only. The view from the site is average, compared to the other similar sites, the access (egress and ingress) is average, the topography is suitable for the intended use, the water drainage is good, and the soil type is suitable to support the structure. These lots are increasing approximately 10% per year. Therefore the time adjustment of 10% reflects the sales that occurred one year ago.

Two of the comparables reveal location features that are unique. Comparable 3 is a corner lot, which matched pairs (discussed in Chapter 4) has revealed is worth an additional 20% in price. Comparable 4 is a lot that has been combined from two smaller lots and this plottage effect has been shown from matched pairs to be equal to an additional 5% in price. Comparable 5 is located on a block such that it may be called the "best lot" on the block, which matched pairs has revealed raises the price by 10%. An adjustment for the view has been shown to be worth $2500 from matched pair analysis.

Comparable 5 was purchased with an installment note for $20,000 down and a balance of $38,000. Local data indicate that a similar cash transaction

Exhibit 5.1
Site analysis using market sales comparison

	Subject	Comparable 1	Comparable 2	Comparable 3	Comparable 4	Comparable 5
Date	January 1982	January 1982	January 1981	January 1981	January 1982	January 1982
Size	150 × 250	150 × 250	160 × 250	145 × 250	150 × 250	160 × 250
Sq. feet	37,500	37,500	40,000	36,250	37,500	40,000
Sales price	------	$54,000	$50,000	$56,000	$57,000	$62,500
Financing terms	cash	cash	cash	cash	cash	$20,000 cash with an installment note for $38,000
View	average	average	average	less than average	less than average	average
Access	good	good	good	good	good	good
Topography	suitable	suitable	suitable	suitable	suitable	suitable
Water drainage	good	good	good	good	good	good
Soil type	suitable	suitable	suitable	suitable	suitable	suitable
Location	average	average	average	corner lot	plottage effect	best lot in area location

Adjustments:					
Time	0	+10% = +$5,000	+10% = +$5,600	0	0
Location					
1. corner lot, plottage, best lot	0	0	−20% = −$11,200	−5% = −$2,850	−10% = −$6,250
2. view	0	0	+$2,500	+$2,500	0
Physical	0	0	0	0	0
Financing	0	0	0	0	−$2,813
Adjustments	0	+$5,000	−$3,100	−$350	−$9,063
Adjusted selling price	$54,000	$55,000	$52,900	$56,650	$53,437
Value trends:					
Adjusted sales price per sq. ft.	$1.44	$1.38	$1.46	$1.51	$1.34
Adjusted sales price per front foot	$360.	$344.	$365.	$378.	$334.

would probably sell for approximately 4.5% less. The higher price of $62,500 reflects a premium price that is charged for a larger payment period.

The adjusted selling prices range from $52,900 to $56,650. When these prices are translated into value trends, the adjusted sales price per square foot ranges from $1.34 to $1.51, and the adjusted sales price per front foot ranges from $334 to $378. The adjusted selling price of $54,000 was selected as the best indication of the value of the subject. The value trend appeared to be the adjusted sales price per square foot of $1.44.

In this analysis, the factors such as financing terms, view, access, topography, water drainage, soil type, and location were selected by the analyst to be the best indicators of value. The market sales technique involves identifying these factors and making adjustments for the dissimilarities between the subject and the comparable.

Development Method[3]

The development method of estimating land value is useful when recent comparable land sales are not available and the property has an obvious potential for subdivision into individual residential sites, an office or industrial park, or recreational camping sites. This method of estimating value is based upon the principle of anticipation, which says that the present value of the parcel equals the discounted future income and benefits.

Essentially, this method involves estimating the future income stream from the development and sales, estimating the expenses from the development, and discounting the net revenue to present value. This analysis involves nine steps:[4]

1. Create a sound development plan, covering the health department site requirements, proposed water and sewage systems, topography, subsoil conditions, maximum utilization of prominent views, and areas left undeveloped.

2. Forecast a realistic pricing schedule. The cost of on-site improvements must be estimated to be consistent with the probable prices that the finished product will bring.

3. Forecast accurately the absorption rate and mix of sites to be sold. The first year pricing schedule for the sites should be determined.

4. Accurately estimate the staging and expense of land development and related expenses. The engineer(s) and the marketing staff must develop the annual land development expenses.

5. Forecast the marketing and related expenditures.

6. Estimate the annual real property taxes during the development and marketing periods.
7. Estimate a reasonable overhead and profit allowance.
8. Analyze the market to determine the appropriate discount rate expected by investors for this type of investment. A discount rate that will be applied to the anticipated net revenue must be market determined to produce an estimate of market value.
9. Select a discount factor that reflects the timing of the site sales. The timing of the income flow must be determined. For example, will the anticipated net revenue arrive regularly each month, regularly twice per year, or once per year at the end?

Exhibit 5.2 shows these nine steps applied to a parcel that the analyst felt would be suitable for recreational use (as camping sites) and the estimate of present value using a discount rate of 12%.

Capitalized Ground Rent Method[5]

If the site is leased separately from any improvement that may exist, an estimate of its value may be derived by

Value = present value of the net contract rent over the life of the lease + present value of the site at the termination of the lease

The net contract rent is determined by subtracting any expenses from the annual lease payment. This should be estimated for each year of the remaining lease term. The site value at the termination of the lease must be estimated from local market trends. Consider the following example.

- A site of 150,000 square feet is leased separately from its improvement at $.20 per square foot or $30,000 per year.
- Annual expenses are expected to equal $.03 per square foot or $4500.
- Annual contract rent is $25,500 ($30,000 – $4500).
- The lease has ten years to expiration.
- Your research of local market trends indicates that the site should be priced at approximately $270,000 by the expiration of the lease.
- Local market trends indicate that an appropriate rate to be used with these types of sites is 11%.

Exhibit 5.2
Development cost method

	Annual expense schedule		
Year 1			
Camping site sales (900 sites)		$4,050,000	
Utility installation charge @ $299		269,100	
		$4,319,100	
Less:			
Marketing expenses @ 35% of sales	$1,417,500		
General and administrative @ 5%	202,500		
Development expenses	2,450,000		
Construction loan interest	229,700		
Legal and recording @ $50/site	45,000		
Estimated real estate taxes	500		
Overhead and profit on sales @ 22%	891,000	$5,236,200	
Value of net sales receipts			($ 917,100)
Year 2			
Camping site sales (1,400 sites)		$7,000,000	
Utility installation charge @ $299		418,600	
		$7,418,600	
Less:			
Marketing expenses @ 35%	$2,450,000		
General and administrative @ 5%	350,000		
Development expenses	1,815,000		
Construction loan interest	170,200		
Legal and recording @ $50/site	70,000		
Estimated real estate taxes	50,000		
Overhead and profit on sales @ 22%	1,540,000	$6,445,200	
Value of net sales receipts			$ 973,400

Year 3			
Camping site sales (1,100 sites)		$6,160,000	
Utility installation charge @ $299		328,900	
		$6,488,900	
Less:			
Marketing expenses @ 35%	$2,156,000		
General and administrative @ 5%	308,000		
Development expenses	—		
Construction loan interest	—		
Legal and recording @ $50/site	55,000		
Estimated real estate taxes	70,000		
Overhead and profit on sales @ 22%	1,355,200	$3,944,200	
Value of net sales receipts			$2,544,700

Present value of net sales receipts discounted at an annual rate of 12%

Year 1	($ 917,100) × .892857 =	($818,839)
Year 2	973,400 × .797194 =	775,989
Year 3	2,544,700 × .711780 =	1,811,267
Present value		1,768,417
Rounded to		1,768,000
or $2,210 per acre for 800 acres		

Source: Selected portions of this exhibit were taken from James H. Boykin, "Developmental Method of Land Appraisal," *The Appraisal Journal* 44 (April 1976): 190–191.

An estimate of the site value can be found as follows:

Value = (\$25,500) (5.889232)
P.V. ordinary annuity factor of 11%, ten years
+ (\$270,000) (.352184)
P.V. reversion factor of 11%, ten years
Value = \$150,175 + \$95,090
Value = \$245,265 rounded to \$245,300.

The reader will find an explanation of discounting and factors in Chapter 6.

Land Residual Technique

The land residual technique is discussed in detail in Chapter 15. Briefly, this technique attempts to identify the portion of the income generated by the whole property that can be attributed to the building only. Any income remaining must be attributed to the site. The income for the building is identified because the building is typically relatively new. In addition, good comparable sales for the site may not be readily available.

Extraction/Allocation Method

These methods are used for improved sites that have recently sold. In both cases, the site value is not estimated directly, but is derived indirectly. The extraction/allocation methods involve some subjectivity and should be viewed as only a first approximation of the site value.[6]

Allocation is a term applied to the calculation of the market price of the site as a percent of the total selling price. This percent may then be applied to the subject. For example, consider the recent sales of the following improved properties:

Comparable	*Recent Selling Price*	*Estimated Market Price of Site*	*Site Value as a % of Total*
A	\$900,000	\$180,000	20.0
B	\$950,000	\$199,500	21.0
C	\$975,000	\$209,600	21.5
D	\$910,000	\$177,450	19.5

If the analyst concluded that these comparables reveal that site value is approximately 20% of the total selling price, this ratio may be applied to the subject.

Extraction is the term applied to the calculation of the site value by deductive reasoning. For example, if a comparable property recently sold for $950,000 and reliable cost estimates for the structure equal $750,000, the residual selling price of $200,000 could be attributed to the site.

REPRODUCTION COST NEW

One method of estimating the value of an improvement is to derive its cost. Reproduction cost new may be defined as "the cost to reconstruct an exact replica at current prices."[7] The phrase *exact replica* is important since the building is reconstructed on paper with all of its deficiencies and obsolescence.[8] All of these are measured and the appraisal report is dated on the day that the property is seen by the appraiser. All cost figures are current price estimates.

Reproduction cost-new includes an estimate of accrued depreciation for the improvements. For this reason, this estimate of cost is often called *depreciable cost*. Examples are shown later in this chapter.

Steps in the Cost Approach

The steps for deriving an estimate of reproduction cost-new include the following:[9]

1. Estimate the reproduction cost-new of the existing structure.
2. Estimate the accrued depreciation.
3. Deduct the accrued depreciation from the reproduction cost-new.
4. Estimate the depreciated cost-new of any supplemental improvements such as the parking, detached buildings, etc.
5. Estimate the value of the site.
6. Add the estimates in steps 3, 4, and 5.

Advantages and Disadvantages of the Cost Approach

A structure's cost is not always its value since it may not represent what a knowledgeable buyer would pay a knowledgeable seller. Nevertheless, a cost figure can serve as an approximation of market value under the following conditions:

1. Few reliable comparable sales exist, and the direct sales comparison approach cannot be accurately applied.

2. Comparable sales exist, but the properties are too dissimilar.
3. An income stream does not exist, and the income approach cannot be accurately applied.

This method does *not* provide a good estimate unless the following hold:[10]

1. The reproduction cost-new has been estimated correctly using reliable price data.
2. The building is nearly new or new and represents the highest and best use of the property.
3. Physical and functional obsolescence are measurable.
4. All types of obsolescence can be correctly estimated.

REPLACEMENT COST

Replacement cost may be defined as "the cost of reconstructing at current prices a structure with all of the same utility but having no functional obsolescence."[11] The same utility is given to the structure in terms of modern materials, design, and layout, but an exact replica is not constructed on paper. In this type of cost estimate, all functional obsolescence may be eliminated. If obsolescence is to be measured, physical and environmental (economic) are the only two remaining. The cost figures are estimated, and the appraisal report is dated on the day the property is inspected.

By its very nature, this type of cost does not include an estimate of accrued depreciation. A structure having no functional utility would have the newest technology available in the area, which implies new rather than old materials. If an estimate of physical deterioration and environmental obsolescence is derived and subtracted from the replacement cost estimate, the estimate becomes a *replacement depreciable cost.*

Steps in Estimating Replacement Cost

The steps used to estimate replacement cost are identical to the steps used to estimate reproduction cost, except that several modifications are inserted to comply with the definition.

1. Estimate replacement cost for the existing structure using current prices.
2. Estimate accrued depreciation from physical deterioration and economic obsolescence only.
3. Estimate the depreciable (physical and environmental) replacement cost of any additional improvements to the property.

4. Estimate the value of the site.
5. Sum the estimates found in steps 3 and 4.

This estimate suffers from the same disadvantages as the estimate of reproduction cost.

METHODS OF MEASUREMENT

Three methods of estimating cost may be used in the cost approach. Each is discussed.

Square Foot and Cubic Foot

Sometimes called *calculator cost,* a square foot estimate of "$________per square foot" is derived and then multiplied by the square foot in the structure. Adjustments can then be added or subtracted, depending upon the unique features of the structure such as the perimeter and height. Another measurement of "$________per cubic foot" can be used where the air space is important such as a warehouse used for storage.

Costs per square foot and cubic foot can be derived from the market using comparable properties. Recently constructed buildings that are comparable to the subject can be used to derive a cost per square foot or cubic foot that should be applicable to the subject. Second, estimates of costs per square foot can be taken from one of several cost services. These services report costs periodically on different types and qualities of structures that can be purchased for office use.

Trade-Breakdown

This technique summarizes the costs charged by the trades performing the work. A figure is added for indirect expenses such as overhead, legal fees, property taxes, etc. An example of this method is shown later in this chapter.

Segregated Cost

This procedure sums the cost of major components such as the roof, foundation, walls, floors, etc. This method may be more appropriate in situations where a structure has experienced some remodeling to some parts.

A *unit-in-place method* is often used to complement the segregated cost or the square foot method. It is similar to the segregated cost method in that it contains more detailed costs of the structure's components. The unit-in-place method may not contain sufficient costs to complete a whole structure, and is meant to provide additional detail where desired. An example of this method is shown later in this chapter.

METHODS OF COMPUTING ACCRUED DEPRECIATION

This section examines the various methods of estimating accrued depreciation.

Indirect Method

The indirect method means that the accrued depreciation is not directly observed or estimated. It is a difference between two other numbers. Typically, the amount of accrued depreciation using this method is found by subtracting the present worth of the property from the reproduction cost-new. The example shows that accrued depreciation is the difference between the two estimates, which is equal to $50,000.

Reproduction cost-new	$550,000
Present worth of the total property from the income approach	$500,000
Difference	$ 50,000

The biggest advantage of this method is that the estimate of accrued depreciation is entirely market derived using two known estimates of the property's value. Human error is minimized. The biggest disadvantage is that the analyst has little knowledge as to its source. In addition, the accrued depreciation has not actually been observed.

Age-Life Method

One of several age-life methods can be used.

Composite physical life Composite physical life is one rate based upon the physical life only that is applied to the total structure. The one rate is found by

$$100\,(\text{chronological age}/\text{physical life}) = \text{accrued physical deterioration percent}$$

where

chronological age = the actual age found by subtracting the date the structure was built from the date of the appraisal, expressed in fractions of years,

physical life = the estimated time that the building will exist when built.

Consider the following example:

- An apartment building has an estimated physical life of sixty years. The building was built on January 5, 1971, and the date of the value estimate is January 5, 1981.

- The chronological age is January 5, 1981 − January 5, 1971, which equals ten years.
- Thus (10/60)100 = 16.67%.
- This figure of 16.6% is then multiplied by the actual reproduction cost to estimate accrued physical deterioration. In this case, the reproduction cost-new estimate was \$550,000, and .1667 × \$550,000 = \$91,685.

The advantage of this method is that it is based upon physical life concepts only and is very simple. The disadvantage is that it measures only one element of accrued depreciation. Accrued depreciation comes from factors in addition to physical features only such as functional and economic factors.

Composite effective age Composite effective age calculates one figure, which is applied to the total structure. This figure is found by

100 (effective age/economic life) = accrued depreciation percent.

Effective age is the observed age of the property relative to comparable properties. For example, a structure with a chronological age of ten years may be comparable to other structures that are twelve years old if the level of maintenance, style, and location suggest a loss in value for that property. A structure that has a chronological age of ten years may be comparable with others that are eight years old if the level of maintenance has been higher than the average. The appraiser starts with the chronological age of the structure and adjusts this figure up or down according to what is observed with respect to the level of maintenance, style, and location on the subject property, and his or her knowledge of the condition of the comparables. Thus, effective age may be defined as chronological age ± an adjustment for observed conditions relative to similar conditions in comparable properties.

For example, a property that is ten years old has received a level of maintenance above average, which makes this property equivalent to similar properties that are eight years old, and has a forty-year economic life, would have an effective age percent of

$$\left(\frac{10 - 2}{40}\right) 100 \text{ or } \left(\frac{8}{40}\right) 100 = 20\%.$$

Alternatively, if this same property had received below average maintenance, making it equivalent to similar properties that are twelve years old, it would have an effective age percent of

$$\left(\frac{10 + 2}{40}\right) 100 \text{ or } \left(\frac{12}{40}\right) 100 = 30\%.$$

Economic life is the period over which the improvements contribute to the value of the property. Economic life is typically judged by using comparable properties. Consider the following example:

- An apartment building is judged to have an economic life of forty-five years by using comparable properties. An appraiser visits the premises and concludes that the level of maintenance, style, and location is higher than average for similar properties and, as a result, the building is actually comparable to structures that are eight years old. The building's chronological age is ten years.
- Thus the accrued depreciation percent is $(8/45)100 = 17.78\%$.
- This figure is then multiplied by the reproduction cost-new of the structure, which is \$550,000, to give $.1778 \times \$550{,}000 = \$97{,}790$.

The advantage of this method is that it is simple. The disadvantage is that it is too simple in that it stresses physical observed features while possibly underemphasizing the influence of functional and environmental obsolescence.

Component effective age The component age-life method computes a depreciation percent for each of the major components of the structure, multiplies each percent by the appropriate reproduction cost-new, and sums the results. The total items in the structure can typically be depreciated more rapidly, resulting in a larger total than the composite method.

The Economic Recovery Tax Act of 1981 eliminated component depreciation for properties placed into service after 1980 except for special cases involving improvements. This is discussed in chapter 12.

Breakdown Method

The breakdown method separates accrued depreciation into the categories of physical, functional, and economic, and estimates each. The results are totaled to represent the accrued depreciation estimate.

Exhibit 5.3 shows the definitions and measuring tools contained within the required readings of the AIREA. Exhibit 5.4 gives the definitions and measuring tools contained within the required readings of the SREA. Both are presented since some differences do exist. For example, under the category of "incurable," the SREA has three classifications for short lived, long-lived, and indirect costs. The AIREA uses only one category of "incurable."

The purpose of this section is not to debate the relative merits of the contents of each exhibit. Our objective is to inform the reader. Consequently, both are presented to inform the future appraiser that some differences exist between the two organizations in their tools to measure accrued depreciation, whether the difference is in semantics, concept, or application.

Exhibit 5.3
Summary of accrued depreciation measured by the breakdown method taught by the American Institute of Real Estate Appraisers

Obsolescence	Definition	Measurement tool
I. PHYSICAL	Adverse effect on value caused by deterioration or impairment of condition as a result of wear and tear and disintegration.	------------
a. Curable (deferred maintenance)	Cost to cure less than or equal to increase in utility (value or benefits).	Cost to cure
b. Incurable	Cost to cure is greater than increase in utility (value or benefits). Relates to all components of the structure not included in the physical curable category.	(age/life adjusted for observed condition/total physical life expectancy) times (reproduction cost new less reproduction cost of physical curable items)
II. FUNCTIONAL	Adverse effect on value resulting from defects in design that impair utility. It can also be caused by changes over the years that have made some aspect of the structure, material, or design obsolete by current standards.	------------
a. Curable	Cost to cure less than or equal to the increase in utility (value or benefits) and a deficiency that can be corrected through modernization.	------------

Source: Textbook Revision Subcommittee, *The Appraisal of Real Estate, Seventh Edition* (Chicago: American Institute of Real Estate Appraisers, 1978), pp. 251–260.

(continued)

Exhibit 5.3 (continued)

Obsolescence	Definition	Measurement tool
1. Deficiency from age	Comparable structures reveal that the subject was deficient when originally built.	Excess cost of adding this item over the cost of including this item in reproduction cost new
Deficiency from style	Comparable structures reveal that the subject has a feature that is out-of-date.	Cost to cure
2. Excess (overadequacy)	Comparable structures reveal that the subject has an item that is over-built.	Reproduction cost new of the excess less physical deterioration already charged + cost to cure
b. Incurable	Cost to cure is greater than the increase in utility (value or benefits).	------------
1. Deficiency	Comparable structures reveal that the subject has an item that is deficient.	1. Capitalized value of net rent loss due to the condition OR 2. gross rent loss × GRM applicable to the subject
2. Excess	Comparable structures reveal that the subject has an item that is excessive or obsolete and no longer contributing to the economic whole.	Reproduction cost new of item less physical deterioration already charged + present worth (if any) of added cost of ownership due to the item.
III. ECONOMIC-ENVIRONMENTAL	Adverse environmental factors that result in some degree of market rejection and loss in market value. The adverse effect may be on the land value, improvement value, or both.	1. Capitalization of the estimated net rental loss due to the condition OR 2. net rental loss by comparison × GRM applicable to the subject OR 3. Comparison with similar properties not affected.

Exhibit 5.4
Summary of accrued depreciation measured by the breakdown method taught by the Society of Real Estate Appraisers

Obsolescence	Definition	Measurement tool
I. PHYSICAL	Diminished utility caused by physical factors.	------------
a. Curable Deterioration (deferred maintenance or rehabilitation)	Economic life = 0; a typical buyer would repair it immediately.	Cost to cure
b. Incurable Deterioration	------------	------------
1. Short-lived	Remaining economic life of the item is greater than 0 but less than the remaining economic life of the structure.	(reproduction cost) times $\left(\frac{\text{effective age by observation}}{\text{economic life}}\right)$

Source: John D. O'Flaherty, "An Appraiser's Dilemma: The Cost Approach to Value," *The Real Estate Appraiser,* Vol. 35 (January-February, 1969), pp. 5–15.

Exhibit 5.4 (continued)

Obsolescence	Definition	Measurement tool
2. Long-lived	Remaining economic life of the item = the remaining economic life of the structure.	[reproduction cost of direct costs for the structure − (reproduction cost of direct costs from physical curable items and physical incurable short-lived items)] times (effective age of structure by observation after curing physical curable and incurable short-lived and functional curable obsolescence / economic life)
c. Allocation of Indirect Costs	Labor and materials not placed directly into the structure such as profit, survey, legal fees, insurance, taxes, etc.	[(curable physical + incurable short-lived physical + incurable long-lived physical)/(reproduction direct costs of the structure)] × total indirect costs for the structure.
II. FUNCTIONAL	Decreased capacity of the structure to perform its intended function.	------------
a. Curable	Cost to cure is less than or equal to increase in utility (value or benefits).	------------
1. Deficiency	Comparable structures reveal that this item was deficient.	Cost to cure minus the reproduction cost of the item in the original structure.
2. Modernization	Comparable structures reveal that this item is out-of-date.	Cost to cure by installing a new item minus the depreciated value of the existing item.

a. 3. Superadequacy (excess)	Comparable structures reveal that this item is excessive. This excess is *curable* if the cost to cure is less than or equal to the increase in utility (value or benefits).	Reproduction cost new less physical deterioration already charged plus the cost to cure by installing a new item.
b. Incurable	Cost to cure is greater than the increase in utility (value or benefits).	------------
1. Deficiency	Comparable structures reveal that this item is deficient.	1. direct sales comparisons OR 2. rent loss from deficiency as determined by comparables × GRM applicable to the subject.
2. Superadequacy (excess)	Comparable structures reveal that this item is excessive. This excess is *incurable* if the cost to cure is greater than the increase in utility (value or benefits).	Capitalized value of rent loss from the condition: rent loss is measured by added expenses plus excess reproduction cost over the cost supported by an increase in the market rental caused by the existence of the item.
III. ECONOMIC LOCATION	Diminished utility originating from neighborhood influences that are external to the site. It is exists, it is almost always *incurable*.	1. comparison of similar neighborhoods where one has the negative influence and one does not. OR 2. estimated rent loss attributable to the negative influence × GRM for the subject property.

Characteristics of Accrued Depreciation

One source[12] has summarized in a required SREA reading several of the characteristics of accrued depreciation to include the following:

1. It is not a historical fact, nor a loss from a historical fact.
2. It should be viewed as a loss in utility rather than value. Accrued depreciation is only one step in estimating the depreciated reproduction cost of the property. This latter estimate of cost will be used to estimate value.
3. It is an estimate of diminished utility that occurs on the day of the appraisal when the appraiser actually sees the property and compares the subject to the property's highest and best use.

The AIREA teaches a slightly different definition, which includes the following:[13]

1. Accrued depreciation should be viewed as a loss in value from all causes.
2. It should be viewed as being caused by any historical factor through the date of the appraisal.
3. It is the accrued depreciation existing in the improvements at a given date.
4. It should be considered as the difference between reproduction cost-new of the improvements on the date of the appraisal and the property's present value (excluding site value).[14]

Reconciliation The two views can be reconciled into one composite interpretation suggested by the authors.

1. It should be viewed as a loss in utility, which is most likely measured as a loss in value, on the date of the appraisal, which is the date the property is viewed.
2. Whether it is caused by historical factors is not important to the actual measurement. Whatever factors cause a loss in utility on the day the property is seen is part of accrued depreciation.
3. It is not historical or predictable in the same sense as accounting depreciation that is used to determine tax liability. However, accounting depreciation tools such as straight line may be used to help measure its magnitude.

CHARACTERISTICS OF THE COST APPROACH

Several characteristics about the estimates derived from the cost approach need to be identified.

First, the estimate of reproduction cost-new or replacement cost is not value. They should be interpreted as cost figures which, under certain market conditions, may be used as proxies for market value. Cost figures, however, do not replace good estimates of market value from samples of recently sold, comparable properties.

Second, cost estimates may or may not serve as maximums for the estimate of market value derived from the appraisal. If the property is new, at its highest and best use, and the market conditions of demand and supply do not create extreme shortages or surpluses of properties, the cost estimate is probably the maximum that a knowledgable buyer will pay for the property. Other conditions can exist that can cause the cost estimate to be higher or lower than the actual market value. For example, the reproduction cost-new of a structure can be $3.0 million, but a willing buyer may pay only $2.8 million since the area is economically depressed and several alternative properties are for sale on the market.

Third, cost figures are typically more accurate on lower-priced properties than higher-priced properties. The reason for this is that higher-priced properties may have more custom features that must be priced individually. If the features are unusual but expensive, the appraiser may have a tendency to be conservative. Lower-priced properties with features that are seen often in the market and found in many comparable structures can be priced more confidently and accurately.

Fourth, the cost estimate tends to become less accurate and reliable in older buildings. The reason for this is tied to the appraiser's inability to estimate accurately functional and economic obsolescence.

Fifth, a disproportionate amount of time is spent between the amount of instruction given to mastering the concepts and methods of calculating cost versus the figures often desired by the client. Typically, in lower-priced assignments, the client does not want lengthy cost estimates, but prefers these figures to be reduced to briefer summaries that may be used to judge the accuracy of the market value estimate derived from other procedures.

The competent appraiser should not reduce the amount of time spent on a good cost estimate just because the client does not want all of the details. The information desired by the client can be reported, and the remaining information retained in the appraiser's files.

COST ESTIMATES IN A DEMONSTRATION REPORT

One source[15] recently identified the common causes for a candidate's failure in a demonstration report. Although not every report is a demonstration report done for designation credit, this discussion provides a good insight that can be utilized in all estimates of cost. The same source says that the two major reasons for weakness in this section are (1) the lack of justification for the estimated depreciation, and (2) the inconsistent application of the cost technique. Quoting from this article,

Depreciation features should have been identified in the description of improvements and previous report sections and should not make their first appearance in the cost approach section. Depreciation must be market demonstrated; therefore, if comparables are not available to demonstrate the existence of obsolescence in the market, the property is not a good demonstration report property. The cost approach need only summarize the reasons for the depreciation and estimate the dollar amount.

Market justification is recommended for all forms of depreciation. The physical curable cost-to-cure estimate source should be stated and its credibility established, e.g., estimates by local building repair contractors represent market justification. Physical incurable depreciation is market supported if the effective age, remaining economic life, or remaining physical life are market supported or this or other report sections. Functional curable depreciation is market supported if the loss in income or value due to the obsolescence is backed up by comparable income, expense, and cost-to-cure. The basic cost approach question to be answered is this: What market facts and reasoning validate the conclusion that the property value is reduced by the estimated dollar amount because the obsolescence exists? Also, why is it increased by a specific amount when it is cured? Reliable references are available in this area that have stood the test of time. The depreciation analysis objective is to estimate all the depreciation in the various forms only once. Errors most often occur in the areas of:

1. *Not market-justifying the loss in rent or change in expenses due to the obsolescence.*
2. *Underdepreciation due to the application of remaining physical life rather than remaining economic life.*
3. *Excessive depreciation due to deducting the cost of curing obsolescence when the cure is the addition of an item not in the replacement cost.*[16]

ILLUSTRATIONS

The purpose of this section is to provide illustrations of many of the concepts explained earlier. Specifically, two examples are included to illustrate the following points:

- Illustration 1
  Trade breakdown method of estimating reproduction cost new Estimation of physical and functional depreciation using the SREA procedure explained in Exhibit 5–2
- Illustration 2
  Dollars-per-square-foot method of estimating replacement cost from a cost service

Segregated cost method of using costs from a cost service to be used in the replacement cost method

Illustration 1

The first illustration is an eight-unit apartment complex in a midwestern city. Many of the background facts have been omitted.

Builders Trade-Breakdown Method of Reproduction Cost-New

Direct costs (labor and materials)—This cost is separated into groups of probable suppliers.		
Site improvements		
a. Excavation and backfill	1500	
b. Landscaping (trees, shrubs, and grass)	3000	
c. Fencing	850	
d. Asphalt parking	12,000	
		17,350
Concrete and steel		
e. Iron and steel	2300	
f. Footings and foundations including concrete finishwork	2000	
Lumber and accessories		
g. Framing	2200	
h. Exterior shingle and roofing shingle	1500	
i. Plywood sheathing	7850	
j. Finish trim, doors	2500	
k. Kitchen cabinets	15,350	
l. Insulation	1225	
m. Drywall	9000	
n. Exterior stucco	8500	
o. Hardware fixtures	250	
p. Windows and shades	2250	
q. Guttering	375	
		55,300
Plumbing		
r. Plumbing	5500	
s. Bath and kitchen fixtures including kitchen equipment	13,950	
t. Heating and cooling	65,450	
Electrical		
u. Wiring	5500	
v. Lighting fixtures	975	
Painting and tile		
w. Paint	1175	
x. Ceramic tile	565	
y. Labor	3000	
Carpet	8500	
		104,615
	TOTAL	$177,265

Indirect Costs (taxes, sales commission, engineering fees, permits, legal fees, loan points, insurance)—Used 16% of the direct costs which was justified from the costs of other similar properties

$.16 \times \$177{,}265 =$		28,362
	Reproduction Cost-New	$205,627

All of the figures shown in the trade-breakdown method were derived from local suppliers. Classifying the direct costs according to the most probable supplier (excavation, lumber yard, heating and plumbing, electrical, painting, title, etc.) was done for convenience. The figure of 16% that was used to estimate indirect costs has been justified by examining the construction costs of other similar structures.

The total for reproduction cost-new corresponds to step 1 of the cost procedure shown earlier in the chapter. Also included is the supplemental reproduction cost of any detailed improvements included in step 4. If this estimate of cost, $205,627, is used as an estimate of value, accrued depreciation must be estimated next and subtracted.

A. Physical Deterioration

Curable (direct costs) The structure is two years old. Using the criteria that curable physical deterioration applies to all items that are in immediate need of repair (something a buyer would repair immediately), three items were judged by the appraiser to be in this category:

	Cost to cure
1. Painting	
a. Exterior stain was not applied correctly when constructed and needs to be redone.	$1500
b. Interior halls show wear and tear.	500
c. The walls and ceiling are cracked in three rooms on one side of the building.	450
2. Landscaping	
a. The front has a dead shrub.	400
b. The side yard has a water drainage problem.	50
3. Cracked Drive	
a. The driveway is cracked, which will create a larger crack after the winter freeze if not repaired.	125
Total curable:	$3,025

The reproduction cost-new of these items (direct cost) with no indirect cost was estimated to be $5465.

Incurable: short-lived (direct costs) This section identifies those items that have a remaining economic life that is greater than zero, but shorter than the remaining economic life of the structure. These items might show some wear, could need to be replaced soon, but probably will wear out before the structure does. Examples include the following:

	Reprod. Cost-New	*Effect Age by Observ.*	*Normal Life Expect.*	*Dep. %*	*Dep. $*
Roofing	$1200	2 yrs.	16 yrs.	12.5	150.0
Plumbing					
hot water tanks	950	2	8	25.0	238.0
fixtures	545	2	25	8.0	44.0
pipes	4,000	2	25	8.0	320.0
Carpet	8,500	3	5	60.0	5100.0
Kitchen and bath					
dishwasher	1,800	2	7	28.6	515.0
disposal	950	2	5	40.0	380.0
hood and fan	950	2	10	20.0	190.0
range and oven	2,700	2	12	16.7	451.0
refrigerator	3,000	2	12	16.7	501.0
exhaust fan in bath	600	2	12	16.7	100.0
Electrical					
fixtures	975	2	15	13.3	130.0
wiring and service	5500	2	25	8.0	440.0
Heating and Cooling					
air cond. unit	40,000	2	15	13.3	5320.0
heating unit	10,000	2	20	10.0	1000.0
ductwork	15,450	2	25	8.0	1236.0
Drapes and Shades	2,250	2	8	25.0	563.0
	$99,370		Total incurable short-lived:		$16,678

Incurable: long-lived (direct costs) The incurable long-lived items are those that will last only as long as the structure.

Direct costs of the improvements (no indirect costs)	$177,265.
Less all direct reproduction costs shown for (a) physical curable short-lived, and (b) physical incurable short-lived. These costs were (a) $5465 and (b) $99,370	– 104,835.
Total for the long-lived components:	$72,430.
(Observed effective age is two years)/(estimated economic life of sixty years)	× .033
Total physical long-lived:	$2,390.

Total Physical Deterioration

Direct Costs	
Curable	$3,025
Incurable: short-lived	16,678
Incurable: long-lived	2,390
	22,093

Indirect Costs
(physical direct cost of $22,093)/(total direct cost of $177,265) = 12.46%. 12.46% total indirect costs of $28,362 is $3,534.

Total	
Direct	$22,093
Indirect	3,534
	$25,627

B. Functional Obsolescence

Curable This unit was thought by the appraiser to have functional obsolescence from a deficiency in the amount of kitchen cabinets. Several of the tenants have complained to the property manager that kitchen storage space is inadequate and not as much as provided by other comparable rental units. The estimate was made as follows:

1. The cost to cure the deficiency now by adding the extra space is estimated to about $550 per unit × 8 units, which equals $4400.
2. Less the cost of installing the space when the units were built two years ago, which is estimated to be $3000.
3. Loss in value from this obsolescence is $1400.

Incurable No incurable functional obsolescence was observed.

C. Environmental (Economic) Obsolescence

The key to this adjustment is whether the appraiser has estimated the value of the site previously. If so, and this is likely the case, then any loss in value due to neighborhood adverse influence will attach to the improvements only. The following procedure is used to estimate the impact of environmental influences:

1. Ascertain that the site value has been estimated.
2. Estimate GIM for the unaffected property.
3. Estimate rent loss x GIM = environmental impact.
4. Multiply figures in steps 2 and 3 by ratio found from bldg. value/property value.
5. Answer in step 4 is the environmental obsolescence applied to the building.

In this neighborhood, six comparable complexes have been constructed or sold. Sufficient sales exist to perform a limited matched pair analysis. The results tend to indicate that when compared to other neighborhoods throughout the community, the subject was suffering from monthly rent loss of \$10, which was attributed to the constant smog. The site has been estimated by comparable sales to be worth approximately \$25,600, comprising about 13% of the property value. Thus the adjustment is found by

(monthly rent loss) (GIM) (bldg. value/property value)

or,

(\$10) (115) (.87) = \$1001.

This figure was cross-checked by examining the sales in each neighborhood. Four recent sales in neighborhood A were around \$210,000; neighborhood B sales were around \$211,000; and sales in the subject's neighborhood were around \$209,000.

The figure of \$1,001 was selected to represent the loss in value from location.

Summary of Accrued Depreciation	
Physical	
Curable	3,025
Incurable: short-lived	16,678
Incurable: long-lived	2,390
Indirect cost	3,534
Functional	
Curable-deficiency	1,400
Environmental	1,001
	\$28,028

Estimate of Market Value from the Reproduction Cost New Approach		
Reproduction cost-new of the improvements		$205,627
Less accrued depreciation		– 28,028
Value of site (estimated by comparables)		+ 25,600
	Estimate of market value:	$203,199
	rounded to	$203,200

Illustration 2

This example covers a multiple residence and the use of a cost service to estimate replacement cost using dollar-per-square-foot and segregated costs. Also, computerized cost systems have been developed and are available from various cost services.

SUMMARY

Under certain conditions, a cost estimate may serve as a reliable approximation for market value. The cost estimate can be measured as reproduction cost or replacement cost. Reproduction cost is the current price estimate of reproducing an exact replica. Replacement cost is the current price estimate of building a structure that satisfies the same utility with no functional obsolescence. Reproduction cost includes an estimate of accrued depreciation. Replacement cost may or may not include an estimate of accrued depreciation.

Cost estimates can be generated by any of several methods: dollars-per-square- or cubic-foot, segregated cost, or the trade breakdown method. Dollars-per-square- or cubic-foot multiplies a dollar figure times the square or cubic feet in the structure. Segregated cost estimates the costs for each of the major components of the structure like the roof, walls, flooring, etc., and sums the result. The trade breakdown method sums the costs charged by the subcontractors performing the work.

Accrued depreciation may be measured by one of several methods. These include the indirect approach, age-life techniques, or the breakdown method. The latter is the most comprehensive and includes separate estimates for physical, functional, and economic obsolescence.

REPLACEMENT COST EXAMPLE

11 UNIT APARTMENT BUILDING

AVERAGE QUALITY

Presented by

MARSHALL and SWIFT

Publication Company

1617 BEVERLY BOULEVARD • P.O. BOX 26307 • LOS ANGELES, CALIFORNIA 90026

Copies of this material are available, without charge, to current subscribers or qualified instructors for free distribution to appraisal students.

6R1-90 RCH

PLOT PLAN

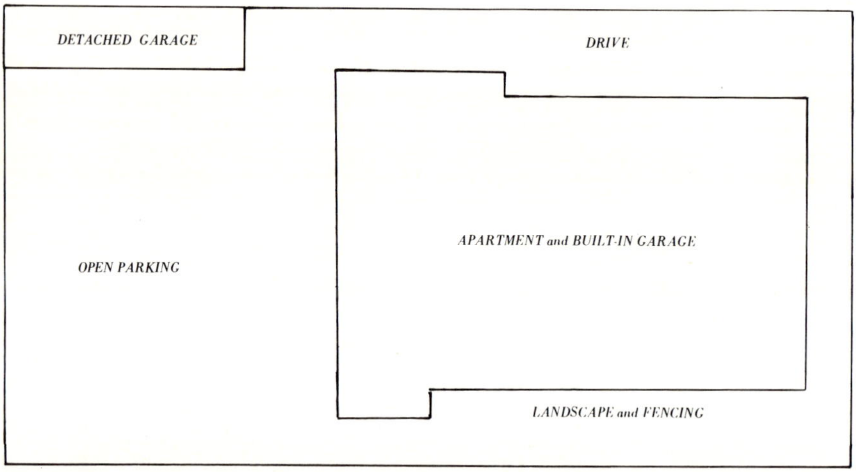

3 BEDROOM and 2 BATHS (ONE UNIT)

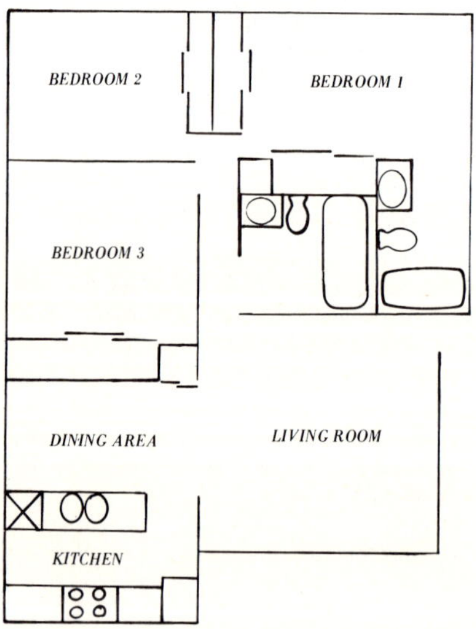

2 BEDROOM and 1½ BATHS (TEN UNITS)

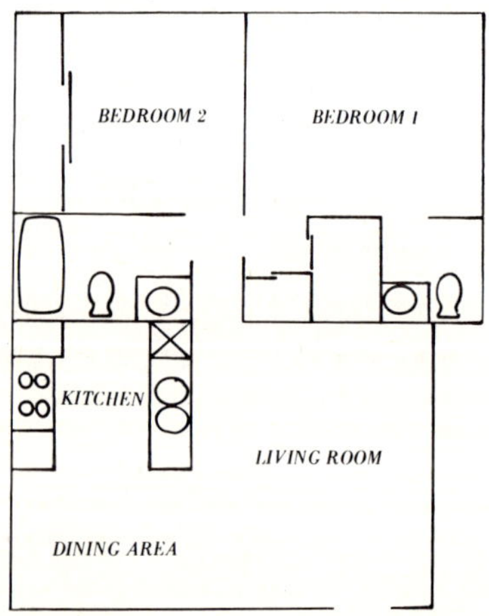

N

GENERAL BUILDING DESCRIPTION

This is a two story, 11 unit, apartment building of 9,761 square feet. It has 10 units with 2 bedrooms, 1-1/2 baths; an additional unit with 3 bedrooms and 2 baths. Included in the living area are laundry and storage facilities. There is also a 600 sq. ft. built-in garage under one of the living units and a 1,626 sq. ft. carport which can be priced as a detached garage. There are 11 additional spaces of open parking.

FOUNDATION:	Continuous perimeter foundation with continuous foundation under interior bearing walls. The site was level with no unusual soil conditions.
FLOOR STRUCTURE:	First floor is a concrete slab on the ground. The second floor is a wood structure, 2"x12" @ 16" o.c. with 5/8" plywood sheathing.
FLOOR COVER:	Carpet throughout with vinyl asbestos tile in the kitchen and the baths. There is also 1-5/8" foamed concrete on the upper level for soundproofing.
EXTERIOR WALL:	Wood frame, 2"x4" @ 16" o.c. with stucco and wood shingles exterior cover. Exterior doors are solid core. Windows and sliding glass doors are aluminum.
ROOF:	Rafters consist of 2"x6" @ 16" o.c. for the gable portion and 2"x10" @ 16" o.c. which double as ceiling joists for the flat portion. Both sections have 1/2" CDX plywood sheathing. The roof covers are a 3-ply composition with small gravel on the flat portion and wood shingles on the gable portion.
INTERIOR FINISH:	Walls are taped and painted drywall. There are vaulted ceilings in the living room areas of the second floor units. Ceiling finish is sprayed drywall with enamel painted ceilings in the kitchens and baths. Adequate wardrobe closets with sliding wardrobe doors. Cabinets are natural wood. Counter tops and splash are laminated plastic and simulated marble. Stock hollow core doors and hardware throughout the interior.
HEATING/COOLING:	Ten units are heated by an electric ceiling radiant system with thermostat controls and cooled by 1/2 ton wall air conditioning. One unit has a warm and cooled air system.
ELECTRICAL:	Wiring is flexible conduit. The quality and quantity of the fixtures is average.
PLUMBING:	Fixtures include: tubs which are plastic one piece units with a wainscot, lavatories of average quality porcelain enamel, white tank type toilets, and double compartment kitchen sinks. Hot water is from a 100-gal. circulating system, which is considered the equivalent of one plumbing fixture per unit. There are two plumbing rough-ins. Ten units have seven fixtures each and one unit has eight fixtures.
INSULATION:	There is 3-1/2" batt insulation on the exterior surfaces with sound insulation between units. Ceiling insulation on the upper level.
BUILT-INS:	There are: 11 range & ovens, electric; 11 range hoods and fans; 11 dishwashers; 11 garbage disposers; 22 bath heaters and 22 exhaust fans. All built-ins are Fair Quality.
BALCONIES:	Wood frame with ornamental iron railing and a cement composition deck. Both the soffit and the balcony ceiling are finished.
GARAGES:	There is a built-in garage with a concrete slab floor, supporting columns and small storage. There is also a carport with a concrete slab floor, flat roof structure, built-up composition roof cover and small storage.
QUALITY:	The overall quality of the building is average.

SQUARE FOOT APPRAISAL FORM

for use with the **RESIDENTIAL COST HANDBOOK**

Appraisal for ____________ Property owner ____________

Address ____________

Appraiser ____________ Date ____________

TYPE		QUALITY		STYLE		EXTERIOR WALLS		GARAGE TYPE	
Single Family	☐	Low	☐	No. Stories 2		Hardboard	☐	Detached	☒
Apartment	☒	Fair	☐	Split Level	☐	Stucco	☒	Attached	☐
Town House	☐	Average	☒	1½ story - Fin.	☐	Siding or Shingle	☐	Built-In	☒
Row House	☐	Good	☐	1½ story - Unf.	☐	Masonry Veneer	☐	Carport	☐
		Very Good	☐	End Row	☐	Common Brick	☐	Subterranean	☐
				Inside Row	☐	Face Brick or Stone	☐		
						Concrete Block	☐	Garage Area 1626 SQ. FT./600 SQ. FT.	

FLOOR AREA	BASEMENT AREA	PORCH AREA	PLUMBING	NUMBER OF MULTIPLE UNITS
1st 4,463 SQ. FT.	Unf. ____			
2nd 5,298 SQ. FT.	Fin. ____			
3rd ____	BALCONY AREA	(a) 208 SQ. FT.	Fixtures 78	
Total 9,761 SQ. FT.	360 SQ. FT.	(b) ____	Rough-In 2	11

INTERPOLATED FOR 12 UNITS: \$19.08 (8 UNITS) + \$21.46 (16 UNITS) ÷ 2	Quan.	Cost	+	−	Extension
1. COMPUTE RESIDENCE BASIC COST: Floor area x selected sq. ft. cost	9,761	\$20.27			\$ 197,855
2. Basic residence cost adjustments Lines 3-13. Describe and indicate plus or minus			+	−	
3. Roofing BUILT-UP (BASE): ½ ROOF = SHINGLE @ +\$.22 = \$.11 ÷ 2 (STORIES ADJ.)	9,761	.06	+		586
4. Flooring 1st floor CONCRETE SLAB (1ST FLOOR)	4,463	.76		−	3,392
5. Flooring upper floors SEE NOTES	9,761	1.22	+		11,908
6. Heating - Cooling SEE NOTES	9,761	.10	+		976
7. Plaster NONE					
8. Plumbing 78 FIXT. (55 = BASE) = 23 @ \$275 = \$6,325 + 2 R.I. @ \$105 = \$210	1	6,535	+		6,535
9. Built-in appliances R & O ELEC. @ \$340; GARB. DISP. @ \$95					
10. RANGE HOOD & FAN @ \$85; DISHWASHER @ \$280 (FAIR QUALITY)	11	800	+		8,800
11. Fireplace NONE					
12. Miscellaneous WALL A/C, ½ TON (FAIR QUALITY)	10	265	+		2,650
13. EXHAUST FAN @ \$50 + BATH HEATER @ \$50 (FAIR QUALITY)	22	100	+		2,200
14. SUBTOTAL ADJ. RESIDENCE COST: Line 1 plus or minus Lines 3-13					\$228,118
15. BASEMENT, UNFINISHED					
16. Add for basement garage: Single ☐ Double ☐					
17. Add for basement outside entrance					
18. Add for basement interior finish					
19. Porches or balconies, describe CONC. PORCH (SEGREGATED COSTS)	208	1.54	+		320
20. BALCONY: WOOD ORN. IRON, PLASTER @ \$11.45 + CEIL. @ \$1.07	360	12.52	+		4,507
21. SUBTOTAL RESIDENCE COST: Total of Lines 14-20					\$232,945
22. GARAGE OR CARPORT – sq. ft. area x selected sq. ft. cost BUILT-IN GARAGE	600	5.58	+		3,348
23. Attached garage – deduct for common wall				−	
24. Garage roofing adjustment					
25. Garage miscellaneous DETACHED GARAGE @ \$6.50 MINUS DOOR @ \$1.03	1,626	5.47	+		8,894
26. SUBTOTAL GARAGE COST: Line 22 plus or minus Lines 23-25					12,242
27. SUBTOTAL OF ALL BUILDING IMPROVEMENTS: Sum of Lines 21 and 26					\$245,187
28. Current Cost Multiplier 1.09 x Local Multiplier 1.00 x Line 27					\$267,254
29. Depreciation: Age ____ Condition ____ Deduction ____ % of Line 28					
30. Depreciated cost of building improvements: Line 28 less Line 29					
31. Yard improvements cost: List, total, apply local multiplier and depreciate on reverse side					
32. Landscaping cost: List and compute on reverse side					
33. Lot or land value					
34. **TOTAL INDICATED VALUE**: Total of Lines 30-33					

FORM 1007

4 RCH 6R4-90

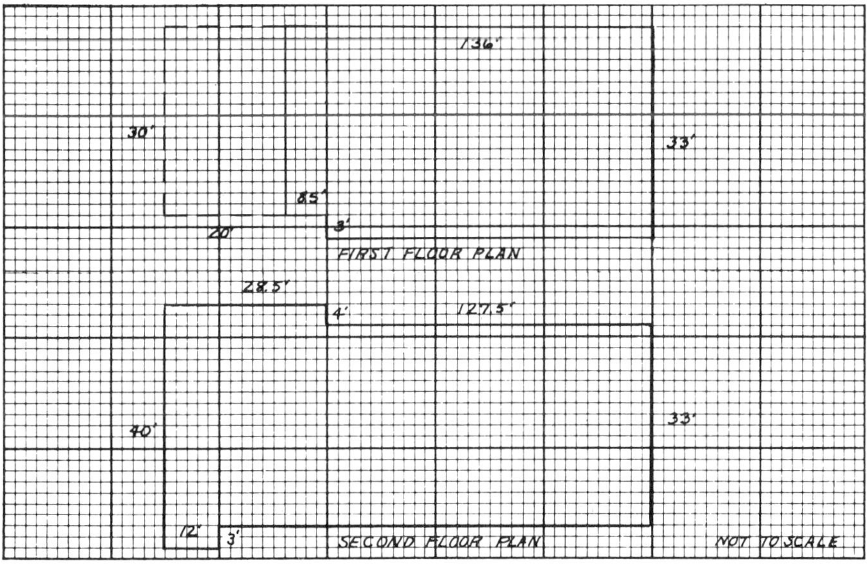

NOTES AND COMPUTATIONS

FLOOR AREAS:

APARTMENT

1ST FLOOR: 127.5' x 33' = 4,208 S.F.
8.5' x 30' = 255 S.F.
4,463 S.F.

2ND FLOOR: 156' x 33' = 5,148 S.F.
28.5' x 4' = 114 S.F.
12' x 3' = 36 S.F.
5,298 S.F.

TOTAL FLOOR AREA = 9,761 S.F.

GARAGES

BUILT-IN: 20' x 30' = 600 S.F.
DETACHED: 80' x 20.33' = 1,626 S.F.

ADJUSTMENTS:

FLOOR COVER

80% CARPET @ \$1.12 = \$ .90
20% RES. FLR. COVER @ \$.63 = .13
54% LT. WT. CONC. @ \$.36 = .19
\$1.22

HEATING/COOLING

10% WARM & COOLED AIR @ \$.90 = \$ .09
90% CEILING RADIANT @ \$.01 = .01
\$ .10

FORM 1007

Square Foot Costs
Average Quality Multiples

BASIC DESCRIPTION

The following description and costs apply to multiple residences of the most common quality, up to three stories, usually constructed to meet or exceed the minimum uniform building codes. By most standards, the quality of materials and workmanship are quite acceptable but do not reflect custom craftsmanship or special features. They are usually built from stock plans with some exterior ornamentation. Interior finish is average with few refinements. Compute costs separately for basements, balconies, exterior stairways and garages.

FOUNDATION	Concrete perimeter footing and wall with continuous foundation or piers under interior bearing walls.
FLOOR STRUCTURE	Wood structure and subfloor on first and upper story floors. Use Square Foot Adjustments to correct basic cost for concrete slab.
FLOOR COVER	Carpet, asphalt or vinyl asbestos tile. Floor cover costs are not included in the basic cost. Use the Square Foot Adjustments to add for floor cover.
EXTERIOR WALL	Wood frame and stucco with adequate fenestration using standard grade sash. Some ornamentation. Quality of materials and workmanship are generally average. Use percentage adjustments to correct for variations in exterior wall type.
ROOF	Wood frame and sheathing with either medium weight asphalt shingles or built-up, small rock cover. Use Square Foot Adjustments to correct basic cost for other types of roofing.
INTERIOR FINISH	Walls are taped and painted drywall with few surface imperfections. Ceilings are generally sprayed drywall with enamel painted ceilings in the kitchens and baths. Adequate wardrobe type bedroom closets and guest closet or shelved linen closet. Stock cabinets of finished hardwood veneer or paint grade wood. Countertops and splash of laminated plastic, simulated marble or ceramic tile. Medium grade, stock hollow core slab or flat panel interior doors. Softwood base and casing, medium grade hardware. Use Square Foot Adjustments to correct for plaster interior.
HEATING	Gas fired forced air furnace. Use Square Foot Adjustments to correct for other types of heating or cooling.
ELECTRICAL	Minimum number of outlets and inexpensive fixtures.
PLUMBING	Five competitively priced white fixtures per unit, which can include any of the following: water heater, tiled or fiberglass stall shower, toilet, lavatory sink, tub with shower over, kitchen sink. Use Lump Sum Adjustments to correct basic cost for more or less than five plumbing fixtures.
INSULATION	Wall and ceiling insulation are included in the basic cost. Use the Segregated Cost Section to correct the basic costs for no wall or ceiling insulation.
BUILT-IN APPLIANCES	None included in basic cost. Add from Lump Sum Adjustments when applicable.
BASEMENT	Refer to Segregated Cost Section, pages B-6 and B-7.
GARAGE	Concrete slab floor, overhead doors. Conforms to multiple residence in quality.
ELEVATORS	Refer to Unit-in-Place Cost Section, page C-14.

Square Foot and Lump Sum Adjustments not listed on the cost pages may be determined by reference to Segregated Cost Section B. For detailed cost adjustments or the pricing of specialty items, refer to Unit-in-Place Cost Section C.

Refer to Section F for the appropriate Current Cost and Local Multiplier.

All costs in Section A include a normal allowance for plans, specifications and general contractor's overhead and profit.

page A-124

MULTIPLES

Square Foot Costs
Average Quality

FRAME AND STUCCO MULTIPLES COSTS (per sq. ft. of total floor area)

TOTAL FLOOR AREA	3	4	8	16	25	40	60	80	100
2,000	$22.61	$23.41							
3,000	20.92	21.52							
4,000	19.89	20.51	$23.35						
6,000	18.80	19.38	20.88						
10,000		18.08	19.08	$21.46					
14,000			18.03	19.75	$22.11				
20,000			17.03	18.50	20.15	$22.81			
30,000				17.23	18.49	20.45	$22.61		
40,000				16.50	17.59	19.02	20.69	$22.49	
60,000					16.44	17.67	18.92	20.17	$21.14
80,000						16.77	17.95	18.82	19.77

For larger projects deduct 1% to 3%. For other than frame and stucco exterior walls, adjust the above costs as follows: Siding or shingle, +3%; masonry veneer, +10%; brick, +12%; face brick or stone, +18%; concrete block, +6%.

SQUARE FOOT ADJUSTMENTS (Additions or deductions to the above costs)

ROOFING (Divide by number of stories)		HEATING (Apply to total flr. area)	
Asph. shingle or B.U. rock	(base)	Forced air, gas	(base)
Wood shingle	+ $ .22	Forced air, electric	+ $ .12
Wood shake	+ .50	Floor or wall furnace	- .33
Composition roll	- .25	Gravity furnace	- .11
FLOORS (Apply to individual floors)		Floor radiant, hot water	+ 1.05
Wood subfloor only	(base)	Ceiling radiant, electric	+ .01
Concrete slab only	- $ .76	Baseboard, electric	- .07
Add for: Hardwood	+ [illegible]	Hot water, baseboard	+ .44
Carpet	+ 1.12	Warm and cooled air	+ .90
Resilient floor cover	+ .63	Heat pump	+ .95
Lt. Wt. conc.	+ .36	PLASTER INTERIOR	+ $ .54

LUMP SUM ADJUSTMENTS PER UNIT (*) Indicates only item included in base cost.

PLUMBING (* 5 fixtures)	(base)	BUILT-IN APPLIANCES	
Per fixture	+ or - $275	Range & oven, gas	+ $ 355
Plbg. fixture, rough-in	+ 105	Range & oven, electric	+ 400
Tub enclosure	+ 100	Electric bath heater	+ 55
		Garbage disposer	+ 110
		Range hood & fan	+ 100
		Kitchen or bath exhaust fan	+ 55
FIREPLACES, ea.		Dishwasher	+ 320
Single, 1 story	$ 825 to $1215	Radio-intercom	+ 155
Single, 2 story	1000 to 1470	Wall air cond., 3/4 ton	+ 340

BALCONIES (sq. ft. cost all sizes)

Soffit (Underside of Balcony)	Wood: Or. Iron Rail	Wood: Wood Rail	Cement Comp.: Or. Iron Rail	Cement Comp.: Wood Rail
Unfinished	$9.25	$7.36	$10.38	$8.47
Plaster	10.32	8.43	11.45	9.54

For plastered balcony ceiling, add $1.07 per sq. ft.

EXTERIOR STAIRWAYS (cost per flight)

Soffit (Underside of Stairway)	Wood	Cement Comp.	Steel
Unfinished	$440	$705	$795
Plaster	515	780	-----

For sq. ft. cost of landings, use applicable balcony costs.

PORCHES AND BASEMENTS (Refer to Segregated Cost Section B.)

DETACHED GARAGES (with overhead doors)

Exterior Wall	800	1600	3200	4800
Frame & Stucco	$6.77	$6.50	$6.17	$5.91
Siding or Shingle	7.31	[illegible]	6.50	6.26
Masonry Veneer	8.15	7.61	7.23	6.97
Brick	8.77	8.18	7.70	7.37
Face Brick & Stone	9.96	9.18	8.68	8.33
Concrete Block	8.05	7.41	7.09	6.83

If no overhead doors, deduct $1.03 per sq. ft.

BUILT-IN GARAGES

Exterior Wall	800	1600	3200	4800
Frame & Stucco	$5.58	$5.46	$5.33	$5.20
Siding or Shingle	6.02	5.88	5.75	5.60
Masonry Veneer	6.73	6.57	6.41	6.26
Brick	7.23	7.07	6.89	6.73
Face Brick & Stone	8.21	8.03	7.84	7.64
Concrete Block	6.63	6.49	6.33	6.17

Ceiling and wall finish included.

ADJUSTED SUBTERRANEAN GARAGE COSTS (per sq. ft. of floor area)

3000	6000	9000	12000	15000	18000	21000	24000	Add for Mech. Vent	Add for Sprinklers
$7.25	$7.00	$6.76	$6.56	$6.31	$6.13	$5.91	$5.74	$ .33	$ .77

When concrete roof of subterranean garage is utilized as courtyard deck or sidewalk on top side, add **$4.39** per sq. ft. for courtyard or walk area. Where utilized as first floor of apartment, add **$1.89** per sq. ft. to basic floor cost.

page A-125

MULTIPLES

Square Foot Costs
Fair Quality

FRAME AND STUCCO MULTIPLE COSTS (per sq. ft. of total floor area)

TOTAL FLOOR AREA	3	4	8	16	25	40	60	80	100
2,000	$18.94	$19.62							
3,000	17.52	18.03							
4,000	16.66	17.18	$19.56						
6,000	15.75	16.24	17.49						
10,000		15.14	15.99	$17.98					
14,000			15.11	16.54	$18.52				
20,000			14.26	15.50	16.88	$19.11			
30,000				14.43	15.48	17.13	$18.94		
40,000				13.83	14.74	15.94	17.34	$18.84	
60,000					13.77	14.80	15.85	16.90	$17.71
80,000						14.04	15.04	15.77	16.56

For larger projects deduct 1% to 3%. For other than frame and stucco exterior walls, adjust the above costs as follows: Siding or shingle, +2%; masonry veneer, +10%; brick, +13%; face brick or stone, +19%; concrete block, +7%.

SQUARE FOOT ADJUSTMENTS (Additions or deductions to the above costs)

ROOFING (Divide by number of stories)

Asph. shingle or B.U. gravel	(base)
Wood shingle	+ $ .22
Wood shake	+ .47
Composition roll	- .21

FLOORS (Apply to individual floors)

Wood subfloor only	(base)
Concrete slab only	- $ .70
Add for: Hardwood	+ 1.46
Carpet	+ .93
Resilient floor cover	+ .50

HEATING (Apply to total flr. area)

Floor or wall furnace	(base)
Forced air, gas	+ $ .31
Forced air, electric	+ .42
Gravity furnace	+ .21
Ceiling radiant, electric	+ .32
Baseboard, electric	+ .26
Hot water, baseboard	+ .72
Evaporative cooling	+ .49
Warm and cooled air	+ 1.18
Heat pump	+ 1.21

PLASTER INTERIOR + $ .49

LUMP SUM ADJUSTMENTS PER UNIT (*) Indicates only item included in base cost.

PLUMBING (* 5 fixtures) (base)

Per fixture	+ or – $240
Plbg. fixture, rough-in	+ 95
Tub enclosure	+ 85

FIREPLACES, ea.

Single, 1 story	$685 to $1030
Single, 2 story	830 to 1235

BUILT-IN APPLIANCES

Range & oven, gas	+ $ 300
Range & oven, electric	+ 340
Electric bath heater	+ 50
Garbage disposer	+ 95
Range hood & fan	+ 85
Kitchen or bath exhaust fan	+ 50
Dishwasher	+ 280
Radio-intercom	+ 135
Wall air cond., 1/2 ton	+ 265

BALCONIES (sq. ft. cost all sizes)

Soffit (Underside of Balcony)	Wood: Or. Iron Rail	Wood: Wood Rail	Cement Comp.: Or. Iron Rail	Cement Comp.: Wood Rail
Unfinished	$8.28	$6.55	$9.32	$7.58
Plaster	9.24	7.51	10.28	8.54

For plastered balcony ceiling, add $ .96 per sq. ft.

EXTERIOR STAIRWAYS (cost per flight)

Soffit (Underside of Stairway)	Wood	Cement Comp.	Steel
Unfinished	$355	$590	$665
Plaster	425	660	----

For sq. ft. cost of landings, use applicable balcony costs.

PORCHES AND BASEMENTS (Refer to Segregated Cost Section B.)

DETACHED GARAGES (with overhead doors)

Exterior Wall	800	1600	3200	4800
Frame & Stucco	$6.01	$5.70	$5.40	$5.13
Siding or Shingle	6.44	6.09	5.73	5.53
Masonry Veneer	6.95	6.53	6.21	5.90
Brick	7.59	7.08	6.82	6.43
Face Brick/Stone	8.69	8.16	7.83	7.40
Concrete Block	7.00	6.58	6.25	5.93

If no overhead doors, deduct $ .93 per sq. ft.

BUILT-IN GARAGES

Exterior Wall	800	1600	3200	4800
Frame & Stucco	$4.96	$4.85	$4.73	$4.62
Siding or Shingle	5.30	5.20	5.06	4.94
Masonry Veneer	5.71	5.60	5.46	5.32
Brick	6.25	6.12	5.97	5.83
Face Brick/Stone	7.16	7.01	6.84	6.67
Concrete Block	5.77	5.65	5.51	5.36

Ceiling and wall finish included.

page A-123

Segregated Costs
Balconies, Attics, Porches

PORCHES

BALCONIES OR STAIR LANDINGS . . . Apply cost to floor area.

QUALITY	WOOD FLOOR: WOOD RAIL	WOOD FLOOR: ORN. IRON RAIL	CEMENT COMPOSITION FLOOR: WOOD RAIL	CEMENT COMPOSITION FLOOR: ORN. IRON RAIL
Low	$ 6.55	$ 8.45	$ 7.80	$ 9.80
Fair	7.15	9.20	8.45	10.60
Average	7.80	10.00	9.15	11.45
Good	9.25	11.85	10.80	13.40
Very Good	10.10	12.85	11.70	14.50
Excellent	11.00	14.00	12.70	15.65

Note: *Add for balcony roofs and ceiling or soffit finish from porch roof tables below.*

ATTICS . . . Attic finish may be priced from the appropriate Segregated components or Unit-in-Place Cost tables or from the following cost range below computed on square foot of floor area. Costs include softwood floor cover and stairway, drywall ceiling, and minimum electrical. Plumbing and partition walls are not included and may be added from Section C.

	LOW	FAIR	AVG.	GOOD	V.GOOD	EXCL.
Attic Finish	$2.55	$2.84	$3.17	$3.94	$4.39	$4.89

PORCHES . . . Apply all component costs to porch floor area.

Open Concrete Porches - Including Perimeter Foundation

QUALITY	25 SQ. FT.: WITH STEPS	25 SQ. FT.: SLAB	100 SQ. FT.: WITH STEPS	100 SQ. FT.: SLAB	200 SQ. FT.: WITH STEPS	200 SQ. FT.: SLAB
Low	$4.86	$1.62	$4.02	$1.43	$3.78	$1.35
Fair	5.22	1.75	4.32	1.53	4.06	1.45
Average	5.60	1.89	4.63	1.63	4.36	1.54
Good	6.46	2.20	5.34	1.85	5.04	1.74
Very Good	6.94	2.37	5.73	1.97	5.41	1.85
Excellent	7.45	2.56	6.15	2.10	5.81	1.97

Note: *Use $1.20 per square foot for slab porches or patios without perimeter foundation.*

Open Wood Porches or Decks - With Wood Steps

QUALITY	25 SQ. FT.	100 SQ. FT.	200 SQ. FT.	300 SQ. FT.
Low	$6.50	$5.45	$4.72	$4.13
Fair	7.22	6.08	5.27	4.61
Average	8.02	6.78	5.89	5.14
Good	9.90	8.43	7.36	6.41
Very Good	11.00	9.40	8.22	7.15
Excellent	12.22	10.48	9.18	7.98

Note: *Increase cost 5% for each foot of height above 3 feet.*

Add For Porch Roof and Posts - (No Ceiling Included)

TYPE	LOW	FAIR	AVG.	GOOD	V.GOOD	EXCL.
Asphalt shingle	$2.88	$3.11	$3.35	$3.90	$4.21	$4.54
Built-up, rock	2.98	3.21	3.46	4.03	4.34	4.68
Composition, roll	2.71	2.90	3.10	3.54	3.78	4.04
Wood shingle	3.57	3.79	4.02	4.52	4.80	5.09
Rigid asbestos shingle	3.58	3.87	4.18	4.87	5.26	5.68
Wood shakes	3.67	3.92	4.19	4.79	5.12	5.47
Clay (mission) tile	4.09	4.48	4.90	5.87	6.42	7.03
Concrete tile (lightweight)	3.56	3.86	4.19	4.93	5.35	5.08
Slate	4.65	5.00	5.38	6.24	6.71	7.22

Note: *For pitched roof, use residence roof slope multipliers.*

Add For Porch Ceiling or Soffit Finish

TYPE	LOW	FAIR	AVG.	GOOD	V.GOOD	EXCL.
Plaster	$ .88	$ .99	$1.11	$1.41	$1.58	$1.78
Wood, painted	1.01	1.13	1.26	1.56	1.74	1.94
Hardboard, painted	.91	1.03	1.15	1.47	1.65	1.86

page B-T4

CURRENT COST MULTIPLIERS

CURRENT COST MULTIPLIER . . . Apply these multipliers to the costs on the following pages in the handbook to arrive at a current cost level.

PAGES	FRAME	MASONRY
SECTION A		
A-1 thru A-82 (Single Family Residences)	1.00	1.00
A-113 thru A-130 (Apartments)	1.09	1.10
A-131 thru A-148 (Town Houses)	1.06	1.07
A-149 thru A-162 (Urban Row Houses)	1.03	1.04
SECTION B		
B-1 thru B-13 (Segregated Costs)	1.02	1.02
SECTION C		
C-1 thru C-14 (Yard Improvements & Unit-in-Place)	1.14	1.16
C-15 thru C-26 (Unit-in-Place & Mobile Homes)	1.11	1.13

LOCAL MULTIPLIERS

LOCAL MULTIPLIERS . . . Apply these multipliers to the costs in the handbook to arrive at a local cost level.

UNITED STATES

	FRAME	MASONRY
ALABAMA		
ANNISTON	.93	.93
AUBURN,OPELEIKA,PHENIX C.	.81	.83
BESSEMER	.93	.93
BIRMINGHAM	.95	.95
DOTHAN	.83	.84
FLORENCE	.91	.92
GADSDEN	.96	.96
HUNTSVILLE	.93	.94
MOBILE	.96	.97
MONTGOMERY	.84	.85
TUSCALOOSA	.89	.90
ALASKA		
ANCHORAGE	1.47	1.51
FAIRBANKS	1.59	1.61
JUNEAU	1.50	1.52
KENAI PENINSULA	1.49	1.55
KETCHIKAN	1.53	1.60
KODIAK	1.58	1.65
SITKA	1.51	1.60
ARIZONA		
DOUGLAS	1.04	1.05
FLAGSTAFF	1.06	1.08
NOGALES	1.04	1.04
PHOENIX	1.05	1.06
PRESCOTT	1.06	1.07
TUCSON	1.04	1.04
YUMA	1.01	1.02
ARKANSAS		
BLYTHEVILLE	.85	.87
FAYETTEVILLE	.88	.89
FORT SMITH	.88	.89
HOT SPRINGS	.88	.89
JONESBORO	.86	.87
LITTLE ROCK	.87	.88
TEXARKANA	.88	.89
WEST MEMPHIS	.87	.89
CALIFORNIA		
ANTELOPE VALLEY	1.12	1.13
BAKERSFIELD	1.13	1.13
BARSTOW	1.12	1.13
BISHOP-MAMMOTH LAKES	1.18	1.18
BLYTHE	1.15	1.16
BUTTE CO.	1.09	1.11
CALAVERAS CO.	1.10	1.12
COALINGA	1.10	1.12
CONTRA COSTA CO.	1.15	1.17
EL DORADO CO.	1.12	1.13
EUREKA	1.14	1.15
FRESNO	1.06	1.07
HANFORD	1.07	1.08
CALIFORNIA (Cont'd)		
HUNTINGTON-NEWPORT B.	1.12	1.13
IMPERIAL CO.	1.16	1.17
LAGUNA-SAN CLEMENTE	1.13	1.14
LAKE ARROWHEAD-BIG BEAR	1.16	1.17
LAKE TAHOE	1.16	1.18
LOS ANGELES	1.12	1.12
MADERA	1.05	1.06
MARIN CO.	1.16	1.17
MARIPOSA CO.	1.12	1.14
MENDOCINO CO.	1.11	1.12
MERCED	1.04	1.05
MODESTO	1.02	1.04
MONO CO.	1.15	1.16
NAPA CO.	1.17	1.18
NEVADA CO.	1.14	1.16
OAKLAND-ALAMEDA	1.15	1.17
ORANGE CO. (X/BEACHES)	1.12	1.12
PALM SPRINGS-INDIO	1.14	1.15
PASO ROBLES	1.10	1.11
PLACER CO.	1.10	1.12
REDDING	1.10	1.11
RIVERSIDE	1.11	1.11
SACRAMENTO	1.11	1.12
SALINAS	1.14	1.15
SAN BERNARDINO	1.11	1.11
SAN DIEGO	1.10	1.10
SAN FRANCISCO	1.16	1.17
SAN JOSE	1.15	1.16
SAN LUIS OBISPO	1.11	1.12
SAN MATEO CO.	1.15	1.16
SANTA BARBARA	1.14	1.15
SANTA CLARA	1.15	1.16
SANTA CRUZ	1.14	1.16
SANTA MARIA-LOMPOC	1.11	1.12
SANTA ROSA	1.14	1.16
SOLANO CO.	1.14	1.16
STOCKTON	1.07	1.09
SUSANVILLE	1.14	1.14
TULARE CO.	1.06	1.07
TUOLUMNE CO.	1.10	1.13
VENTURA CO.	1.11	1.11
VICTORVILLE-HESPERIA	1.13	1.14
YOLO CO.	1.09	1.10
YUBA CITY-MARYSVILLE	1.09	1.11
COLORADO		
BOULDER	1.01	1.02
COLORADO SPRINGS	1.00	1.01
DENVER	.99	1.00
GRAND JUNCTION	1.02	1.03
GREELEY	1.01	1.02
PUEBLO	.99	1.00

REVIEW QUESTIONS

1. What is the difference between reproduction cost and replacement cost?
2. What are the steps that are followed in deriving an estimate of value by the cost approach? What are the disadvantages of these steps?
3. What is the difference among the square foot, segregated cost, and trade-breakdown method of measuring cost?
4. Explain and give examples of the following methods of estimating accrued depreciation:

   indirect

   age-life

   breakdown
5. Discuss several characteristics of the cost approach.
6. Explain the common mistakes made by candidates in completing the cost section of their demonstration report.

ENDNOTES

1. Byrl N. Boyce, *Real Estate Appraisal Terminology* (Cambridge, Mass.: Ballinger Publishing Co., 1975), p. 189.
2. Ibid.
3. This section draws heavily on James H. Boykin, ''Developmental Method of Land Appraisal,'' *The Appraisal Journal* 44 (April 1976): 181–192.
4. Ibid.
5. William N. Kinnard, Jr., *Income Property Valuation* (Lexington, Mass: D. C. Health and Co.—Lexington Books, 1971), p. 324.
6. Textbook Revision Subcommittee, *The Appraisal of Real Estate* (Chicago: AIREA, 1978), pp. 145–147.
7. Boyce, *Real Estate Appraisal Terminology,* p. 176.
8. Ibid.
9. Textbook Revision Subcommittee, *Appraisal of Real Estate,* pp. 66–67.
10. Ibid., p. 507.
11. This definition is similar to Boyce, *Real Estate Appraisal Terminology,* p. 176.
12. John O'Flaherty, ''An Appraiser's Dilemma: The Cost Approach to Value,'' *The Real Estate Appraiser* 35 (January–February 1969): 7.
13. Textbook Revision Subcommittee, *The Appraisal of Real Estate,* p. 237.
14. emphasis added by authors.
15. Robert Heinrich, ''A Candidate's Guide to Writing a Passing MAI Demonstration Appraisal Report,'' *The Appraisal Journal* 47 (October 1979): 567.
16. Ibid.

ADDITIONAL READINGS

Ames, Ronald. "Appraisal and Feasibility Analysis of Bowling Centers." *The Real Estate Appraiser* 44 (March-April 1978): 15-18.

Bateman, Ronald H. "Appraising the Going Concern." *The Appraisal Journal* 39 (October 1971): 526-534.

Baumgarten, Judy. "Market Value When there is No Market." *The Appraisal Journal* 46 (January 1978): 79-89.

Callaway, Robert J. "Condominiums Revisited." *The Appraisal Journal* 43 (October 1975): 517-526.

Dix, S. M. "Appraisal for Assessment of a Major Industrial Property." *Assessor Journal* 14 (March 1979): 1-4.

Entreken, Henry C., Jr. "More Applications of the Cost Approach." *The Real Estate Appraiser* 43 (November-December 1977): 13-15.

Fredman, Albert J., and White, R. Dean. "A Logical Method of Depreciating Buildings." *The Appraisal Journal* 42 (October 1974): 549-564.

Gaines, James P. "Residential Rehabilitation Appraisals: Problems and Prospects." *The Appraisal Journal* 48 (April 1980): 236-248.

Goldman, Theodore R. "Apartment Construction: Quality Versus Costs." *The Appraisal Journal* 37 (July 1969): 330-336.

Hartman, Donald J. "Industrial Real Estate: Cost Approach with Caution." *The Appraisal Journal* 45 (July 1977): 444-449.

Heidrick, Harold H. "Determining Utility Market Value." *The Appraisal Journal* 38 (April 1970): 253-272.

Higgins, J. Warren. "Depreciation: Real Property." *The Real Estate Appraiser and Analyst* 42 (January-February 1976): 51-54.

Knowles, Jerome, Jr. "Estimating Accrued Depreciation." *The Appraisal Journal* 45 (January 1976): 34-43.

Ludy, Victor R. "The Why of Depreciation." *The Appraisal Journal* 33 (January 1965): 41-47.

Parker, John M. "A Conceptual Route to Replacement Cost of Productive Capacity." *Valuation* 23 (October-November 1976): 120-128.

Reeves, L. T. "The Depreciated Incremental Cost Concept." *The Appraisal Journal* 39 (October 1971): 556-561.

Roche, John K. "The Assessor's View of Depreciation." *The Appraisal Journal* 35 (April 1967): 223-225.

Sunley, Emil M. "Changes in Depreciation and Recapture—Impact on Real Estate Investments." *The Appraisal Journal* 38 (October 1970): 524-535.

Waldron, William D. "Toward an Honest Cost Approach." *The Appraiser's Journal* 39 (July 1971): 370-373.

Zimmerman, Paul. "Reproduction Cost New is 'Cute.' " *The Real Estate Appraiser and Analyst* 40 (July-August 1974): 43-47.

MODULE VI
Tools for Income Valuation

The third indicator of market value comes from the income approach, which is next in the text. But first, several tools and definitions used in later chapters must be developed, explained, and, in some cases, illustrated. Chapter 6 covers the basics of discounting and compounding, and Chapter 7 contains additional explanations and definitions.

CHAPTER 6

LEARNING OBJECTIVES

When a student finishes this chapter, he or she should be able to:

- Explain the reasons for discounting and compounding.
- Explain the difference between discounting and compounding.
- Define and discuss the six functions of $1.
- Outline several typical applications of the six functions of $1.

Discounting and Compounding

IMPORTANT TERMS AND PHRASES

amortization factor: $1/a_{\overline{n}|}$ The present value of a series of equal payments over n equal periods that will fully amortize \$1.

beginning of period: Income collected at the beginning of the period.

compound amount of a constant repeated investment of \$1 over n equal periods: $S_{\overline{n}|}$ A future value that is the amount of accumulated principal and interest resulting from a series of equal investments of \$1 over n equal periods.

compound amount factor: S^n A future value that is the amount to which an investment today of \$1 will compound with interest over n equal periods.

end of period: Income is collected at the end of the period.

factors: Financial functions based on \$1 that are found in tables.

future value: The worth of money at some point in the future.

Inwood factor: $a_{\overline{n}|}$ The present value of a series of equal investments of \$1 over n equal periods and discounted at the appropriate interest rate.

present value: The worth of money received at the present date.

reversion factor: $1/S^n$ A present value of \$1 where the \$1 occurs in the future at the end of n equal periods.

sinking fund factor: $1/S_{\overline{n}|}$ The periodic payment over n equal periods where the principal and interest will total \$1.

time value of money: An assumption that a consumer places a higher value on money received today than money received in the future.

The purpose of this chapter is to explain the basics of discounting and compounding. These two tools are used in many different applications discussed in later chapters.

PURPOSE OF DISCOUNTING AND COMPOUNDING

Before entering the mechanics of discounting and compounding, the student should understand the purpose of these tools. Both concepts rest on the concept called the *time value of money*. Sometimes called the opportunity cost of money, both discounting and compounding assume that the owner of the funds would rather have the money today than tomorrow. In other words, present consumption is more important than future consumption.

In order for the owner to release this money for investment, he or she must forego current consumption. That payment for the consumption given up takes the form of interest earnings, which are typically expressed as

$$\text{Interest earnings} = \text{principal} \times \text{interest rate} \times \text{time.}$$

The magnitude of the interest rate is dependent upon several items. First, the owner of the funds must be compensated for interest earnings that have been lost from not investing in another competing investment. The rate paid on the investment in question must at least cover the rates paid by the competition. Second, the owner of the funds will consider his or her loss of liquidity. These funds are committed and used by the borrower for a predetermined time period, meaning the owner cannot use them. Third, the owner must consider the risk that the borrower may not repay the funds. A larger risk would typically mean a higher interest rate, and vice-versa.

DEFINITIONS AND SYMBOLS

The appropriate compounding and discounting definitions and symbols used in this chapter and later chapters are explained in this section.

Factors

The first six definitions and symbols represent the "Six Functions of $1." These *functions*, sometimes called *factors*, represent calculations that are all based on $1. These factors may be used with any dollar amount other than $1 to derive the needed results in the problem at hand.

Future Value (FV)

S^n = a future value that is the amount to which an investment today of \$1 will grow with compound interest over n equal periods.

$S_{\overline{n}|}$ = a future value that is the amount of accumulated principal and interest resulting from a series of equal investments of \$1 over n equal periods.

$\frac{1}{S_{\overline{n}|}}$ = *sinking fund factor:* the periodic payment over n equal periods where the principal and interest will total \$1.

Present Value (PV)

V^n = *reversion factor:* a present value of \$1 where the \$1 occurs in the future at the end of n equal periods.

$a_{\overline{n}|}$ = *Inwood coefficient:* the present value of a series of equal investments of \$1 over n equal periods and discounted at the appropriate interest rate.

$\frac{1}{a_{\overline{n}|}}$ = the present value of a series of equal payments over n equal periods that will fully amortize \$1.

Dollar Amounts

When any of these six factors is used with a dollar amount, the desired dollar answer can be derived. The symbols and definitions shown in this chapter and later chapters for dollar amounts are defined below.

PV = current dollar investment.

pay = a series of equal dollar payments over n equal periods.

FV = *future value:* sometimes called the compound amount, this will appear in the future after n periods.

USES OF THE FACTORS AND THE DOLLAR AMOUNTS: END OF THE PERIOD (EOP) PAYMENTS

This section defines and demonstrates the uses of the factors and the dollar amount.

Future Amounts

Sometimes called *compound amounts,* these represent a value that will occur at some point in the future. The reader should always remember that these factors and dollar amounts represent dollar figures that appear at the *end* of the period in question. Sometimes these are called end-of-the-period (EOP) payments. Finding compound amounts is sometimes called *compounding.*

A. Future Amount of $1

$$FV = S^n \text{ (PV)}$$

where

FV = final balance, total sum, *compound amount,* future amount, or future value of one investment, (PV), over n equal periods,

S^n = *compound amount factor* which is $(1 + i)^n$ where i = the interest rate and n = number of annual payments at the end of each period.

Example: You invest one amount of $1000 today for three years at 12% annual interest paid at the end of each year. What is the $1000 worth at the end of three years?

Solution 1

$$\begin{aligned} FV &= S^n \text{ (PV)} \\ FV &= (1 + .12)^3 \, \$1000 \\ FV &= (1 + .12)\,(1 + .12)\,(1 + .12)\, \$1000 \\ FV &= (1.404928)\, \$1000 \\ FV &= \$1404.928. \end{aligned}$$

Solution 2

$$\begin{aligned} FV &= S^3 \text{ (PV)} \\ FV &= (1.404928)\, \$1000 \end{aligned}$$

factor from financial tables for $i = 12\%$, $n = 3$

$$FV = \$1404.928.$$

B. Future Value of a Constant Repeated Investment of $1 for *n* Equal Periods

$$FV = S_{\overline{n|}} \times \text{pay}$$

where

FV = final balance, total sum, compound amount, future amount, or future value of a repeated investment of a constant amount with interest, i, at the end of each period n,

$S_{\overline{n|}}$ = *compound amount factor,* which is $\left[\dfrac{(1 + i)^n - 1}{i}\right]$ or $\left[\dfrac{S^n - 1}{i}\right]$ where i = interest rate and n = number of annual payments made at the end of each period.

Example: You invest $1000 at the end of each year for three years at 12% annual interest paid at the end of each year. What is the $1000 worth at the end of three years?

Solution 1

$$FV = S_{\overline{n|}} \times \text{pay}$$

$$FV = \left[\frac{(1 + .12)^3 - 1}{.12}\right] \$1000$$

$$FV = \left[\frac{(1.12)(1.12)(1.12) - 1}{.12}\right] \$1000$$

$$FV = \left[\frac{1.404928 - 1}{.12}\right] \$1000$$

$$FV = [3.3744]\ \$1000$$

$$FV = \$3374.40.$$

Solution 2

$$FV = S_{\overline{n|}} \times \text{pay}$$

$$FV = [3.374400]\ \$1000$$

factor from financial tables for $i = 12\%$, $n = 3$

$$FV = \$3374.40.$$

C. Sinking Fund Factor

$$\text{pay} = \frac{1}{S_{\overline{n|}}} \times (FV)$$

where

pay = a constant repeated dollar amount invested at the end of n equal periods,

$\frac{1}{S_{\overline{n|}}}$ = *sinking fund factor* for n periods, which equals

$$\left[\frac{i}{S^n - 1}\right] \text{ or } \left[\frac{i}{(1 + i)^n - 1}\right] \text{ for } n \text{ periods.}$$

Example: You must possess \$1000 at the end of three years. How much must you invest at the end of each year at 12% annual interest to equal \$1000?

Solution 1

$$\text{pay} = \frac{1}{S_{\overline{n|}}} \times (FV)$$

$$\text{pay} = \frac{1}{\dfrac{(1 + i)^n - 1}{i}} \times (FV)$$

$$\text{pay} = \frac{1}{\dfrac{(1.12)(1.12)(1.12)-1}{.12}} \$1000$$

$$\text{pay} = \frac{1}{3.3744} \$1000$$

$$\text{pay} = (.2963489)\ \$1000$$

$$\text{pay} = \$296.3489.$$

Solution 2

$$\text{pay} = \frac{1}{S_{\overline{n|}}} \times (\text{FV})$$

$$\text{pay} = (.2963489)\ (\$1000)$$

factor from financial tables for $i = 12\%$, $n = 3$

$$\text{pay} = \$296.3489.$$

Solution 3

$$\text{pay} = \frac{1}{S_{\overline{n|}}} \times (\text{FV})$$

$$\text{pay} = \left[\frac{i}{(1+i)^n - 1}\right] \text{FV}$$

$$\text{pay} = \left[\frac{.12}{.404928}\right] \$1000$$

$$\text{pay} = (.2963489)\ \$1000$$

$$\text{pay} = \$296.3489.$$

Present Value (Present Worth)

These figures represent the current value or current worth. Finding present value is sometimes called *discounting*. All of the dollar amount figures are assumed received at the end of each period (EOP).

D. Reversion Factor: Sometimes Called the Present Value of $1

$$\text{PV} = \frac{1}{S^n} \times (\text{FV})$$

where

PV = present worth of a future value, FV, that will occur at the end of n periods,

$\frac{1}{S^n}$ = *present value of $1 factor* where i = interest rate and n = number of annual payments made at the end of each period.

Example: You will receive \$1000 at the end of three years from today. What is this amount worth today if it is discounted at 12% annually?

Solution 1

$$PV = \frac{1}{S^n} (FV)$$

$$PV = \frac{1}{(1 + i)^3} (FV)$$

$$PV = \frac{1}{(1 + .12)(1 + .12)(1 + .12)} \$1000$$

$$PV = \frac{1}{1.404928} \$1000$$

$$PV = (.7117802) \$1000$$

$$PV = \$711.7802.$$

Solution 2

$$PV = \frac{1}{S^n} (FV)$$

$$PV = (.711780) \$1000$$

factor from financial tables for $i = 12\%$, $n = 3$

$$PV = \$711.780.$$

E. Present Value of an Ordinary Annuity: Sometimes Called the Inwood Coefficient

$$PV = a_{\overline{n}|} \times \text{pay}$$

where

PV = present value of a stream of constant payments, pay, made at the end of n equal periods,

$a_{\overline{n}|}$ = *present value of an annuity factor,* which is

$$\left[\frac{1 - \frac{1}{(1 + i)^n}}{i}\right] \quad \text{or} \quad \left[\frac{1 - V^n}{i}\right].$$

Example: You will invest \$1000 per year for three years. What is the present worth of these three payments if these amounts are discounted at 12% annually?

Solution 1

$$PV = a_{\overline{n}|} \times \text{pay}$$

$$PV = \left[\frac{1 - \dfrac{1}{(1+i)^n}}{i}\right] \times \text{pay}$$

$$PV = \left[\frac{1 - \dfrac{1}{(1+.12)^3}}{.12}\right] \$1000$$

$$PV = \left[\frac{1 - .7117802}{.12}\right] \$1000$$

$$PV = (2.4018316)\ (\$1000)$$

$$PV = \$2401.8316.$$

Solution 2

$$PV = a_{\overline{n}|} \times \text{pay}$$

$$PV = (2.401831)\ \$1000$$

factor from financial tables for $i = 12\%$, $n = 3$

$$PV = \$2401.831.$$

F. Amortization Factor: Sometimes Called the Installment to Amortize $1 and the Ordinary Annuity which has a Present Value of $1

$$\text{pay} = (PV)\frac{1}{a_{\overline{n}|}}$$

where

pay = a series of constant dollar payments over n equal periods that will fully amortize a predetermined amount, PV, with interest,

PV = predetermined amount such as a loan balance to be amortized over n equal periods with a series of constant payments, P,

$\dfrac{1}{a_{\overline{n}|}}$ = *amortization factor* over n equal periods, which is

$$\left[\frac{i}{1 - \dfrac{1}{(1+i)^n}}\right] \quad \text{or} \quad \left[\frac{1}{1 - V^n}\right].$$

Example: You borrow $1000 for three years at 12% interest and agree to repay it with interest in three equal installments at the end of each period, n. What is the amount of each payment?

Solution 1

$$\text{pay} = (\text{PV})\frac{1}{a_{\overline{n}|}}$$

$$\text{pay} = \$1000\left[\frac{.12}{1 - \dfrac{1}{(1 + .12)^3}}\right]$$

$$\text{pay} = \$1000\left[\frac{.12}{.2882198}\right]$$

$$\text{pay} = \$1000\ (.4163489)$$

$$\text{pay} = \$416.3489.$$

Solution 2

$$\text{pay} = (\text{PV})\frac{1}{a_{\overline{n}|}}$$

$$\text{pay} = \$1000\ (.416349)$$

from financial tables for $i = 12\%$, $n = 3$

$$\text{pay} = \$416.349.$$

USES OF THE FACTORS AND THE DOLLAR AMOUNTS: BEGINNING OF THE PERIOD PAYMENTS (BOP)

The previous section illustrated discounting and compounding with end of the period payments. The purpose of this section is to illustrate discounting and compounding where the dollar amount is paid at the *beginning of the period* (BOP) rather than at the end of the period.

In times where creative financing arrangements are common, BOP factors may be needed. The following present value and future value factors are for illustrative purposes only. The appraiser must be careful to select the appropriate factor for the problem at hand.

Future Amounts

A future amount may be needed that includes income received at the beginning of the period.

A. Future Value of $1

$$\text{FV} = (S^n)\ (\text{PV})$$

where

FV = future value,
(S^n) = *compound amount factor* for n equal periods.

Example: You invest $1000 today and the interest at 12% is paid in advance in four equal payments over three periods. What is the total at the end of the third year?

Solution 1

If the solution is worked by hand, n is set equal to the number of *periods.*

$$\text{FV} = (S^n)\ (\text{PV})$$
$$\text{FV} = [(1 + i)^3]\ (\text{PV})$$
$$\text{FV} = [(1 + .12)^3]\ \$1120 \text{ including } \$120 \text{ prepaid interest}$$
$$\text{FV} = [1.404928]\ \$1120$$
$$\text{FV} = \$1{,}573.5193.$$

Solution 2

If the solution is found by using a table of factors, the value of n in the formula is set equal to <u>(n − 1) payments</u>

$$\text{FV} = (S^n)\ (\text{PV})$$
$$\text{FV} = (1.404928)\ (\$1120)$$

factor from financial tables for $i = 12\%$, $n = 2$

$$\text{FV} = (1.404928)\ (\$1120)$$
$$\text{FV} = \$1{,}573.5193.$$

B. Compound Amount of a Constant Repeated Investment of $1 for *n* Periods

$$\text{FV} = S_{\overline{n}|} \times \text{pay} + \text{PV}(1 + i)^n$$

where

FV = compound amount,

pay = the payments,

$S_{\overline{n}|}$ = *compound amount factors* for n equal periods,

PV = the first payment.

Example: You invest $1000 today and agree to make three additional investments at the beginning of three equal periods for a total investment of $4000, at 12% interest. What are these investments worth at the beginning of the fourth period?

Solution 1

If the solution is calculated by hand, the value for n is set equal to the <u>number of periods or (n − 1) payments.</u>

$$\text{FV} = S_{\overline{n}|}\text{pay} + \text{PV}\ (1 + i)^n$$

$$\text{FV} = \left[\frac{(1 + .12)^3 - 1}{.12}\right] 1000 + \$1000\ (1 + .12)^3$$

$$FV = (3.3744)\ \$1000 + \$1000\ (1.404928)$$
$$FV = \$3374.40 + \$1404.928$$
$$FV = \$4779.328.$$

Solution 2

If the solution is calculated using factor tables, n is set equal to $(n - 1)$ payments or the number of periods.

$$FV = S_{\overline{n|}}\,\text{pay} + PV\ (1 + i)^n$$
$$FV = (3.3744)\ \$1000 + \$1000\ (1.404928)$$
$$FV = \$3374.40 + \$1404.928$$
$$FV = \$4779.328.$$

C. Sinking Fund

$$\text{pay} = \frac{1}{S_n}\ (FV)$$

where

$\frac{1}{S_n}$ = sinking fund factor for payments made in time 0 and the beginning of each period thereafter.

Example: You must possess \$1000 by the end of three periods. You will make a payment to an investment account today at 12% and commit to three other equal payments at the beginning of each period for a total of four payments. What is the amount of each payment?

Solution 1

If the solution is worked by hand, n is set equal to $(n + 1)$ periods or the number of payments.

$$\text{pay} = \left(\frac{1}{S_n}\right)\ (FV)$$

$$\text{pay} = \left[\frac{i}{(1 + i)^4 - 1}\right]\ (\$1000)$$

$$\text{pay} = \left[\frac{.12}{(1 + .12)^4 - 1}\right]\ (\$1000)$$

$$\text{pay} = [.2092344]\ (\$1000)$$

$$\text{pay} = \$209.2344.$$

Solution 2

If the solution is worked using a table of factors, the value of n is set equal to $(n + 1)$ periods or the number of payments.

$$\text{pay} = \frac{1}{S_n} \text{(FV)}$$

$$\text{pay} = (.209234)\ (\$1000)$$
from financial tables for $i = 12\%$, $n = 4$

$$\text{pay} = \$209.234.$$

D. Reversion Factor

$$\text{PV} = \frac{1}{S^n} \text{(FV)}$$

where

$\frac{1}{S^n}$ = reversion factor for a future amount that appears at the beginning of a future period.

Example: You will receive $1000 at the beginning of the third year from today. What is this amount worth today using an interest rate of 12%?

Solution 1

If the solution is worked by hand, n is set equal to the *number of periods.*

$$\text{PV} = \frac{1}{S^n} \text{(FV)}$$

$$\text{PV} = \frac{1}{(1 + i)^2} (\$1000)$$

$$\text{PV} = \frac{1}{1.2544} (\$1000)$$

$$\text{PV} = (.7971938)\ (\$1000)$$

$$\text{PV} = \$797.1938.$$

Solution 2

If the solution is found by using a table of factors, the value of n in the formula is set equal to the *number of periods.*

$$\text{PV} = \frac{1}{S^{n-1}} \text{(FV)}$$

$$\text{PV} = (.797194)\ (\$1000)$$
factor from financial tables for $i = 12\%$, $n = 2$

$$\text{PV} = \$797.194.$$

E. Present Value of an Ordinary Annuity

$$\text{PV} = a_{\overline{n-1}|}\ \text{pay} + \text{first payment}$$

where

$a_{\overline{n-1}|}$ = present value for an annuity factor for $(n - 1)$ periods,

pay = stream of constant payments.

Example: You receive \$1000 today and will receive another payment of \$1000 at the beginning of three equal periods for a total of \$4000. Interest is paid on the \$3000 at 12% annually. What is the annuity's present value?

Solution 1

If the solution is calculated by hand, n is set equal to the number of payments or $(n + 1)$ periods.

$$\text{PV} = a_{\overline{n-1}|} \text{ pay} + \$1000$$

$$\text{PV} = \left[\frac{1 - \dfrac{1}{(1+i)^3}}{i}\right] \$1000 + \$1000$$

$$\text{PV} = (2.401831)\ \$1000 + \$1000$$

$$\text{PV} = \$2401.831 + \$1000$$

$$\text{PV} = \$3401.831.$$

Solution 2

If the solution is calculated by the use of factor tables, the value of n in the table is set equal to the number of periods or $(n - 1)$ payments.

$$\text{PV} = a_{\overline{n-1}|} \text{ pay} + \$1000$$

$$\text{PV} = (2.401831)\ \$1000 + \$1000$$

factor from financial at $i = 12\%$ for $n = 3$

$$\text{PV} = \$3401.831.$$

F. Amortization Factor

$$\text{pay} = (\text{PV}) \frac{1}{a_{\overline{n-1}|}}$$

where

$\dfrac{1}{a_{\overline{n-1}|}}$ = *amortization factor* for n payments made at the *beginning* of each period.

Example: You borrow \$1000 for three years at 12% interest and agree to repay it with interest by making one payment today of \$200, followed by three consecutive equal payments at the beginning of each period. What is the amount of each payment?

Solution 1

If the solution is calculated by hand, the value of n is set equal to the number of payments after the first or the number of periods.

$$\text{pay} = \text{PV}\frac{1}{a_{\overline{n-1}|}}$$

$$\text{pay} = \$800\left[\frac{1}{\dfrac{1-\dfrac{1}{(1+.12)^3}}{.12}}\right]$$

$$\text{pay} = \$800\ [.4163489]$$

$$\text{pay} = \$333.08.$$

Solution 2

If the solution is calculated by the use of factor tables, the value of n in the table is set equal to the number of periods or the number of payments after the first.

$$\text{pay} = \text{PV}\frac{1}{a_{\overline{n-1}|}}$$

$$\text{pay} = \$800\ (.416349)$$

factor from financial tables for $i = 12\%$, $n = 3$

$$\text{pay} = \$333.08.$$

SUMMARY

This chapter explained and illustrated the concepts and techniques of discounting and compounding. Discounting is the technique of converting future income into present worth. Compounding is the technique of converting present dollars into future dollars. Either may involve dollar amounts that appear at the end of the period(s) or at the beginning of the period(s).

PROBLEMS

The following represent several calculator problems that provide drill on the keystrokes. These problems are reprinted with the permission of the Hewlett-Packard Co., for use with a HP-38E/38C hand calculator. Also, the student can check his or her mastery of the concepts by working them by hand.

Example: Your good friend needs a loan to start his latest enterprise. He has requested that you lend him \$450 for 60 days. You lend him the money at 7%

simple interest, based on a 360-day year. What is the amount of accrued interest he will owe you in 60 days? What is the net amount?

	Keystrokes	Display
	60 [n]	60.00
	7 [i]	7.00
	450 [CHS] [PV]	-450.00
Accrued interest.	[f] [INT]	5.25
Net amount paid back (received).	[+]	455.25

Example: What is the accrued interest and net amount on $450 for 60 days at 7%, figured on a 365-day year?

	Keystrokes	Display
	60 [n]	60.00
	7 [i]	7.00
	450 [CHS] [PV]	-450.00
Accrued interest.	[f] [INT] [g] [R↓] [x≷y]	5.18
Net amount paid back (received).	[+]	455.18

Example: Fur trapper Bill Buckskin wishes to invest in a $22,000 log cabin to keep the rain off. A local merchant has offered to loan Bill the $22,000 at 10.5% interest. Making $200 monthly payments, how long will it take Bill to repay his mortgage?

Set the payment switch D.MY BEGIN [switch] M.DY END to END.

	Keystrokes	Display
	[f] CLEAR [FIN]	
% monthly interest rate.	10.5 [g] [12÷]	0.88
Negative for money paid out.	200 [CHS] [PMT]	-200.00
Loan amount (recieved).	22000 [PV]	22,000.00
Months.	[n]	376.89
Years.	12 [÷]	31.41

Example: What is the annual interest rate on a 25-year, $32,500 mortgage with $230 monthly payments?

Set the payment switch D.MY BEGIN [switch] M.DY END to END.

	Keystrokes	Display
	[f] CLEAR [FIN]	
Months.	25 [g] [12×]	300.00
Remember the sign convention.	230 [CHS] [PMT]	-230.00
Mortgage amount.	32500 [PV]	32,500.00
% monthly interest rate.	[i]	0.58
% annual interest rate.	12 [×]	7.01

Example: What annual interest rate must be obtained to accumulate $10,000 in 8 years on an investment of $6,000, with quarterly compounding?

	Keystrokes	Display
	[f] CLEAR [FIN]	
Quarters.	8 [ENTER↑] 4 [×] [n]	*32.00*
Investment.	6000 [CHS] [PV]	*-6,000.00*
Total returned.	10000 [FV]	*10,000.00*
% quarterly interest rate.	[i]	*1.61*
% annual interest rate.	4 [×]	*6.44*

What if the compounding were monthly?

	Keystrokes	Display
Months.	8 [g] [12×]	*96.00*
% monthly interest rate.	[i]	*0.53*
% annual interest rate.	12 [×]	*6.40*

Example: Property values in an unattractive area are declining at the rate of 2% per year. What will property presently valued at $32,000 be worth in 6 years if this trend continues?

	Keystrokes	Display
	[f] CLEAR [FIN]	
	6 [n]	*6.00*
% interest rate.	2 [CHS] [i]	*-2.00*
	32000 [CHS] [PV]	*-32,000.00*
Property value.	[FV]	*28,346.96*

Example: An investor pays $65,000 for a duplex that he intends to keep 5 years and then sell. The first year he knows he will have to spend a considerable amount for repairs. Will he achieve a desired 9% after-tax yield with the following after-tax cash flows? Note that the duplex is sold for $74,500 at the end of the fifth year.

	Keystrokes	Display
Clear financial and storage registers.	[f] CLEAR [ALL]	*0.00*
Desired yield.	9 [i]	*9.00*
Initial investment.	65000 [CHS] [g] [CF_0]	*-65,000.00*
First cash flow.	100 [CHS] [g] [CF_j]	*-100.00*
Second cash flow.	4900 [g] [CF_j]	*4,900.00*
Third cash flow.	5300 [g] [CF_j]	*5,300.00*
Fourth cash flow.	4800 [g] [CF_j]	*4,800.00*
Fifth cash flow.	74500 [g] [CF_j]	*74,500.00*
Net present value.	[f] [NPV]	*-5,054.61*

REVIEW QUESTIONS

1. Explain the reasons for compounding and discounting.
2. What is the difference between discounting and compounding?
3. Explain the meaning of each of the six functions of $1. When is each applied?
4. Make your own drill questions covering the concepts and techniques shown in this chapter.

ADDITIONAL READINGS

Epley, Donald R., and Millar, James A. *Basic Real Estate Finance and Investments* (New York: John Wiley & Sons, 1980), chapter 14.

Kelso, Donald E., and Weygandt, Jerry J. *Intermediate Accounting* (New York: John Wiley & Sons, Inc., 1974), pp. 215–238.

Smith, Keith V., and Eiteman, David K. *Essentials of Investing* (Homewood, Ill.: Richard D. Irwin, 1974), parts I and II.

Sprecher, C. Ronald. *Essentials of Investment* (Boston: Houghton Mifflin Co., 1978), chapter 4.

Thorndike, David. *The Thorndike Encyclopedia of Banking and Financial Tables* (Boston: Warren, Gorham, and Lamont, 1973), chapters 5–12.

Mason, James J. (ed. and comp.), American Institute of Real Estate Appraisers. *Financial Tables* (Chicago: AIREA, 1981).

MODULE VII
Income Approach to Value

The next eight chapters deal with the income approach to value. Chapter 7 attempts to develop tools and assumptions, Chapter 8 covers the estimation of net operating income (NOI), Chapter 9 discusses mortgage-equity including Akerson, Chapter 10 covers mortgage-equity including Ellwood, Chapter 11 deals with the extraction of *R* from market comparables, Chapter 12 presents contemporary methods including estimates of investment value and discounted cash flow, and the next three chapters cover the physical residual techniques. These eight chapters give the student explanations, techniques with and without algebra, and many illustrations.

CHAPTER 7

LEARNING OBJECTIVES

When a student finishes this chapter, he or she should be able to:

- Discuss the basis of real estate values.
- Discuss the present value estimation of use and exchange and the derivation of $V = I/R$.
- Explain the contribution of appraisal to the I/R technique of valuation.
- Explain the importance of market derived data.
- Contrast the definitions and use of the holding period, useful life, and remaining economic life.
- Identify the difference between equity and debt funds.
- Explain the differences among the equity dividend rate, equity yield rate, discount rate, return *on* investment, and the return *of* investment.

Important Assumptions and Tools Used in Estimating Value

IMPORTANT TERMS AND PHRASES

appreciation (app.): A capital gain used in estimating value.

band of investment: A technique for computing a rate by averaging a weighted mortgage interest rate, *i,* and the owner's expected return on the equity. This technique can be used with different terms to estimate the overall rate, *R,* as explained in Chapter 9.

cash throw-off (CTO): Before-tax income, found by subtracting debt service from the net operating income.

debt funds: The use of assets belonging to others to purchase property.

depreciation (dep.): A capital loss used in estimating value: tax depreciation is discussed in Chapter 12.

discounted cash flow: A technique for estimating value by summing the discounted values of all future income flows to the property.

economic life (useful life): The period of time over which the improvements contribute to the value of the property; for income-producing property, this may be viewed as the ability of the property to generate an income stream.

equity dividend rate, R_E: Defined as the before-tax cash or cash throw-off divided by the original equity.

equity funds: The use of one's own personal assets to purchase property.

income projection period, *p*: The period of time over which the typical owner-investor will expect to own the property, *p*.

internal rate of return (IRR): The yield rate that causes future income flows on the property to equal the cost.

mortgage reduction (equity buildup): Payments to the remaining debt through amortization.

overall rate of return, R_o: The overall capitalization rate used in the estimation of value.

recapture: Recovery of the owner's equity.

remaining economic life (remaining useful life): The period of time from the present date to the end of the economic or useful life.

return "of": A recapture of the property value.

return "on": Expected payment such as interest or dividends from the use of the equity.

reversion: the proceeds from the property at the end of the ownership period, Rev.

The purpose of this chapter is to define and explain several critical concepts used in income property valuation. Understanding these should be very helpful in following the development and application of techniques explained in later chapters.

THE BASIS OF VALUE

Chapter 1 explained that all property is held for a motive, which originates from a desire to (1) hold a property and collect an income stream or subjective benefits, and (2) collect a capital gain from increasing property values when the property is resold or refinanced at some future time.[1] Both of these motives permeate a decision to buy and must be evaluated simultaneously. In some specific market transactions, one motive may have more emphasis than the other. For example, an owner-manager purchases a Speedy Hamburger Stand to operate and earn an income to support his or her family. The owner certainly wants a capital gain, but the purchase is transacted primarily for its value in use. In contrast, an investor might purchase undeveloped acreage on the urban fringe to hold for two years and resell with the expectation of a large capital gain since the city is growing in that direction and property values are increasing. This investor will certainly accept an income that can be earned from the property in the interim, but the primary motive behind the transaction is capital gain.

Since value in use and value in exchange are part of every transaction, they must be valued in every transaction. The value in use is valued as an income flow from the sale of a product such as pizzas, cars, clothes, or condominiums. In addition, a value in use can be derived from subjective benefits such as the view from a vacation home in the mountains or on the seashore, and the satisfaction from owning one's residence. The value in exchange is the income flow that the owner receives from the resale or refinancing of the property at a future date. Typically, the selling price must be estimated by the appraiser to determine the amount of the capital gain. Since the client typically wants to know the value of the property today, the present value of both income streams must be estimated and summed.

PRESENT VALUE IN USE AND EXCHANGE

The present value of a parcel of income producing property can be written as

$$V = \sum_{i=1}^{\infty} \frac{I_i}{(1 + R_i)^i} \tag{7-1}$$

where

V = present value of the income expected in each year i,

I_i = net operating income for each year i,

R_i = rate of return for each year i.

The present value of this property equals the income expected in each year to infinity discounted by the discount factor $(1 + R_i)^i$ for each year *i*. The appraiser can account for varying levels of income, *I,* in each year and different levels of risk, which will help determine the level of the overall rate of return, R_i. The income is expected to last in perpetuity or until infinity.

One might typically assume that properties where this approach is used would experience level *gross* income and a declining *net* income from an increasing amount of obsolescence.

Simplifying Assumptions

This definition of present value can be simplified further by making two additional assumptions. The first is that the level of net income, *I,* remains the same in each year *i*. The second is that the overall rate of return, *R,* remains the same in each year *i*. These two, combined with the assumption of an income projection period that lasts to infinity, simplifies the preceding equation (7–1) to the following (Appendix A shows this derivation):

$$V = \frac{I}{R} \qquad (7\text{–}2)$$

where

I = net operating income in year 1,

R = rate of return in year 1.

This definition of market value is very easy to use in the market. If the assumptions can be satisfied, an estimate of present value can be derived readily.

These assumptions have several limitations.[2] First, very few properties produce an income stream that exists until infinity. Second, the income levels quite often vary from year to year because of factors such as seasonal swings, recession, expansion, remodeling, and variations in the expenses. Third, the overall rate of return will typically not remain the same in every year from various market factors, especially money market conditions and levels of risk.

The simplified equation (7–2) is used frequently after attempts have been made to minimize the influence of the limitations. For example, the income stream can be "stabilized". A stabilized income stream is one figure that has been adjusted to reflect the equal level of annual income that does not fluctuate. In addition, the overall rate of return, *R,* can be computed by various techniques, which allow several levels of risk and rates of return to be included and weighted. Also, the formula can be altered to include a "holding period," allowing a value to be calculated only for the period of time that a typical investor will own the property. Each of the procedures is shown in later chapters.

Reversionary Value

This definition of present value in equation (7–2) is based upon value in use and the expected flow of income. An exchange value would equal the present value above. Thus, V = value in use + value in exchange.

NATURE OF VALUATION

A question frequently asked by a layperson is, "Isn't valuation simply an income figure divided by a capitalization rate? If yes, what's so difficult about it?" While it's true that the numerator is an income figure, it is constructed by measuring gross potential income from all acceptable sources and adjusting it for typical market expenses. All of these estimates must be *documented* for accuracy and *justified* by using acceptable procedures for measurement.[3] Figures should be taken from market trends.

In addition, the estimate for the capitalization rate must be justified and documented. It should include appropriate assumptions for weighted returns on the downpayment, equity buildup from the mortgage reduction, and possible changes in the equity from a capital gain (or loss).

MARKET DERIVED DATA

The figures used in the calculations of I and R are always derived from the local market. The use of figures that are not market derived make the value of the property a function of the management of the property, which it is not. If the figures that management uses are inserted to calculate V, the value of the property could be changed by changing the management, which is not consistent with the definition of market value.

For example, assume that the subject property was an apartment complex containing two-bedroom units, which the current management is renting for $325 per month. Your market estimates indicate that these units could rent for $350 per month. The $350 should be used since the value for V could be raised by changing managers and raising the rents as soon as possible.

PERIODS OF TIME

Holding Period (Income Projection Period)

A holding period is a period of time that a typical investor would desire to own this property before disposing of it by sale or exchange. The typical holding period is usually estimated by examining the periods of time between resales of the same property.

Economic Life

The economic life is defined as the period over which improvements contribute to the value of the property.[4] For income properties, this can be viewed as its ability to generate an income flow.

The phrase *remaining economic life* means the same as the remaining useful life, which is the "number of years remaining in the useful life of the structure."

EQUITY vs. DEBT FUNDS

Equity and debt funds are used in real estate finance and play a critical role in valuing property.

Equity

Equity funds are those personal assets used for the purchase of property. Typically, equity is composed of three parts that are of interest to the appraiser. The first is the *downpayment,* which is anything of value that the seller is willing to accept, but typically is cash. The size of downpayment is determined by negotiation between the buyer and seller or the buyer and the lender. If a financial lender is involved, it may have its own requirements imposed upon the transaction, which the buyer must accept. The second is *mortgage reduction* (called *equity buildup*), assuming a mortgage exists. Every amortization payment on the outstanding mortgage balance reduces the indebtedness on the property and increases the equity to the owner. The third is *appreciation* in the selling price caused by inflation of overall values. This type of equity is simply capital gain acquired by the owner from buying at a lower price and expecting inflation to increase the property value. This figure can be zero or negative in a declining market.

Debt

Debt funds are those assets belonging to others that are used for the purchase of property. These funds typically are large loans given by financial institutions, although debt funds can originate from small syndicates and individuals.

RATES OF RETURN

Several definitions of rates of return are critical in appraisal.

Return "On" vs. Return "Of"

Return "on" refers to a flow of income that the owner-investor expects for the use of his or her equity. Examples include interest, dividend earnings, and income after taxes. Return "of" is a charge that the owner-investor makes to *recapture* the property value. When using a return rate, one must always verify whether it represents only the *return on, return of,* or both.

Overall Rate of Return, R_o

The overall rate of return, R_o, is the *capitalization rate* used in equation (7–2), $V = I/R$, to derive an estimate of value, V.

Equity Dividend Rate, R_E

The equity dividend rate, R_E, may be defined as the annual before-tax cash flow (cash throw-off) derived by the original equity investment,

$$R_E = \frac{\text{cash throw-off}}{\text{original equity investment}}. \tag{7-3}$$

This rate is assumed to reflect the net cash flow expectation of similar investors in the market. An estimate for the subject property can be derived directly from the market by the use of *current* cash throw-off and original equity figures for comparable properties. This rate, R_E, reflects the "cash-on-cash" return. The appendix gives other definitions and uses of this rate.

Equity Yield Rate Y_E

The equity yield rate, Y_E, can be defined as

$$Y_E = \frac{\begin{array}{c}\text{annualized cash throw off + annualized gain or}\\ \text{loss in equity at the resale}\end{array}}{\text{original equity}}.$$

Its amount typically is estimated after the property is sold since the last figure in the numerator can only be estimated after the resale.

The appendix gives other definitions, uses of the rate, and market conditions that would cause the equity dividend and the equity yield rate to be equal.[5]

Band of Investment

The band of investment is a technique for calculating a rate composed of a weighted average of the other rates. This technique may be used with or without algebra. The following examples review the concepts with no amortizing mortgages.

With algebra

$$R_L = (\%\ \text{debt})\ i + (\%\ \text{equity})\ Y_E$$

Without algebra

	%		*interest or yield*	
1st mortgage:	(% debt)	×	i	= total
+ Downpayment:	(% equity)	×	Y_E	= total
				R = sum

Consider the following example:

1st mortgage = $500,000 at 10.5% interest

Downpayment = $100,000 and the investor expects a 11% return

R_L may be found by either of the two methods mentioned.

With algebra

$$R_L = (.833333).105 + (.166667).110$$
$$R_L = .1058332 \text{ or } 10.6\%$$

Without algebra

	%		*interest or yield*	
1st mortgage	$500,000:(.833333)	×	.105	= .0874999
+ Downpayment	100,000:(.166667)	×	.110	= .0183333
	$600,000:1.0000			.1058332
				or 10.6%

The band of investment technique shown here is simply calculating a weighted average of the mortgage interest rate, *i*, and the equity yield rate, Y_E. Equity build-up and recapture are ignored. Appendix B shows other concepts of the band of investment technique and comparisons with other rates.

Internal Rate of Return and Discounted Cash Flow

The internal rate of return is defined as the rate that will make the present value of the income stream plus the present value of the reversion (if any) equal to the present value of the initial equity. This may be shown by the equation

$$V_E = \sum_{i=1}^{p} \frac{I_i}{(1 + \text{IRR})^i} + \frac{\text{Rev}}{(1 + \text{IRR})^p}$$

where

V_E = present value of the initial equity,
I_i = net operating income in each year i,
IRR = internal rate of return,
REV = before-tax cash flow on the reversion
p = holding period.

One of the biggest criticisms of the IRR is that it assumes that the income stream, I, is automatically reinvested immediately at the same rate as the IRR.[6] This assumption ignores the magnitude of the income flow, I_i, and the current market conditions that might create a higher or lower rate. A problem illustrating the methods for calculating the IRR[7] and a discussion of its shortcomings are contained in Chapter 12.

Discounted cash flow Discounted cash flow refers to the technique of calculating the present value of future levels of income. The income received in each time period is treated as a reversion and multiplied by a present worth of $1 factor. All results are summed, and the result is said to equal the present value of the initial equity. This technique is illustrated in Chapter 12.

FINANCIAL RATIOS

Several financial ratios that are used in later chapters are defined and discussed briefly here.

Loan to Value Ratio, *M*

The loan to value ratio, M, refers to the dollar amount of the debt funds loaned for the purchase of the subject property divided by the estimated value of the property. The equity to value ratio may be found by $1 - M$. Multiplying $1 - M$ by the property value gives the amount of the equity funds or the downpayment.

Sometimes the phrase *high ratio loan* is used to describe the situation where the lender allows the purchaser to borrow funds in a loan that is a large percent of the property value. Conversely, a "low ratio loan" refers to a loan that is a smaller percent of the property value.

Debt Service Coverage Ratio, DSCR

The debt service coverage ratio refers to the annual net operating income divided by the annual mortgage payment. This ratio serves as an indicator of whether the property will generate sufficient income to make the mortgage payment. Obviously, if the ratio falls below one, the required mortgage payment is more than the net operating income, causing justifiable concern from the lender. Chapter 12 illustrates the use of the DSCR in estimating property value.

Operating Expense Ratio

The operating expense ratio refers to the level of annual operating expenses divided by the level of annual gross or effective income, usually effective income. This ratio serves as an indicator of the property's expenses as a percent of its income.

Breakeven or Default Ratio

This ratio refers to annual mortgage payments and operating expenses divided by the annual gross income. This ratio serves as an indicator of the property's ability to generate sufficient income to make the required payments.

Vacancy and Bad Debt Ratio

This ratio refers to annual revenue lost from vacancy and bad debts divided by gross income. It serves as an indicator of the revenue that will be lost.

Sources of Information on Ratios

Sources of information containing these ratios or containing information that can be used to calculate these ratios include *The Appraiser, The Appraisal Briefs, Institute for Real Estate Management Income/Expense Analysis,* and the appraiser's own files.

CASH EQUIVALENCY

The sale of property may involve financial terms that are more favorable than those provided within the local mortgage market on similar properties. Typically, this situation arises when the seller is involved in providing the buyer with financing. Examples involve sales where the buyer assumes the existing mortgage, the seller agrees to extend credit on a first or second mortgage, the seller pays points to acquire financing, or the seller exerts influence to acquire credit for the buyer. If the seller provides any type of financial advantage, the

Exhibit 7.1
Cash equivalency

	1	2	3
A. sale price	$1,010,000	$1,085,000	$1,160,000
B. downpayment	0	$200,000	$225,000
C. type of financing for 12-year monthly pay	cash	installment: level payment: $885,000	purchase money: level payment: $935,000
D. mortgage interest	none	10%	10%
E. monthly payment to seller	none	$11,300	$12,000
F. market yield for similar properties	not applicable	14%	14%
G. present value and annuity $1 per period = $a_{\overline{n}\rvert}$	not applicable	69.583269 at 14% for 12 yrs	69.583269 at 14% for 12 yrs
H. value of mortgage at 14% (E × G)	not applicable	$11,300 × 69.583269 = $786,291	$12,000 × 69.583269 = $834,999
I. add downpayment (B + H)	0 + $1,010,000	$200,000 + 786,291 = $986,291	$225,000 + 834,999 = $1,059,999
J. cash equivalent value (rounded)	$1,010,000	$986,300	$1,060,000
K. value of favorable financing (A − J)	$1,010,000 − 1,010,000 = 0	$1,085,000 − 986,300 = $98,700	$1,160,000 − 1,060,000 = $100,000

added value of this service most likely will be added to the asking price. In these cases, an adjustment may be necessary to convert the contract price to the cash equivalent price.[8]

Definition

Cash equivalency analysis may be defined as the process of equating various sale prices with different interest rates by using a mechanical process of discounting future income generated by the mortgage loan to its present value.[9] Cash equivalency involves breaking the sales price into two components: the cash price today and the value of the favorable financing terms that are paid to the seller.

An Illustration

Consider the recent sales of three similar properties shown in Exhibit 7.1. Sale 1 was for $1,010,000, cash. Sale 2 involved a contract for deed with an installment note for $1,085,000, with payments of $11,300 monthly for twelve years at a face interest rate of 10%, which is the usury limit for personal contracts in this state. The downpayment was $200,000, and the installment note was written for $885,000. Sale 3 was a purchase money mortgage for $1,160,000, with a mortgage for $935,000 at 10% interest with level monthly payments of $12,000 for twelve years. Similar sales revealed that a 14-percent yield rate was realistic for these types of properties.

The cash equivalency value for sale 2 was $986,300, and for sale 3, $1,060,000. The value of the lower interest rate to the seller is found by subtracting these prices from the sale price, which resulted in $98,700 and $100,000, respectively. These latter two figures represented the additional price that the seller charged for the lower interest rate, a possible lower downpayment, and the wait of twelve years to receive the full purchase price.

Now consider the situation where the seller in sale 3 needs more cash and approaches another investor attempting to sell the purchase money mortgage. The investor examines the local market and discovers that purchase money mortgages with good underlying buyer credit are being sold at a discount to generate a yield of approximately 25% (assume that this does not violate the usury limit). The discount and cash equivalency are computed as follows:

Discount

$$1 - \frac{R_M(10\%)}{R_M(25\%)} = \text{Discount}$$

$$1 - \frac{.01195078}{.02196093} = \text{Discount}$$

$$1 - .5441807 = \text{Discount}$$

$$.4558193 = \text{Discount}$$

Cash equivalency

Downpayment	$225,000.
+ Value of Mortgage	
$834,999 × .4558193 =	+ $380,609.
	$605,609.

SHORT PROBLEMS

Question: You receive an appraisal assignment to estimate the present value of a small group of apartments. Your market surveys lead you to believe that the typical rate on a one-bedroom unit with 1000 square feet is $250 per month, and the rate for a 1200-square foot apartment is $300 per month. You discover that the present apartment management is charging $260 and $325 respectively. Which rental rates do you use? Why? What is the result if you use the other set of rates?

Answer: If the assignment is to estimate market value, then market rates must be inserted regardless of what the current management is charging. If the rates charged by the management are used, the appraiser has made the value estimate directly dependent upon the ability of the management, and the value estimate becomes more like investment value.

Question: An engineer, agricultural economist, or an accountant might estimate the value of income-producing real estate by dividing the net operating income earned in year one by a rate paid by financial lenders on long-term CDs. How does an appraiser's estimate of value differ?

Answer: An appraiser would probably project the next twelve month's income, stabilize the income flow over the projection period, and use the stabilized figure in the numerator. This technique is discussed in Chapters 8 and 12. In addition, the capitalization rate typically would be compiled by using a weighted aggregate by including the downpayment, equity buildup, and capital gain (or loss) and perhaps the DSCR.

Question: Under what market conditions would the equity yield rate and the equity dividend rate be equal?

Answer: These two will be equal when the purchase and sales prices are not expected to increase or decrease. (See the Appendix.)

Question: You estimate that a farm should be valued at $1200 per acre since you have estimated the net operating income and discounted it to present value. But four farms have recently sold in the area for $2000 per acre. Which figure would estimate the market? Why does this difference exist?

Answer: A selling price that is considerably higher than the capitalized value most likely indicates a rising market, significant speculation, and an incorrect capitalization rate in the first estimate of value. Buyers are buying and paying higher prices because they anticipate the market to increase in the near future and they can resell the land at even a higher price. If these sales are between a knowledgeable buyer and seller, and neither are under duress, the appraiser must conclude that the market value is above $1200 and closer to the $2000 price. This conclusion is consistent with the definition of market value.

SUMMARY

Valuation of real estate is future oriented. Value in use and value in exchange comprise the demand for properties and are essential in determining its value. Market estimates of these must be estimated and used in the appraisal process.

Appraisal makes a unique contribution to the valuation technique of I/R by including several types of weighted equity within the estimate of R. The formula, I/R, is derived from a more complicated estimate of value, V, and relies upon restrictive assumptions.

Valuation is typically estimated for an expected holding period over which a typical owner-investor will own the property.

Various rates of returns such as the equity dividend rate, equity yield rate, return on investment, return of investment, and the discount rate are included in various appraisal techniques. Their relationships are critical.

REVIEW QUESTIONS

1. Why is the value of real estate estimated from future events rather than historical patterns?
2. Explain the derivation of $V = I/R$.
3. What does appraisal technique contribute to the valuation of real property through the construction of the capitalization rate, R?
4. Why is the use of market derived data important?
5. Explain the differences among economic life, holding period, income projection period, and useful life.
6. What is the difference between equity and debt funds?
7. Contrast each of the following:

   equity dividend rate, R_E

   equity yield rate, Y_E

   return on

   return of

   overall capitalization rate, R_o

8. What is the band of investment?

9. Compute a discount rate by the band of investment method given the following data: (1) first mortgage is $.5 million at 11.5% interest, (2) downpayment is $100,000 and the expected return is 12%.

ENDNOTES

1. William M. Shenkel, "Value in Use, Value in Exchange, and Investment Value," *Real Estate Appraiser and Analyst* 46 (May–June 1980): 28–29.
2. C. F. Sirmans and Austin Jaffe, "Some Myths About Real Estate," *Real Estate Review* 8 (Spring 1978): 39–42.
3. Society of Real Estate Appraisers, *Guide to Narrative Demonstration Appraisal Reporting* (Chicago: SREA, 1976).
4. Byrl Boyce, *Real Estate Appraisal Terminology* (Cambridge, Mass.: American Institute of Real Estate Appraisers and Society of Real Estate Appraisers, 1975), p. 74.
5. Robert Zerbst and Daniel Kohlhepp, "The Use of Equity Rates in Appraisal Theory," *Real Estate Appraiser* 43 (May–June 1977): 26–30.
6. Joseph Strung, "The Internal Rate of Return and the Reinvestment Presumptions," *The Appraisal Journal* 44 (January 1976): 23–33.
7. A good example of IRR calculations can be found in Stephen Messner, Irving Shreiber, and Victor Lyon, *Marketing Investment Real Estate: Finance, Taxation, Techniques* (Chicago: REALTORS National Marketing Institute, 1975), chapter 4.
8. Joseph B. Lipscomb, "Discount Rates for Cash Equivalent Analysis," *The Appraisal Journal* 49 (January 1981): 23–33.
9. Jack P. Friedman and Bruce Lindeman, "Cash Equivalent Analysis," *The Appraisal Journal* 47 (January 1979): 35–43.

ADDITIONAL READINGS

Boyce, Bryrl. *Real Estate Appraisal Terminology* (Cambridge, Mass.: American Institute of Real Estate Appraisers and the Society of Real Estate Appraisers, 1975).

Coulter, William. "A Current and Objective Equity Yield Rate." *The Appraisal Journal* 45 (January 1977): 16–24.

Epley, Donald, and Millar, James. *Basic Real Estate Finance and Investments* (New York: John Wiley & Sons, Inc., 1980), chapter 1.

Hanford, Lloyd. "The Capitalization Process Revisited." *The Appraisal Journal* 44 (July 1976): 393–404.

Stehm, Robert J. "Equity Dividend/Equity Yield Conversions." *Real Estate Appraiser and Analyst* 44 (March–April 1978): 23–25.

Appendix A
Derivation of $\dfrac{I}{R}$

Prove that

$$V = \sum_{i=1}^{n} \frac{I_i}{(1 + R_i)^i} = \frac{I}{R}$$

when

$I_1 = I_2 = \ldots I_n$, and
$R_1 = R_2 = \ldots R_n$.

Proof:

Consider a series of numbers:

$1, X, X^2, X^3, \ldots X^n$ where X is any number.

Their sum is, S:

$$S = 1 + X + X^2 + X^3 + \ldots X^n. \tag{A–1}$$

Multiply both sides by X:

$$X \times S = X + X^2 + X^3 + \ldots X^{n+1}. \tag{A–2}$$

From equation (A–2), add (1 − 1) to both sides:

$$(1 - 1) + X(S) = (1 - 1) + X + X^2 + X^3 + \ldots X^n + X^{n+1}.$$

Rewrite:

$$0 + X(S) = -1 + (1 + X + X^2 + X^3 + \ldots X^n) + X^{n+1}.$$

or,

$$X(S) = -1 + S + X^{n+1}.$$

Simplify,

$$S - X(S) = 1 - X^{n+1}$$

or,

$$S = \frac{1}{1 - X} - \frac{X^{n+1}}{1 - X}.$$

For large *n*,

$$X = \infty, \text{ and } S = \frac{1}{1 - X} \quad \text{for } X \text{ less than } 1.$$

Know that,

$$V = \frac{I_1}{1 + R} + \frac{I_2}{(1 + R)^2} + \frac{I_3}{(1 + R)^3} + \ldots$$

Add (I − I) to both sides

$$(\mathrm{I} - \mathrm{I}) + V = (-I + I) + \frac{I_1}{1 + R} + \frac{I_2}{(1 + R)^2} + \frac{I_3}{(1 + R)^3} + \ldots$$

$$V = -I + I\left[1 + \frac{1}{1 + R} + \left(\frac{1}{1 + R}\right)^2 + \left(\frac{1}{1 + R}\right)^3 + \ldots\right]$$

$$V = -I + I(S).$$

Know that,

$$S = \frac{1}{1 - X}.$$

Let

$$X = \frac{1}{1 + R}.$$

$$V = -I + I\left(\frac{1}{1 - \frac{1}{(1 + R)}}\right)$$

$$V = -I + I\left(\frac{1 + R}{R}\right)$$

$$V = -I + \frac{I}{R} + I$$

$$V = \frac{I}{R}.$$

Appendix B
Band of Investment and the Equity Dividend Rate

The purpose of this appendix is to provide further elaboration on several of the concepts and definitions defined in the chapter.

Band of Investment

A recent survey[1] found that two types of band of investment analysis were being used in the appraisal industry. These are,

$$R = Y_E(1 - M) + \text{Mi}$$

and

$$R = R_E(1 - M) + \text{MR}_M.$$

The first derives R as a weighted average of the equity yield rate and the mortgage interest rate. The second derives R as a weighted average of the equity dividend rate and the mortgage constant.

A recent article[2] argues that the two equations above should be written as they appear below to give the same answers with no capital gain or loss.

$$R = Y_E(1 - M) + \text{Mi} + \left(R_M - i - \frac{1}{S_{\overline{n}|}}P\right)$$

and

$$R = R_E(1 - M) + \text{MR}_M$$

where

$$R_E = Y_E - \frac{M}{(1 - M)}\left(\frac{1}{S_{\overline{n}|}}P\right).$$

Equity Dividend Rate

The preceding equation provides a definition of the equity dividend rate, which should be equal to the same figure derived by dividing the before-tax cash flows by the equity investment. Another definition of the equity dividend rate and the equity yield rate in another article is,[3]

$$R_E = Y_E - \text{app.}\frac{1}{S_{\overline{p}|Y_E}}$$

or

$$R_E = Y_E + \text{dep.}\frac{1}{S_{\overline{p}|Y_E}}$$

where

app. = expected percent change in the property value over the holding period,

$\frac{1}{S_{\overline{p}|Y_E}}$ = sinking fund factor over the holding period p at the equity yield rate Y_E.

Obviously, R_E and Y_E are equal only when market conditions are such that no capital gains or losses in the resale value occur.

ENDNOTES

1. Kenneth Lusht, "Appraising Income Property: Empirical Evidence on the Relationships Between Appraisal Theory and Appraiser Behavior," working paper, College of Business Administration, Pennsylvania State University, February, 1979.
2. Anthony B. Sanders and C. F. Sirmans, "A Comparison of the Ellwood and Simple Weighted-Average Overall Capitalization Rates," *The Appraisal Journal* 48 (July 1980): 432–438; see also Jeffrey D. Fisher and Anthony B. Sanders, "Capitalization Rates and Market Information," *The Appraisal Journal* 49 (April 1981): 186–198.
3. Robert Zerbst and Daniel Kohlepp, "The Use of Equity Rates in Appraisal Theory," *The Real Estate Appraiser* 43 (May–June 1977): 26–30.

CHAPTER 8

LEARNING OBJECTIVES:

When a student finishes this chapter, he or she should be able to:

- Explain the difference between income and cash flow.
- Outline the contents of a real estate financial statement.
- Explain in detail the following: gross potential income; vacancy allowance, bad debts and income losses; operating expenses, fixed expenses; and reserves for replacements.
- Evaluate the issues surrounding the reserves for replacement account.
- Reconstruct a real estate financial statement from a financial statement prepared by an accountant.
- Work a problem that requires the levels of NOI to be projected over the expected holding period.
- Stabilize NOI into one figure.
- Explain the importance of the residual (reversion) worth of the property at the end of the expected holding period, p.
- Discuss important points that should be covered in justifying and documenting the computation of NOI.
- Summarize several questions that should be answered to assure the accurate estimation of NOI.
- Explain several likely sources of information for data that can be used in the estimation of NOI.

Estimate of Net Operating Income, *I*

IMPORTANT TERMS AND PHRASES

cash: One asset on the balance sheet.

expenses: Outflows from operations.

fixed expenses: Outflows of revenue because of long-term commitments not related to current level of activity but due to passage of time.

gross income from all sources: All revenues that the subject property can earn.

income: The difference between the inflows and outflows of assets due to operations.

net operating income: The terms applied to the difference between all operating outflows and all inflows.

operating (variable) expenses: Outflows of assets for the operation of the business in order to maintain the income flow; relates to the level of activity.

real estate financial statement (reconstructed income statement): A financial worksheet illustrating the accounting method and adjustments used to derive net operating income for real estate purposes.

reserves for replacement: A special deduction to replace short-lived assets that are going to wear out prior to the expiration of the building's useful life.

revenue: Inflows of assets not limited to cash from operations.

reversion: The net sale value received by the owner at the end of the holding period.

stabilized NOI: One figure selected to represent all future NOIs.

vacancy allowance: An allowance for loss of potential gross income caused by unrented space.

Estimating future levels of net operating income for the subject is a critical step in deriving market value. This chapter demonstrates the typical procedure used to derive *I*, and presents contemporary controversies surrounding several key steps.

DEFINITION OF NET OPERATING INCOME, NOI

Income vs. Cash Flows

An important distinction must be made early between income and cash flows. For most real estate investments, the two will not be equal.

Income[1] Income is defined as the difference between inflows and outflows of assets as a result of operations. The inflows are called *revenues,* and the outflows are called *expenses.* Income is the net difference found by subtracting all outflows from all inflows caused by all assets. Net operating income (NOI) is the term applied to this difference.

Net operating income (NOI) for real estate purposes is comparable to Net Income Before Recapture (NIBR) and Net Income Before Depreciation (NIBD). All three concepts are used in practice, but their use indicates that their concepts and application are the same. Net operating income is the term used in this book. This concept and definition is consistent with the definition of NOI in *Real Estate Appraisal Terminology,* which states that NOI is "annual net income remaining after deducting all fixed and operating expenses but before deducting financial charges such as recapture or debt service."[2]

Cash[3] Cash is only one asset. A net cash flow is the difference between inflows of cash only and outflows of cash only not restricted to changes resulting from operations.

Real Estate Financial Statement

Typically, a real estate financial statement is constructed by the appraiser to follow the following format:

Gross Potential Income from All Sources

Less: Vacancy allowances, bad debts, and income losses

Result: Effective Gross Income

Less: Operating expenses (variable expenses)

Fixed Expenses: Property taxes, insurance, and long-term leases (if applicable)

Reserves: Replacements for short-lived assets

Result: Net Operating Income (NOI)

If debt service (amortization and interest payments) and income taxes are subtracted from NOI, the result is the *net cash flow,* a concept that can be important to the investor.

Each of these income and expense categories used to estimate NOI is discussed below.

Gross Potential Income from All Sources

A convenient starting point for estimating gross potential income from all sources is to examine the previous year's income statement that has been audited, compiled, or reviewed by the owner's accountant. The next step is to reconstruct a real estate financial statement, which is shown in a later section of this chapter. The following step is to verify that the gross potential income earned by the subject property is typical of the market. Is it too low, high, typical, and by what amount? This information is gathered by market surveys and the examination of the gross potential incomes from comparable, competitive properties.

Care must be exercised to guarantee that market trends that are typical of the competition are used, as opposed to figures that are a function of the current management. For example, the *contract rent* for an apartment may be $375 per month. But an examination of market trends indicates that the *fair market rent* may be $400 per month. The prevailing market rent figure is used since the objective is to estimate market value, which is not a function of the management that is operating the property at the moment the property is appraised. Gross potential income from rents alone, such as apartments, refers to the *rent roll* of the unit that is "rented up."

Any additional income that is typically earned by competitive properties is added. Examples would include assessments for parking spaces, laundry fees, clubhouse rental and dues, concessions of any kind, and dues from a homeowners' association.

Vacany Allowances, Bad Debt, and Income Losses

An estimate of losses from potential income must be subtracted to derive Effective Gross Income, which is a more realistic level of income that the owner can expect. If the subject is a rental, such as apartment or office space, a vacancy percent should be estimated from local market trends and examinations of competitive properties that reflects the typical vacancy allowance. The percent is multiplied by the gross potential income from that particular type of unit. For example, the local typical vacancy rate for one-bedroom apartments may be 5 percent, for two-bedroom units, 6.5 percent, and 7.5 percent for three-bedroom units. If the subject is a business, an estimate of bad debts is made for comparable properties and expressed as a percent of gross potential income. This percent is multiplied by gross income and subtracted from the gross potential income figure.

Operating Expenses (Variable Expenses)

Operating expenses are expenses for the operation of the business in order to maintain or increase the income flow. They are considered to be variable expenses since they vary proportionately with the level of the income flow. Examples include electricity, gas, water, advertising, payroll, management expenses, office supplies, and general maintenance.

These expenses should include only those items necessary for the maintenance of the income flow. In addition, they should be viewed as variable, or fluctuating with the size of the income flow. They should be compared with the operating expenses of comparable properties to assess their accuracy and amount. Once these expenses have been assessed for accuracy and amount and related to the market by examining the operating expenses in comparable properties for reasonableness, they have been *stabilized.*[4]

Typically, all of the expenses included under this category can be stabilized at a percent of the gross potential income from one source such as the rental income. For example, operating expenses can be stabilized at 25 percent of the rental from apartment lease income.

Fixed Expenses

Fixed expenses include those accounts that are not directly related to the income flow and relate to the passage of time. In addition, these expenses are relatively long-term in nature because of long-term obligations to pay or long-term leases. Typically, three types of expenses are included. The first is property taxes calculated at the prevailing local rates. The appraiser is interested in what should be paid in taxes as opposed to what is actually being paid. Second, property insurance premiums are determined at the prevailing local market rates. The local insurance industry may quote a rate of $5.50 per $1000 of valuation, exclusive of the site. A ball-park estimate of the property value may be used to determine the approximate insurance premium. Third, the building may have been constructed on a site that has a long-term ground lease between the previous owner and the current owner. The payments on the lease would be included here since a contractual lease arrangement exists.

Reserves for Replacement

A special account may be established to replace short-lived items that are going to wear out before the building. These items are essential to the income flow. For example, if the subject is an apartment building, the stoves, carpets, refrigerators, range hoods, water heaters, and washers and dryers for the laundry need replacing in the near future. Typically, the roof is included under this account also.

The useful life of each item is estimated. A percent equal to 1/(useful life) is multiplied by the reproduction cost of the item. The result is deducted as an expense each year. For example, a stove might have a useful life of eight years and cost $300 to replace. The amount deducted is,

$$1/8 \times \$300 \times 24 \text{ units} = \$900$$

Several issues surround the handling of this account and should be identified at this point. First, a recent survey reported that of 640 multifamily residential appraisals, a specific entry for reserves for replacement did not appear in 58% of the reports. A typical argument for not including this account is that the appraiser is attempting to estimate market value and the typical owner may not deduct from income regularly to cover the expense of anticipated expenses for short-lived items. Instead, the owner simply pays for the needed item from his or her personal assets at the time it occurs, or floats a short-term loan at the bank. If the latter is normal procedure, then appraisal procedure should reflect the market.

One response to this argument is that these expenses will be needed at some future time and the owner should provide for that eventuality. Prudent management of the subject property to assure that the income stream to the property is maintained requires that this account exist since these items will need to be replaced and the expense paid by someone.

Second, what is the responsibility of the appraiser if the subject is, say, three years old, several short-lived items have a useful life of four years, and no reserves for replacement account has been established at any time? The proper answer is that the appraiser could establish the account for the current year, estimate three years of use, and deduct it all in the current year. These items are in need of replacing in the following year, and the funds must be generated from some source. The fact that this account has not been established in the past means that the owner has simply received an artificially high level of NOI in previous years, which is justifiably lower in the current year. The failure to recognize these needed requirements is to overstate the property income and in turn inflate its value.

A third issue is the handling of inflation in the cost of the items. The issue is whether the reproduction cost should be measured on the day of the appraisal or the date that the item is replaced at the end of its useful life. To be consistent with the rest of the estimates used to derive NOI, the reproduction cost estimates at current prices measured on the date of the appraisal are the figures used. The owner could invest these funds in interest-bearing accounts so that interest earnings will somewhat match over time any price increases that may occur in the cost of the item to be replaced.

Another issue is whether to take these reserves out of NOI using straight-line techniques or a sinking fund pattern. Straight line deducts the same amount each year. Assuming that new replacement items have the same useful lives as older ones, and that replacement costs have not changed, the same amount is deducted each year. If a useful life changes or a replacement cost changes, a separate reserve schedule must be computed and added.

For example, consider a case where the useful life of a stove is seven years and the replacement cost is $300. After five years, the stove needs to be replaced from hard use at a cost of $300. If the second stove has the same useful life, the deduction from NOI for reserves on both stoves is the same.

Another method of handling the reserve account is to use the sinking fund technique. The owner is assumed to have a dollar figure in mind that must be accumulated over all of the reserve items to replace them at the end of their useful lives. The amount deducted each year from NOI could be placed in an interest-bearing account, which, in effect, will reduce the annual deduction. Any premature withdrawal to pay for appliances that have expired will change the targeted amount and change the annual deduction.

A frequent question asked here is, "Why not estimate the replacement costs of these items at the end of their useful lives since that is a more realistic price?" The answer to this question and any others that may be posed around handling inflation in the derivation of NOI is that any estimate of future price due to inflation must not conflict with any estimate for an increase in property value that might be placed in the capitalization rate. The essential problem is to avoid double counting.

In addition, a prudent owner-investor who subtracts these reserves regularly from NOI has the option of placing them in an interest-bearing account to accumulate until the items in question need replacing. If the interest rates earned are directly related to the level of inflation, the interest earned will offset any price increases in the replacement cost from price increases.

Annual Data

The real estate financial statement shown earlier is always in *annual* data. The use of annual figures is consistent with the annual terms used in the construction of the overall *R*. In addition, annual data minimizes the influence of seasonal trends.

Typically, this annual estimate of NOI is viewed as arriving to the owner at the end of the period (EOP). It may be viewed as a reversion that occurs at the EOP.

RECONSTRUCTED INCOME STATEMENT

The current property manager has provided a statement of the previous year's cash flow and expenses shown in Exhibit 8.1. These have been audited, compiled, or reviewed by the accountant employed by the partnership that owns the property. All these figures are directly attributable to the current property management. Good management can cause high income and low expenses,

Exhibit 8.1
Previous year's income and expenses

Income		
Rent (if every unit is rented for 12 months)		
12, units at $300 × 12 months (1 Bedroom) $43,200		
8, units at $300 × 12 months (2 Bedrooms) $28,800		
4, units at $425 × 12 months (3 Bedrooms) $20,400		
Actual rent received		$92,400
Laundry receipts (coin-operated washers and dryers)		10,250
Clubhouse rental (special events)		4,500
Renters' Association dues ($20 annually per unit)		480
Parking (excess vehicles such as boats, recreational vehicles, motorcycles, etc.) ($15 annually per space)		300
	Total	$107,930
Expenses		
1. Electricity		$ 4,200
2. Gas		2,520
3. Water		1,310
4. Office supplies		1,000
5. Telephone		755
6. Advertising		5,000
7. General maintenance		3,696
8. Property manager (5% of gross rental income)		4,620
9. Interest payments on mortgage		55,240
10. Property taxes		9,200
11. Insurance		3,150
12. Depreciation (1/40 × $600,000)		15,000
13. New appliances		
1 Refrigerator $300		
1 Stove 300		
3 Disposals 300		900
	Total	$106,591
Operating Income		
Income		$107,930
– Expenses		– 106,591
	Total	$ 1,339

and mediocre management can create some combination that is unique to the subject property but not typical of the current, local market. Consequently, the income and expenses figures for the subject must be reconstructed. The objective of the reconstruction is to provide a cross-sectional view of net operating income under management that is normal in the local market and includes the collection of income and paying of expenses that are typical to similar properties.

In sum, the objective of the reconstruction is to insert typical, normal market figures for similar properties. If NOI is calculated in this manner, the value of the building does not depend upon the ability of the property manager.

After considerable investigation of local market trends and other similar properties, the following figures appear to be appropriate for competitive properties:

- Rent:
  1-bedroom apartments: \$300 per month
  2-bedroom apartments: \$350 per month
  3-bedroom apartments: \$425 per month
- Vacancy Rates:
  5.0% of income for the 1-bedroom apartments
  6.5% of income for the 2-bedroom apartments
  7.5% of income for the 3-bedroom apartments
- Laundry Income:
  the income received on this project is typical of usage: \$10,250
- Clubhouse Income:
  the income received on this project is typical of usage: \$4,500
- Renters' Association Dues:
  most competitive properties do not have these dues
- Parking Income:
  other competitive properties limit and enforce parking to two vehicles; no extra charges are assessed the tenants.

Expenses

Expenses on 1 through 8 of Exhibit 8.1 were accumulated for competitive properties. Each individual category of expense was compared to the identical expense for similar properties to determine whether the expense was justified and the amount was appropriate. In addition, the total of 1 through 8 was computed and expressed as a percentage of the gross rental income. Similar properties revealed that these variable expenses were approximately 25 percent of the gross rental income, including a 5-percent payment to the property manager.

Property taxes showed some variation, but \$9200 was typical. Property insurance was \$5.25 per \$1000 of value, and typical coverage was for \$600,000, which created a premium of \$3,150.

Items in the structure that were critical to the maintenance of the rental income were the stoves, range hoods, refrigerators, water heaters, air conditioner units, and carpets. The roof will probably need replacing every fifteen years. The useful lives and replacement costs were found to be the following:

	Useful life	*Cost*
Stoves	8	300
Range hood	8	100
Refrigerators	8	350
Water heaters	8	125
Carpets	8	1500
Roof	15	5000
Washer (coin-operated)	10	350
Dryer (coin-operated)	10	800
Air conditioner units	15	1500

This market information was used to reconstruct a normal year's operating statement with normal management, which is shown later in the first column of Exhibit 8.3.

PROJECTED LEVELS OF NOI

Column one of Exhibit 8.3 shows the reconstructed NOI for the subject. This total alone is not sufficient to determine the value of the property. The valuation of income producing property is based upon the *present value of future income streams or benefits,* which is the principle of anticipation. NOI must be projected for each year over the holding period, *p*.

Projecting the level of NOI involves the projection of the individual components as shown in Exhibit 8.2. Individual assumptions can be made about the patterns of increase (decrease) if applicable. For example, Exhibit 8.3 shows the projections of individual components using the following assumptions. Each has been determined using market rents and examining the histories of comparable properties.

1. Market rents will remain competitive with other competitive properties since this project is new. After the tenth year, the rents may not be compe-

titive since the building must compete with the appeal of newer structures. Rents in all three types of units are expected to grow $180 per year per unit ($15 per month) in the absence of rent controls.

2. The vacancy allowance will remain comparable with other competitive properties for the first ten years. The rates used for the first year NOI are typical.

3. Insurance premiums will increase by 8 percent per year. Property taxes will remain the same for the first five years only. At that time, the tax levy most likely will increase to the level where the property tax bill could increase by $150.

Exhibit 8.2
Reconstructed net operating income statement

Without reserves for replacement	Year 1
Gross potential income from all sources	
Rent	
12, 1-Bedroom units at $300 × 12 = $43,200	
8, 2-Bedroom units at $350 × 12 = $33,600	
4, 3-Bedroom units at $425 × 12 = $20,400	
24 units	$ 97,200
Laundry income	+ 10,250
Minus: vacancy, bad debt, or income loss	
12, 1-Bedroom units: .05 × $43,200 = $2,160	
8, 2-Bedroom units: .065 × $33,600 = $2,184	
4, 3-Bedroom units: .075 × $20,400 = $1,530	
24 units	– 5,874
Result: effective gross income	$101,576
Minus: expenses	
Variable (25% of gross rental income: .25 × $97,200 = $24,300)	– 24,300
Electricity	
Gas	
Water	
Office supplies	
Telephone	
Advertising	
General maintenance	
Property manager (5% of income)	
Fixed	
Property taxes $9,200	– 9,200
Insurance $3,150	– 3,150
Result: net operating income	$64,926

Exhibit 8.3
Reconstructed net operating income statement

Gross potential income from all sources	Year 1	Year 2	Year 3	Year 4	Year 5	Year 6
Rent						
12, 1-Bedroom units at \$300 × 12 = \$43,200						
8, 2-Bedroom units at \$350 × 12 = \$33,600						
4, 3-Bedroom units at \$425 × 12 = \$20,400						
24 units	\$97,200	\$101,520	\$105,840	\$110,160	\$114,480	\$118,800
Laundry income	+ 10,250	+ 10,250	+ 10,250	+ 10,250	+ 10,250	+ 10,250
Clubhouse income						
Minus: vacancy, bad debt, or income loss						
12, 1-Bedroom units: .05 × \$43,200 = \$2,160						
8, 2-Bedroom units: .065 × \$33,600 = \$2,184						
4, 3-Bedroom units: .075 × \$20,400 = \$1,530						
24 units	− 5,874	− 6,135	− 6,396	− 6,657	− 6,918	− 7,179
Result: effective gross income	101,576	105,635	109,694	113,753	117,812	121,871

(continued)

Exhibit 8.3 (continued)

Gross potential income from all sources	Year 1	Year 2	Year 3	Year 4	Year 5	Year 6
Minus: expenses						
Variable (25% of gross rental income:						
.25 × $97,200 = $24,300)	– 24,300	– 25,380	– 26,460	– 27,540	– 28,620	– 29,700
Electricity						
Gas						
Water						
Office supplies						
Telephone						
Advertising						
General maintenance						
Property manager (5% of income)						
Fixed						
Property taxes $9,200	$ – 9,200	$ – 9,200	$ – 9,200	$ – 9,200	$ – 9,200	$ – 9,350
Insurance $3,150	– 3,150	– 3,402	– 3,674	– 3,968	– 4,286	– 4,628
Reserves for Replacements						
Stoves (1/8 × $300 = $37.50 × 24 = $900)						
Range hoods (1/8 × $100 = $12.50 × 24 = $300)						
Refrigerators (1/8 × $350 = $43.75 × 24 = $1,050)						
Water heaters (1/8 × $125 = $15.63 × 24 = $375)						
Air conditioners (1/15 × $1500 = $100 × 24 = $2,400)						
Carpets (1/8 × $1,500 = $187.50 × 24 = $4500)						
Roof (1/15 × $5,000 = $333.33)						
Washer (1/10 × $350 = $35 × 10 machines = $350)						
Dryer (1/10 × $800 = $80 × 10 machines = $800)						
	$ – 11,008 (rounded)	– 11,008	– 11,008	– 11,008	– 11,008	– 11,008
Result: net operating income	$53,918	56,645	59,352	62,037	64,698	67,185

Exhibit 8.3 shows that NOI increases every year of the expected holding period, six years. Any type of pattern could be illustrated depending upon the assumptions covering the rents, vacancy rates, variable expenses, or fixed expenses.

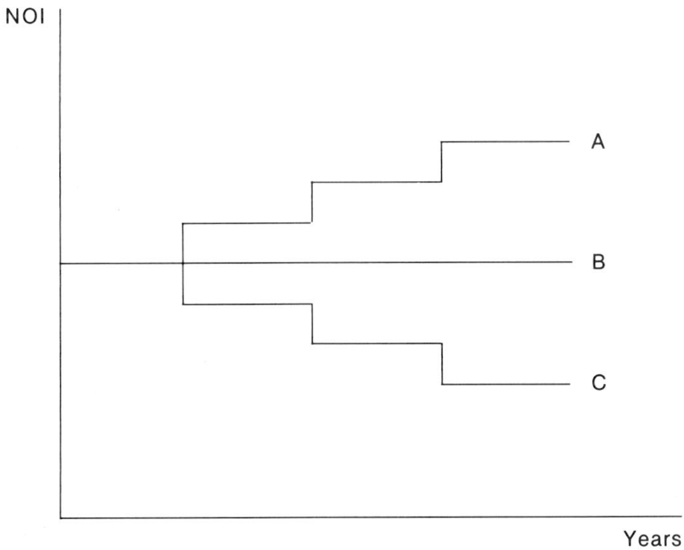

Path A reflects the NOI pattern in Exhibit 8.3. Path C, or some pattern similar to it, could easily occur if market rents do not keep pace with the competition or if expenses are not watched closely.

Using a Typical Current Year Income

Evidence[6] exists that most appraisers would prefer to derive NOI for only the current year and use it in place of a stabilized NOI, I_S. This view suggests that the current year NOI should be derived using market figures that reflect the actions of comparable competitive properties. Proponents for using the current year NOI only argue that the estimate of NOI is for the lender who wants to be assured that the owner can pay the debt service in early years where the high risk of default occurs. In addition, they may argue that the current year's estimate of NOI is a estimate of expected income of the year, rather than a discounted value of a large stream of expected, projected benefits of the property.

The use of a current year's estimate of NOI may be combined with the omission of any deduction for reserves for replacement. The argument says that the owner does not actually make this deduction and therefore should be omitted. Exhibit 8.2 shows a current year reconstructed real estate financial statement without the reserves for replacement account.

NOI from Comparable Properties

The two methods described for estimating NOI should present a warning to an appraiser to check NOI estimates from comparable properties to assure that they were derived using comparable techniques. The results may be quite different if the concepts are different.

STABILIZATION OF NOI

Once the annual level of NOI has been projected for each year of the expected holding period, all NOI figures can be stabilized. The reason for stabilization is that one technique of valuation shown in Chapter 7 is $V = I/R$. This valuation technique assumed that I or NOI was the same in each year, and that R was the same in each year. Since the levels of projected NOI vary in each year, one estimate must be derived to use in the numerator. That one estimate is the stabilized NOI. An estimate of R is derived in later chapters.

To stabilize NOI, the NOI derived in each year of the holding period is treated as a reversion that appears at the end of the year. In Exhibit 8.3, the NOI of \$53,918, in year one is considered as a reversion that occurs at the end of the year. The NOI of \$56,645 is a reversion that occurs at the end of year two, and so on through the holding periods.

Each of these reversions is discounted by the appropriate factor for a known equity yield rate, Y_E.

Equity Yield Rate = 10.5%

Year	*NOI*	*Present value reversion of \$1*		*Present value*
1	\$53,918	× .904977	=	\$48,795
2	\$56,645	× .818984	=	46,391
3	\$59,352	× .741162	=	43,989
4	\$62,037	× .670735	=	41,610
5	\$64,698	× .607000	=	39,272
6	\$67,185	× .549321	=	36,906
			Sum =	\$256,963

The appropriate present value reversion of \$1 factor is used for each NOI reversion. The sum of the present value column, \$256, 963 represents the present value of the NOI stream over the next six years.

Stabilized NOI *(I_s)*

If the appraiser desires to use a stabilized NOI, one method that can be used to estimate I_s is,[7]

$$I_s = \frac{\text{present value of NOI reversions}}{\text{present value of an ordinary annuity of \$1 per period}}$$

$$I_s = \frac{\$256{,}963}{4.292179}$$

$$I_s = \$59{,}868.$$

The result, $59,868, is stabilized NOI, which can now be used in the formula $V = I/R$. *Since the levels of NOI varied and have now been stabilized, this formula changes to* $V = I_s/R$.

The method of stabilizing income shown here is only one technique. If the appraiser attempts to derive NOI directly from the market by rearranging the terms of the equation, $V = I/R$, into $I = VR$, the estimate of the market derived I may not be equal to the stabilized I. Both estimates should be viewed as tools in the appraiser's toolkit that can be used when appropriate.

J, Adjusted *J*, and *G* Factors

Changing levels of NOI are incorporated into the Ellwood analysis in Chapter 10, and into discounted cash flow analysis in Chapter 12.

THE RESIDUAL

If the investor-owner expects to sell, refinance, or exchange the subject at the end of the holding period, p, additional income in the form of net sale proceeds may be received (lost). The net sale proceed is considered income that is received as a *lump sum* at the end of the holding period, as opposed to NOI, which is received *regularly*. Both are income to the owner even though the net sale proceed *may be* taxed as *gains,* as opposed to the NOI, which is taxed as ordinary *income.* This *residual* or *reversion* received by the owner at the end of the holding period, p, must be discounted and added to the present value of the income flow, NOI. After-tax cash flows are discounted to present value in Chapter 12.

Zero Residual

If the property is expected to have a zero residual worth at the end of the holding period, p, no residual income exists to discount. A negative amount may be discounted reflecting the present value of the salvage costs if the highest and best use of the property suggests a change in the land use. In this case, one estimate of market value could be derived by

$$V = \frac{I_s}{R}$$

where

I_s = stabilized NOI for the holding period, p,

R = rate.

Capital Gain (Loss)

If the property is expected to have a gain (loss) in worth at the end of the holding period, this gain (loss) must be discounted. The amount of income to discount would be estimated by subtracting any unpaid mortgage balances at the time of sale from the estimated selling price. The net may be called *equity* since it is claimed on the owner's asset side of his or her balance sheet.

Estimating the future worth of the property at the end of the holding period is a market research problem. Conditions of local demand and supply must be carefully evaluated to determine trends. Typically, past patterns of growth illustrated by competitive properties are applied to the subject and projected into the future which ignores the influences of the competition and changing market conditions.

In this case, one estimate of market value could be estimated by

$$V = \frac{I_s}{R} + (\text{SP} - \text{UM}) \times (\text{present value of reversion of \$1 for } p \text{ and } Y_E)$$

where

SP = projected selling price at p,

UM = unpaid mortgage balance at p.

ACCURATE ESTIMATION OF NOI

Several questions must be asked and evaluated in estimating future levels of NOI to assure that the results are accurate and reflect the decision-making process.[8]

1. Is the first year's income projected into perpetuity?
   Some users might argue that this often-used method of projection is not accurate.

2. Should a reversionary value be considered?
   If the property generates income for a holding period, p, that is shorter than the life of the property, a future resale value may exist. Should it be estimated?

3. Will the projected levels of NOI vary in various years?
If the answer is yes, perhaps a projection for each year should be made.
4. Should expenses be allowed to vary to comply with local market conditions?
Most expenses will change over the holding period.
5. How should inflation be handled?
Inflation assumptions should be consistent and double-counting avoided.
6. Will conditions external to the property cause the projected levels of NOI to vary?
If the answer is yes, varying income levels are treated in the analysis in the same manner as constant income levels.
7. If this market is profitable, will new competitors enter?
If the answer is yes, perhaps the vacancy rate should be adjusted upward in future years.
8. Does a probability exist that rent control or mandatory expense expenditures legislation be passed?
If the answer is yes, perhaps the limits on expected income and expenses should be included in future years.

No riskless projections exist. The analyst attempts to uncover past and current market trends and uses this information to estimate future income.

JUSTIFICATION AND DOCUMENTATION

All estimates of income and expenses must be justified and documented. A paper by one AIREA grader[9] covering the weaknesses of demonstration reports emphasizes several points that appraisers should remember in estimating the necessary figures:

> *. . . the failure of candidates to include in the report all the market data and reasoning supporting the income, vacancy, expenses, and rate of return estimates.*
>
> *A narrative presentation of the reasons the existing lease may or may not indicate current market rent should be included.*
>
> *Each comparable analysis should include a detailed narrative of how its rental value characteristics compare to those of the subject property. Adjustments should be market supported. The adjusted comparables should then be reconciled to the final estimated rent.*
>
> *. . . other properties (not comparables) that may be superior rent indicators should be considered.*
>
> *Market support for the vacancy and collection loss estimate should include evidence of competitive properties survey. . . The question to be an-*

swered and supported is what the applicable vacancy and collection loss is for the subject property. . . A very good vacancy estimate should relate in some manner to the previous city and neighborhood analysis.

A strong estimate (for expenses) will illustrate the subject property's recent experience, comment on its adequacy for projecting future expense, and then report and reconcile comparable property expenses to the subject property. Opinions of property managers, insurance agents, and others may be used in conjunction with the primary sources.

The income approach must reflect, in a very obvious way, all the depreciation features identified in the cost approach. In summary, the candidate should use market data facts, relate their applicability to the subject property, and reconcile conflicting market data and conclusions.

SOURCES OF INFORMATION

Information reflecting market trends and competitive properties must be obtained to complete the appraisal. Data on income producing properties might be obtained from the following:

1. The appraiser's own files.
   Data on past assignments and comparables visited is a prime source.
2. Other appraisers.
   In some cases, other appraisers can be a source of data on local trends and competitive properties.
3. Local brokers and lending institutions.
   Any individual or institution associated with a sale is a source of information.
4. Supporting individuals or firms.
   Any individual or firm that supported the sale is a source of information. Examples include the title company, real estate attorney, and title insurance agent.
5. Local and state data banks.
   The local board of REALTORS, appraisal chapter, or property management chapter may have established a data bank on comparable properties. In addition, some colleges and universities maintain this information for classroom purposes and for policy decisions on land acquisition and housing.
6. National data sources.
   Trends at the national level can be delineated by examining the census and time series reported in publications such as the *Federal Reserve Bulletin, Journal of the Federal Home Bank Board, The Appraiser,* and *The Appraisal Briefs.*
7. Publications on survey results.
   The Institute of Real Estate Management publishes annually three vol-

umes containing their survey. These volumes are *Income/Expense Analysis: Apartments, Income/Expense Analysis: Suburban Office Buildings,* and *Income/Expense Analysis: Condominiums, Cooperatives, and Planned Unit Developments.*

PROBLEMS

Question: You receive an assignment to estimate the NOI of a twelve-unit apartment complex. You ask the owner for a copy of the previous year's income statement that has been audited, compiled, or reviewed by an accountant. You receive the following information:

Previous Year's Income Statement

Income		
Rent received		$50,400
12, 2-Bedroom units at $350 per month		
Laundry income		5,000
Extra parking charges		1,500
Renters' Association dues		360
Clubhouse charges		500
	Total	$57,760
Expenses		
1. Electricity		400
2. Gas		400
3. Water		350
4. Telephone		250
5. Office supplies		300
6. Advertising		3,000
7. Property manager (5% of rents collected)		2,520
8. General maintenance		11,500
9. Interest payments on mortgage		25,500
10. Property taxes		4,500
11. Property insurance		1,500
12. Depreciation (1/40 × $400,000)		10,000
13. New appliances replacement		1,025
2 stoves ($300 each)		
1 refrigerator ($300 each)		
1 water heater ($125 each)		
	Total	$61,245
Operating income		
Income		57,760
– Expenses		– 61,245
		($3,485)

You review your files covering comparable properties. Also, you review a recent survey that contains information on market rents and costs of operation. You uncover the following information pertaining to local market trends concerning properties similar to the subject:

- Prevailing market rental for two-bedroom apartments is $350 per month.
- Other properties collected a laundry concession, and the $5,000 figure is typical. Other competitive properties did *not* collect parking, clubhouse, or renters' association dues.
- A typical vacancy rate is 6.5% of the rent.
- Items 1 through 8 listed as expenses tend to average about 25% of the gross rent.
- The figures for property taxes and property insurance are typical.
- You want to establish a reserve for replacement account. After viewing the property, you feel the following items should be included:

	Useful life	*Cost*
stove	7	$300 each
refrigerator	7	$300 each
water heater	7	$125 each
range hood	7	$125 each
roof	15	$2000

- The property is three years old, and no reserves account has been established to date. Reconstruct a real estate financial statement from this information given.

Answer: Reconstructed Real Estate Financial Statement

Gross potential income from all sources		
Rent		
12, 2-Bedroom units at $350		$50,400
Laundry income		5,000
Less: Vacancy allowance, bad debt, and income loss		
$50,400 × .065		– 3,276
Result: Effective gross income		$52,124
Less: Expenses		
Operating		
.25 × $50,400		– 12,600
Fixed		
Property taxes 4,500		
Property insurance 1,500		– 6,000
Reserves for replacement		
stoves	(1/7 × 300 × 12 = $514)	
refrigerator	(1/7 × 300 × 12 = 514)	
water heater	(1/7 × 125 × 12 = 214)	
range hood	(1/7 × 125 × 12 = 214)	
roof	(1/15 × $2,000 = 133)	
	$1,589	
3 years × 1,589 = 4767		– 4,767
Result: Net Operating Income		$28,757

Question: Stabilize the following projected levels of NOI at $Y_E = 12$ percent.

Year	NOI_1	NOI_2	NOI_3
1	$25,000	$23,000	$22,500
2	20,000	21,000	22,500
3	21,500	24,000	22,500
4	25,500	22,000	22,500
5	18,500	20,500	20,500

Answer:

Year	NOI_1	*Present value of \$1 at 12%*	
1	$25,000 ×	.892857	= $22,321.43
2	20,000 ×	.797194	= 15,943.88
3	21,500 ×	.711780	= 15,303.27
4	25,500 ×	.635518	= 16,205.71
5	18,500 ×	.567427	= 10,497.40
			$80,272 (rounded)

$$I_s = \frac{\text{present value of NOI reversions}}{\text{present value of an ordinary annuity of \$1 per period}}$$

$$I_s = \frac{\$80{,}272}{3.604776} = \$22{,}268$$

Year	NOI_2	*Present value of \$1 at 12%*	
1	$23,000 ×	.892857	= $20,535.71
2	21,000 ×	.797194	= 16,741.07
3	24,000 ×	.711780	= 17,082.72
4	22,000 ×	.635518	= 13,981.40
5	20,500 ×	.567427	= 11,632.25
			$79,973 (rounded)

$$I_s = \frac{\$79{,}973}{3.604776} = \$22{,}185$$

Year	NOI_3	Present value of $1 at 12%	
1	$22,500 × .892857		= $20,089.28
2	$22,500 × .797194		= 17,936.87
3	$22,500 × .711780		= 16,015.05
4	$22,500 × .635518		= 14,299.16
5	$20,500 × .567427		= 11,632.25
			$79,973 (rounded)

$$I_s = \frac{\$79{,}973}{3.604776} = \$22{,}185$$

Question: For those readers interested in hand calculator applications, the following problem covering income flow was submitted to "The Calculating Appraiser," *The Appraiser,* March, 1981. Reprinted with permission. The Keystrokes are designed for a HP-38 calculator.

> *Dear Calculating Appraiser:*
>
> *I am appraising a small, residential income property. The trend in NOI has been for an annual increase approximating 7% compounded and I feel that it is appropriate to expect a similar pattern in the foreseeable future. I have estimated that the NOI for the coming year will be $10,000.*
>
> *Leaving aside the consideration of the future value of the property, I wish to value this income stream over a five-year period using a discount rate of 12%. I know that once the cash flows are laid out I can determine their present worth using individual reversion factors, either calculated or from a table. Is there an easier method of doing this?*
>
> *R.G.*

Answer:

Dear R.G.:

Yes, there is an easier method—especially if you are interested in analyzing the sensitivity of your answer to changes in your assumptions. The type of income stream you have described is known as an *ordinary annuity changing in constant ratio.* Given this pattern, a single factor may be applied to the initial cash flow, just as you would with an ordinary level annuity. The result will be the present value of a series of cash flows that increase or decrease at a compound rate.

This PVF may be computed by formula or found in some books of financial tables. Fortunately, however, its calculation is a simple matter on any standard financial calculator. The steps are:

1. Enter the projection period in [n].
2. Find the percent difference between the change base and the yield base. In your problem this calculates as (1.12 − 1.07) × 100/1.07 = 4.67. Many calculators have a Δ% key to make this calculation for you. Enter this amount in [i].
3. Enter the reciprocal of the change base (1/1.07) in [PMT].
4. Solve for the [PV].

The HP-38 keystrokes below illustrate this procedure.

1	f FIN		8	i	
2	5	(Years)	9	x><y	1.07
3	n		10	f1/x	
4	1.07	(^ Base)	11	PMT	
5	ENTER		12	PV	− 4.08
6	1.12	(Y Base)	13	f 6	− 4.083090
7	fΔ%				

Thus, a PVF of 4.083090 times a net income of $10,000 yields a present value of $40,830.90. The intermediate step of solving for a factor may be bypassed by substituting these steps in the routine above:

9	10,000	(NOI)
10	x><y	1.07
11	÷	
12	PMT	
13	PV	− 40,830.90

In either case, the result is the same as a more detailed approach using reversion factors from a book of tables:

Year		
1	$10,000.00 × .892857 =	$8,928.57
2	$10,000.00 × 1.07 = $10,700.00 × .797194 =	8,529.98
3	$10,700.00 × 1.07 = $11,449.00 × .711780 =	8,149.17
4	$11,449.00 × 1.07 = $12,250.43 × .635518 =	7,785.37
5	$12,250.43 × 1.07 = $13,107.96 × .567427 =	7,437.81
	Present Value	$40,830.90

Although the latter format may be desirable if you wish to lay out the detail of the problem, the obvious advantage in the use/calculation of the present value factor is the time saved. This advantage becomes substantial if you are making a sensitivity analysis. Imagine the amount of work involved in the layout and calculation of ten years of individual cash flows, presuming that they increase at 3, 5, 7, and 9% compounded, and are to be discounted at 10, 12, 14, and 15%!

SUMMARY

Income is the difference between inflows and outflows of all assets. Cash is only one asset. Net operating income is found by estimating gross potential income from all sources and subtracting vacancy allowance, bad debts, and losses in income; operating expenses; fixed expenses and reserves for replacements. A real estate financial statement may need to be reconstructed from available data to derive NOI in an efficient and straightforward manner.

Several issues surround the handling of the reserves for replacement account. One is whether the account should be included since some investors do not maintain a reserve account. Another is that future replacement costs should be included rather than current replacement costs to account for inflation. Another issue is whether past reserves for replacements that have not been charged should be charged totally in the current year.

Assumptions covering future levels of income and expenses typically must be made to derive NOI for each year of the holding period. These assumptions must be justified and documented through market trends and surveys and comparisons with competitive properties.

All of the NOI estimates for the holding period years can be treated as a series of annual end-of-the-year reversions and discounted. The sums of these discounted values can be divided by the present value of the annuity to receive the stabilized NOI, I_s.

The property may have a residual value at the end of the owner's holding period. This residual must be discounted and added to the value estimate using I_s.

To assure that the value estimate is accurate, the appraiser should always evaluate the assumptions that underlie the estimate of NOI. For example, was one year's NOI projected into perpetuity? How should inflation be handled? Will conditions external to the property cause the projected levels of NOI to vary?

All estimates of NOI must be justified and documented. This includes steps such as including all relevant market data, a discussion of whether the current lease reflects current market rents, examination of other properties (not comparables) which may reflect rent trends, and a strong reconciliation of the expenses of comparable properties to the subject property.

All sources of data should be examined as to its usefulness. These range from the appraisers own files to publications containing national trends and survey results.

REVIEW QUESTIONS

1. What is the difference between net operating income and net cash flow?
2. Explain in detail the real estate financial statement.
3. Explain how to reconstruct a real estate financial statement from a financial statement that might be prepared by an accountant.
4. Define and explain each of the following:

   gross potential income from all sources

   vacancy allowance, bad debts, and loss of income

   operating expenses

   fixed expenses

   reserves for replacement

   net operating income
5. Evaluate the controversies surrounding the reserve for replacement account.
6. Identify the typical assumptions that must be made to project NOI over the holding period.
7. Demonstrate and explain precisely how a stabilized NOI is derived from the projected levels of NOI.
8. Assume that the property you are appraising *has* a residual worth at the end of the holding period. How is this worth treated in valuing the property? Why?
9. Assume that the property you are appraising has *no* worth at the end of the holding period. How is this zero worth treated in valuing the property? Why?
10. Outline several pointers for an appraiser to remember in justifying and documenting the income approach.
11. What are typical sources of information for data to use in the income approach?

ENDNOTES

1. Donald R. Epley and James A. Millar, *Basic Real Estate Finance and Investments* (New York: John Wiley & Sons, Inc., 1980), p. 469.

2. Byrl N. Boyce, *Real Estate Appraisal Terminology* (Cambridge, Mass.: Ballinger Publishing Co., 1975), p. 148.

3. Epley and Millar, *Basic Real Estate Finance and Investments.*

4. William N. Kinnard, Jr. *A Guide to Appraising Apartments* (Chicago: Society of Real Estate Appraisers, 1977), pp. 30–35.

5. Kenneth M. Lusht, "The Behavior of Appraisers in Valuing Income Property," *The Real Estate Appraiser and Analyst* 45 (July–August 1979): 43–52.

6. Robert Zerbst and Gary Eldred, "The Specification of Net Operating Income," *Real Estate Appraiser and Analyst* 45 (November–December 1979): 39–43; see also Lusht, "The Behavior of Appraisers."

7. Jeffrey D. Fisher, *Computer Assisted Investment Analysis and Valuation of Income Property* (Columbus, Ohio: OSU Center for Real Estate and Education and Research, Research Report No. 6, August 1979), p. 22.

8. James Cooper, *Real Estate Investment Analysis* (Lexington, Mass.: Heath-Lexington Books, 1974), p. 14; see also Stephen Pyhrr, "Mathematics of Finance," in *Financing Income Producing Real Estate* (New York: McGraw Hill, Inc., 1977), pp. 322–324.

9. Robert J. Heinrich, "A Candidate's Guide to Writing a Passing MAI Demonstration Appraisal Report," *The Appraisal Journal* 47 (October 1979): 561–573.

ADDITIONAL READINGS

Cannaday, Roger E., and Colwell, Peter F. "A Unified Field Theory of the Income Approach to Appraisal—Part I," *The Real Estate Appraiser and Analyst* 47 (First Quarter, 1981): 5–9.

Carpenter, Michael D., and Shannon, Donald S. "The Effect of Inflation on Value." *The Real Estate Appraiser and Analyst,* 47 (First Quarter, 1981): 51–55.

Ellwood, L. W. "The Income Forecast: Straight Line or Curve?" *The Appraisal Journal* 39 (April 1971): 200–206.

Gibbons, James E., and Rushmore, Stephen. "Using Total Project Analysis to Compete for Investment Capital." *The Appraisal Journal* 43 (October 1975): 491–516.

Hemmer, Edgar H., and Fisher, Jeffrey D. "Dealing With Uncertainty in Income Valuation." *The Appraisal Journal* 46 (April 1978): 230–244.

Lusht, Kenneth M. "Inflation and Real Estate Investment Value." *American Real Estate and Urban Economics Association Journal* 6 (Spring 1978): 37–49.

Lusht, Kenneth M. "Inflation and Real Estate Investment Value." *Real Estate Appraiser and Analyst* 45 (November–December 1979): 23–29.

Martin, William B., Jr. "A Risk Analysis Rate-of-Return Model for Evaluating Income-Producing Real Estate Investments." *The Appraisal Journal* 46 (July 1978): 424–442.

Shipp, Royal. "Property Income Streams—Measuring and Evaluating Their Size and Certainty." *The Appraisal Journal* 38 (July 1970): 357–375.

CHAPTER 9

LEARNING OBJECTIVES

When a student finishes this chapter, he or she should be able to:

- Explain the importance of using market-derived data in the appraisal.
- Contrast the techniques used in estimating value when the loan terms are known and unknown.
- Discuss the difference between using the equity yield rate and using the equity dividend rate in estimating value.
- Develop the Akerson R by tracing the method for including the various types of equity with and without algebra.
- Explain the influence on the estimate of V when switching from annual to monthly amortization.

Estimate of V and R by Mortgage-Equity Analysis

IMPORTANT TERMS AND PHRASES

Akerson *R*: A rate used in estimating the value of property that relies on a mortgage equity procedure.

Akerson with algebra: A mortgage equity procedure for estimating value using algebraic terms.

Akerson without algebra: A mortgage equity procedure for deriving the value of property without using algebraic terms.

mortgage equity analysis: A procedure whereby the value of property is assumed to be equal to the present value of the mortgage principal and the present value of the equity.

mortgage equity analysis with equity buildup over an expected holding period and an expected capital gain (loss): A mortgage equity procedure for valuing property where equity comes from debt reduction and a capital gain (loss).

mortgage equity analysis with equity buildup through mortgage reduction: A mortgage equity procedure for valuing property where equity comes from debt reduction.

simplified mortgage equity analysis: A mortgage equity procedure for valuing property under simplified assumptions.

The purpose of this chapter is to explain several techniques for valuing income-producing property that has been purchased using debt financing.

MARKET VALUE AND FINANCING

The first question that arises in valuing income-producing property that has been purchased using financing is, "Does the financing influence the market value? After all, isn't the market value an independent value determined separately from the terms of the financing?" The correct answer is that the financing *does influence* the market value. The objective of the appraisal is to estimate a value that reflects the market. If financing is not considered, the value estimate could underemphasize current market trends. Consequently, the financing must be considered.

Market Derived Data

The loan terms used in the analysis are those that are currently available in the market for similar types of properties. Could the valuation of a structure be changed by replacing the management and seeking new terms? The answer should be "no." Two adjacent structures that are identical and are built according to the same specifications, having the same amount of maintenance and obsolescence, should have the same value. If they are financed differently, however, they will have different levels of V. To avoid this problem, the appraiser should use the terms of financing that are available to a typical investor for this type of structure as determined by the market.

MORTGAGE-EQUITY ANALYSIS

Mortgage-equity analysis is the procedure for valuing property whereby the value of property, V, is assumed to be equal to

$$V = V_M + V_E \tag{9–1}$$

where

V_M = the present value of the mortgage investment (mortgage principal),

V_E = present value of the equity.

The present value of the property, V, can be estimated in one of two ways, depending upon the available data. One way is simply to estimate V_M and V_E and sum the two. The amount of the mortgage, V_M, can be given in (a) dollar figures, or (b) a loan-to-value ratio. The present value for V_E is typically found by dividing the before-tax income (cash throw off) by the R_E.

The second method relies upon equation 9–2,

$$V = I/R. \tag{9–2}$$

I and R are rewritten into their components,

$$I = \text{annual debt service on the mortgage} + \text{before-tax income}.$$

$$R = R_M\left(\frac{V_M}{V}\right) + R_E\left(1 - \frac{V_M}{V}\right)$$

or

$$R = i\left(\frac{V_M}{V}\right) + Y_E\left(1 - \frac{V_M}{V}\right)$$

where

$$R_M = \text{mortgage constant,}$$

$$\frac{V_M}{V} = \text{loan-to-value ratio,}$$

$$1 - \frac{V_M}{V} = \text{equity-to-value ratio,}$$

$$i = \text{interest rate on the mortgage,}$$

$$Y_E = \text{equity yield rate,}$$

$$R_E = \text{equity dividend rate.}$$

Thus

$$V = \frac{\text{annual debt service + before tax income}}{R_M\left(\frac{V_M}{V}\right) + R_E\left(1 - \frac{V_M}{V}\right)}$$

or

$$\text{V} = \frac{I}{i\left(\frac{V_M}{V}\right) + Y_E\left(1 - \frac{V_M}{V}\right)}.$$

Net operating income, I, can be estimated and divided by an estimate of the overall R. The reader should remember that Appendix B to Chapter 7 gives a recent correction to the calculation of R, which makes the result more precise.

The unique contribution of mortgage-equity analysis to appraisal technique is that the overall rate, R_0, is composed of an initial rate which has been adjusted for three types of equity: downpayment and equity buildup through mortgage reduction, and equity change through appreciation or loss which can be easily added.

AVERAGE vs. MARGINAL RATES

The capitalization rate, R, presented in the previous section is a *weighted average rate* that can be used to discount an income flow when the debt-to-equity ratio does not change. If the ratio is constant, amortization of the debt is not occurring or happens in one lump payment at the end of the time period.[1]

If the debt-to-equity ratio changes over time from amortization and/or equity change through capital gain (loss), the estimates of R_E and Y_E will change.[2] For example, if the mortgage is amortized over time, the debt, V_M, decreases and the equity, $1 - V_M/V$, increases. If this ratio changes and all other factors remain constant, the estimate of Y_E should change in each succeeding year. These new changing rates are called *marginal rates.*[3] The reader should refer to Appendix B in Chapter 7 for one interpretation of the correct estimate of R using R_E or Y_E.

MORTGAGE-EQUITY ANALYSIS WHEN THE ORIGINAL LOAN TERMS ARE KNOWN

Mortgage equity can be used to value income-producing property when *the original loan terms are known.* The property value is thought to be equal to

$$V = \text{original loan amount} + \text{present value of the equity.} \tag{9–3}$$

One method of finding the present value of the equity is to use the equity dividend rate, R_E, which is[4]

$$R_E = \frac{\text{before tax income}}{\text{original equity}}.$$

By rearranging terms,

$$\text{original equity} = \frac{\text{before tax income}}{R_E}.$$

The present value of the equity (original equity) can be approximated by dividing before-tax income (cash throw off) by the equity dividend rate, R_E.

A second method is to sum the discounted net operating income earned in each year and add it to the discounted reversion using the equity yield rate. The result should be present value of the equity. The equity yield rate, Y_E, must be used because the income is before taxes and an estimate of capital gain (or loss) is included. The equity yield rate may be thought of as the internal rate of return.

The present value of the equity, V_E, is[5]

$$\text{present value of equity} = \sum_{i=1}^{p} \frac{(\text{before tax income})_i}{(1 + Y_E)^i} + \frac{\text{reversion}}{(1 + Y_E)^p} \tag{9–4}$$

If applied correctly, both techniques should produce the same value for the equity. For example, consider the following problem.

- Cash throw off is \$9000.
- Reversion is \$152,640.

- Mortgage loan is $300,000.
- Equity yield rate is .12.
- Equity dividend rate is .09.
- The expected holding period, p, is ten years.

The present value of the equity, V_E, is

$$V_E = \frac{\text{before tax income}}{R_E}$$

$$V_E = \frac{\$9{,}000}{.09}$$

$$V_E = \$100{,}000.$$

The value, V, is

$$V = V_M + V_E$$

$$V = \$300{,}000 + \$100{,}000$$

$$V = \$400{,}000$$

or

$$V_E = \sum_{i=1}^{p} \frac{(\text{before tax income})_i}{(1 + Y_E)^i} + \frac{\text{reversion}}{(1 + Y_E)^p}$$

$$V_E = \frac{9000}{(1 + .12)^1} + \frac{9000}{(1 + .12)^2} + \frac{9000}{(1 + .12)^3} + \cdots \frac{9000}{(1 + .12)^{10}} + \frac{152{,}640}{(1 + .12)^{10}}$$

$$V_E = \$100{,}000.$$

The present value, V, is

$$V = V_M + V_E$$

$$V = \$300{,}000 + \$100{,}000$$

$$V = \$400{,}000.$$

MORTGAGE-EQUITY ANALYSIS WHEN THE ORIGINAL LOAN TERMS ARE NOT KNOWN

Other techniques of mortgage-equity analysis can be used when the *original loan terms are not known but the loan as a percentage of the property value is known*. In these cases, the property value is thought to be equal to $V = I/R$. Mortgage-equity analysis is used here to derive an estimate of R.

Typically, the value for R in these situations is derived by one of four techniques, depending on the available data. The first is the use of *Akerson with or without algebra,* explained in the following section of the chapter. The second is the use of the *Ellwood procedures,* described in the next chapter. The third is *direct extraction from comparable market properties,* discussed in Chapter 11. The fourth is the use of *contemporary computer procedures,* explained in Chapter 12. All four methods should give the same answer if applied correctly.

AKERSON WITH OR WITHOUT ALGEBRA

Charles Akerson developed a procedure for estimating R with and without algebra.[6] Estimates of R from both procedures are equal to the R derived from the Ellwood procedure described in the next chapter. The appendix at the end of Chapter 10 proves that the Akerson R is equivalent to the Ellwood R.

Simplified Mortgage-Equity Analysis

Simplified mortgage-equity analysis estimates R under the following assumptions.

1. Original mortgage loan is not known, but the loan as a percentage of the property value is known.
2. Equity from a buildup of mortgage reduction is ignored.
3. Equity from an increase or decrease in the property value over time is ignored.
4. The property is held until the debt expires.

The estimate for R is obtained by the following procedures.

With algebra

$$R = M\,R_M + (1 - M)\,Y_E$$

where

$$\begin{aligned} M &= \text{initial percent debt,} \\ (1 - M) &= \text{initial percent equity,} \\ R_M &= \text{mortgage constant,} \\ Y_E &= \text{equity yield rate.} \end{aligned}$$

Without algebra

	%	rate
1st mortgage	M	$\times R_M$
+ downpayment	$(1-M)$	$\times Y_E$
		Sum = R

Consider the following data as an example.

- First mortgage is $500,000 at 10.5% interest for twenty-five years.
- Downpayment is $100,000 and expected return is 11.0% interest.
- Payments on the loan are *annual* at the end of the year.

With algebra

$$R = M(R_M) + (1 - M)\,Y_E$$
$$R = .833333 \times .113302 + .166667 \times .11$$
$$R = .1127515 \text{ or } 11.3\%$$

Without algebra

	%	rate
1st mortgage	M	$\times R_M$
+ downpayment	$(1 - M)$	$\times Y_E$
		Sum = R

	%	rate		
1st mortgage	.833333	× .113302	=	+ .0944182
+ downpayment	.166667	× .11	=	+ .0183333
			R =	.1127515 or 11.3%

Simplified mortgage equity analysis is identical to the band of investment technique for estimating the overall rate, R. Chapter 7 illustrated the use of the band of investment technique for deriving a discount rate, R_L, which simply calculated a weighted average of two rates. This approach did not include equity buildup or any recapture. Simplified mortgage equity calculates a weighted average of the mortgage constant, R_M, and the equity yield rate, Y_E.

In some cases, the owners of the subject and similar properties may be more interested in cash-on-cash return than the equity yield rate. They may be more concerned with current return than the equity yield rate which includes expectations of value changes. In this situation, the equity yield rate, Y_E, would be changed to the equity dividend rate, R_E. The approach developed by Akerson used the equity yield rate.

Mortgage-Equity Analysis with Equity Buildup through Mortgage Reduction

If the appraiser wants to consider the buildup in equity through mortgage reduction, an adjustment must be made to the simplified method. Equity buildup can be considered (1) for the life of the mortgage, or (2) over an expected holding period. Thus the assumptions in this case are:

1. Original mortgage loan is not known, but the loan as a percentage of the property value is known.
2. Equity from a buildup of mortgage reduction is considered for (1) the life of the mortgage, or (2) an expected holding period.
3. Equity from an increase or decrease in the property value over time is ignored.
4. The property is (1) held until the mortgage is paid off, or (2) held only for an expected holding period. This assumption must be consistent with assumption 2.

The estimate for R *if the property were held until the end of the mortgage* would be:

With algebra

$$R = M(R_M) + (1 - M)Y_E - M\frac{1}{S_{\overline{n}|Y_E}}$$

where

$\dfrac{1}{S_{\overline{n}|Y_E}}$ = sinking fund factor for the maturity of the debt, n, at the equity yield rate Y_E.

Without algebra

	%		rate
1st mortgage	M	×	R_M
+ downpayment	$(1 - M)$	×	Y_E
− credit for equity buildup	M	×	$\frac{1}{S_{\overline{n}\|Y_E}}$
			Sum = R

The subtraction of the amount

$$M\frac{1}{S_{\overline{n}|Y_E}}$$

eliminates double-counting. The amortization factor, R_M, has already been used and already includes a payment to the mortgage balance. The following data can be used as an example.

- First mortgage is \$500,000 at 10.5% for twenty-five years and the payments are made *annually* at the end of each year.
- Downpayment is \$100,000 at 11.0% expected yield.

With algebra

$$R = MR_M + (1 - M)Y_E - M\frac{1}{S_{\overline{n}|Y_E}}$$

$$R = .833333(.113302) + .166667(.110) - .833333(.008740)$$

$$R = .1127515 - .0072833$$

$$R = .1054682 \text{ or } 10.5\%.$$

Without algebra

	%		rate
1st mortgage	M	×	R_M
+ downpayment	$(1-M)$	×	Y_E
− credit for equity buildup	M	×	$\frac{1}{S_{\overline{n}|Y_E}}$
		Sum =	R

	%	rate		
1st mortgage	.833333 ×	.113302 =	+ .0944182	
+ downpayment	.166667 ×	.110 =	+ .0183333	
− credit for equity buildup	.833333 ×	.008740 =	− .0072833	
		R =	.1054682	or 10.5%

The estimate for R *if the property were held only until the end of a holding period* would be:

With algebra

$$R = MR_M + (1 - M)Y_E - MP\frac{1}{S_{\overline{p}|Y_E}}$$

where

P = percent of the debt paid off at the end of the holding period, p,

$\frac{1}{S_{\overline{p}|Y_E}}$ = sinking fund factor for the holding period p at the equity yield rate Y_E.

Without algebra

	%		rate
1st mortgage	M	$\times$	R_M
+ downpayment	$(1-M)$	$\times$	Y_E
− credit for equity buildup	MP	$\times$	$\frac{1}{S_{\overline{p}\rceil Y_E}}$
		Sum =	R

A number of methods can be used to calculate P. Perhaps one of the easiest methods to remember is the following.

$$P = \frac{R_M \text{ for the mortgage} - i}{R_M \text{ for the mortgage} - i \text{ for the holding period}}$$

or,

$$P = \frac{R_M - i}{R_{M_p} - i}$$

where

R_M = the annual constant (12 × monthly installment to amortize \$1, 4 × quarterly installment to amortize \$1, 2 × semi-annual installment to amortize \$1),

i = nominal annual interest rate on the mortgage loan (12 × effective monthly rate, 4 × effective quarterly rate, 2 × effective semi-annual rate).

These data can be applied as an example.

- First mortgage is \$500,000 at 10.5% interest for twenty-five years and the payments are made *annually* at the end of each year.
- Downpayment is \$100,000 at 11.0% expected yield.
- Investor-owner is expected to hold the property for ten years.

With algebra

$$R = M R_M + (1 - M) Y_E - M(P) \frac{1}{S_{\overline{p}\rceil Y_E}}$$

$$R = .833338(.113302) + .166667(.11) - .833333(P)\ .059801$$

where

$$P = \frac{R_M \text{ for the mortgage} - i}{R_M \text{ for the mortgage} - i \text{ for the holding period}}$$

$$P = \frac{.113302 - .105}{.161922 - .105}$$ [7]

$$P = .1458487$$

$$R = .1127515 - .0072682$$

$$R = .1054833 \text{ or } 10.5\%.$$

Without algebra

	%		rate
1st mortgage	M	×	R_M
+ downpayment	$(1 - M)$	×	Y_E
− credit for equity buildup	$M\,P$	×	$\frac{1}{S_{\overline{p}\rceil Y_E}}$
		Sum =	R

	%	rate		
1st mortgage	.833333	× .113302	=	+ .0944182
+ downpayment	.166667	× .11	=	+ .0183333
− credit for equity buildup	.833333(.1458487)	× .059801	=	− .0072682
			R =	.1054833 or 10.5%

where

$$P = \frac{R_M \text{ for the mortgage} - i}{R_M \text{ for the mortgage} - i \text{ for the holding period}}$$

$$P = \frac{.113302 - .105}{.161922 - .105}$$ [8]

$$P = \frac{.008302}{.056922} = .1458487.$$

Mortgage-Equity Analysis with Equity Buildup Over an Expected Holding Period and an Expected Capital Gain (Loss)

The most sophisticated mortgage-equity analysis is used in a more realistic situation involving the following assumptions.

1. Original mortgage loan is not known, but the loan as a percentage of the property value is known.
2. Equity buildup from the mortgage reduction is considered for an expected holding period.
3. Equity from a change in the property value over time is considered.
4. The property is held only for an expected holding period.

The estimate for R is found by the following procedures.

With algebra

$$R = M R_M + (1 - M) Y_E - M P \frac{1}{S_{\overline{p}|Y_E}} - \text{app.} \frac{1}{S_{\overline{p}|Y_E}} \text{ or } + \text{dep.} \frac{1}{S_{\overline{p}|Y_E}}$$

where

− app. = percent increase expected in property value (capital gain),

+ dep. = percent decrease expected in property value (capital loss).

Without algebra

	%		*rate*
1st mortgage	M	×	R_M
+ downpayment	$(1 - M)$	×	Y_E
− credit for equity buildup	$M P$	×	$\frac{1}{S_{\overline{p}|Y_E}}$
− capital gain	− app.	×	$\frac{1}{S_{\overline{p}|Y_E}}$
or			
+ capital loss	+ dep.	×	$\frac{1}{S_{\overline{p}|Y_E}}$
			Sum = R

Expected capital gain is subtracted from R, which in turn increases the estimate for V. Expected capital loss is added to the estimate for R, which in turn lowers the estimate for V. The levels of app. or dep. must be estimated from market trends. The following data can be used to illustrate these calculations.

- First mortgage is \$500,000 at 10.5% for twenty-five years and payments are made *annually* at the end of each year.
- Downpayment is \$100,000 at 11.0% expected yield.
- Expected holding period is ten years.
- The resale value of the property is projected to reflect an increase in value of 50%.

With algebra

$$R = M R_M + (1 - M)Y_E - M P \frac{1}{S_{\overline{p}|Y_E}} - \text{app.} \frac{1}{S_{\overline{p}|Y_E}}$$

$$R = .1054833 - .50\ (.059801)$$

$$R = .1054833 - .0299005$$

$$R = .0755828 \text{ or } 7.6\%.$$

Without algebra

	%		*rate*
1st mortgage	M	×	R_M
+ downpayment	$(1 - M)$	×	Y_E
− credit for equity buildup	$M P$	×	$\frac{1}{S_{\overline{p}|Y_E}}$
− capital gain	− app.	×	$\frac{1}{S_{\overline{p}|Y_E}}$
			Sum = R

	%	*rate*	
1st mortgage	.833333	× .113302	= +.0944182
+ downpayment	.166667	× .11	= +.0183333
− credit for equity buildup	.833333(.1458487)	× .059801	= −.0072682
− capital gain	−.50	× .059801	= −.0299005
		Sum =	.0755828 or 7.6%

MONTHLY AMORTIZATION

In the preceding examples, amortization payments on the mortgages are assumed to be made annually. If the amortization schedule requires that payments be made on a different basis such as monthly, quarterly, or semi-annually, the R_M factors change. For example, a monthly amortization schedule requires that the R_M factor be read from the monthly table using the proper years and interest rate and then annualized by multiplying by 12. For a quarterly amortization schedule, the appropriate factor is read from the quarterly table and then multiplied by 4. For a semi-annual amortization schedule the factor is read from the semi-annual table and multiplied by 2. Otherwise, the derivation of R is identical to the solutions previously shown. For example, consider the following data.

- First mortgage is \$500,000 at 10.5% interest for twenty-five years and the payments are made *monthly* at the end of each month.
- Downpayment is \$100,000 at 11.0% expected yield.
- Expected holding period is ten years.
- The resale value of the property is projected to reflect an increase in value of 50%.

With algebra

$$R = MR_M + (1 - M)Y_E - MP\frac{1}{S_{\overline{p}|Y_E}} - \text{app.}\frac{1}{S_{\overline{p}|Y_E}}$$

where

$$R_M = \text{monthly mortgage constant for the mortgage} \times 12,$$

$$P = \frac{\text{monthly } R_M \text{ for the mortgage } \times 12 - .105}{\text{monthly } R_M \text{ for the holding period} \times 12 - .105}.$$

Solve for R_M:[9]

$$R_M = .009441 \times 12 = .113292.$$

Solve for P:[10]

$$P = \frac{.113292 - .105}{.013493 \times 12 - .105}$$

$$P = \frac{.113292 - .105}{.161916 - .105}$$

$$P = \frac{.008292}{.056916}$$

$$P = .1456883$$

$$R = .833333(.113292) + .166667(.11) - .833333(.1456883)(.059801) - .50\,(.059801)$$

$$R = .0944099 + .0183333 - .0072602 - .0299005$$

$$R = .1127432 - .0371607$$

$$R = .0755825 \text{ or } 7.56\%.$$

Without algebra

	%	rate
1st mortgage	M	$\times$ annualized monthly R_M
+ downpayment	$(1-M)$	$\times Y_E$
− credit for equity buildup	MP	$\times \dfrac{1}{S_{\overline{p}\rceil Y_E}}$
− capital gain	− app.	$\times \dfrac{1}{S_{\overline{p}\rceil Y_E}}$
		Sum = R

	%	rate		
1st mortgage	.833333	× .113292	=	+ .0944099
+ downpayment	.166667	× .11	=	+ .0183333
− credit for equity buildup	.833333(.1456883)	× .059801	=	− .0072602
− capital gain	−.50	× .059801	=	− .0299005
		Sum = R	=	.0755825 or 7.56%

OVERALL R WITH THE REQUIRED DEBT SERVICE

One technique encompasses several concepts developed in the chapter and adds the required debt service for estimating the overall R.[11] This technique is

R = mortgage loan ratio × annual mortgage constant × debt service coverage ratio.

Consider the example for annual amortization where,

mortgage loan ratio = .833333

annual mortgage constant = .114429.

If the lender required a debt service coverage of 1.25, the overall R would be

$$R = .833333 \times .114429 \times 1.25$$

$$R = .1191967 \text{ or } 11.9\%.$$

The required debt service reflects the borrower's most probable financing arrangement, and thus leads to the estimate of V, which can be viewed as the most probable selling price. Some analysts believe that techniques such as these are more useful since they reflect the lender's debt service cover ratio and estimate most probable selling price. Chapter 12 includes two other techniques incorporating the lender's requirements.

TAX ASSESSMENT PROBLEMS

Situations can occur within the market where the client wants an estimate of value that will be used for taxation purposes. Specifically, an estimate of value may be needed when the assessment of the property is the primary issue, construction is proposed and the tax rate is known but the assessed value is unknown, or the client wants to examine the equity and fairness of existing taxes. In these situations, the following technique is often used to generate an estimate of value:

$$V = \frac{\text{NOI before the property tax deduction}}{R_o + \left(\dfrac{\begin{matrix}\text{equalization} \\ \text{rate}\end{matrix} \times \begin{matrix}\text{jurisdiction} \\ \text{tax rate}\end{matrix}}{\text{\$ units used by jurisdiction}} \right)}$$

where

R_o = overall capitalization rate,

equalization rate = local jurisdiction rate for standardizing the tax bill on similar properties,

jurisdiction tax rate = the effective tax rate for the subject, sometimes approximated by the effective tax rate of (ad valorum property taxes/value),

\$ units used by jurisdiction = typically \$100 or \$1000.

Consider the following example. Your client wants to estimate the value of an office building for taxation purposes. Recent sales of comparable properties indicate that the overall capitalization rate for similar properties is 10.24%. The equalization rate for the local taxing jurisdiction is 30.92%, and the existing tax rate is \$152.82 per \$1000 of assessed valuation. The dollar unit used locally by taxing authorities is \$1000. The NOI for the subject has been estimated to be \$2,544,500. before the deduction of ad valorum taxes. The estimated value is,

$$V = \frac{\$2,544,500}{.1024 + \left(\dfrac{.3092 \times 152.82}{1000} \right)}$$

$$V = \frac{\$2,544,500}{.1024 + .0472519}$$

$$V = \frac{\$2,544,500}{.1496519}$$

$$V = \$17,002,791.$$

AN ILLUSTRATION

An appraiser in a midwestern city receives an assignment to determine the market value of two adjacent structures, each consisting of eight townhouse rental units that are four years old. Four other similar structures in the community are used to gain comparable data. These structures and the opinions expressed by several local appraisers reveal that the current most likely financing for this type of structure is a 75% L/V ratio with a 10% interest rate and monthly amortization for twenty years. Consultations with local appraisers suggest that an equity yield rate of 14% is typical and sales of the comparables support this figure. Resales of such properties through time indicate that the typical investor holds the property about seven years. One of the comparable properties sold three times in the past two years with a total appreciation in value of 23%. Demand for housing appears to be strong and likely to remain strong, and thus could readily be interpreted into a 30% increase in the reversionary value. Using this information, calculate an Akerson R with and without algebra.

With algebra

$$R = M R_M + (1 - M) Y_E - M(P) \frac{1}{S_{\overline{p}|Y_E}} - \text{app.} \frac{1}{S_{\overline{p}|Y_E}}.$$

Solve for P:

$$P = \frac{R_M \text{ for the mortgage} \times 12 - i}{R_M \text{ for the mortgage} \times 12 - i \text{ for the } p}$$

$$P = \frac{.009650 \times 12 - .10}{.016601 \times 12 - .10}$$

$$P = \frac{.1158 - .10}{.199212 - .10}$$

$$P = \frac{.0158}{.099212}$$

$$P = .1592549.$$

Solve for R:

$$R = .75\,(.1158) + .25\,(.14) - .75\,(.1592549)\,(.093192) - .30\,(.093192)$$

$$R = .08685 + .035 - .0111309 - .0279576$$

$$R = .12185 - .0390885$$

$$R = .0827615 \text{ or } 8.28\%.$$

Without algebra

	%		rate
1st mortgage	M	$\times$	$R_M \times 12$
+ downpayment	$(1 - M)$	$\times$	Y_E
− credit for equity buildup	$-M(P)$	$\times$	$\frac{1}{S_{\overline{p}\|Y_E}}$
− appreciation	−app.	$\times$	$\frac{1}{S_{\overline{p}\|Y_E}}$
			Sum = R

	%	rate	
1st mortgage	.75	× .009650 × 12	= +.08685
+ downpayment	.25	× .14	= +.035
− credit for equity buildup	−.75(.1592549)	× .093192	= −.0111309
− appreciation	−.30	× .093192	= −.0279576
		Sum = R =	.0827615 or 8.28%

SUMMARY

Mortgage-equity analysis is the procedure for valuing property whereby the value is assumed to be equal to the present value of the loan plus the present value of the equity. When the original loan terms are known, the present value of the equity is estimated and added to the loan. When the original loan terms are unknown, but the loan as a percentage of the property value is known, the value is estimated by using I/R.

The Akerson technique is one method of deriving an R with or without algebra. This R is then divided into an estimate of I to obtain the property value.

Market-derived figures are always used rather than the figures on revenue, expenses, or loan terms for an individual property because the property value is not a function of the management's ability.

Two criticisms of this type of mortgage-equity analysis are that the debt-to-equity ratio remains constant through time and any requirements of debt service imposed by the lender are ignored. These issues are addressed further in Chapter 12.

REVIEW QUESTIONS

1. Why are market data used rather than figures obtained from an individual property?
2. How is the property value estimated if the loan terms are known? If the loan terms are unknown? Explain the differences.
3. Develop an Akerson R by tracing the various types of equity. Show the algebraic and nonalgebraic techniques.
4. Explain a simplified method of estimating the percentage of the mortgage balance paid off, p, at the end of the holding period.
5. How does the period in which amortization payments are made influence the calculation of the Akerson R?

ENDNOTES

1. Jeffrey D. Fisher and Anthony B. Sanders, "Capitalization Rates and Market Information," *The Appraisal Journal* 49 (April 1981): 186–198.
2. Ibid. p. 191.
3. Ibid.
4. Anthony B. Sanders and C. F. Sirmans, "A Comparison of the Ellwood and Simple Weighted-Average Overall Capitalization Rates," *The Appraisal Journal* 48 (July 1980): 432–439.
5. This example was developed in Robert Zerbst and Daniel Kohlhepp, "The Use of Equity Rates in Appraisal Theory," *Real Estate Appraiser and Analyst* 43 (May–June 1977): 26–31.
6. For further reading and detail, see Charles Akerson, "Ellwood Without Algebra," *The Appraisal Journal* 38 (July 1970): 325–335; *An Introduction to Mortgage-Equity Capitalization* (Chicago: American Institute of Real Estate Appraisers, 1970).
7. See L. W. Ellwood, *Ellwood Tables for Real Estate Appraising and Financing,* 4th ed. (Cambridge, Mass.: Ballinger Publishing Company, 1977), p. 316.
8. Ibid.
9. Ibid., p. 265.
10. Ibid.
11. For a discussion of this technique, see Henry C. Entreken, Jr., "Are We Really Seeking Market Value?" *The Appraisal Journal* 48 (July 1980): 428–431; and Kenneth Lusht and Robert Zerbst, "Valuing Income Property in an Inflationary Environment," *The Real Estate Appraiser and Analyst* 46 (July–August 1980): 11–18.

ADDITIONAL READINGS

Akerson, Charles B. *An Introduction to Mortgage-Equity Capitalization* (Chicago: American Institute of Real Estate Appraisers, 1970).

Akerson, Charles B. "Ellwood Without Algebra," *The Appraisal Journal* 39 (July 1970): 325-335.

Akerson, Charles B. "Appraisal Nomograms." *The Appraisal Journal* 40 (April 1972): 189-194.

Archer, Wayne. "Valuation Under Uncertainty: Will the Real Highest and Best Use Please Stand Up?" *Real Estate Appraiser and Analyst* 43 (May-June 1977): 32-40.

Barrett, G. Vincent. "Appraisal Should be Market Study." *The Appraisal Journal* 47 (October 1979): 538-555.

Berger, Allan. "Putting People in Their Place: The Highest and Best Use of Land." *Real Estate Appraiser and Analyst* 43 (October 1977): 45-47.

Crean, Michael J. "Are Capitalization Rates Obsolete?" *The Appraisal Journal* 49 (April 1981): 248-258.

Ellwood, L. W. *Ellwood Tables for Real Estate Appraising and Financing* (Cambridge, Mass.: Ballinger Publishing Co., 1977).

Gau, George, and Kohlhepp, Daniel. "The Estimation of Equity Yield Rates Based on Capital Market Returns." *Real Estate Appraiser and Analyst* 44 (November-December 1978): 40-46.

Jaffe, Austin, and Sirmans, C. F. "Some Myths About Real Estate." *Real Estate Review* 8 (Spring 1978): 30-42.

Miles, Mike, and Estey, Arthur. "The Relevant Required Rate of Return." *The Appraisal Journal* 47 (October 1979): 511-522.

Paulsen, John, and Sherman, Larry. "The Problem of Going Concern: The Relationship Between Cost and Income Approach." *Real Estate Appraiser and Analyst* 45 (September-October 1979): 16-18.

Sirmans, C. F., and Webb, James R. "Mortgage-Equity Analysis: Again?" *The Appraisal Journal* 47 (January 1979): 44-52.

Stehm, Robert. "Equity Dividend/Equity Yield Conversion." *Real Estate Appraiser and Analyst* 44 (March-April 1978): 23-25.

Strung, Joseph. "The Internal Rate of Return and the Reinvestment Presumptions." *The Appraisal Journal* 44 (January 1976): 23-24.

Treadwell, Donald. "Value in Use in Perspective." *The Appraisal Journal* 46 (April 1978): 223–229.

Zerbst, Robert, and Kohlhepp, Daniel. "The Use of Equity Rates in Appraisal Theory." *Real Estate Appraiser and Analyst* 43 (May–June 1977): 26–31.

CHAPTER 10

LEARNING OBJECTIVES

When a student finishes this chapter, he or she should be able to:

- Explain the market conditions in which Ellwood can be used.
- Compare the Akerson R with the Ellwood R.
- Explain the contribution of Ellwood to appraising.
- Contrast the three types of equity that may be included in the Ellwood R.
- Calculate an Ellwood R using a set of tables where appropriate.
- Compare graphically the relationships between app. or dep. and Y_E for a given R and various holding periods.

Estimate of *R* By Mortgage-Equity and Ellwood Analysis

IMPORTANT TERMS AND PHRASES

adjusted *J* factor: A figure derived within the Ellwood technique that accounts for changing levels of NOI by a linear amount.

Ellwood *G* factor: A figure derived within the Ellwood technique that accounts for changing levels of NOI at a constant rate each year.

Ellwood *J* factor: A figure derived within the Ellwood technique that accounts for changing levels of NOI at a constant amount each period.

Ellwood *R*: A rate derived from the Ellwood technique.

Ellwood technique: A type of mortgage equity analysis that is used in estimating the value of property.

equity yield analysis: A relationship between the reversionary value and the equity yield rate for the property given the level of *R*.

mortgage coefficient: A figure derived within the Ellwood technique.

This chapter is devoted entirely to the mortgage-equity analysis technique developed by L. W. Ellwood. For additional detail on the procedures discussed here, a student should refer to L. W. Ellwood, *Ellwood Tables for Real Estate Appraising and Financing, Part I* (Cambridge, Mass.: Ballinger Publishing Co., 1977).

ESTIMATING *R* WHEN THE EXACT LOAN TERMS ARE NOT KNOWN

Since the late 1950's, Ellwood's technique for estimating R has been widely used in the appraisal community for several reasons. First, it starts with an initial rate of return and adjusts it for equity buildup from mortgage reduction and a capital gain or loss. Second, it is presented in convenient equations that permit quick derivation of an R. Third, Ellwood precomputed many of the variables that can be used in the equations according to various combinations of years and interest rates to ease the computations. These figures are compiled in a book of tables.

The Ellwood technique derives exactly the same estimate of R as does the Akerson technique shown in the preceding chapter. In fact, Akerson's technique has been labeled "Ellwood without algebra"[1] because the Akerson R can be estimated without algebraic techniques, whereas the Ellwood R must be found by using his equations. Appendix A contains a proof that the two R's are identical. Both techniques derive capitalization rates that are *weighted average rates* since the loan to value ratios in both do not change over time for one specific property.

The Ellwood estimate of R is derived under the same conditions as the Akerson estimate of R. Typically, the exact loan terms are unknown. The estimate of V is computed by deriving a composite R and dividing it into a stabilized estimate of net operating income, I. Estimates of I and stabilizing procedures are shown in Chapter 8.

Several authors have recently criticized the Ellwood technique by arguing that it does not correctly estimate the debt capacity of the lender and the equity investor, and it omits the lender's debt service coverage ratio. Several of these models are shown in Chapter 12.

DERIVATION OF THE ELLWOOD TECHNIQUE

The Ellwood technique can be derived by referring to the basic assumption that the value of property that has outstanding financing can be estimated by[2]

$$V = V_M + V_E \tag{10–1}$$

where

V_M = present value of the mortgage position (mortgage principal),

V_E = present value of the equity position.

Ellwood defined the present value of the equity,

$$V_E = \sum_{i=1}^{p} \frac{I_s - \text{VMR}_M}{(1 + Y_E)^i} + \frac{V(1 + \text{app.}) - \text{VM}(1 - P)}{(1 + Y_E)^p} \tag{10–2}$$

where

p = expected holding period,
I_s = stabilized NOI,
M = loan-to-value ratio,
P = proportion of loan paid off at the end of p,
Y_E = equity yield rate,
$(1 - P)$ = portion of loan *not* paid off at the end of p,
VM = loan size,
VM$(1 - P)$ = balance of loan due at time of sale,
$V(1 + \text{app.})$ = expected selling price, assuming appreciation.

Substituting equation (10–2) into (10–1) and solving for V produces the result shown in Appendix B.

$$V = \frac{I_s}{Y_E - M(Y_E) + M(R_M) - MP\left(\frac{1}{S_{\overline{p}|Y_E}}\right) - \text{app.}\left(\frac{1}{S_{\overline{p}|Y_E}}\right)}$$

Rewriting, one obtains

$$V = \frac{I_s}{Y_E - M\left(Y_E + P\frac{1}{S_{\overline{p}|Y_E}} - R_M\right) - \text{app.}\left(\frac{1}{S_{\overline{p}|Y_E}}\right)}$$

or

$$\text{V} = \frac{I_s}{Y_E - \text{MC} - \text{app.}\frac{1}{S_{\overline{p}|Y_E}}} \tag{10–3}$$

where

$$V = \frac{I_s}{\text{Ellwood } R}$$

where

C is defined as the mortgage coefficient,

$$C = Y_E + P\left(\frac{1}{S_{\overline{p}|Y_E}}\right) - R_M.$$

If the property is expected to decline in value through time, equation (10–2) is changed to

$$V_E = \sum_{i=1}^{p} \frac{I_s - \text{VMR}_M}{(1 + Y_E)^i} + \frac{V(1 - \text{dep.}) - \text{VM}(1 - P)}{(1 + Y_E)^p}$$

where

$V(1 - \text{dep.})$ = expected selling price, assuming depreciation.

Equation 10–3 changes to

$$\text{V} = \frac{I_s}{Y_E - \text{MC} + \text{dep.}\dfrac{1}{S_{\overline{p}|Y_E}}}.$$

The denominator shows that the Ellwood technique starts with the equity yield rate, Y_E, and adjusts it for equity buildup and appreciation (or capital loss). By rewriting the denominator, one can find the overall R

$$R = Y_E - M\left(Y_E - R_M + P\frac{1}{S_{\overline{p}|Y_E}}\right) - \text{app.}\left(\frac{1}{S_{\overline{p}|Y_E}}\right) \text{or dep.}\left(\frac{1}{S_{\overline{p}|Y_E}}\right).$$

The estimates for app. or dep. are percentages of capital gain or loss in the reversion (resale value). For convenience, the result of,

$$\left(Y_E - R_M + P\frac{1}{S_{\overline{p}|Y_E}}\right)$$

is called the *mortgage coefficient, C,* and is rewritten into

$$C = \left(Y_E + P\frac{1}{S_{\overline{p}|Y_E}} - R_M\right).$$

Several methods[3] can be used for estimating P. One method used in the preceding chapter was:

$$P = \frac{R_M \text{ for the mortgage} - i}{R_M \text{ for the mortgage} - i \text{ for the holding period}}.$$

Ellwood used another formula,

$$P = (R_M/i - 1)(S_P - 1)$$

where

R_M = annual constant (12 × monthly installment to amortize \$1, 4 × quarterly installment to amortize \$1, 2 × semi-annual installment to amortize \$1),

i = nominal annual interest rate on the mortgage loan (12 × effective monthly interest rate, 4 × effective quarterly interest rate, 2 × effective semi-annual interest rate),

S_P = amount to which \$1 will grow with interest at the effective rate during the hold period, p.

Both methods of estimating P will produce similar answers.

An Illustration

The data from the problems in the preceding chapter can be used to illustrate the Ellwood technique.

- First mortgage is \$500,000 at 10.5% interest for twenty-five years and payments are made *annually* at the end of each year.
- Downpayment is \$100,000 at 11% return.
- The investor-owner is expected to hold the property for ten years.
- The property value is expected to have increased by 50% upon resale.

$$R = Y_E - \text{MC} - \text{app.}\frac{1}{S_{\overline{p}|Y_E}}$$

where

$$C = Y_E + P\frac{1}{S_{\overline{p}|Y_E}} - R_M$$

and

$$P = \frac{R_M \text{ for the mortgage} - \text{i}}{R_M \text{ for the mortgage for the holding period} - \text{i}}.$$

Solve for P:

$$P = \frac{.113302 - .105}{.161922 - .105}$$

$$P = .1458487.$$

Solve for C:

$$C = .110 + .1458487\ (.059801) - .113302$$

$$C = .110 + .0087218 - .113302$$

$$C = .1187218 - .113302$$

$C = .0054198$. (Similar to the value found on page 361 of the Ellwood tables.)

Solve for app. $\frac{1}{S_{\overline{p|}Y_E}}$:

$$\text{app.}\frac{1}{S_{\overline{p|}Y_E}} = .50\ (.059801)$$

$$= .0299005.$$

Now, solve for R:

$$R = .11 - .833333\ (.0054198) - .0299005$$

$$R = .11 - .0045164 - .0299005$$

$$R = .11 - .0344169$$

$$R = .0755831 \text{ or } 7.6\%.$$

MONTHLY AMORTIZATION

When the *amortization* schedule changes from annual to another period such as monthly, the Ellwood technique remains the same, but different R_M factors are inserted. For convenience, Ellwood precomputed these factors and included them in Part II of his book.[4] Amortization periods and corresponding factors are shown for monthly, quarterly, semi-annual, and annual payments on the loan at various interest rates. Only the use of *monthly* amortization factors is illustrated here. The student could test his or her mastery of the tables and the Ellwood procedure by working the problem shown in this chapter with the other amortization periods.

Consider the foregoing problem with all data the same except that the amortization payments on the mortgage are *monthly* rather than *annual.*

- First mortgage is \$500,000 at 10.5% interest for twenty-five years and the amortization payments are made *monthly* at the end of each month.
- Downpayment is \$100,000 at 11% return.
- The investor-owner is expected to hold the property for ten years.
- The property value is expected to have increased by 50% upon resale.

$$R = Y_E - \text{MC} - \text{app.}\frac{1}{S_{\overline{p|}Y_E}}$$

where

$$C = Y_E + P\frac{1}{S_{\overline{p|}Y_E}} - (\text{monthly } R_M \text{ for the mortgage} \times 12)$$

and

$$P = \frac{\text{monthly } R_M \text{ for the mortgage} \times 12 - i}{\text{monthly } R_M \text{ for the mortgage} \times 12 - i \text{ for the holding period}}.$$

All R_M factors are read from the monthly tables for the appropriate number of years and interest rate. The factor read from the table is "annualized" by multiplying the result by 12. If the payments on the mortgage were quarterly, this R_M factor would be read from the quarterly table and the result multiplied by 4. For a semi-annual payment the factor would be multiplied by 2. Otherwise, the problem is worked exactly the same as in the preceding example.

Solve for P:

$$P = \frac{.009441 \times 12 - .105}{.013493 \times 12 - .105}$$

$$P = \frac{.113292 - .105}{.161916 - .105}$$

$$P = \frac{.008292}{.056916}$$

$$P = .1456883.$$

Solve for C:

$$C = .110 + .1456883\ (.059801) - .113292$$

$$C = .110 + .0087123 - .113292$$

$$C = .1187123 - .113292$$

$$C = .0054203.$$

Solve for app. $\dfrac{1}{S_{\overline{p|}Y_E}}$:

Solution derived before was .0299005.

Solve for R:

$$R = .11 - .8333\ (.0054203) - .0299005$$

$$R = .11 - .0045167 - .0299005$$

$$R = .11 - .0344172$$

$$R = .0755828 \text{ or } 7.6\%.$$

TWO OR MORE MORTGAGES

The influence of two or more mortgages on the magnitude of R may be estimated by

$$R = Y_E - M_1C_1 - M_2C_2 - \ . \ . \ . \ M_iC_i \begin{matrix} + \text{ dep} \\ - \text{ app} \end{matrix} \left(\frac{1}{S_{\overline{p|}Y_E}}\right)$$

where

M_1 = loan to value ratio for mortgage 1,

M_2 = loan to value ratio for mortgage 2,

C_1 = mortgage coefficient for mortgage 1,
C_2 = mortgage coefficient for mortgage 2,
M_iC_i = figures for mortgages i.

Consider the same problem worked earlier:

- First mortgage is \$500,000 at 10.5% for twenty-five years and payments are made monthly at the end of each month.
- Downpayment is \$100,000 at 11%.
- The typical owner-investor expects to hold the property for ten years.
- The property is expected to increase in value by 50 percent upon resale.
- Estimate of R was .0755828.
- Now change the first mortgage to \$400,000 at 10.5% for twenty-five years with payments made monthly at the end of each month, and add a second mortgage for \$100,000 at 10.75% for ten years with payments made monthly at the end of each month. The overall R would be derived as follows:

$$R = Y_E - M_1C_1 - M_2C_2 - \; . \; . \; . \; M_iC_i \begin{matrix} + \text{ dep} \\ - \text{ app} \end{matrix} \left(\frac{1}{S_{\overline{p}|Y_E}} \right)$$

$$R = .11 - .666666\ (.005424) - .166667\ (.006199) - .50\ (.059801)$$

$$R = .11 - .0345495$$

$$R = .0754505.$$

A GRAPHICAL ANALYSIS COMPARING Y_E TO app. OR dep.

A graphical analysis showing the interaction of Y_E and app. and dep. given a predetermined R can be very useful in judging the accuracy of the appraisal. The procedure for calculating and graphing the yield analysis is shown here.

The yield ranges are calculated for the one R that has been estimated. Various levels of Y_E values and holding periods are inserted into the familiar Ellwood equation and solved for app. and dep. The results are then graphed. In this manner, the appraiser can view the influence of app. and dep. upon Y_E and the property value for various holding periods and a given R.

The Equations

The Ellwood R equals the following:

$$R = Y_E - \text{MC} - \text{app.} \frac{1}{S_{\overline{p}|Y_E}}$$

or,

$$R = Y_E - \text{MC} + \text{dep.} \frac{1}{S_{\overline{p}|Y_E}}.$$

These two may be rewritten as

$$\text{app.} = \frac{r - R}{\frac{1}{S_{\overline{p|}Y_E}}} \text{ or } \frac{Y_E - \text{MC} - R}{\frac{1}{S_{\overline{p|}Y_E}}}$$

$$\text{dep.} = \frac{R - r}{\frac{1}{S_{\overline{p|}Y_E}}} \text{ or } \frac{R - (Y_E - \text{MC})}{\frac{1}{S_{\overline{p|}Y_E}}}.$$

Difference between app. and dep.

The only difference between app. or dep. in the two preceding formulas is the numerator. The numerator for app. is $(r - R)$ and the numerator for dep. is $(R - r)$. *If* R *is greater than* r, *the result will be dep.; if* r *is greater than* R, *the result will be app.*

Consequently, the appraiser simply calculates R and r, determines which is the larger, and labels the result app. or dep. The last step is to divide the numerator by the appropriate sinking fund factor to calculate the estimate of the app. or dep.

Question to be Answered

The question that the appraiser wants to answer is:

> *Given* R, *what is the amount of* (app. or dep.) *in the reversion that the property will have to experience at any time during the next* (number) *years to give an equity yield rate of* (amount) *percent?*

Typically, this question is answered several times using various combinations of Y_E and years. In this manner, various market conditions can be simulated.

An Example

Consider the example worked in earlier sections.

- First mortgage is $500,000 at 10.5% for twenty-five years and payments are made *monthly* at the end of each month.
- Downpayment is $100,000 at 11.0%.
- The typical owner-investor expects to hold the property for ten years.
- The property is expected to increase in value by 50% upon resale.
- Estimate of R was .0755828.

First, try $Y_E = .09$ for $p = 5$ years. Calculate $r = Y_E - \text{MC}$, where

$r = .09 - (.833333)\ \text{C},$
$C = -.014221$ from *Ellwood Tables,* page 361 for $Y_E = .09$, $p = 5$ years, and $i = .105$. When $Y_E < i$, the effect of C on r is positive. Thus, the sign is changed to a minus which changes $r = Y_E - \text{MC}$ to $r = Y_E + \text{MC}$. (See Ellwood Tables, p.80.)

Then

$$r = .09 + (.833333)\ (.014221)$$
$$r = .09 + .0118508$$
$$r = .1018508.$$

Compare r to R:

$$\begin{matrix} r & & R \\ .1018508 & > & .0755828. \end{matrix}$$

Therefore the result is labeled *app.*

Calculate the amount of app. by dividing by the appropriate sinking fund factor,

$$\frac{1}{S_{\overline{5|}.09}} = .167092$$

$$\text{app.} = \frac{r - R}{\dfrac{1}{S_{\overline{5|}.09}}}$$

$$\text{app.} = \frac{.1018508 - .0755828}{.167092}$$

$$\text{app.} = \frac{.026268}{.167092}$$

$$\text{app.} = .1572068 \text{ or } 15.7\%.$$

The appraiser may say: Given $R = .0755828$, the reversionary value of the property being appraised will have to *increase* by *15.7%* over the next five years to give a Y_E of *.09* percent.

Tabular form For convenience, these calculations may be placed in a table. Exhibit 10.1 shows the calculation of app. and several additional combinations of Y_E and various holding periods, p.

For ease in interpretation, these results can be graphed. Figure 10.1 shows the graphical analysis of the yields in Exhibit 10.1. For the R of .0755828, the property would have to appreciate by approximately 15.7% at any time within

Exhibit 10.1
Equity yield analysis (R = .0755828 and p = 5 years)

Y_E	C*	R	$Y_E - (.833333)C =$ r	R-r or r-R		$\frac{1}{S_{\overline{5}\rceil Y_E}}$		app. or dep.
.09	−.014221	.0755828 <	.1018508	.026268	÷	.167092	=	.1572068 app.
.10	−.004402	.0755828 <	.1036683	.0280855	÷	.163797	=	.1714652 app.
.12	.015246	.0755828 <	.1072951	.0317123	÷	.157409	=	.2014643 app.
.13	.025076	.0755828 <	.1090134	.0335206	÷	.154314	=	.2172233 app.

R = .0755828 and p = 10 years

Y_E	C*	R	$Y_E - (.833333)C =$ r	R-r or r-R		$\frac{1}{S_{\overline{10}\rceil Y_E}}$		app. or dep.
.09	−.013686	.0755828 <	.1014049	.0258221	÷	.065820	=	.3923138 app.
.10	−.004140	.0755828 <	.1034499	.0278671	÷	.062745	=	.4441326 app.
.12	.015009	.0755828 <	.1074926	.0319098	÷	.056984	=	.5599782 app.
.13	.024611	.0755828 <	.1094909	.0339081	÷	.054289	=	.624585 app.

*All values for C were taken from the *Ellwood Tables*. When $Y_E < i$, the effect of C on r is positive. Thus, the sign is changed to a minus which changes $r = Y_E - MC$ to $r = Y_E + MC$. See *Ellwood Tables*, p. 80.

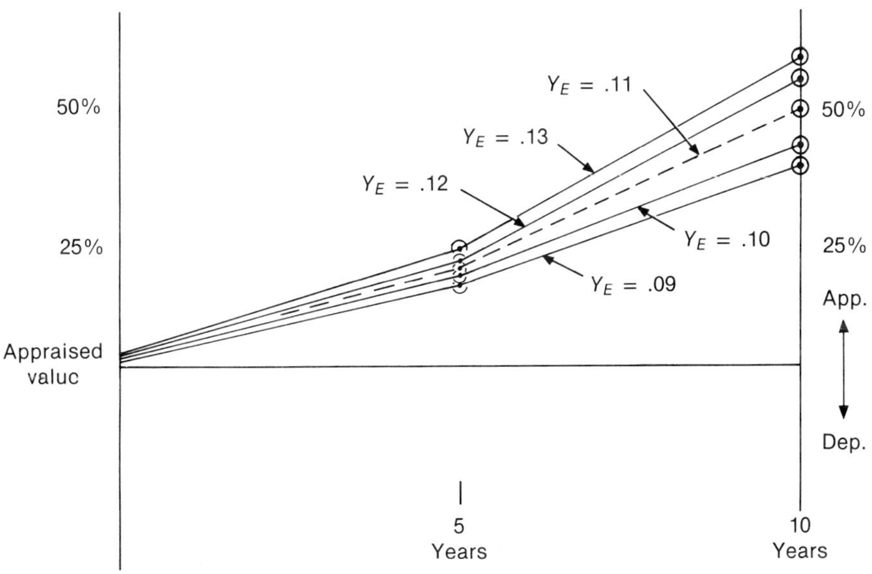

Fig. 10.1 Graphic analysis of equity yields

the next five years to give an equity yield rate of 9%. This property would have to increase by approximately 39.2% within the next ten years to give the same 9% equity yield rate. To give a Y_E of 13% in five years, the property would have to increase approximately 21.7%; a Y_E of 13% within ten years would require an appreciation of approximately 62.5%. The dotted line illustrates the assumptions used in appraising the subject property.

MORTGAGE COEFFICIENT *C* WITH A DISCOUNTED MORTGAGE

Sometimes the borrower may receive a mortgage where the interest is taken out in advance.[5] In this case, amortization and interest payments are computed and paid on the face amount of the loan, which is more money than the borrower received. This discounting has three effects: the effective mortgage interest rate is increased, the ratio of the loan to the property value, M, is lowered, and the equity buildup through amortization is decreased.

The definition of the mortgage coefficient, C, changes to

$$C = Y_E - \frac{R_M - \frac{1}{S_{\overline{p}|Y_E}}(P - k)}{(1 - k)}$$

where

k = the mortgage discount,

R_M = mortgage constant when no discount exists,

P = proportion of the mortgage paid-off when no discount exists.

The definition of the loan-to-value ratio, M, changes to adjusted $M = (1 - k)M$. Once these adjustments are made to the definitions of C and M, the overall rate, R, is computed the same as the preceding, using these new terms.

Consider the illustration shown earlier in this chapter. Using the same data with a mortgage discount of 18%, the value of C changes to

$$C = Y_E - \frac{R_M - \frac{1}{S_{\overline{p}|Y_E}}(P - k)}{(1 - k)}$$

$$C = .11 - \frac{.113302 - (.059801)(.1458487 - .18)}{(1 - .18)}$$

$$C = .11 - \frac{.113302 + .0020422}{.82}$$

$$C = .11 - .1406636$$

$$C = -.0306636.$$

ELLWOOD J FACTOR AND RECENT DEVELOPMENTS

Ellwood recognized that the actual, initial level of NOI may increase or decrease by a constant amount each period. To account for either case, he incorporated into his analysis the J factor.[6] The overall R with a J factor is found by

$$R = \frac{r \begin{smallmatrix} + \text{dep} \\ - \text{app} \end{smallmatrix} \left(\frac{1}{S_{\overline{p}|Y_E}} \right)}{1 \begin{smallmatrix} - \text{dep} \\ + \text{app} \end{smallmatrix} J}$$

where

$$J = \frac{1}{S_{\overline{p}|Y_E}} \left(\frac{p}{1 - V^p} - \frac{1}{Y_E} \right)$$

where

V^p = reversion factor (present worth of $1 collected in the future for p years at Y_E rate).

Consider the following example[7]:

- The NOI for the property in the previous year is $10,000 and is expected to increase by 20% over the holding period.
- The property value is expected to increase by 20% over the holding period.
- The expected holding period is five years.
- The property has a first mortgage at 75% of the value with an interest rate of 10% amortized with monthly payments over a twenty-year period.
- The expected return on the equity is 20%.

What is the overall rate, R, using the Ellwood technique?

$$r = Y_E - M(Y_E + P\left(\frac{1}{S_{\overline{p}|Y_E}} \right) - R_M)$$

$$r = .20 - .75(.20 + .10198\ (.13438) - .11580)$$

$$r = .12657$$

and

$$R = \frac{r - \text{app}\left(\frac{1}{S_{\overline{p}|Y_E}} \right)}{1 + \text{app}\ J}$$

$$R = \frac{.12657 - .20\ (.13438)}{1 + .20\ (.45145)}$$

where

$$\text{Ellwood } J = \frac{1}{S_{\overline{p}|Y_E}}\left(\frac{p}{1 - V^p} - \frac{1}{Y_E}\right)$$

$$J = .13438\left(\frac{5}{1 - .401878} - \frac{1}{.20}\right)$$

$$J = .45145$$

and

$$R = .09144.$$

Adjusted *J* and *G* Factors

Jeffrey Fisher developed an adjusted J factor[8] to give exact answers for a linear increase or decrease in income estimates. Also, Fisher developed a G factor that allows income to change at a constant rate rather than a constant amount. A discussion of each follows.

Adjusted *J* factor This J factor assumes a linear increase or decrease in NOI over the holding period.

$$R = \frac{r - \text{app}\left(\dfrac{1}{S_{\overline{p}|Y_E}}\right)}{1 + \text{app}.\ J}$$

where

$$\text{adjusted } J = \frac{1}{p} + \frac{\left(1 - p\dfrac{1}{S_{\overline{p}|Y_E}}\right)}{pY_E}$$

Consider the example above:

$$\text{adjusted } J = \frac{1}{p} + \frac{1 - p\left(\dfrac{1}{S_{\overline{p}|Y_E}}\right)}{pY_E}$$

$$\text{adjusted } J = \frac{1}{5} + \frac{1 - 5\,(.13438)}{5(.20)}$$

$$\text{adjusted } J = .5281$$

and

$$R = \frac{.12657 - .20\,(.13438)}{1 + .20\,(.5281)}$$

$$R = .09017.$$

The value of the property is,

$$V = \frac{\text{NOI}}{R}$$

$$V = \frac{\$10{,}000}{.09017}$$

$$V = \$110{,}901.$$

G factor The G factor[9] can be used when the level of NOI increases or decreases at a constant rate each year.

$$R = \frac{r - \text{app}\left(\dfrac{1}{S_{\overline{p}|Y_E}}\right)}{G}$$

where

$$G = \frac{1 - \left(\dfrac{1 + g}{1 + Y_E}\right)^p}{Y_E + g} \times \frac{(1 + g)}{a_{\overline{p}|Y_E}},$$

and

G = factor for an income stream increasing or decreasing at a growth rate, g,

g = compound annual growth rate,

$a_{\overline{p}|Y_E}$ = present value of an annuity for p years at the equity yield rate, Y_E.

Consider the following example for a subject property[10]:

r = .12657,

app. = the property appreciation of 20% over five years,

g = the increase in the income stream of 4% annually,

Y_E = expected equity yield rate of 20%,

$\dfrac{1}{S_{\overline{p}|Y_E}}$ = sinking fund factor at 20% for five years,

$a_{\overline{p}|Y_E}$ = present value of an annuity for five years at 20%,

p = holding period of five years.

$$G = \frac{1 - \left(\frac{1+g}{1+Y_E}\right)^p}{Y_E - g} \times \frac{(1+g)}{a_{\overline{p}|Y_E}}$$

$$G = \frac{1 - \left(\frac{1+.04}{1+.20}\right)^5}{.20 - .04} \times \frac{(1+.04)}{2.990612}$$

$$G = 3.1941031 \times .3477549$$

$$G = 1.110765.$$

Then

$$R = \frac{\text{r} - \text{app.}\left(\frac{1}{S_{\overline{p}|Y_E}}\right)}{G}$$

$$R = \frac{.12657 - .20\,(.13438)}{1.110765}$$

$$R = .08975.$$

Prepayment Penalties and Selling Expenses

Two authors[11] argued that the Ellwood technique ignored prepayment penalties and selling expenses. Because of these omissions, they argued that the traditional overall rate, *R*, found by the Ellwood technique is too low and results in a higher valuation of the property.

They correct for these omissions by inserting two additional factors as follows:

$$R = Y_E - \text{MC} - \text{app}\left(\frac{1}{S_{\overline{p}|Y_E}}\right) + \pi M(1-P)\left(\frac{1}{S_{\overline{p}|Y_E}}\right) + \beta(1+\text{app.})\left(\frac{1}{S_{\overline{p}|Y_E}}\right)$$

where

π = prepayment penalty as a proportion of unpaid balance,

β = selling expenses as a proportion of the selling price.

The inclusion of these extra two variables will make the Ellwood *R* higher and the resulting value of the property lower. Consider the following example:

- Stablized NOI is \$132,998.
- Equity yield rate is 25%.
- The loan to value ratio is 80%.
- The mortgage rate is 11.25% over twenty-five years with monthly amortization.
- The property is expected to increase by 35% over the expected holding period of five years.

The following values have been computed or taken from a table:

$$P = \frac{R_M - i}{R_{M_p} - i} = \frac{.009982 \times 12 - .1125}{.021867 \times 12 - .1125} = \frac{.007284}{.149904} = .048591$$

$$C = Y_E + P\frac{1}{S_{\overline{5}|.25}} - R_M \times 12 = .25 + (.048591)\,(.121847) - .119784$$

$$C = .1361366$$

$$\beta = .05$$

$$\pi = 0.$$

Find the overall rate, R, and the resulting value, V:

$$R = .25 - .8(.1361366) - .35(.121847) + .05(1 + .35)\,(.121847)$$

$$R = .25 - .1089092 - .0426464 + .0082246$$

$$R = .106669$$

and

$$V = \frac{\$132{,}998}{.10669}$$

$$V = \$1{,}246{,}584$$

CRITICISMS OF THE ELLWOOD *R*

Much discussion has been conducted during recent years on the proper R to use in appraisal problems. One trend has been to use an estimate of the internal rate of return (equity yield rate, Y_E) instead of an Ellwood R.[12] Perhaps one of the most convincing arguments for using this rate to value property is the fact that it is used widely in the finance and security markets to value financial interests and instruments. A legitimate question is why the real estate appraisal community insists on using their own unique terminology and techniques rather than the terms and tools already tested and applied in financial circles.

Another argument has been presented for using discounted cash flow analysis including an internal rate of return to value property. This technique is shown in equation (7–2) and is discussed in Chapters 8 and 12.

Perhaps the biggest criticism to Ellwood has appeared in recent years through the development of appraisal models, which include the assumption that the debt and equity funds loaned to the property are a function of the operating income and debt service coverage ratio. These authors contend that Ellwood assumed in his model that lenders and equity investors would loan and invest, respectively, unlimited amounts determined by the loan-to-value proportion of the market value. But in an inflationary economy, the reversion equity may be growing faster and contributing more to the market value of the property than the net operating income. Thus the resulting income stream may not be sufficiently large to pay the debt service. These models are discussed in Chapter 12.

The purpose of this text is to cover adequately the important contemporary techniques for valuing property, but not to emphasize any certain one. Consequently, all are discussed and the user can apply whichever procedure coincides with his or her training and needs.

PROBLEMS

Question: Refer to the townhouse assignment discussed on page 225 of Chapter 9. The Akerson R calculated with and without algebra is equal to .0827615. For drill, calculate an Ellwood R for the same case and verify that the two approaches give the same result.

Answer:

$$R = Y_E - \text{MC} - \text{app}\frac{1}{S_{\overline{p|}\,Y_E}}.$$

Solve for C:

$$C = Y_E + P\frac{1}{S_{\overline{p|}\,Y_E}} - R_M.$$

Solve for P:

$$P = \frac{R_M \text{ for the mortgage} \times 12 - i}{\begin{array}{c}R_M \text{ for the mortgage} \\ \text{for the } p \qquad \times 12 - i\end{array}}$$

$$P = \frac{.009650 \times 12 - .10}{.016601 \times 12 - .10}$$

$$P = \frac{.1158 - .10}{.199212 - .10}$$

$$P = .1592549.$$

Solve for C:

$$C = .14 + .1592549\ (.093192) - .1158$$
$$C = .14 + .0148412 - .1158$$
$$C = .1548412 - .1158$$
$$C = .0390412.$$

Solve for R:

$$R = .14 - .75\ (.0390412) - .30\ (.093192)$$
$$R = .14 - .0292809 - .0279576$$
$$R = .14 - .0572385$$
$$R = .0827615 \text{ or } 8.28\%.$$

Question: An appraiser is given an assignment to estimate the market value of a four-unit office building in a southern city. Five comparable properties are located to provide data for interpreting the market trends. A typical L/V ratio for this type of property is 62% at 11% with equal monthly payments over twenty years. Resales of the comparables and conversations with other local appraisers indicate that the equity yield rate is about 15%. Also, the resales of the comparables show that these properties are held about fourteen years. Resales of the comparables and strong market demand for office space can be interpreted into a 40% increase in the reversion.

Calculate an Ellwood R for this property. Do a graphic analysis of the equity yield rates equal to .12, .15, and .18 for holding periods of ten and fifteen years and discuss the results.

Answer:

$$R = Y_E - \text{MC} - \text{app.}\frac{1}{S_{\overline{p|}\,Y_E}}.$$

Solve for C:

$$C = Y_E + P\frac{1}{S_{\overline{p|}\,Y_E}} - R_M.$$

Solve for P:

$$P = \frac{R_M \text{ for the mortgage} \times 12 - i}{\begin{array}{c}R_M \text{ for the mortgage} \\ \text{for the } p \quad \times 12 - i\end{array}}$$

$$P = \frac{.010321 \times 12 - .11}{.011690 \times 12 - .11}$$

$$P = \frac{.123852 - .11}{.14028 - .11}$$

$$P = \frac{.013852}{.03028}$$

$$P = .4574636.$$

Solve for C:

$$C = .15 + .4574636\ (.024688) - .123852$$
$$C = .15 + .0112938 - .123852$$
$$C = .1612938 - .123852$$
$$C = .0374418.$$

Solve for R:

$$R = .15 - .62\ (.0374418) - .40\ (.024688)$$
$$R = .15 - .0232139 - .0098752$$
$$R = .15 - .0330891$$
$$R = .1169109.$$

Exhibit 10.2 and Figure 10.2 show the tabular and graphical analysis, respectively.

Exhibit 10.2
Equity-yield analysis (R = .1169109 and p = 10 years)

Y_E	C	R	$Y_E - (.62)C =$ r	R-r or r-R	$\frac{1}{S_{\overline{10}\rceil Y_E}}$	app. or dep.
.12	.010425	.1169109 >	.1135365	.0033744 ÷	.056984 =	.0592166 dep.
.15	.038473	.1169109 <	.1261468	.0092359 ÷	.049252 =	.1875233 app.
.18	.066772	.1169109 <	.1386014	.0216905 ÷	.042514 =	.5101966 app.

R = .1169109 and p = 15 years

Y_E	C	R	$Y_E - (.62)C =$ r	R-r or r-R	$\frac{1}{S_{\overline{15}\rceil Y_E}}$	app. or dep.
.12	.010228	.1169109 >	.1136587	.0032522 ÷	.026824 =	.1212421 dep.
.15	.037157	.1169109 <	.1269627	.0100518 ÷	.021017 =	.4782699 app.
.18	.064716	.1169109 <	.1398761	.0229652 ÷	.016402 =	1.4001463 app.

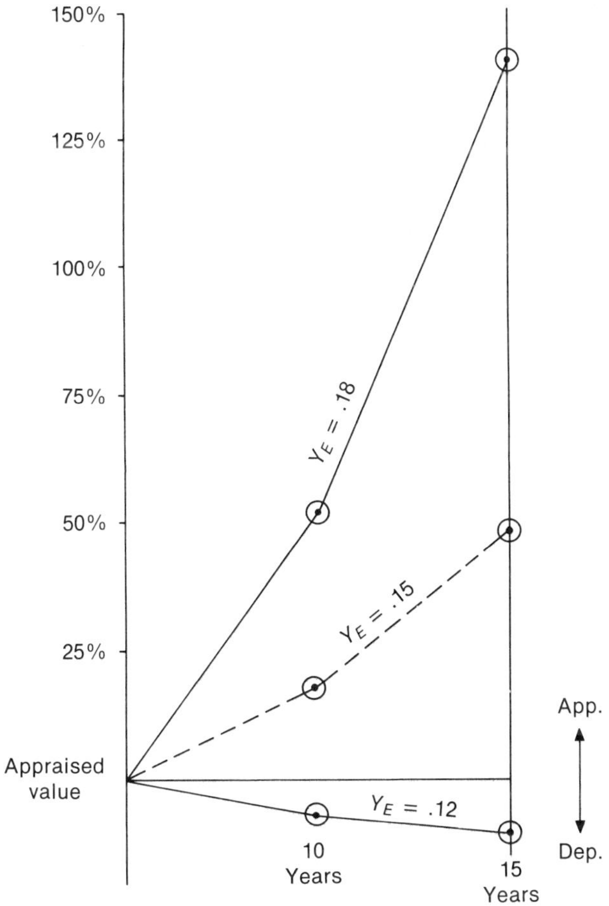

Fig. 10.2 Graphical analysis of equity yield.

SUMMARY

The Ellwood technique is a method of estimating *R* by starting with an equity yield rate, Y_E, and adjusting it for equity buildup through mortgage reduction and a capital gain (or loss). The technique is presented in a small number of equations that can be used with a set of tables that include some precomputed factors.

The Ellwood *R* can be shown to be equal to the Akerson *R*. Ellwood can be derived by algebraic equations. Akerson can be derived with or without algebraic equations.

The Ellwood technique uses mortgage constants that are determined according to the amortization schedule on the loan. If the payments are monthly, quarterly, or semi-annual, they are annualized.

For a given R, the level of app. or dep. that must occur over a holding period to achieve a predetermined level of Y_E can be computed. A graphic analysis of the Y_E and app. or dep. over the holding period is very useful in interpreting the market.

Critics of the Ellwood approach argue that it omits factors such as prepayment and selling expenses. Other researchers argue that the lender's loan and debt servicing requirements are ignored.

REVIEW QUESTIONS

1. Under what market conditions is the Ellwood technique typically used?
2. Derive the Ellwood technique, starting with the basic assumption about the value of income-producing property that has been financed.
3. Explain in your own words the Ellwood technique's contribution to appraising.
4. Define and explain the meaning of each of the following.

R	C	k
Y_E	P	J
r	R_M	adjusted J
M	$\frac{1}{S_{\overline{p}\rceil Y_E}}$	G

5. What is the difference between the mortgage constant, R_M, and the mortgage coefficient, C?
6. How does a discounted mortgage influence the magnitude of C and M?
7. What three types of equity are included in the Ellwood R?
8. What adjustments are made in the Ellwood technique when the amortization schedule is changed from monthly payments to quarterly? Semiannual?
9. How do the Akerson R and the Ellwood R compare in magnitude?
10. Can the relationship between the app. or dep. and Y_E be shown graphically for a given R and p? How? Why?

ENDNOTES

1. See Charles Akerson, "Ellwood Without Algebra," *The Appraisal Journal* 39 (July 1970): 325–335.
2. Peter Colwell and Phillip Rushing, "To Ellwood and Beyond," *The Appraisal Journal* 47 (July 1979): 352–358.

3. See Stephen D. Messner and Byrl Boyce, "Calculation of Amortization Schedule and Mortgage Balance," *The Appraisal Journal* 40 (January 1972): 76–82.
4. L. W. Ellwood, *Ellwood Tables for Real Estate Appraising and Financing* (Cambridge, Mass.: Ballinger Publishing Co., 1977), Part II.
5. Ibid., pp. 101–103.
6. Ibid., p. 93.
7. Jeffrey D. Fisher, "Ellwood *J* Factors: A Further Refinement," *The Appraisal Journal* 47 (January 1979): 65–75; see also James Mason, *Financial Tables* (Chicago: AIREA, 1981).
8. Ibid., p. 68.
9. Ibid., p. 71.
10. Ibid., p. 73.
11. Colwell and Rushing, "To Ellwood and Beyond."
12. See McCloud B. Hodges, Jr., *Annotated Bibliography for Modernization in Valuation of Investment Classed Real Estate,* unpublished bibliography, Arlington, Virginia, 1980.

ADDITIONAL READINGS

Bradley, David M. "Ellwood Through Algebra—New Horizons." *The Appraisal Journal* 44 (January 1976): 98–110.

Cannaday, Roger E., and Colwell, Peter F. "A Unified Field Theory of the Income Approach to Appraisal—Part I." *The Real Estate Appraiser and Analyst* 47 (First Quarter, 1981): 5–9.

Coulter, William H. "A Current and Objective Equity Yield Rate." *The Appraisal Journal* 45 (January 1977): 16–24.

Crean, Michael J. "Are Capitalization Rates Obsolete?" *The Appraisal Journal* 49 (April 1981): 248–258.

Ellwood, L. W. "All Rights to Future Benefits." *The Appraisal Journal* 42 (January 1974): 38–43.

Ellwood, L. W. "Selection of Capitalization Rates in Today's Market." *The Appraisal Journal* 45 (July 1977): 325–330.

Fisher, Jeffrey. "Ellwood After Taxes." *The Appraisal Journal* 45 (July 1977): 331–342.

Fisher, Jeffrey, and Sanders, Anthony B. "Capitalization Rates and Market Information." *The Appraisal Journal* 49 (April 1981): 186–189.

Gibbons, James E. "A Second Look." *The Appraisal Journal* 46 (July 1978): 331–339.

Howcroft, Paul A. "A Review of Appraisal Practices and Methods of Analysis." *The Appraisal Journal* 46 (July 1978): 419–423.

Johnson, Irvin. *The Instant Mortgage-Equity Technique* (Lexington, Mass.: Lexington Books, 1972).

Kinnard, William. "Counseling Investor-Clients Through Mortgage-Equity Analysis." *The Appraisal Journal* 40 (July 1972): 356–368.

Lusht, Kenneth. "Financing Risk, Value, and Capitalization Rates." *The Appraisal Journal* 45 (October 1977): 601-612.

Nelson, Roland D., and Allen, Laurence G. "Market Testing of Ellwood." *The Appraisal Journal* 44 (April 1976): 262-269.

Nelson, Roland D., and Allen, Laurence G. "Market Testing of Ellwood: Part 2." *The Appraisal Journal* 45 (January 1977): 59-65.

Raleigh, James C. "The Ellwood System—Simplified Applications." *The Appraisal Journal* 39 (July 1971): 422-429.

Raleigh, James C. "Ellwood Converts Income into Market Value." *The Appraisal Journal* 41 (April 1973): 264-268.

Ramsland, Maxwell O. "Ellwood: A Practitioner's Observations." *The Appraisal Journal* 39 (July 1971): 430-437.

Steele, Robert. "Application of Equity Yield Analyses in Appraisal Reports." *The Appraisal Journal* 43 (April 1975): 194-201.

Steele, Robert A. "The *J* Factor: A Valuable Ellwood Legacy." *The Appraisal Journal* 46 (October 1978): 581-587.

Wendt, Paul. "Ellwood, Inwood, and the Internal Rate of Return." *The Appraisal Journal* 35 (October 1967): 561-600.

Wiley, Tom. "Equity Risk Analysis by Ellwood Graph Technique." *The Appraisal Journal* 45 (October 1977): 541-549.

Zartolas, George. "Graphic Analysis: The Easy Way." *Real Estate Appraiser and Analyst* 45 (September-October 1979): 31-35.

Zerbst, Robert, and Kohlhepp, Daniel. "The Use of Equity Rates in Appraisal Theory." *Real Estate Appraiser and Analyst* 43 (May-June 1977): 26-31.

Appendix A: Akerson and Ellwood R

The following proves that the R derived from Akerson and Ellwood are identical.

Akerson's R is found by

$$R_0 = M(R_M) + (1 - M)Y_E - \text{app.}\frac{1}{S} - \text{MP}\frac{1}{S_{\overline{n}|}}. \tag{A-1}$$

Ellwood's R is found by

$$R_E = Y_E - M(C) - \text{app.}\frac{1}{S_{\overline{n}|}}. \tag{A-2}$$

where

M = initial percent debt,

R_M = mortgage constant,

Y_E = equity yield rate,

app. = percent expected appreciation in the reversion,

$\frac{1}{S_{\overline{n}|}}$ = sinking fund factor,

C = mortgage coefficient equal to $(Y_E + P\frac{1}{S_{\overline{n}|}} - R_M)$.

Proof

Set equation (A-1) equal to equation (A-2):

$$R_E = R_A$$

$$Y_E - M(C) - \text{app}\frac{1}{S_{\overline{n}|}} = M(R_M) + (1 - M)Y_E - \text{app.}\frac{1}{S_{\overline{n}|}} - M(P)\frac{1}{S_{\overline{n}|}}$$

or

$$Y_E - M(C) = M(R_M) + (1 - M)Y_E - M(P)\frac{1}{S_{\overline{n}|}}.$$

Substitute value for C:

$$Y_E - M(Y_E + P\frac{1}{S_{\overline{n}|}} - R_M) = M(R_M) + (1 - M)Y_E - M(P)\frac{1}{S_{\overline{n}|}}$$

$$Y_E - M(Y_E) - M(P)\frac{1}{S_{\overline{n}|}} - M(R_M) = M(R_M) + (1 - M)Y_E - M(P)\frac{1}{S_{\overline{n}|}}$$

$$Y_E - M(Y_E) = (1 - M)Y_E$$

Divide both sides by Y_E:

$$1 - M = 1 - M.$$

This result states that the percent equity must equal the percent equity which is true by definition.

Appendix B: Derivation of Ellwood

Derive the Ellwood technique of valuation*

$$V = \frac{I}{Y_E - M(Y_E) + M(R_M) - M(P)\dfrac{1}{S_{\overline{n}|}} - \text{app}\dfrac{1}{S_{\overline{n}|}}}$$

Know that

$$V = V_M + V_E \tag{B-1}$$

where

$$V_E = \sum_{i-1}^{p} \frac{I - \text{VM}R_M}{(1 + Y_E)^i} + \frac{V(1 + \text{app.}) - \text{VM}(1 - P)}{(1 + Y_E)^p} \tag{B-2}$$

and

I = stabilized NOI,
Y_E = equity yield rate,
p = number of periods property will be held,
app = appreciation in property value,
$V(1 + \text{app})$ = projected selling price,
P = proportion of loan paid off,
$(1 - P)$ = proportion of loan not paid off,
M = loan to value ratio,
VM = loan size,

*See David Bradley, "Ellwood Through Algebra—New Horizons," *The Appraisal Journal* 44 (January 1976): 98–110; Peter Colwell and Phillip Rushing, "To Ellwood and Beyond," *The Appraisal Journal* 47 (July 1979): 352–358.

VM $(1 - P)$ = balance due at time of sale,

$\frac{1}{S_{\overline{n|}}} =$ sinking fund factor.

Substitute equation (B–2) into equation (B–1):

$$V = \text{VM} + A(I - \text{VMR}_M) + B(V + V\text{app} - \text{VM} + \text{VMP})$$

where

A = present value of ordinary annuity,

B = reversion factor.

Gather the M terms,

$$V = \text{AI} + \text{BV} + B\text{app}V + \text{MV} - \text{AVM}(R_M) - \text{BMV} + \text{BPMV}.$$

Factor the M,

$$V = \text{AI} + \text{BV} + B\text{app}V + M(V - A(R_M)V - \text{BV} + \text{BPV}).$$

Divide through by V,

$$1 = A\frac{I}{V} + B + B\text{app.} + M(1 - A(R_M) - B + \text{BP}).$$

Know that

$$\frac{I}{V} = R,$$

$$1 = \text{AR} + B + B\text{app.} + M(1 - \text{A}(R_M) - B + \text{BP}).$$

Solve for R:

$$\text{AR} = 1 - B - B\text{app.} - M(1 - A(R_M) - B + \text{BP})$$

$$R = \frac{1}{A} - \frac{1}{A}B - \frac{1}{A}B\text{app} - M(\frac{1}{A} - \frac{\text{A}(R_M)}{A} - \frac{1}{A}B + \frac{1}{A}\text{BP}).$$

Know that

$$\frac{1}{A}B = \frac{1}{S} = \text{sinking fund factor at } Y_E.$$

Then

$$R = \frac{1}{A} - \frac{1}{S} - \frac{1}{S}\text{app.} - M(\frac{1}{A} - \frac{1}{S} - R_M + \frac{1}{S}P).$$

Know that

$$\frac{1}{A} - \frac{1}{S} = i.$$

Then

$$R = i - \frac{1}{S}\text{app.} - M(i - R_M + \frac{1}{S}P).$$

Know that

$$i = Y_E,$$

$$R = Y_E - \frac{1}{S}\text{app.} - M(Y_E - R_M + \frac{1}{S}P).$$

Rewriting,

$$R = Y_E - M(Y_E) + M(R_M) - \frac{1}{S}\text{MP} - \frac{1}{S}\text{ app.}$$

Know that

$$R = \frac{I}{V}.$$

Then

$$\frac{I}{V} = Y_E - M(Y_E) + M(R_M) - \frac{1}{S}\text{MP} - \frac{1}{S}\text{ app.}$$

Cross multiply

$$I = V(Y_E - M(Y_E) + M(R_M) - \frac{1}{S}\text{ MP} - \frac{1}{S}\text{ app.}).$$

Solve for V:

$$\text{V} = \frac{I}{Y_E - M(Y_E) + M(R_M) - \frac{1}{S}\text{MP} - \frac{1}{S}\text{ app.}}.$$

CHAPTER 11

LEARNING OBJECTIVES

When a student finishes this chapter, he or she should be able to:

- Demonstrate the method for estimating an overall rate from the recent sales of comparable properties.
- Explain the assumptions that should be satisfied in selecting the comparables and performing the calculations.
- Demonstrate the method for extracting the risk rate and the recapture rates from the recent sales of comparable properties.
- Discuss the relationship among the overall rate, the risk rate, the recapture rate, and the building capitalization rate.

Estimate of *R*, the Risk Rate, and the Recapture Rate by Market Extraction

IMPORTANT TERMS AND PHRASES

building capitalization rate: The sum of the recapture rate and the risk rate.

composite recapture rate: A rate that is equivalent to the composite rate used for accrued depreciation.

market extraction: A procedure for deriving rates from data gathered on the recent sales of comparable properties.

remaining economic life: The number of years left before the expiration of the property's economic life.

risk rate: A rate that does not include recapture and is sometimes used in the valuation of a site.

The purpose of this chapter is to discuss and demonstrate the extraction of rates, especially the overall rate, R, from the market. The problems that can be encountered in deriving market rates are discussed also.

NEED FOR A MARKET ESTIMATE OF THE RATE, R

Chapter 9 discussed and showed that the value of property, V, when the original loan amount is unknown but is expressed as a percent of the property value can be found by

$$V = \frac{I}{R}$$

where

I = net operating income,

R = overall rate.

An estimate of R has been derived in earlier chapters by using (1) the band of investment method, (2) the Akerson method with and without algebra, and (3) the Ellwood method. Chapter 12 discusses additional contemporary methods of approximating R and V. This chapter discusses the extraction of an R from the market using the sales of comparable properties.

EXTRACTION OF R FROM THE SALES OF COMPARABLE PROPERTIES

An estimate of the overall rate, R, for the subject property can be derived from recent sales of comparable properties by rewriting the definition of V,

$$V = \frac{I}{R}$$

$$R \cdot V = I$$

$$R = \frac{I}{V}.$$

If I and V can be generated for a recent sale of a comparable rental property, an estimate of R can be derived by I/V.

Critical Assumptions

Several criteria[1] should be satisfied before the estimate of R will be accurate and meaningful. These criteria are:

1. *An audited annual report should be reviewed for the year preceding and the year following the sale.* The estimate of I is net operating income prior to debt service and taxes. Audited reports can provide justification for the figures used.

2. *A relationship must be established between market rent and contract rent.* The appraiser must make sure that the rental used in the estimate of I is realistic when compared to prevailing economic rentals. For example, a sale that included contract rents significantly below the market level with leases that expire soon probably would indicate a property value different from the value justified by market rent.

3. *The total sales price must be carefully analyzed.* The appraiser must determine the total price paid for the property. Additional questions are: Are the mortgages worth their face value (or less?) Does the summation of the cash plus the debt equal the purchase price? Were any items exchanged that should be valued? Was the sale an arm's length transaction?

4. *The motivations of the buyer should be scrutinized.* Is there a probability that any marked changes will occur in the income flow or the level of expenses? Either could influence the value.

5. *Closely related to number 4 are additional factors pertaining to the type of property, its riskiness as an investment, and motivations of the investor.* The comparable properties should be very comparable in reflecting the motivations of the investor/buyer. For example, properties generating a negative cash flow could be grouped, others purchased mainly for tax shelter purposes could be grouped, similar economic lives could be grouped, and those purchased only for purposes of capital gain upon resale may form another group. Other appropriate criteria could be used for grouping such as financial ratios and the site to property value ratio.

THE RECAPTURE RATE AND THE RISK RATE

The same data that are used to derive an estimate of the overall rate can be used to estimate the composite recapture rate and the risk rate. The purpose of this section is to illustrate the derivation of the two and to discuss their relationship to the overall rate.

Composite Recapture Rate

The composite recapture rate is the same as the composite method of estimating accrued depreciation discussed in Chapter 12. Also this rate is sometimes called the composite return *of* the investment. Data on the recent sales of comparable properties may be used to derive an estimate of the composite recapture rate, which is said to be *documented* since it has been observed and derived from the market. Consider the following example:

Recent comparable sale		
Sale price		\$600,000
NOI		\$ 66,000
Site value from comparable sales		\$100,000
Rate of return *on* similar investments found by market analysis (land and buildings)		9%
The recapture rate could be derived as follows:		
Sale price	\$600,000 × .09	
NOI attributable to site and building	\$ 54,000 annual	
Total NOI	\$ 66,000 annual	
–NOI attributable to site and building	54,000 annual	
Residual NOI for recapture	\$12,000 annual	
(Residual NOI for recapture)/(bldg. value)		= 12,000/500,000 = .024 annual

Using four pieces of information from recent comparable sales—sales price, total NOI, site value, and the rate of return on the site and building—a recapture rate may be derived. Thus the analyst has an overall rate (\$66,000/\$600,000 = .11) and a recapture rate (.024) that are justifiable from market data.

Remaining Economic Life

The estimate for the recapture rate above (.024) has been justified from market data. This figure may be used to derive an estimate of how the market views the remaining economic life.

Remaining economic life may be found by dividing 1 by the recapture rate. Thus

$$\begin{aligned}\text{remaining economic life} &= 1/(\text{recapture rate})\\ &= 1/.024\\ &= 41.7, \text{ say 42 years.}\end{aligned}$$

Risk Rate

These same data on the recent sale of a comparable property may be used to derive an estimate of the risk rate, sometimes called the yield rate, which is defined as the rate of return on capital that is required by the investor to attract investment capital.[2] Since by definition this rate does *not* include recapture, it is sometimes used as a rate that is applicable to the site only, and is known as the site capitalization rate. This rate may be derived as follows:

Sale price	$600,000.	
− site value	100,000.	
Bld. value	$500,000.	
× recapture rate	× .024	
NOI attributable to recapture of bldg.	$ 12,000.	
Total NOI	$ 66,000.	
− NOI attributable to recapture of bldg.	− 12,000.	
NOI attributable to site	$ 54,000.	
(NOI attributable to site/sales price)		= $54,000./600,000 = .09 risk rate

Comparison of the Overall Rate, the Recapture Rate, and the Risk Rate

Relative to the above derivations, each rate may be defined as follows:

overall rate = NOI/sales price

recapture rate = (residual NOI for recapture)/(bldg. value)

risk rate = (NOI attributable to the site/sales price)

In addition, the analyst can derive a *building capitalization rate* which is defined as

building capitalization rate = recapture rate + risk rate

The relationship among these rates can best be seen in the band of investment method. The recapture rate, the risk rate, and the building capitalization rate are weighted and averaged in the band of investment method to derive *R*.

Thus,

		Rate	*Total*
Building:	83.33% ×	(.09 + .024 = .114) =	.095
Site:	16.66% ×	.09 =	.015
			.110

Thus the reader should remember the following relationships:

1. The risk rate is often applied to the site only.
2. The building capitalization rate is the sum of the risk rate and the recapture rate.
3. The overall rate is the weighted average of the risk rate and the building capitalization rate.
4. The building capitalization rate can be larger than the overall rate.

Number of Comparables

One example of deriving these rates from one recent sale has been shown. Several recent comparable sales should be used to derive a final estimate of *R*, the risk rate, the recapture rate, and the building capitalization rate.

AN ILLUSTRATION

Consider the following illustration: You want to derive a market estimate of *R*, the risk rate, the recapture rate, and the building capitalization rate for your subject. After searching the market, you locate four good comparables, which you reduce to three. The relevant information for each is the following:

Comparable 1

sale price: $200,000

NOI: $24,000

site value from comparables: $50,000

rate of return on similar investments: 10%

Comparable 2

sale price: $225,000

NOI: $26,500

site value from comparables: $50,000

rate of return on similar investments: 10%

Comparable 3

sale price: $215,000

NOI: $25,500

site value from comparables: $50,000

rate of return on similar investments: 10%

Each of the estimates of NOI has been taken from audited, compiled, or reviewed annual reports for the year prior and the year following the date of the sale. The level of contract rents is very close if not equal to the level of market rent. The sales price is an accurate reflection of what the buyer paid for the property. The buyers have no intentions of changing the level of income or expenses in the foreseeable future. All of the properties have been purchased for the purpose of generating an acceptable cash flow to the buyers.

Question: Derive one estimate of the overall rate, risk rate, recapture rate, and the building capitalization rate. Use the straight-line method of recapture where appropriate.

Answer:

Comparable 1

Recapture Rate	
Sales price	$200,000
	× .10
NOI attributable to site and building	$ 20,000
NOI	$ 24,000
− NOI attributable to site and building	− 20,000
Residual NOI	$ 4,000
4,000/150,000 = .027	
Risk Rate	
Bldg. value	$150,000
× Recapture rate	× .027

NOI attributable to recapture	$ 4,050
Total NOI	$ 24,000
– NOI attributable to recapture	– 4,050
NOI attributable to site	19,950

19,950/200,000 = .09975 or .10

Bldg. Capitalization Rate

.10 + .027 = .127

Comparable 2

Recapture Rate

Sales price	$225,000
	× .10
NOI attributable to site and building	$ 22,500
NOI	$ 26,500
– NOI attributable to site and building	– 22,500
Residual NOI	$ 4,000

4,000/175,000 = .0229

Risk Rate

Bldg. value	$175,000
× recapture rate	× .0229
NOI attributable to recapture	$4,007.5
Total NOI	$ 26,500
– NOI attributable to recapture	– 4,007.5
NOI attributable to site	$22,492.5

22,492.5/225,000 = .09997 or .10

Building Capitalization Rate

.10 + .0229 = .1229

Comparable 3

Recapture Rate

Sales price	$215,000
	× .10

NOI attributable to the site and building	$ 21,500
NOI	$ 25,500
– NOI attributable to site and building	– 21,500
4,000/165,000 = .024	$ 4,000

Risk Rate

Bldg. Value	$165,000
× Recapture rate	× .024
NOI attributable to recapture	$ 3,960
NOI	$ 25,500
– NOI attributable to recapture	3,960
NOI attributable to the site	$ 21,540

21,540/215,000 = .100

Building Capitalization Rate

.10 + .024 = .124

Summary	*Risk Rate*	*Recapture Rate*	*Bldg Cap. Rate*
Comparable 1:	.10	.027	.127
Comparable 2:	.10	.0229	.1229
Comparable 3:	.10	.024	.124

A good choice for the final risk rate is .10. Comparables 2 and 3 were judged to be more comparable than 1; therefore the final recapture rate was selected to be .0235. The resulting building capitalization rate was then .1235 or (.10 + .0235).

SUMMARY

An estimate of the overall rate may be derived from the recent sales of comparable properties by dividing each respective NOI by its sales price. Each sale should be examined carefully to assure that it is an accurate reflection of the true price paid, that the NOI comes from audited, compiled, or reviewed statements, that no significant changes might occur in the income stream or expenses, and that the properties have been purchased for the same motivations such as income or capital gain.

The same comparables that are used to derive an estimate of the overall *R* may be used to estimate the risk rate and the recapture rate. The summation of the risk rate and the recapture rate will give an estimate of the building capitalization rate. The weighted average of the risk rate and the building capitalization rate will give the overall rate.

REVIEW QUESTIONS

1. Explain the formula that is used to estimate the overall rate.
2. Outline the assumptions that should be followed in selecting the comparables and performing the calculations in deriving the overall rate.
3. Demonstrate the technique for estimating the risk rate. The recapture rate.
4. Explain the relations among the following: overall rate, risk rate, recapture rate, and the building capitalization rate.
5. What is the relationship between the remaining economic life and the recapture rate?

ENDNOTES

1. Arthur C. Cohen, ''Extracting Cap Rates 'From the Market': Beware,'' *The Appraisal Journal* 47 (July 1979): 370–373.
2. Byrl N. Boyce, *Real Estate Appraisal Terminology* (Cambridge, Mass.: Ballinger Publishing Co., 1975), p. 180.

ADDITIONAL READINGS

Akerson, Charles B. ''Income-Approach-Determining the Adequate Rates. *The Appraisal Journal* 48 (April 1980): 172–181.

Brown, Ralph J., and Johnson, Dennis A. ''Inflation, Valuation, and the Discount Rate.'' *The Appraisal Journal* 48 (October 1980): 549–555.

Coulter, William. ''A Current and Objective Equity Yield Rate.'' *The Appraisal Journal* 45 (January 1977).

Dilmore, Gene. ''Income Property Return Ratios.'' *The Real Estate Appraiser* 44 (March–April 1978): 39–40.

Ellwood, L. W. ''Selection of Capitalization Rates in Today's Market.'' *The Appraisal Journal* 45 (July 1977): 325–330.

Gau, George W., and Kohlhepp, Daniel B. ''Estimation of Equity Yield Rates Based on Capital Market Returns.'' *The Real Estate Appraiser and Analyst* 44 (November–December 1978): 33–39.

Jaffe, Austin J. ''A Note on the Use of Capitalization, Discount, and Forward Rates.'' *The Appraisal Journal* 48 (January 1980): 24–30.

Lane, David E. ''Comparable Sales on Trial.'' *The Appraisal Journal* 45 (July 1977): 435–441.

Tchira, Arnold. "Comparable Sales Selection—A Computer Approach." *The Appraisal Journal* 47 (January 1979): 86–93.

Zerbst, Robert H., and Kohlhepp, Daniel B. "The Use of Equity Rates in Appraisal Theory." *The Real Estate Appraiser* 43 (May–June 1977): 26–31.

CHAPTER 12

LEARNING OBJECTIVES

When a student finishes this chapter, he or she should be able to:

- Contrast market value with investment value.
- Derive *after-tax cash flow.*
- Explain and compute the amount of capital gains taxes owed after the sale of property under pre-1981 and post-1980 tax laws.
- Discuss the types of depreciation that may be taken on property.
- Explain the difference between straight line and accelerated depreciation.
- Present the concepts used in net present value analysis.
- Explain the internal rate of return and illustrate its calculation.
- Contrast the IRR with the financial management rate of return and illustrate the technique for calculating the FMRR.
- Discuss the techniques for estimating an overall *R,* which includes lender requirements.

Contemporary Methods of Estimating *R* and *V*

IMPORTANT TERMS AND PHRASES

accelerated cost recovery system: Depreciation deductions that are allowed under the Economic Recovery Tax Act of 1981.

after-tax cash flow: Net operating income minus debt service and income taxes plus any tax loss saving.

component depreciation: A number of deductions taken on the components of one property that may be used for taxation purposes.

composite depreciation: A deduction for taxation purposes that is applied to the complete structure.

financial management rate of return: A rate of return on a series of cash flows where some may be negative.

internal rate of return: The rate of return that causes the discounted sum of the income flows to equal the initial equity.

investment value: The after-tax worth of property to an individual investor.

The material in this chapter covers several topics. First, the differences between market value and investment value are discussed. This section includes a discussion of the types of depreciation that may be applied to real property investments and the current recapture rules under pre-1981 and post-1980 tax laws. Second, a discussion of net present value and the internal rate of return are included. Both analytical methods are contemporary tools for real property investment analysis. Third, a discussion of the financial management rate of return is included. This rate is allegedly designed to overcome the inadequacies of the IRR. Fourth, additional estimates of an overall *R*, which include the lender's requirements, are discussed. Fifth, a brief discussion on the treatment of inflation is covered.

The material in this chapter is not a thorough discussion of investment analysis. These additional tools and techniques are introduced to supplement and compare to the techniques discussed in earlier chapters to derive market value.

INVESTMENT VALUE VERSUS MARKET VALUE

A client may be interested in his or her *investment* value in addition to the *market* value. The investment value estimates the worth of the property to a specific individual. Consideration is given to the individual's ability to obtain special financing terms in the market, the individual's choice of depreciation schedules, and the individual's marginal tax rate. In addition, investment value includes the time value of money, and examines the residual worth that occurs when the property is sold at the end of the holding period.

In investment analysis, the concept of NOI typically used is one that *includes* the reserves for replacement account. If this account has been subtracted from NOI during an earlier stage of analysis, an equivalent amount typically is added back here. The reasoning is that this account may not be a cash expenditure.

When investment value is estimated, NOI is typically transformed into *after-tax cash flow*. This involves a discussion of several additional steps including the types of depreciation that may be used in real estate. A brief discussion of each step follows.

After-Tax Cash Flow (ATCF)

In most investment situations, an early step in estimating investment value is to derive ATCF[1] for each year of the holding period, *p*. ATCF is found for each year by,

NOI
– Debt service
Before-tax cash flow (sometimes called *cash throw-off*)
– Income taxes
or + Tax loss saving
After-tax cash flow

The amount deducted for income taxes may require additional calculations,

NOI
– Depreciation
– Interest
Before-tax income × taxpayer's marginal tax rate = – income taxes or + tax loss saving

Income taxes are computed on *before-tax income* according to the taxpayer's marginal tax rate. For example, a taxpayer in the 40% bracket would pay 40% of before-tax income in taxes. If the taxes are subtracted from *before-tax income,* the result is called *after-tax income.*

Tax-loss saving represents the amount of tax saving from a negative figure for *after-tax income.* This negative amount may be taken as a deduction against income from another source that shelters that income from taxes. The resulting reduction in income taxes on other income can be added here. This tax loss is of benefit to the taxpayer *only* to the extent that taxable income from other sources exists.

A slight modification of the previous steps is used by some[2] to derive the same answer for *after-tax cash flow:*

NOI
– Interest
– Depreciation
Taxable income
– Income taxes
After-tax income
+ Depreciation
– Mortgage amortization payments
+ Tax-loss savings
After-tax cash flow

Either method can be used. The first one is shown in this chapter.

The reader should remember that *income* is the difference between inflows and outflows from all assets. *Cash* is simply one asset. The concepts "before-tax income" and "after-tax income" reflect all of the assets, while "before-tax cash flow" and "after-tax cash flow" reflect only the movement of cash.

Reversionary Value and Taxes

The property may show a capital gain (loss) at the time of resale, exchange, or refinancing at the end of the holding period. This gain (loss) is considered to be future income that is received irregularly and is taxed differently than regular income such as NOI.

Property that is a capital asset (depreciable real estate) qualifies as a long-term capital gain if it has been owned for over twelve months. Real estate investments used in a trade or business (called "1231 assets") and other types of "income assets" are not considered here.

The procedure for computing the *after-tax cash flow from the sale or exchange of the property at the end of the holding period is:*[3]

Net sale price
 – Unpaid mortgages
 – Depreciation recapture taxes
 – Capital gains taxes

After-tax cash flow from the sale

Each item is discussed:

Net Sales Price: This figure is the projected selling price of the total property minus any expected selling expenses.

Unpaid Mortgages: All unpaid mortgage balances are liabilities and are paid from the sales proceeds.

Depreciation Recapture Taxes: Any excess depreciation over the straightline amount may need to be recaptured according to the rules given later in this section. Income taxes are paid on the recapture amount using the individual's marginal tax rate.

Capital Gains and Tax: The capital gains tax is applied to the capital gain which may be computed as follows:[4]

Selling price
—Selling expenses (such as agent's commission and fix-up expenses)
—tax basis (original purchase price plus improvements minus total dep. charged)

Gains before recapture
—Depreciation recapture (if applicable)

Taxes are figured on the *capital gain* depending upon whether the taxpayer is an individual or a corporation. For an individual, 60% of the capital gain is excluded, and the remaining 40% is taxed at the individual's marginal income tax rate. A corporation is not allowed the 60% exclusion that the individual taxpayer can use. The maximum a corporation can pay is 20% of the net capital gain for post-1980 transactions.

Depreciation for Real Property Placed in Service Prior to 1981

Any property that has a definite useful life, is used for the production of income, and is subject to obsolescence or physical wear-and-tear is typically qualified for a depreciation deduction.[5] This deduction is claimed by the owner of the property rights and not the party(s) liable for the mortgage. Exhibit 12.1 shows the allowable types of depreciation deductions.

The taxpayer may select initially *composite* or *component* depreciation. *Composite* depreciation is estimated by multiplying one figure, which in some cases may vary from year-to-year, by the appropriate dollar figure for the depreciable asset. The result produces one total representing the depreciation for the whole structure. Examples are shown later in the chapter. *Component* depreciation estimates annual depreciation for the building components, which are summed to represent the total for the building. For example, an estimate of depreciation could be derived for each item in the structure such as the wiring, plumbing, ceiling, paving, etc., and the results summed to represent the depreciation for the building.

Composite depreciation Three methods of estimating composite depreciation are straight line, declining balance, and sum-of-the-years-digits. The last two are commonly known as *accelerated* since they give larger deductions in the early years. Each is considered below briefly.

1. *Straight-line.* This method takes depreciation deductions in equal annual amounts. The annual *rate* is (1/useful life of the improvement). The annual *amount* is found by multiplying the rate by the cost of the improvement less any salvage value if applicable.[6]

2. *Declining balance.* This method takes depreciation deductions using an annual *rate* that is a multiple of the straight line rate. The annual *amount* is calculated by multiplying the rate by the declining balance of the undepreciated book value of the improvement. Salvage value is not subtracted from the cost.

3. *Sum-of-the-years-digits.* This method takes depreciation deductions using a *rate* that is computed each year. The denominator is the sum of the digits of the life of the asset, which is a constant. The numerator each year is each digit in reverse order. The *amount* is found by multiplying the rate by the original cost of the improvement less the salvage value if applicable.[7]

Exhibit 12.1
Allowable types of depreciation for real property (section 1250 Property)

I. *Used* property acquired after July 24, 1969 (owner is not the first user)

Residential Real Property	*Nonresidential Real Property*
straight line, 125% declining balance if useful life is at least 20 years	(commercial, industrial, etc.) straight line

II. *New* property acquired after July 24, 1969 (owner is the first user)

Residential rental real property	*Nonresidential (new commercial) real property*
straight-line, 200% declining balance; 150% declining balance; 125% declining balance, sum-of-the-years digits	150% declining balance; 125% declining balance, straight line

Source: Commerce Clearing House, *1980 Federal Tax Course,* (Chicago: CCH, 1979), pp. 1315–1316; see also Lawrence Phillips and William Hoffman, *1980 Annual Edition West's Federal Taxation: Individual Income Taxes* (St. Paul, Minn.: West Publishing Co., 1979 and 1981), pp. 200–201 and 278–283, respectively.

Consider the following example:

- John Smith purchased property for $500,000 ($400,000 for the improvement and $100,000 for the site).
- The anticipated useful life is forty years.
- The property qualifies for 150% declining balance and straight-line depreciation methods.
- The building salvage value will equal 0 in forty years.

Figure 12.1 illustrates the depreciation deductions for the first five years. The calculations are as follows: (sum-of-the-years-digits is shown as an illustration although the property is not qualified)

		150% Declining Balance		*Sum of the year's digits (illustration only)*	
Year	*Straight line*	*Undepreciated Book Value*	*Deduction*	*Original Cost*	*Deduction*
1	$10,000	$400,000. × .0375 =	$15,000.	$400,000 × $\frac{40}{820}$ =	$19,512.
2	10,000	385,000. × .0375 =	14,438.	400,000 × $\frac{39}{820}$ =	19,024.
3	10,000	370,562. × .0375 =	13,896.	400,000 × $\frac{38}{820}$ =	18,537.
4	10,000	356,666. × .0375 =	13,375.	400,000 × $\frac{37}{820}$ =	18,049.
5	10,000	343,291. × .0375 =	12,873.	400,000 × $\frac{36}{820}$ =	17,561.
TOTAL	$50,000		$69,582.		$92,683.

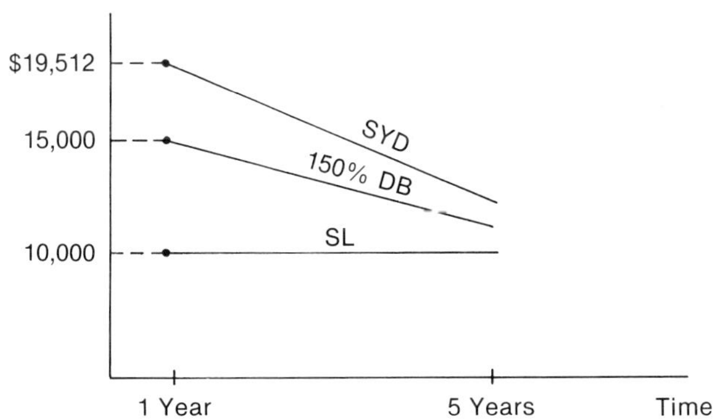

Fig. 12.1 Depreciation methods for real property placed into service prior to 1981.

1. *Straight-line.* The tax rate equals 1/40, which is .025. The annual amount is .025 × $400,000, which is $10,000.
2. *Declining balance.* The rate equals 150% times .025, which equals .0375. The annual amount is found by subtracting the previous year's depreciation and multiplying the result by .0375.
3. *Sum-of-the-years-digits* (illustration only). The denominator of the rate is found by summing the digits of 1 through 40, which equals 820. The numerator for each year represents the digits in reverse. Each respective rate is multiplied by the original cost.

Component depreciation Depreciable items in the structure can typically be depreciated more rapidly than reality, resulting in a larger deduction than the composite method.[8] For example, consider the following: John Smith purchases property that was valued at $500,000. John apportioned $100,000 to the site and $400,000 to the building which was recently constructed. Using straight-line depreciation and a useful life of forty years, the composite deductible amount is $10,000 annually (1/40 × $400,000). Using component depreciation, the first year depreciation deduction was the following:

Component	*Cost*	*Useful life*	*Depreciation*
Building	$300,000	40	$ 7,500
Plumbing	20,000	20	1,000
Wiring	25,000	15	1,667
Heating	25,000	18	1,389
Paving	10,000	10	1,000
Roofing	10,000	10	1,000
Air condition	10,000	10	1,000
	$400,000		$14,556

The component method has provided an additional $4,556 of depreciation above the straight-line method.

The same depreciation methods allowed for composite may be used also for component. For example, a taxpayer who uses 150% declining balance for a new nonresidential real property may use the same method on the components.[9] In addition, component depreciation is not subject to recapture taxation, providing the straight-line method is used. The other accelerated methods are subject to recapture taxes.[10]

Recapture Accelerated depreciation refers to 125%, 150%, 200%, and sum-of-the-years digits. If one of these techniques is used, the excess depreciation taken over the straight-line amount may need to be recaptured when the property is sold. Income taxes may be paid on the recaptured amount. The following recapture rules[11] are in effect for properties after December 31, 1975:

Type	*Depreciation recapture for post-1975 depreciation*
a. All residential and nonresidential if held *less* than 12 months	All depreciation, including straight line
b. All residential and nonresidential subsidized housing if held for *more* than 12 months	All depreciation in excess of straight line
c. Subsidized low-income housing if held between 12 and 100 months	All depreciation in excess of straight line
d. Subsidized low-income housing if held more than 100 months	Recapture of excess depreciation phased out at 1% for each month over 100, with no recapture after 200 months.

A problem Consider the following problem as an example of the concepts previously discussed:

- John Smith purchased property as a sole owner in the 40% tax bracket.
- Purchase price = \$500,000 (\$100,000 for the site and \$400,000 for the building).
- John paid for the site with his own cash.
- First mortgage for \$400,000 at 12% interest for twenty years with quarterly constant payments equal to \$13,245 or \$52,980 annually.
- Straight-line depreciation for a building useful life of forty years with no salvage value (1/40 × \$400,000. = \$10,000).
- Resale value of the property is projected to be \$560,000 at the end of a five-year expected holding period.
- No improvements will be made.
- NOI is projected to be \$60,000 annually.

- Selling expenses are estimated to be $45,000.
- The property was placed in service prior to 1981.

John wants to know his *after-tax cash flow* for each of the five years that he holds the property. In addition, he wants to calculate his *after-tax cash flow from the sale.* Exhibit 12.2 shows the calculations using the information given above.

The after-tax cash flow for each of the five years is $6,128, $5,867, $5,573, $5,242, and $4,869, respectively. The after tax cash flow from the sale is $138,046.

Exhibit 12.3 shows an example of computing *after-tax cash flow* and *after-tax cash flow from the sale* using accelerated depreciation. In this situation, the same data were used as were shown in Exhibit 12.2, except that 150% was used for the depreciation deduction since the building was qualified if the owner wanted to use it. The accelerated depreciation lowered the *after-tax cash flow* for each year of the holding period, but the excess over the straight-line amount was reclaimed at the time of sale and taxes paid at that time.

Tax Preference Items

When the investor is contemplating the use of accelerated depreciation, he or she may need to be aware of additional tax due to a tax preference item as explained in IRS Code 57. A tax preference is the individual benefit received from a fast write-off.

NET PRESENT VALUE AND THE INTERNAL RATE OF RETURN

Net Present Value

Net present value is defined as the present value of the cash inflows less the present value of the cash outflows.[12] The phrase *net present value* has been used to cover two different present value figures. The first is the present value estimate, which is thought to be equivalent to the present cost (purchase price) of the project,

$$\text{Purchase price} = \sum_{i=1}^{p} \frac{(\text{NOI})_i}{(1+R)^i} + \frac{(\text{Selling price})_p}{(1+R)^p}$$

Typically, the single unknown in this equation is the purchase price. The equation illustrates that the current price of the property is equal to the sum of discounted NOI and the discounted selling price.

Exhibit 12.2
After-tax cash flow

	Year 1	Year 2	Year 3	Year 4	Year 5
After-tax income					
NOI	$60,000	$60,000	$60,000	$60,000	$60,000
– Interest	– 47,771	– 47,118	– 46,382	– 45,554	– 44,623
– Depreciation	– 10,000	– 10,000	– 10,000	– 10,000	– 10,000 ($50,000 total)
before-tax income	2,229	2,882	3,618	4,446	5,377
– Income taxes (40%)	892	1,153	1,447	1,778	2,151
after-tax income	1,337	1,729	2,171	2,668	3,226
After-tax cash flow					
NOI	60,000	60,000	60,000	60,000	60,000
– Debt service	– 52,980	– 52,980	– 52,980	– 52,980	– 52,980
– Income taxes above	– 892	– 1,153	– 1,447	– 1,778	– 2,151
after-tax cash flow	6,128	5,867	5,573	5,242	4,869

(continued)

Exhibit 12.2 (continued)

	Year 1	Year 2	Year 3	Year 4	Year 5
Capital gain & tax					
Sales Price					$560,000
– Selling expense					– 45,000
– Tax basis ($500,000 – 50,000 = 450,000)					– 450,000
– Depreciation recapture					0
Capital gain					$ 65,000
– Long-term capital gain exclusion (60%)					– 39,000
Taxable capital gain					$ 26,000
Tax on gain (40% tax bracket)					$ 10,400
After-tax cash flow from sale					
Net Sales Price ($560,000 – 45,000)					$515,000
– Unpaid mortgage					– 366,554 (first mortgage)
– Depreciation recapture taxes					0 (used straight line)
– Capital gains tax					– 10,400
After-tax cash flow from sale					$138,046
Total tax liability on sale					
Capital gain					$ 10,400

Exhibit 12.3
After-tax cash flow

	Year 1	Year 2	Year 3	Year 4	Year 5	
After-tax income						
NOI	$60,000	$60,000	$60,000	$60,000	$60,000	
− Interest	− 47,771	− 47,118	− 46,382	− 45,554	− 44,623	
− Depreciation (150%)	− 15,000	− 14,438	− 13,896	− 13,375	− 12,873	($69,582 total)
before-tax income	(2771)	(1556)	(278)	$1,071	$2,504	
+ Tax loss saving (40%)	+ 1108	+ 622	+ 111	0	0	
or − income taxes (40%)	0	0	0	− 428	− 1,002	
After-tax cash flow						
NOI	60,000	60,000	60,000	60,000	60,000	
− Debt service	− 52,980	− 52,980	− 52,980	− 52,980	− 52,980	
+ Tax loss saving	+ 1108	+ 622	+ 111	0	0	
or − Income taxes	0	0	0	− 428	− 1,002	
After-tax cash flow	8,128	7,642	7,131	6,592	6,018	

(continued)

Exhibit 12.3 (continued)

	Year 1	Year 2	Year 3	Year 4	Year 5
Capital gain and taxes					
Sales price					$560,000
– Selling expenses					– 45,000
– Tax basis (500,000 – 69,582 = 430,418)					– 430,418
– Depreciation recapture (69,582 – 50,000)					– 19,582
capital gain					$ 65,000
– Long-term capital gain exclusion (60%)					– 39,000
Taxable capital gain					$ 26,000
Tax on gain (40% tax bracket)					$ 10,400
After-tax cash flow from sale					
Net sales price ($560,000 – 45,000 = 515,000)					$515,000
– Unpaid mortgage					– 366,554
– Depreciation recapture taxes (69,582 – 50,000 = 19,582 (.40 tax bracket) = 7,833)					– 7,833
– Capital gains tax					– 10,400
After-tax cash flow from sale					$130,213
Total tax liability on sale					
Capital gain $10,400					$ 10,400
+ Recapture depreciation (19,582. × .40 = 7,833)					7,833
					$18,233

One author[13] likens this equation to the uses and assumptions made by Inwood. This equation may be criticized as not including depreciation, the influence of financing, and the impact of taxes. In addition, the overall R that is used is estimated on the total purchase price instead of only the investor's equity.

To overcome these criticisms, the phrase *net present value* has been applied to a modification of this equation:

$$\text{Initial equity} = \sum_{i=1}^{p} \frac{(\text{after tax cash flow})_i}{(1+R)^i} + \frac{(\text{after-tax cash flow from sale})_p}{(1+R)^p}$$

If the overall R can be estimated and inserted in the preceding equation, it can be solved to determine the present value of the owner's initial equity.

Using the after-tax cash flow estimates in Exhibit 12.2, and an estimate of the overall R to be equal to 11.64%, the present value of owner's equity is,

$$V_E = \frac{\$6{,}128.}{(1+.1164)^1} + \frac{\$5{,}867.}{(1+.1164)^2} + \frac{\$5{,}573.}{(1+.1164)^3} + \frac{\$5{,}242.}{(1+.1164)^4} + \frac{\$4{,}869.}{(1+.1164)^5} + \frac{\$138{,}046}{(1+.1164)^5}$$

which is the same as:

$$V_E = \$100{,}000.$$

Internal Rate of Return (IRR)

The IRR is defined as ". . . that rate which discounts all returns to equal the original investment."[14] By a simple rewording of this statement and rewriting of the previous equation that estimates the present value of the equity, the IRR may be defined as the rate that makes the present value of the income flows minus the initial equity to equal zero, or

$$0 = -\$100{,}000 + \sum_{i=1}^{p} \frac{(\text{after-tax cash flow})_i}{(1+R)^i} + \frac{(\text{after-tax cash flow from sale})_p}{(1+R)^p}$$

The IRR can be used to rank projects since the property with the highest IRR will be considered as a better investment than one that is lower, other things being equal. In addition, the IRR is a universal analytical tool that is used to rank investments in the finance field.

A common question asked by the investor is, "I have $______ to invest. Find a property that will give an IRR of at least (amount) since I can receive that amount on an alternative investment." The analyst's role here is to compare the after-tax cash flow on alternative properties, calculate the IRR, and select one that fits the investor's objective.

In addition, the IRR can be used as the objective of sensitivity studies with the figures. For example, what is the influence upon the IRR by lowering the operating expenses by 5%? What is the influence upon the IRR by refinancing the first mortgage? What is the influence upon the IRR by selling the property in the fourth year rather than the fifth? What is the influence upon the IRR from using one of the accelerated methods of depreciation as opposed to straight line?

Techniques for calculation The IRR may be found by (1) use of special calculator that contain an IRR routine, or (2) manual calculations by trial and error. The manual technique is the older method and involves a repetition of discounting using various arbitrarily selected rates. This method is shown here. A reader with a special calculator might estimate the IRR by both procedures to verify understanding of both techniques.

The objective is to make the discounted sum of these reversions equal to the original equity. The interest rate that does this is the IRR. For example, Exhibit 12.4 is the after-tax cash flow for the problem shown in Exhibit 12.2. To begin, select an interest rate equal to, say, 11.5%. The appropriate "present value of $1 reversion factors" are found in a set of financial tables for 11.5%. The discounted sum is $100,555.46, as shown in Exhibit 12.5, which means that the selection of 11.5% is too low. Exhibit 12.6 shows that the next choice of 11.75% is too high since the discounted sum equals $99,541.39. The actual IRR is between 11.5 and 11.75%, and must be interpolated.

Exhibit 12.4
After-tax cash flow

Year	After tax cash flow
1	$ 6,128
2	5,867
3	5,573
4	5,242
5	4,869
Sale	138,046

Exhibit 12.5
Estimate of IRR with 11.5%

Year	After-tax cash flow		Try IRR = 11.5%		
1	$6,128	×	.896861	=	5,495.96
2	5,867	×	.804360	=	4,719.18
3	5,573	×	.721399	=	4,020.36
4	5,242	×	.646994	=	3,391.54
5	4,869	×	.580264	=	2,825.31
Sale	138,046	×	.580264	=	80,103.124
			Sum		$100,555.46

$100,000 < $100,555.46

Conclusion: 11.5% is too low

Exhibit 12.6
Estimate of IRR with 11.75%

Year	After-tax cash flow		Try IRR = 11.75%		
1	$6,128	×	.894855	=	5,483.67
2	5,867	×	.800765	=	4,698.09
3	5,573	×	.716568	=	3,993.43
4	5,242	×	.641224	=	3,361.30
5	4,869	×	.573802	=	2,793.84
Sale	138,046	×	.573802	=	79,211.07
				Sum =	$99,541.39

$100,000 > $99,541.39

Conclusion: 11.75% is too high

Interpolation of Actual IRR

Known:

11.75% gave $ 99,541
$100,000 present value of owner's equity
11.50% gave $100,555.

Then,

$$\frac{11.75\% - 11.50\%}{\$99{,}541. - \$100{,}555.} = \frac{.25\%}{-\ \$1{,}014.}$$

$$= -.0002465\% \text{ per } \$1$$

$$\$100{,}000 \text{ equity} - \$100{,}555 = \$-555.$$

and,

$$-.0002465 \times \$-555. = +.1368\% \text{ per } \$1$$

Thus,

$$11.50\% + .1368\% = 11.6368\% \text{ or } 11.6\%.$$

IRR assumptions The IRR makes several critical assumptions that are considered by some users[15] to be criticisms of this technique:

1. The IRR assumes that cash flows received are immediately reinvested at the project's IRR. This assumption may be erroneous since future cash flows may be irregular and reinvested at the same rate. In addition, the IRR technique assumes that reinvestment is made automatically in this project or another with exactly the same level of risk.
2. The IRR is assumed to be equal to the reinvestment rate.
3. The IRR technique discounts positive cash flows at the same rate as negative cash flows.
4. The IRR technique may have no solution or multiple solutions.

ECONOMIC RECOVERY ACT OF 1981[16]

The ERA included several significant points that will influence after-tax cash flow. The act had just recently been approved by Congress at the printing of this book, and time did not permit a full interpretation of its impact. Several selected features are included here.

Depreciation Deduction

The taxpayer will have a choice to recover the unadjusted basis of the real property placed in service after 1980 through the (1) accelerated cost recovery system (ACRS) over a fifteen-year recovery period, or (2) straight-line method over fifteen, thirty-five, or forty-five years. Taxation of the proceeds from a sale in either case is shown below:

	Residential	*Nonresidential*
Straight-line	Taxed as *capital gain*	Taxed as *capital gain*
ACRS	Any gain over straight-line with fifteen yrs. taxed as ordinary *income*	Gain is taxed as ordinary *income* up to amount of prior recovery deduction; excess is taxed as *capital gain*

The maximum tax rate on all income of individuals is reduced to 50%. Otherwise, the capital gain computation is the same.

Both methods are composite rates applicable to the whole structure. Component depreciation has been eliminated except for a substantial improvement.

ACRS deduction The unadjusted basis of the property is multiplied by the appropriate recovery percentage found in Exhibit 12.7. These recovery per-

Exhibit 12.7
Economic Recovery Tax Act of 1981 accelerated cost recovery system rates: ACRS cost recovery tables for real estate

	1. All real estate (except low-income housing)											
	The applicable percentage is: (Use the column for the month in the first year the property is placed in service)											
If the recovery year is:	*Jan	Feb	Mar	Ap	May	Jun	Jul	Aug	Sept	Oct	Nov	Dec
1	12	11	10	9	8	7	6	5	4	3	2	1
2	10	10	11	11	11	11	11	11	11	11	11	12
3	9	9	9	9	10	10	10	10	10	10	10	10
4	8	8	8	8	8	8	9	9	9	9	9	9
5	7	7	7	7	7	7	8	8	8	8	8	8
6	6	6	6	6	7	7	7	7	7	7	7	7
7	6	6	6	6	6	6	6	6	6	6	6	6
8	6	6	6	6	6	6	5	6	6	6	6	6
9	6	6	6	6	5	6	5	5	5	6	6	6
10	5	6	5	6	5	5	5	5	5	5	6	5
11	5	5	5	5	5	5	5	5	5	5	5	5
12	5	5	5	5	5	5	5	5	5	5	5	5
13	5	5	5	5	5	5	5	5	5	5	5	5

(continued)

Exhibit 12.7 (continued)

If the recovery year is:	*Jan	Feb	Mar	Ap	May	Jun	Jul	Aug	Sept	Oct	Nov	Dec
14	5	5	5	5	5	5	5	5	5	5	5	5
15	5	5	5	5	5	5	5	5	5	5	5	5
16	—	—	1	1	2	2	3	3	4	4	4	5

2. Low-income housing

	The applicable percentage is: (Use the column for the month in the first year the property is placed in service)											
If the recovery year is:	*Jan	Feb	Mar	Ap	May	Jun	Jul	Aug	Sept	Oct	Nov	Dec
1	13	12	11	10	9	8	7	6	4	3	2	1
2	12	12	12	12	12	12	12	13	13	13	13	13
3	10	10	10	10	11	11	11	11	11	11	11	11
4	9	9	9	9	9	9	9	9	10	10	10	10
5	8	8	8	8	8	8	8	8	8	8	8	9
6	7	7	7	7	7	7	7	7	7	7	7	7
7	6	6	6	6	6	6	6	6	6	6	6	6
8	5	5	5	5	5	5	5	5	5	5	6	6
9	5	5	5	5	5	5	5	5	5	5	5	5
10	5	5	5	5	5	5	5	5	5	5	5	5
11	4	5	5	5	5	5	5	5	5	5	5	5
12	4	4	4	5	4	5	5	5	5	5	5	5
13	4	4	4	4	4	4	5	4	5	5	5	5
14	4	4	4	4	4	4	4	4	4	5	4	4
15	4	4	4	4	4	4	4	4	4	4	4	4
16	—	—	1	1	2	2	2	3	3	3	4	4

(Note—These tables do not apply for short taxable years of less than 12 months.)

*Monthly column headings were added by the authors.

Source: *Treasury News,* R-345, September 10, 1981.

centages use a 200% declining balance for low-income housing and a 175% declining balance for other real property in the early years followed by a switch to straight line. Salvage value is not used under the ACRS. In addition, if a fifteen-year ACRS is used, the deduction will reflect only the actual number of months the property is in service. Recovery period by months is calculated from the first day of the month the property is placed in service.

For example, if the taxpayer placed the commercial property in service during July of 1981, the appropriate rate for 1981 is 6%, 11% for 1982, 10% for 1983, etc. The taxpayer reads down the column labeled Jul.

Exhibit 12.8 shows the same example as Exhibit 12 .2 only with the ACRS rates for new commercial property placed into service during July. The property qualifies under the ACRS deduction within the new tax law. The depreciation deduction is calculated as follows:

Year	*Unadjusted Basis*	*ACRS Rate*		*ACRS Depreciation*
1	$400,000	× .06	=	$24,000
2	400,000	× .11	=	44,000
3	400,000	× .10	=	40,000
4	400,000	× .09	=	36,000
5	400,000	× .08	=	32,000
				$176,000

Note that in this example for commercial property, any gain upon sale that is over the $176,000 ACRS deduction is taxed as capital gains, while any gain up to this amount is taxed as ordinary income. If straight-line depreciation had been used, all gain would be capital gain. Also, the reader should compare the after-tax cash flow from each year to the same figure in Exhibit 12.2 which used straight-line depreciation under the previous tax law.

The choice between straight line and ACRS Under the ACRS, the short fifteen-year recovery period and the taxation of all or part of the capital gain upon sale as income might cause the taxpayer to consider seriously the alternative of using straight line and save all of the gain for a capital gain treatment. In some circumstances, the taxpayer may need to seriously evaluate the merit of combining an attractive personal income tax credit from special building design features with a depreciation schedule and an optimum holding period.

Anti-Churning Rules

The new method does *not* apply to depreciable real property-Section 1250 property-acquired after 1980 and (1) owned by the taxpayer or related person during 1980, (2) leased by the taxpayer to a person who owned it during 1980,

Exhibit 12.8
After-tax cash flow

	Year 1	Year 2	Year 3	Year 4	Year 5	
After-tax income						
NOI	$60,000	$60,000	$60,000	$60,000	$60,000	
– Interest	– 47,771	– 47,118	– 46,382	– 45,554	– 44,623	
– Depreciation	– 24,000	– 44,000	– 40,000	– 36,000	– 32,000	($176,000 total)
before-tax income	(11,771)	(31,118)	(26,382)	(21,554)	(16,623)	
+ Tax loss saving (40%)	+ 4,708	+ 12,447	+ 10,553	+ 8,622	+ 6,649	
or – income taxes (40%)	0	0	0	0	0	
After-tax cash flow						
NOI	60,000	60,000	60,000	60,000	60,000	
– Debt service	– 52,980	– 52,980	– 52,980	– 52,980	– 52,980	
– Tax loss saving	+ 4,708	+ 12,447	+ 10,553	+ 8,622	+ 6,649	
or – Income taxes	0	0	0	0	0	
After-tax cash flow	11,728	19,467	17,573	15,642	13,669	

Capital gain and taxes—nonresidential property	
Sales price	$560,000
– Selling expenses	– 45,000
– Tax basis (500,000 – 176,000 = 324,000)	– 324,000
Gross Capital Gain	$191,000
– Amount of ACRS deduction	– 175,000
Capital gain subject to gain tax exclusion	15,000
– Capital gain tax exclusion (.60 × 15,000 = $9,000)	– 9,000
	$6,000
Tax on gain (.40 × 6,000 = $2,400)	$2,400
After-tax cash flow—nonresidential property	
Net Sales Price ($560,000 – 45,000)	$515,000
– Unpaid mortgage	– 366,554
– Income taxes on gain (.40 × 176,000 = 70,400)	– 70,400
– Capital gains tax	– 2,400
After-tax cash flow from sale	$75,646
Total tax due from the sale	
Capital gain	$2,400
Income tax	70,400
	$72,800

or (3) received in a like-kind exchange. Thus in the earlier examples, John Smith would continue to calculate the after-tax cash flow and capital gain taxes in the same manner except for one point. The ERA limited the 40% of capital gain subject to income taxation to a maximum 50% tax rate.

FINANCIAL MANAGEMENT RATE OF RETURN (FMRR)

The FMRR was designed to compensate for the inadequacies in the IRR. It is based upon several assumptions:[17]

1. Funds can be used or reinvested at any time at the after-tax safe rate, i_L.
2. Only after-tax cash flows are used.
3. If positive cash flows are greater than a predetermined amount, x, the positive cash flows may be reinvested in another project of comparable risk at an after-tax rate, i_R, above the after-tax safe rate, i_L.

Consider the following example:

Initial Cash Flows

Period	*Cash Flows*	
0	(125,000)	after-tax cash flow safe rate
1	(35,000)	$i_L = 8\%$
2	(10,000)	Predetermined amount $x =$
3	50,000	\$65,000
4	(15,000)	Risk rate, i_R, = 12%
5	(25,000)	
6	55,000	
7	25,000	
8	(10,000)	
9	(5,000)	
10	550,000	

Step 1: Eliminate all negative cash outflows by using prior cash inflows where possible. The negative cash outflows of \$10,000 and \$5,000 in periods 8 and 9 can be removed by establishing a sinking fund from the \$25,000 in period 7. The present value of \$5,000 for two years at the safe rate of 8% is \$4287, and the present value of \$10,000 for one year at 8% is \$9259. Thus the cash flow in period 7 is adjusted to \$25,000 − \$4287 − \$9259 = \$11,454, and the cash flows in periods 8 and 9 are now zero. The same procedure is repeated for periods 3, 4, and 5. The result is the following revision:

Period	*Cash Flows*
0	($125,000)
1	(35,000)
2	(10,000)
3	14,678
4	0
5	0
6	55,000
7	11,454
8	0
9	0
10	550,000

Step 2: All remaining negative cash flows are discounted to the present at the safe rate. The present value of $10,000 for two years equals $8573, and the present value of $35,000 for one year equals $32,407. Thus the cash flow in period 0 = ($125,000) + (8573) + (32,407) = ($165,981), and the cash flow in periods 1 and 2 are set equal to zero. The results are the following:

Period	*Cash Flows*
0	(165,981)
1	0
2	0
3	14,678
4	0
5	0
6	55,000
7	11,454
8	0
9	0
10	550,000

Step 3: Compound all positive cash flows forward at the appropriate rate. The amount $14,678 is compounded forward three periods at the safe rate, i_L, which gives $18,490. This amount is added to the $55,000 in period 6, which gives $73,490. This amount is compared to the predetermined amount, *X*, which is $65,000. Since the compound amount is greater, it may be reinvested at the rate, i_R. If the compound amount was smaller, it would be rein-

vested at the rate, i_L. Therefore the amount of \$73,490 is compounded to the year 10 at the rate of 12%, and \$103,248 is added to the \$550,000 in period 10. Since the cash flow in period 7 of \$11,454 is less than the predetermined amount of \$65,000, it must be compounded at the safe rate of 8%, added to future cash flows appearing in later years (none in this problem), and compared to *X*. The process continues until all positive cash flows are compounded to the terminal year. The result is the following:

Period	*Cash Flows*
0	(\$165,981)
1	0
2	0
3	0
4	0
5	0
6	0
7	0
8	0
9	0
10	\$680,066

Step 4: The FMRR equation is used to calculate the FMRR.

$$\text{FMRR}_n = \left(\sqrt[n]{\frac{T_n^*}{D_n^*}} - 1\right) 100$$

where

$$\begin{aligned} n &= \text{number of periods,} \\ D_n^* &= \text{resulting cash flow in period 0,} \\ T_n^* &= \text{resulting cash flow in period } n. \end{aligned}$$

In this example,

$$\text{FMRR}_{10} = \left(\sqrt[10]{\frac{680{,}066}{165{,}981}} - 1\right) 100$$

$$\text{FMRR}_{10} = 15.15\%$$

AN OVERALL *R* WITH LENDER LOAN REQUIREMENTS

Several authors have argued recently that during periods of inflation, current appraisal techniques and models inaccurately estimate the magnitude of debt capacity for specific property since it is typically determined by the loan-to-value ratio and market value. One of their arguments is that the size of the equity within the reversion increases and can contribute more to the magnitude of market value than net operating income. When this happens, the NOI for the property may not be sufficient to cover the required debt service on the implied mortgage. Thus these newer models have assumptions that the authors consider to be more relevant during inflationary times.

The discussion in this section should be compared to the material covering Ellwood (Chapter 10). The authors of these newer models contend that under Ellwood, the lenders and equity investors will loan and invest, respectively, unlimited amounts to debt and equity according to the loan-to-value proportion of the market value for the property. Further, they contend that Ellwood has a built-in indifference by the lenders as to whether the market value originates from NOI or the reversion. Thus if most of the market value should come from the reversion equity, the NOI may not be sufficiently high to cover the required debt service.

Overall Rate Using Required Debt Service

One technique that has been used to estimate the overall rate R is[18]

R = mortgage loan ratio × annual mortgage constant × debt service coverage.

This concept has been used by some analysts because it includes the most probable financing requirements. Thus the most probable financing arrangements can be used to derive the most probable selling price. Users must be careful to remember that this technique is considered to derive an R that is used to estimate the most probable selling price. Consider the following example:

- The first mortgage currently available to the subject is for the 70% of the value at 11% for twenty-five years.
- The lender wants a debt service coverage of at least 1.25.

Then

$$R = .70 \times .1176 \times 1.25$$
$$R = .1029.$$

Gettel Model

One author[19] attempted to include the most probable financing arrangements in the estimate of R. His estimate of market value was

$$V = \frac{\text{NOI}}{R}$$

where

$$R = M\,(R_M)\,(\text{DCR}),$$
$$M = \text{loan-to-value ratio},$$
$$R_M = \text{mortgage constant},$$
$$\text{DCR} = \text{debt coverage ratio which is } \left(\frac{\text{stabilized NOI}}{\text{debt service}}\right).$$

Consider the following example:

$$M = 75\%,$$
$$\text{DS} = \$75{,}188,$$
$$Y_E = 15\%,$$
$$\text{Stabilized NOI} = \$100{,}000,$$
$$\text{DCR} = 100{,}000/75{,}188 = 1.33,$$
$$\text{R}_M = .1158 \text{ for a monthly mortgage interest rate of } 10\% \text{ for twenty years},$$
$$p = \text{expected holding period of ten years.}$$

Then

$$\text{V} = \frac{\text{NOI}}{R_M(\text{DCR})M} \qquad V = \frac{100{,}000}{(.1158)(1.33)(.75)} \qquad V = \$865{,}722.$$

Lusht and Zerbst[20]

Kenneth Lusht and Robert Zerbst have developed a model that suggests that debt capacity is a function of net operating income and is measured by the relationship between NOI and the debt service coverage ratio.

$$V = V_{\text{debt}} + V_{\text{equity}}$$

where

$$V_{\text{debt}} = \frac{\text{NOI}}{R_M(\text{DCR})},$$
$$V_{\text{equity}} = (\text{NOI} - \text{DS})\ (\text{present value ordinary annuity of \$1 per period}) + \text{equity reversion (present worth of \$1)}.$$

"Equity reversion" is found by deducting the mortgage balance at the end of the holding period from the projected selling price. Consider the following example:

$$M = 75\%,$$
$$\text{DS} = \$75{,}188,$$
$$Y_E = 15\%,$$

Stabilized NOI = \$100,000,

$$DCR = 100{,}000/75{,}188 = 1.33,$$

R_M = .1158 for a monthly mortgage interest rate of 10% for twenty years,

p = expected holding period of ten years,

app. = property is expected to increase in value by 2% per year,

Projected selling price = \$1,145,404

Outstanding loan balance at the end of ten years = \$474,130.

Then

$$V = V_{\text{debt}} + V_{\text{equity}}$$

$$V_{\text{debt}} = \frac{\text{NOI}}{R_M(\text{DCR})} \qquad V_{\text{debt}} = \frac{100{,}000}{.1158(1.33)} \qquad V_{\text{debt}} = \$649{,}292$$

and

$$V_{\text{equity}} = (\text{NOI} - \text{DS})\,(\text{Present value of \$1 ordinary annuity}) + \text{Equity reversion (present value of \$1)}$$

$$V_{\text{equity}} = (100{,}000 - 75{,}188)\,(5.0188) + \text{Equity reversion } (.2472)$$

$$\text{Equity reversion} = (1{,}145{,}404 - \$474{,}130)\,(.2472)$$

$$= (671{,}274)\,(.2472)$$

$$\text{Equity reversion} = 165{,}939.$$

Then

$$V_{\text{equity}} = \$124{,}526 + 165{,}939 \qquad V_{\text{equity}} = \$290{,}465$$

and

$$V = V_{\text{debt}} + V_{\text{equity}} \qquad V = 649{,}292 + 290{,}465$$

$$V = \$939{,}757.$$

INFLATION

A considerable amount of discussion and research has been devoted recently to the problem in estimating value during periods of extreme inflation. The purpose of this section is to summarize the issues.[21]

Concept of Inflation

Some differences exist among the concepts of inflation presented in the literature and the education material available from the AIREA and the SREA. The relationship between supply and demand analysis and inflation is not always made clear. For example, one set of authors define inflation to be "...the rate of expected appreciation in the subject's value as opposed to a basket of consumer goods as presented by the Consumer Price Index." Another source says that inflation is more than "...rising property values and increasing rentals." In addition, some authors feel that value should always be measured in terms of current constant dollars as opposed to the future purchasing power of the dollar.

Inadequacy of Current Models

One theme presented by several authors is that the current appraisal models, such as Ellwood, have no provision for measuring or including inflation. The figures for appreciation or depreciation are left to the appraiser's judgment.

Several authors have attempted to demonstrate that a biased estimate of value can occur if inflationary impacts are placed within the capitalization rate. One set of authors has argued that inflation has no impact on value if the real expected rate of discount is known and used. This assumes that the appraiser knows the relationship between the discount rate and the inflation rate.

Other authors have argued that the impact of inflation upon other variables used in estimating value is not always known or included. For example, the risk/return relationships for the equity investor and the lender are often unknown. In addition, inflationary impacts upon financing arrangements and leverage are often unestimated.

Current Treatment of Inflation

Perhaps the most widespread treatment of inflation in an appraisal report is to assume that income and expenses will both change at equal rates. Therefore the level of NOI calculated in the first year is the one that is used.

Another technique shown in this chapter is the projection of income and expenses for each year of the holding period and discounting the resulting NOI for each year to present value. This technique provides a good vehicle for incorporating inflation into the analysis, but does not include any technique for actually measuring it.

Summary

At the printing of this book, neither the AIREA nor the SREA have published any educational materials for the treatment of the impacts from inflation within the appraisal. Each appraiser is left to his or her own judgment.

The best technique still appears to be a year-by-year projection of income and expenses within a discounted cash flow model. The discounted cash flows and the discounted value of the reversion can be summed to provide an estimate of value that simulates the investor's behavior. The potential for inflation in the income stream and the reversion can be reflected.

CALCULATOR PROBLEMS

Two drill problems follow for use with the HP-38C/38E hand calculator. These are printed with permission of the Hewlett-Parkard Co.

Example: A development company is purchasing a group of condominiums with an annual net cash flow of $17,500. The expected holding period is 5 years with an estimated selling price of $540,000 at that time. If the company wishes to realize a 12% yield, what is the maximum purchase price of the condominiums?

Set the payment switch D.MY BEGIN / M.DY END to END.

Keystrokes	Display	
[f] CLEAR [FIN]		
5 [n]	*5.00*	
12 [i]	*12.00*	
17500 [PMT]	*17,500.00*	
540000 [FV]	*540,000.00*	
[PV]	*-369,494.09*	Amount that company can pay to realize a 12% yield.

In this case [PV] represents the maximum price, $369,494.09 necessary to achieve the desired yield.

Example: An income property is available for $50,000. The annual income over a 23-year projection period (all payments received at the end of the year) may be grouped as follows:

Cash flow (CFj)	*Number of years (Nj)*
$9,000	First 5 years
$7,500	Next 4 years
$6,000	Next 4 years
$7,500	Next 3 years
$5,000	Last 7 years

What is the annual rate of return?

Keystrokes	Display	
[f] CLEAR [ALL]	*0.00*	
50000 [CHS] [g] [CF_0]	*-50,000.00*	Initial investment.
9000 [g] [CF_j]	*9,000.00*	First cash flow amount.
5 [g] [N_j]	*5.00*	Five years (number of times cash flow occurs).
7500 [g] [CF_j]	*7,500.00*	Second cash flow amount.*
4 [g] [N_j]	*4.00*	Four years.
6000 [g] [CF_j]	*6,000.00*	Third cash flow amount.
4 [g] [N_j]	*4.00*	Four years.
7500 [g] [CF_j]	*7,500.00*	Fourth cash flow amount.*
3 [g] [N_j]	*3.00*	Three years.
5000 [g] [CF_j]	*5,000.00*	Fifth cash flow amount.
7 [g] [N_j]	*7.00*	Seven years.
[RCL] [n]	*5.00*	Verify number of cash flows entered.
[f] [IRR]	*15.27*	Annual IRR of 15.27%

Check your answer with [NPV].

*Note that $7,500 occurs two different places in the time scheme. Since the timing of cash flows is important for an IRR calculation, we can only lump together *consecutive* equal payments.

SUMMARY

The purpose of this chapter was to introduce modifications of the typical appraisal procedure and new developments in estimating *R* and *V*. The first part of the chapter explained the differences between investment value and market value. Investment value works with *after-tax cash flow,* which includes the individual's choice of depreciation schedules, the individual's selection of debt service, and the individual's income tax liability. Market value stops with NOI rather than after-tax cash flow, uses accrued depreciation that are typical to other similar properties in the market, and does not consider the individual's tax liability.

Net present value is sometimes used to determine present worth of the property or the present worth of the owner's equity. The latter is held by some to be a more accurate statement of the owner's intentions since it reflects a cash-on-cash return.

Closely related to the concept of net present value is the internal rate of return. This interest rate causes the discounted sum of future income to equal the cost, sometimes called *present value of the equity.* This rate is useful for comparison purposes. Similar rates calculated on all types of investments may be compared to locate the property or investment that yields the highest IRR.

Some analysts feel that the IRR has incorrect assumptions that may be solved by using the financial management rate of return. The calculations for this rate assume that funds can be reinvested at any time at the after-tax safe rate, only after-tax cash flows are used, and the investor has the opportunity to invest positive cash flows greater than a predetermined amount in another project at another rate above the after-tax cash flow rate.

Several attempts have been made to include lender requirements within the estimation of the market value. The authors' rationale is that the market value can be useless if the lender's loan requirements are not satisfied.

The treatment of inflation within the appraisal procedure has been the subject of considerable recent discussion and research. At the printing of this book, neither the AIREA nor the SREA have distributed any educational materials covering its measurement. The best technique still appears to be the projection of income and expenses over each year of the holding period using whatever information is available.

REVIEW QUESTIONS

1. Contrast investment value with market value.
2. Explain the steps for deriving the *after-tax cash flow.*
3. Explain the steps for calculating the capital gains taxes owed upon resale.
4. Explain the rules for selecting a depreciation schedule.
5. Explain the rules for recapture.
6. What is the difference between depreciation deductions under the pre-1981 and post-1980 tax laws.
7. Discuss the two types of net present value calculations.
8. Define the internal rate of return. Explain the methods by which it is calculated.
9. Explain the assumptions inherent to the IRR.
10. Explain the financial management rate of return. How is it better (worse) than the IRR? Explain the steps by which it is calculated.
11. Why are lender requirements important in estimating R and V?
12. Explain how lender requirements can be included in the estimation of R and V.
13. What types of refinements to the Ellwood technique have been developed? Discuss and illustrate them.

ENDNOTES

1. Donald R. Epley and James A. Millar, *Basic Real Estate Finance and Investments* (New York: John Wiley & Sons, Inc., 1980), chapter 19.
2. Ibid., chapter 18.
3. Ibid.
4. Mason J. Sacks and Jack Kusnet, *Real Estate Tax Shelter Techniques; Revised and Expanded Edition Including Revenue Act of 1978* (Boston: Warren, Gorham, and Lamont, 1979), chapter III.

5. Commerce Clearing House, *Standard Federal Tax Reports, Revenue Act of 1978, Number 48, November 2, 1978* (Chicago: Commerce Clearing House), p. 107; see also Editorial Staff Publication, *1980 Federal Tax Course* (Chicago: Clearing House Inc., 1979), pp. 1010–1011; also Lawrence Phillips and William Hoffman, *1980 Annual Edition West's Federal Taxation: Individual Income Taxes* (St. Paul, Minn: West Publishing Co., 1979), pp. 13–15.
6. Salvage value may be reduced by 10% prior to the depreciation calculation. See IRS Code 167 (f), 1954.
7. Ibid.
8. Charles Gilliand, "Component Depreciation—The Appraiser's Role," *The Appraisal Journal* 48 (January 1980): 78–84.
9. C. F. Sirmans, "Minimum Tax, Recapture, and Choice of Depreciation Methods," *Journal of the American Real Estate and Urban Economics Association* 8 (Fall 1980), p. 256.
10. Ibid.
11. Sacks and Kusnet, *Real Estate Tax Shelter Techniques,* chapter X.
12. Epley and Millar, *Basic Real Estate Finance and Investments.* pp. 353–356.
13. Robert Wiley, *Real Estate Investment Analysis and Strategy* (New York: Ronald Press (now John Wiley & Sons), 1977), pp. 117–118.
14. Byrl Boyce, *Real Estate Appraisal Terminology* (Cambridge, Mass.: Ballinger Publishing Co., 1975), p. 117.
15. Gary M. Tenzer and R. Tarantello, "FMRR: A Programmable Calculator Implementation," *The Real Estate Appraiser and Analyst* 45 (November–December 1979): 12, see also Michael S. Young, "FMRR: A Clever Hoax," *The Appraisal Journal* 47 (July 1979): 359–369; also H. S. Kerr, "A Final Word on FMRR," *The Appraisal Journal* 48 (January 1980): 95–103.
16. The material in this section relied heavily upon *The Economic Recovery Tax Act of 1981,* Peat, Marwick, and Mitchell & Co., August 5, 1981, Section IV; *Special Supplement; Economic Recovery Tax Act of 1981,* Deloitte, Haskins, and Sells, August 7, 1981; and *Concise Explanation of the Economic Recovery Tax Act of 1981,* Prentice-Hall, Inc., August, 1981, pp. 20–31.
17. This discussion and the examples were taken from Tenzer and Tarantello, "FMRR: A Programmable Calculator Implementation," pp. 11–16. Reprinted with permission from the November–December, 1979, issue of *The Real Estate Appraiser and Analyst,* published by the Society of Real Estate Appraisers, Chicago, Illinois.
18. For one discussion of this technique, see Henry C. Entreken, "Are We Really Seeking Market Value?" *The Appraisal Journal* 48 (July 1980): 428–431.
19. Ronald E. Gettel, "Good Grief, Another Method of Selecting Capitalization Rate," *The Appraisal Journal* 46 (January 1978): 90–100.
20. Kenneth M. Lusht and Robert H. Zerbst, "Valuing Income Properties in an Inflationary Economy," *The Real Estate Appraiser and Analyst* 46 (July–August 1980): 11–18.
21. This section relies heavily upon the following sources: Kenneth Lusht and Robert Zerbst, "Valuing Income Properties in an Inflationary Environment," *The Real*

Estate Appraiser and Analyst 46 (July-August, 1980): 11-18; Kenneth Lusht, "Inflation and Real Estate Investment," *The Real Estate Appraiser and Analyst* 45 (November-December 1979): 23-29; John P. Blair, "Estimating Price Expectations," *The Real Estate Appraiser and Analyst* 46 (September-October 1980): 45-48; Kenneth Lusht, "Inflation and Real Estate Investment Value," *Journal of the American Real Estate and Urban Economics Association* 6 (Spring 1978): 37-49; Twelfth Annual Young Advisory Council, "Report and Recommendations," *The Real Estate Appraiser and Analyst* 46 (September-October 1980): 34-36; James E. Gibbons, "Point of View: Influence of Inflation on Real Estate Valuation and Investment Analysis," *The Appraisal Journal* 48 (October 1980): 485-502; Ralph Brown and Dennis Johnson, "Inflation, Valuation, and the Discount Rate," *The Appraisal Journal* 48 (October 1980): 549-555; Michael Young, "Inflation, Valuation, and the Petersburg Paradox," *The Appraisal Journal* 48 (January 1980): 85-94.

ADDITIONAL READINGS

Akerson, Charles B. *The Internal Rate of Return in Real Estate Investments* (Chicago: American Society of Real Estate Counselors and American Institute of Real Estate Appraisers, 1976).

Boyce, Byrl. *Real Estate Appraisal Terminology* (Cambridge, Mass.: Ballinger Publishing Co., 1975), p. 117.

Colwell, Peter F., and Rushing, Phillip J. "To Ellwood and Beyond." *The Appraisal Journal* 47 (July 1979): 352-358.

Commerce Clearing House. *Standard Federal Tax Reports, Revenue Act of 1978,* Number 48, November 2, 1978 (Chicago: Commerce Clearing House), p. 107.

Editorial Staff Publication. *1980 Federal Tax Course* (Chicago: Clearing House Inc., 1979), pp. 1010-1011, also Lawrence Phillips and William Hoffman, *1980 Annual Edition West's Federal Taxation: Individual Income Taxes* (St. Paul, Minn.: West Publishing Co., 1979), pp. 13-15.

Ellwood, L. W. *Ellwood Tables for Real Estate Appraising and Financing* (Cambridge, Mass.: Ballinger Publishing Co., 1977), p. 93.

Fisher, Jeffery D. "Ellwood *J* Factors: A Further Refinement." *The Appraisal Journal* 47 (January 1979): 65-75.

Gilliand, Charles. "Component Depreciation—The Appraiser's Role. *The Appraisal Journal* 48 (January 1980): 78-84.

Messner, Stephen D.; Schreiber, Irving; and Findley, Chapman M. "Real Estate Investment Analysis: IRR Versus FMRR." *Real Estate Appraiser* 91 (July-August, 1975): 5-30.

Sacks, Mason J., and Kusnet, Jack. *Real Estate Tax Shelter Techniques: Revised and Expanded Edition Including Revenue Act of 1978,* (Boston: Warren, Gorham, and Lamont, 1979), chapter III.

Young, Michael S. "FMRR: A Clever Hoax." *The Appraisal Journal* 47 (July 1979): 359-369.

CHAPTER 13

LEARNING OBJECTIVES

When a student finishes this chapter, he or she should be able to:

- Explain how the physical residual technique evolved.
- Discuss the circumstances under which the property residual method is best applied and its relative merits.
- Apply the different applications of the property residual method.

Physical Residual: Property

IMPORTANT TERMS AND PHRASES

direct capitalization: A technique used to derive market value, using a market-derived overall capitalization rate, ignoring any residual property value, and assuming that the property's income stream is unchanging.

liquidation value: A term used interchangeably with reversionary value. This value may apply to either the investment holding period or the remaining economic life of the improvements.

overall capitalization rate (R_0): A capitalization rate that provides for return on and of an investment, but without identifying these provisions; net operating income divided by sale price or value.

residual: That which remains, such as income left over to the site after deducting the income assigned to the building from the net operating income.

reversionary value: The value of an owner's reversionary right to repossess and resume full and exclusive use of the property that has been temporarily alienated by a lease or other means.

The purpose of this chapter is to discuss and illustrate the property residual technique of estimating property value. This procedure is one of three methods (property, building, and land) collectively known as the physical residual method.

The building and land residual techniques are covered in the following two chapters. The property residual technique discussion is preceded by a review of how this technique has been viewed over the years.

HISTORY OF PHYSICAL RESIDUAL TECHNIQUES

As part of a land economic series written early in this century, Frederick M. Babcock wrote *The Appraisal of Real Estate* in 1927. He correctly pointed out that the value of land and a building for an income-producing property was genuinely merged, and any division in value was purely a theorectical concept. Further, the value of a vacant site was based on the present value of future net income caused by an improvement.[1] Later, in 1932, Babcock wrote his classic *Valuation of Real Estate.* He referred to a residual land value, which was the discounted future value—allowing for a construction and planning period as well as development expenses.[2] Additionally, he assigned a different rate of return to the building and to the land. The building return was constructed first, and the land returns followed. The latter residual income was capitalized to reveal the land value.[3]

In a subsequent book, in 1933, entitled *Real Estate Appraisal and Valuation,* Philip W. Kniskern observed in evaluating improved real estate by the income approach that the income from the property was produced by a combination of land and building. He made the significant point that neither the land nor the building produced any particular part of the income. Kniskern elaborated that one portion of the income could not be characterized solely by land conditions, which would be entirely eliminated when measuring the other portion of the income. Any net operating income for one property use was judged to have only one set of characteristics that were attached uniformly to each and every individual dollar of the total net income. These characteristics were created by a combination of land and building. Therefore, the entire net operating income for any one year from a particular interest in real estate must be capitalized at the same rate.

Kniskern went on to say that a division of the whole property value between land and building is an arbitrary allocation by the appraiser, but it is proper for the appraiser to make such an allocation when the sum of the two parts equals the whole.[4] He also pointed out that all land has a potential value that is entitled to receive a proportionate return if the land were improved with a building suited to its highest and best use. Any earnings to the land would be residual after paying a fair return on the fair cost of the building and providing for the replacement of the investment in the building during its economic life.[5]

Another early writer, Stanley L. McMichael, writing in the third edition of *McMichael's Appraising Manual* in 1937, devoted a chapter to residual methods for treating income. This is one of the first presentations of the land, building, and the property residual methods. McMichael recognized three sets of computations that could be used with either of these three methods:

1. Direct capitalization, where the income is considered perpetual and unchanging in amount.
2. Computation of the present value of future net operating income, which may vary each year.
3. Solving for value where future decreases or increases in net operating income are computed and then subtracted from or added to the present capitalized value.[6]

ASSUMPTIONS UNDERLYING THE PROPERTY RESIDUAL

This residual method considers the total estimated property value as a unit without either the land or the buildings being a residual part of this value. Yet, there is a certain partitioning of the property value since the forecast land value at the end of the building's economic life is discounted back to a present value. This method sometimes is confused with the overall capitalization rate method, which is market derived and applies a single rate to an income stream without the necessity of forecasting a future site value. This method was discussed in previous chapters.

The property residual method is similar in logic to judging the present value of a bond for a fixed term. The value would be a combination of the present value of the payments plus the present value of the value to be received at maturity. Suppose that the annual interest rate is 8%, creating an interest payment of $400 annually ($5000 × .08), the term is fifteen years, and the face amount is $5000. Discounting these two attributes of value reveals a present value of $5000.

$ 400 × 8.559479 =	$3,423.79
$5,000 × .315242 =	1,576.21
Present Value of Bond	$5,000.00

RELATIVE MERITS OF THE PROPERTY RESIDUAL

The property residual technique generally is regarded as being the preferred method of the three physical residual techniques. It is appropriate both for properties with recently constructed buildings as well as properties with older buildings. If it is difficult to derive an overall capitalization rate, this approach may be used in estimating the value of both the site and improvements, but its potential shortcomings should be remembered. It also is widely used in estimating the leased fee interest of a property subject to a long-term lease.

A weakness inherent in this technique is the necessity of the appraiser to estimate the current market rent and discount rate and forecast the value of the underlying site some twenty-five to fifty years into the future. Who could possibly judge the traffic, zoning, market, demand, and technological changes and other influences on value so far into the future? Also, the appraiser is compelled to select a current appropriate discount rate based on an investor's impression of long-term future value. An assumption that the property value will be unchanged over a twenty-five-year period can alter the estimated property value significantly. For instance, if site values were increased at an annual rate of only 5%, a $50,000 site would be worth $169,318 ($50,000 × 3.386355), twenty-five years hence instead of the constant value $50,000.

An improvement in the use of this approach would be to reduce the potential inaccuracy of a long-term constant site value by substituting a prospective or typical investors' holding period for the forecast remaining economic life of the improvements. Hence the total forecast value of the property at the end of the holding period would be used instead of the alleged unchanged value of the site over the remaining economic life, which may be several times as long as a typical investment period.

STEPS IN THE PROPERTY RESIDUAL APPROACH

The steps involved in this approach are outlined in Exhibit 13.1. Begin by estimating the total net operating income available to the entire property. Once having derived this income, it is discounted at an appropriate rate over the forecast income or holding period. Finally, the reversionary value of the site

Exhibit 13.1
Steps in the property residual method

For a forecast holding period that is less than the remaining economic life of the improvements (improvements have value at end of forecast holding period):

A. Net Operating Income for each future year, i (attributable to land and improvements)	NOI_i
B. Discounted at appropriate rate for holding period using (a_n)	$NOI_i\ (a_n)$
C. Plus reversionary value of land and improvements	$(FV_L + I)(V^n)$
D. Equals total present value of property	$B + C$

Exhibit 13.2
Steps in the property residual method

Forecast holding period equals remaining economic life (improvements have no value at end of forecast holding period):

A. Net Operating Income for each future year, *i* (attributable to land and improvements)	NOI_i
B. Discounted at appropriate rate for REL (a_n)	$NOI_i\ (a_n)$
C. Plus reversionary value of land at the end of the building's economic life	$(FV_L)(V^n)$
D. Equals total present value of property	$B + C$

and improvements are added to the discounted income to reveal the present value of the appraised property. Exhibit 13.2 is similar to Exhibit 13.1 except the holding period is equal instead of less than the remaining economic life of the improvements.

A point well worth considering prior to selecting the property residual or any other valuation method is whether it faithfully represents the analytical method used by investors typically associated with this type property. Use of some esoteric and complex method that is not recognized in practice may produce confusing and unreliable results.

VARIATIONS OF REMAINING ECONOMIC LIFE PREMISE

A more realistic value estimate results when the appraiser takes into account any changes in the site value during the period that the building is expected to lose its value. The estimated decline in the building's value should be matched with the probable change (increase or decrease) in the site's value.

In Exhibit 13.3, it can be seen that there is a difference in value when the value of one site is unchanged while another site is expected to increase in value 5% annually. There is not a significant difference using the 5% rate of growth, but nevertheless the second method more nearly reflects actual market expectations. Of course, the forecast annual change in the site value will vary according to the age and nature of the property and the accompanying demand for and availability of such property.

Using Holding Period Instead of Remaining Economic Life

Using the holding period instead of the remaining economic life in the property residual method is preferable since the market and property performance in the shorter period can more accurately be forecast than over the longer term. A shorter period has a greater probability of more nearly resembling cur-

Exhibit 13.3
Effect of anticipated rising site value on present value

No change in site value—	
Given: Present worth of site	$100,000
Discount rate	10%
Remaining economic life	40 years
Net operating income	$ 72,000
PV of $1 ($V^n$)	.022095
PV of $1 per period ($a_n$)	9.779051
PV of NOI = (9.779051)($72,000)	$704,092
Plus $PV_{Reversion}$ = (.022095)($100,000)	2,210
Total present value of property	$706,302
Assume that site value increased 5% annually for forty years	
Given: Same as above, plus	
Amount of 1 at 5% for 40 years = 7.039989	
PV of NOI	$704,092
Plus PV of Reversion = ($2,210)(7.039989)	15,558*
Total present value of property	$719,650

*Same as $100,000 × 7.039989 × .022095.

rent market conditions than those in the distant future, as well as more faithfully reflecting the holding period of typical investors of income properties. Another advantage of the holding period premise is that it avoids keeping the site value fixed while the building value declines at a uniform rate over its remaining economic life. The example in Exhibit 13.4 is similar to the second part of Exhibit 13.3 except the forecast income period is ten instead of forty years, which will produce a different value.

Necessity of Accurately Forecasting Remaining Economic Life

Care must be taken to carefully estimate the remaining economic life of the improvements. The selection of an unreasonably long remaining economic life of the improvements can either *inflate* the present value of the income stream or understate the present value of the building. This potential error, shown in Exhibit 13.5, points out the necessity of realistically forecasting the appraised structure's remaining economic life.

Recall that Exhibit 13.3 had a present site value of $100,000 and an indicated present value of the income stream of $704,092. Mistakenly forecasting the building's remaining economic life as fifty years rather than forty years produces the values indicated in Exhibit 13.5. The result of this "error" is the

Exhibit 13.4
Property value when site value increases 5% annually for 10 years

Given: PV of $1 at 10% ($V^n$)	0.385543
PV of $1 per period at 10% ($a_{\overline{n}\rceil}$)	6.144567
Amount of $1 @ 5%	1.628895
PV_{NOI} ($72,000)(6.144567)	$442,410
PV_R (.385543)(1.628895)($100,000)	62,800
	$505,210
Rounded to $505,000	

Exhibit 13.5
Property value when site increases at 5% annually for 50 years

$PV_{NOI} = (a_{\overline{n}\rceil}$ at 10%)(I)	
PV_{NOI} = (9.914814)($72,000)	$713,867
$PV_{Reversion} = (S^n$ at 5%)(V^n at 10%)(V_L)	
Plus $PV_{Reversion}$ = (11.4674)(.008519)($100,000)	9,769
Total present value of property	$723,636

total property value being overstated by $3986, caused by the discounted value of the income stream being overstated by $9775 ($713,867 – $704,092), and the site reversion being decreased by $5789 ($15,558 – $9,769). It can therefore be seen that it is important to analyze the property and neighborhood to reach as accurate a forecast of remaining economic life as possible.

PROBLEMS

Question: Compute the present value of a new office property that is subject to an absolute net* lease producing an annual rental income of $80,000 for ten years. The present site value is estimated to be $130,000 and the building is worth $520,000. Over the lease term, the land is expected to increase in value by 80% and the building value should decline by 10%. An annual discount rate of 10% is thought to be appropriate.

*A lease in which the tenant pays all taxes, insurance, and maintenance expenses.

1. Find the present value of this property under the terms of this lease.
2. What is the overall capitalization rate?

Answer:

1. $PV_{NOI} = (a_{\overline{n}|}$ at 10%) $(I) = (6.144567)$ ($80,000)	$491,565
$PV_R = (V^n)$(FV of site and building)	
$PV_R = (.385543)$ ($234,000 + $468,000)*	270,651
Present Value	$762,216
Rounded to	$762,000

2. R_o = $80,000/$762,000
 = .1050

Question: You have been requested to estimate the present value of an industrial loft structure and site in an older declining neighborhood. Similar sites have been declining in value at 3% annually for the past several years. This trend appears likely to continue for the foreseeable future. This eighty-year-old property has another six years remaining on the lease, which requires the tenant to pay $48,000 yearly for the balance of this year. The building is expected to have no value at the end of the lease. Although the rental income will rise slightly in each of the remaining years, the operating expenses can be expected to rise as well, leaving approximately the same NOI. Thus the present operating expense ratio† of 60% will be used for this appraisal. A nearby similar site has just sold for $100,000. Investors expect a 14% return from this type of property. What is the present value of this property?

Answer:

$PV_{NOI}(a_{\overline{n}|}$ at 14%, 6 years)(I)	
PV_{NOI}(3.888667) ($19,200)	$74,662
$PV_R(V^n$ at 3%, 6 years)(V^n at 14%, 6 years)(future sale price)	
PV_R (.837484)‡ (.455587) ($100,000)	38,155
Present Value	$112,817
Rounded to	$113,000

*$234,000 = (1.8)($130,000);$468,000 = (.90)($520,000).

†Operating expense ratio is derived from operating expenses divided by gross income, usually effective gross income.

‡Note 0.837484 is the reciprocal of the Amount of One. If the site were expected to increase in value at 3% annually, the PV_R would have been (1.194052) (.455587) ($100,000).

Question: An investor is interested in purchasing a property that is subject to a twelve-year-lease. At the time the lease expires, the property will be resold to the present owner who agrees to become the tenant. Under the conditions of this purchase-leaseback, the repurchase price would be \$1,000,000 and the absolute net annual rent would be \$16,000 for the full term of the lease. An 8% discount rate is appropriate for this property due to the favorable rental income, but because the future sale price is judged to be low, the reversionary value of the property is discounted at 15%. How much could the investor justify paying for this property under these terms?

Answer:

$PV_{NOI}(a_{\overline{n}\rvert}$ at 8%, 12 years) (I)	
PV_{NOI} (7.536078) (\$16,000)	\$120,577
PV_R (V^n at 15%, 12 years)(repurchase price)	
PV_R (.186907) (\$1,000,000)	186,907
Present Value	\$307,484
Rounded to	\$307,000

SUMMARY

In addition to several key terms, this chapter has covered the historical development of the property residual technique. Frederick Babcock correctly pointed out that only a theoretical division of income can be made between site and building. Yet, under certain circumstances, this division of income is proper. There is no separation of income between land and building(s) under this method except to account for the present value of the site at the end of the building's economic life. The present value of both the site and building is considered if they are expected to retain value at the end of the holding period.

An advantage of this residual technique includes its adaptability to new and older buildings. On the other hand, this method is weakened when an estimate of future property income and value are projected over a long period. Therefore the property residual technique produces the most satisfactory results when the income stream and value of the site and building is forecast over a comparatively short period.

REVIEW QUESTIONS

1. Explain how the reversionary value of a property can be used to produce an overall capitalization rate.

2. On what major point concerning the physical residual techniques did Babcock and Kniskern concur?

3. For what appraisal assignments is the property residual method especially well suited?
4. Discuss any weaknesses that you detected in the property residual method.
5. How does the property residual method using a forecast period less than the remaining life of improvements differ from the forecast income period being equal to the remaining economic life?
6. Outline the steps involved in the property residual method.
7. What advantages, if any, are there to using an investment period instead of the remaining economic life with the property residual method?
8. Discuss the potential value distortion of erroneously selecting a property's remaining economic life.

ENDNOTES

1. Frederick W. Babcock, *The Appraisal of Real Estate* (New York: The MacMillan Company, 1927), p. 175.
2. Frederick W. Babcock, *Valuation of Real Estate* (New York: McGraw-Hill Book Company, Inc., 1932), pp. 288–289.
3. Ibid., pp. 270–273.
4. Philip W. Kniskern, *Real Estate Appraisal and Valuation* (New York: The Ronald Press Company, 1933), p. 409.
5. Ibid., p. 437.
6. Stanley L. McMichael, *McMichael's Appraising Manual* (New York: Prentice-Hall, Inc., 1945), pp. 100–101.

ADDITIONAL READINGS

Babcock, Frederick W. *The Appraisal of Real Estate* (New York: The MacMillan Company, 1927), pp. 175–194.

Babcock, Frederick W. *Valuation of Real Estate* (New York: McGraw-Hill Book Company, Inc., 1932), pp. 288–289.

Goulet, Peter G. *Real Estate: A Value Approach* (Encino, California: Glencoe Publishing Company, Inc., 1979), pp. 101–111.

Kniskern, Philip W. "Capitalization," *Real Estate Appraisal and Valuation* (New York: The Ronald Press Company, 1933), pp. 433–444.

McMichael, Stanley L. "Residual Methods for Treating Income," *McMichael's Appraising Manual,* 3rd ed. (New York: Prentice-Hall, Inc., 1945), pp. 100–106.

Schmutz, George L. "The Income Approach—Land, Building, and Property Residual Process(es)," *The Appraisal Process* (Los Angeles: George L. Schmutz, 1941), pp. 142–151.

CHAPTER 14

LEARNING OBJECTIVES

When a student finishes this chapter, he or she should be able to:

- Understand the logic underlying the application of the building residual technique.
- Discuss under what circumstances this physical residual method is appropriately utilized.
- Determine the relative strengths and weaknesses of this appraisal technique.
- Explain the procedures used in this method under several different income-value scenarios.

Physical Residual: Building

IMPORTANT TERMS AND PHRASES

annualizer (*a*): A factor used to convert overall value change during a given period to an annual rate of change.

annuity capitalization: A method used to estimate the present value of a regular, predictable income stream which may be level, increasing, or declining.

discount rate: A rate that provides for a return on an investment. If there is no perceived decline in value of the property component over the forecast period, then the discount rate equals the capitalization rate, such as generally is the case with land.

holding period (*p*): A period over which the income produced by a real property is analyzed. It may be the typical holding period for similar investment properties or the remaining economic life of the appraised property.

overall rate (R_0): A capitalization rate that expresses a relationship between net operating income and property value (or sale price), i.e., NOI/V.

straight-line capitalization: A method used in valuing real property where the value of the land and building(s) is recognized, with the capitalization rate including an annual recapture rate for the building value over its remaining economic life. This method is inapplicable where the value of the building is expected to increase over the forecast period.

yield (Y_0): An annual rate expressing a relationship between earnings and an equity investment. It allows for any change in value during the holding period, and equals R_0 when there is no change in value.

This chapter continues the physical residual method of appraising, but it departs from the previous chapter in two major ways. The previous chapter dealt with the property residual technique, which did not involve an allocation of the net operating income between the site and building. The present value was the total of the discounted income plus the reversionary value of the future value of the site and improvements (if any).

In this chapter, concerned with the building residual method, the property income is allocated between the site and the building. The process begins with the estimated net operating income; a portion is allocated to the site and the balance applied to the building. Once this capitalized residual income is capitalized, the estimated building value is known.

This chapter also differs from the previous chapter in providing for constant and changing income as well as separate value changes for the site and building.

ASSUMPTIONS UNDERLYING THE BUILDING RESIDUAL TECHNIQUE

This technique is applicable to the appraisal of properties where:

1. The site value can be derived satisfactorily from similar market transfers or other acceptable indicators.
2. Buildings are of a peculiar design, reproduction costs-new are difficult to derive, and estimated accrued depreciation is judged to be unreliable.
3. Reliable rental income and operating expense data can be derived for the appraised property.
4. The remaining economic life of the building can be accurately forecast.
5. A reliable risk or discount rate can be estimated for the property.

It may be helpful to the reader to think of the building residual technique being used when the building value is unknown, but the site value can be satisfactorily estimated.

Relative Merits of the Building Residual Technique

This technique can be used under the straight-line capitalization premise (straight-line recapture), as well as under the annuity capitalization method. The former method is deficient since it is based on the assumption that the property value, as well as the rental income, will decline. This ordinarily does not occur. On the other hand, this method is an improvement over the land residual technique (covered in the next chapter) since the land value is market-derived and it is not necessary to estimate the building value via reproduction cost less accrued depreciation.

If the responsibility of the appraiser is to mirror the behavior and practices of real estate investors and tenants, then it can be argued that both the building and land residual techniques are unrealistic. Investors are neither concerned about apportioning income between the site and improvements nor inclined to apply different discount rates or factors to these property components. The only division of a property by an investor normally would be between land and depreciable improvements for federal income tax purposes.

STEPS IN APPLYING THE BUILDING RESIDUAL

The steps involved in applying this residual technique are outlined in the following model (Fig. 14.1). Two illustrations in Exhibit 14.1 follow this model. The first example depicts this method via straight-line capitalization, while the second illustration shows how annuity capitalization can be applied. Note the difference in value derived by these two variations of the building residual technique.

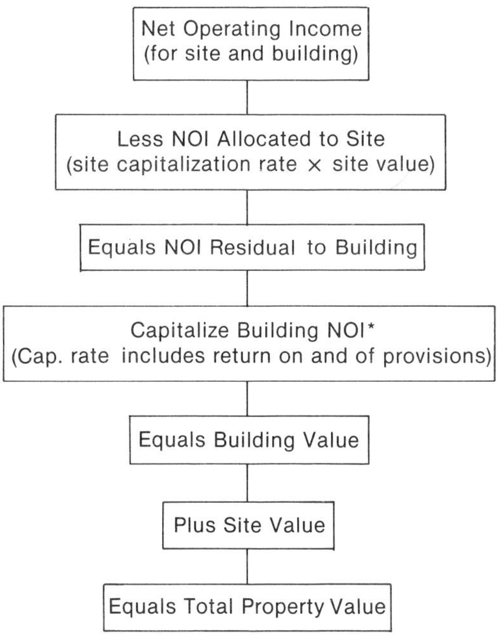

Fig. 14.1 Building residual model

---

*Divide building residual income by building capitalization rate providing for return on and recapture of the building value over its remaining economic life when using straight-line capitalization. The building residual income is multiplied by the PV of one factor for the remaining economic life when using the annuity capitalization method.

Exhibit 14.1
Straight line and ordinary annuity methods illustrated*

Straight line capitalization		Ordinary annuity capitalization	
NOI	$ 72,000	NOI	$ 72,000
Less income to site (10% × $100,000)	−10,000	Less income to site	−10,000
NOI residual to building	$ 62,000	NOI residual to building	$ 62,000
Capitalized† at 12% equals	$516,667	Discounted‡ at 10% for 50 years equals	$614,718
Plus site value	100,000	Plus site value	100,000
Total present worth of property	$616,667	Total present worth of property	$714,718

*Assumptions:
NOI = $72,000
REL = 50 years
Land reversion = $100,000
Discount rate = 10%
$a_{\overline{n}|}$ = 9.914814.

†$62,000/.12 = $516,667.

‡$62,000 × 9.914814 = $614,718.

If the same remaining economic life of the improvements, same discount rate, and site value are used, the same value indications should be produced by the property, building, and land residual techniques. Some minor differences due to rounding, of course, will occur.

APPLICATION OF THE BUILDING RESIDUAL TECHNIQUE

This technique is well suited to the appraisal of real property where the appraiser has difficulty in judging the value of the improvements. Also, it is well suited to valuing buildings that suffer a high degree of accrued depreciation. Finally, it is applicable to properties that are subject to a long-term lease or have a predictable income stream.

If a property is appraised on the basis of the straight-line capitalization method instead of the annuity method, a significantly different value will be indicated. While not immediately apparent, the annuity capitalization rate has a built-in recapture or amortization rate rather than being added on as in the straight-line method. The annuity method will produce a higher property value than the straight-line method, even though both methods provide for capital recapture. This difference is caused by the compounding of interest in the annuity method, which is absent in the straight-line method. In Exhibit 14.1, the annuity method indicates a value 16% greater than revealed by the straight-line method.

Assuming a Change in Site and Building Value

The building residual technique can be used in situations where both the site and building values are expected to change over the forecast income period. This income period could be the typical holding period for investors, the remaining economic life of the building, or for a lease term.

A point to remember is that the appraiser's primary responsibility is to reflect the behavior of real estate owners and users, as well as to accurately depict real property value and income patterns. Thus if the value of the site and building can be separately analyzed, then the appraiser should do so. This actual value behavior can be analyzed with the following procedure that adjusts the site and building capitalization rates to reflect the forecast change in value:

$$R_0 = Y_0 - \Delta a$$

where

R_0 = overall capitalization rate,

Y_0 = yield rate,

Δ = total value change of the site or building over the holding period, a is represented by $1/p$.

This method is illustrated in the following example. Suppose you were asked to find the present value of a property where the present site value of \$100,000 is expected to increase in value 50% over the next ten years; the building value is unknown, but it probably will decline 25% over the same period; $Y_0 = .12$. The present net operating income is \$75,000 and is *expected to rise* to some degree, but you are uncertain as to the amount. The solution to this appraisal assignment follows:

NOI	\$ 75,000
Less income to site (\$100,000)(.12 − .50/10) (\$100,000)(.07)	7,000
NOI residual to building	\$ 68,000
Capitalize building NOI (.12 + .25/10) \$68,000/.1450	\$468,966
Plus site value	100,000
Total property value	\$568,966
Rounded	\$569,000

This building residual technique can be varied slightly to account for a property that has a *constant net operating income,* but changing site and building values. Substitute a sinking fund factor for *a,* computed at the overall yield rate for the holding period. Suppose, for example, that $Y_0 = .08$; the site is worth \$200,000 and is expected to increase 24% over six years; and the sinking fund factor for six years at 8% is .136315. The income assignable to the site is computed as:

$$
\begin{array}{ll}
(V_L) \quad (Y_0 - \Delta a) & \\
(\$200{,}000)[(.08) - (.24 \times .136315)] & = \\
\$200{,}000\,(.08 - .032716) & = \underline{\underline{\$9{,}457}}
\end{array}
$$

PROBLEMS

Question: Find the value of the following property using the straight-line residual method. The forecast effective gross income is \$130,000; the operating expense ratio is 40%;* the expected remaining economic life of the building is thirty years. The site measures 250′ × 400′; similar sites in the area are selling for \$1.60 a square foot and typically bring an annual square foot net rental of \$0.128.

*Total operating expenses divided by gross income (usually effective gross income).

Answer:

Net operating income	
($130,000 × .60)	$ 78,000
Less NOI allocated to site	
(100,000* S.F. × $1.60 = $160,000)	
× ($0.128/$1.60 = .08)	12,800
NOI residual to building	$ 65,200
Capitalize building NOI	
(.08 + 1/30† = .1133)	$575,463‡
Plus site value	160,000
Total property value	$735,463
Rounded	$735,000

*250′ × 400′ = 100,000 square feet.

†.08 = ratio of net rental ($0.128) to sale price ($1.60); 1/30 = .0333 annual recapture rate.

‡$65,200/.1133 = $575,463.

Question: Find the present value of the same property, assuming that the NOI will be constant, while the site value will increase 20% during the next five years. The expected overall yield (Y_0) on this type of property is 12%. (Note: The formula for this income-value situation is $R_0 = Y_0 - \Delta a$, with R_0 = overall capitalization rate, Δ = total value change over the holding or forecast period (p), and a = the sinking fund factor annualizer computed at Y_0 for p.)

Answer:

NOI	$ 78,000
Less income to site	
($160,000)[(.12) − (.20 × .157410)]	14,163
NOI residual to building	$ 63,837
Capitalize building NOI	
.12 − (−.1667* × .157410) = .146240	$436,521
Plus site value	160,000
Total property value	$596,521
Rounded	$597,000

*The value of the building is expected to decline ⅓ or 0.0333 annually for five years. The five-year sinking fund factor of 0.157410 provides for recapture when there is a level income stream and change in property value.

Question: Appraise the same property, but assume that the following facts apply at present and over the next five years:

present site value	$160,000
expected site value change	+ .2000
expected building value change	− .1667
overall yield	.1200

Since the net rental income should also rise, the appropriate formula for estimating the overall rate is $R_0 = Y - \Delta a$, with Δ being the overall value change of the site or building over the holding period, and a is represented by $1/p$.

Answer:

NOI	$ 78,000
Less income to site ($160,000)(.12 − .20/5)	12,800
NOI residual to building	$ 65,200
Capitalize building NOI (.12 + .1667/5)	$425,199
Plus site value	160,000
Total property value	$585,199
Rounded	$585,000

SUMMARY

This chapter has presented several important new appraisal definitions and concepts that the student will want to review carefully. The building residual technique is best applied when the site value and net operating income can be accurately estimated, but the building value cannot be estimated satisfactorily. The straight-line capitalization method may be unrealistic since it is based on the assumption that both the income and property value are assumed to decline; this generally does not happen.

The basic steps involved in this approach are:

1. Estimate net operating income.
2. Deduct NOI allocated to site, which leaves income residual to the building.
3. Capitalize building NOI, which equals the building value.
4. Add site value to reveal the total property value.

The building residual method can be used when the income is rising, and the site and building value is expected to change by use of the equation

$R_0 = Y_0 - \Delta a$, with a equal to the reciprocal of the holding period $(1/n)$. The same method can be used when the income is forecast to be constant. In this case, a equals the sinking fund factor for the holding period, computed at the yield rate.

REVIEW QUESTIONS

1. Briefly comment on the principal similarity and difference between discount and overall capitalization rates.
2. What are two characteristics inherent in the straight-line capitalization method?
3. Can the equity yield on real property differ from the property's overall capitalization rate? Explain.
4. Summarize the assumptions underlying use of the building residual technique.
5. It is sometimes argued that the building residual method does not faithfully reflect the behavior of real estate investors. Explain.
6. Without reference to the book, outline the steps in the building residual model, taking care to distinguish between processing the building NOI for straight-line recapture versus an ordinary annuity.
7. Explain why the ordinary annuity building residual method yields a higher value than the straight-line capitalization method although the discount rate is the same.
8. What effect does an increasing value of the appraised property have on the overall capitalization rate? Explain how this influence on the capitalization rate occurs.
9. Why is it necessary to accurately judge the remaining economic life of a property's building?

ADDITIONAL READINGS

Ratcliff, Richard U. "Net Income Can't Be Split." *The Appraisal Journal* 18 (April 1950): 168–172.

Ratcliff, Richard U. *Valuation for Real Estate Decisions* (Santa Cruz, Calif.: Democrat Press, 1972), p. 212.

Shenkel, William M. "Residual Capitalization Techniques," *Modern Real Estate Appraisal* (New York: McGraw-Hill Book Co., 1978), Chapter 12.

"Straight and Annuity Capitalization," *The Appraisal of Real Estate,* 7th ed. (Chicago: American Institute of Real Estate Appraisers, 1978), Chapter 21.

Wendt, Paul F. "The Residual Approaches," *Real Estate Appraisal: Review and Outlook* (Athens: The University of Georgia Press, 1974), pp. 153–158.

CHAPTER 15

LEARNING OBJECTIVES

When a student finishes this chapter, he or she should be able to:

- Explain the basis for using the land residual technique.
- Explain the comparative merits of the land residual method.
- Discuss how a property's highest and best use is estimated by using the land residual.
- Discuss the importance of accurately perceiving the nature of a property's income pattern before choosing a particular land residual method.

Physical Residual: Land

IMPORTANT TERMS AND PHRASES

building capitalization rate (R_B): A rate that pertains to net operating income available to the building. It provides for a return on capital and capital recovery.

highest and best use: That use or succession of legally permitted uses for which there is sufficient demand and which are adaptable to the site, resulting in the highest present site value.

land capitalization rate (R_L): A rate used to convert net operating income available to a site into capital value. It normally makes no provision for capital recovery; synonymous with risk rate.

This concluding chapter on the three physical residual techniques explains under what circumstances this method is most appropriately applied. Pointed out are the correct ways to handle this technique regarding building value versus building cost. Also considered are how the land residual method can be used to judge the highest and best use of vacant and improved sites. Finally, the income pattern analysis is discussed and illustrated for the land residual method.

ASSUMPTIONS UNDERLYING THE LAND RESIDUAL

This technique is useful not only in estimating site value but also is appropriately used in highest and best use analysis. This latter application will be illustrated later. This technique is best applied to the appraisal of properties where:

1. The building is new or relatively new.
2. The cost-new can be accurately estimated and little, if any, accrued depreciation has occurred.
3. The building contributes a relatively small part of the total property value (and therefore the possibility of misjudging the income available for the site is minimized).

Sometimes it is argued that even though a building is old, the income attributable to the building should be figured on the basis of its reproduction cost-new. This notion seems unrealistic and unduly restrictive. There is no justification for an investor expecting a return on a building costing $400,000 but only worth $300,000. Thus it seems logical that the return *on* and *of* the building should be based on its estimated present value rather than its reproduction cost-new. Otherwise, the building value is overstated and the site value understated, as shown in Exhibit 15.1.

MERITS OF THE LAND RESIDUAL TECHNIQUE

Great care must be taken when using this technique to estimate the reproduction cost-new or present value of the building. Also, caution must be used in developing the income and expense statement, as well as the applicable rates. If the use is both prospective and hypothetical (such as for a vacant parcel) and reproduction costs and income-expense data are scarce, then this technique loses much of its reliability. In the appraisal of a vacant parcel by this method, the appraiser is obliged to base every possible ingredient of value upon reasonable expectations and performances of other comparable properties. Still, this

Exhibit 15.1
Property value via building value instead of cost-new*

Building value $300,000		Building cost $400,000†	
Net Operating Income	$ 50,000		$ 50,000
Less NOI to Building	−36,000		− 48,000
NOI Residual to Site	$ 14,000		$ 2,000
Indicated Site Value ($14,000/.09)(rounded)	$155,550	($2,000/.09)(rounded)	$ 22,200‡

*Assumptions:
Building capitalization rate, 12%
Site capitalization rate, 9%

†overstated

‡understated

method can be unconvincing as related to building costs, income, and operating expenses for a nonexisting structure.

This method is well adapted to estimating the value of a site in a built-up area where there are no recent sales of comparable sites. However, the above mentioned careful analysis of the building's value or cost and income expense analysis and rate selection is mandatory.

If hard pressed, an appraiser can use the land residual method to ascertain the site value. Next, it is possible to judge the value of the building via the building residual technique. This combined site and building valuation is not the preferred method, however. Generally it is preferable to derive the site value with comparable site sales. This residual method then can be used to support the site value developed by use of comparable site sales.

Highest and Best Use Analysis of Vacant Sites

This technique is a valid indicator of a vacant site's highest and best use, which is that use(s) that produces a site's highest present value. This use does not necessarily produce the highest net operating income, as shown in Exhibit 15.2. In fact, it may be misleading to rely on that use having the largest income stream as being the highest and best use. While an initially highest NOI suggests the highest site value, a satisfactory conclusion cannot be reached until the building design, its continued use, and the risk associated with the building is considered. For example, a fast-food service structure will likely have a shorter economic life and higher risk than a multitenant office building.

Exhibit 15.2
Estimating highest and best use by land residual

	Proposed use A		Proposed use B
Assumed building value	$300,000		$400,000
Net operating income	$ 45,000		$ 60,000
Less: building capitalization rate @ 12%	36,000	@ 14%	56,000
NOI residual to site	$ 9,000		$ 4,000
Capitalized at land cap. rate (12% – 4%)*	8%	(14% – 5%)9%	
Indicated site value	$112,500	(rounded)	$ 44,450

*The building capitalization rate of 12% for Proposed use A contains a recapture rate of 4% (to recapture to building value over twenty-five years), leaving a land capitalization rate of 8%; the same procedure is used for Proposed use B, except the estimated remaining economic life (recapture period) is twenty years.

By using several hypothetical buildings and forecast income-expense patterns, a highest and best use can be estimated for a site. This type of highest and best use analysis via the land residual method is especially well applied to an unimproved site where the zoning permits more than one possible use. The use that results in the highest present site value is judged to be the highest and best use.

Highest and Best Use of Improved Sites

Highest and best use analysis via the land residual technique can be applied to an existing structure. First, the unimproved site value is estimated from a study of recent similar site sales. Next, the improved value of the site is judged by use of the land residual method. If the indicated value via land residual for the existing use is less than the value revealed by unimproved site sales, then the property is not realizing its highest and best use. For example, recent sales of similar nearby sites may suggest a value of $100,000 for the appraised site, in contrast to a value of $70,000 by the land residual method.

APPLICATION OF THE LAND RESIDUAL METHOD

After having considered the various assumptions underlying the land residual method and reviewed its relative strengths and weaknesses, this technique now can be applied. The fact that the site value is residual implies that its value is influenced—even determined—by other elements. Primary among these elements is the building constructed on the site.

Changing Income Patterns

The present or prospective building ordinarily generates the bulk of rental income for a property. Given this fact, in order to properly process the residual income, we must first determine the nature of the net operating income. Is it declining, level, or rising? Each of these different income patterns is based on a different premise and requires a different discounting method.

In an older, declining neighborhood, an outmoded property may be expected to show a declining value and income stream. In this case, direct capitalization with straight-line recapture would be appropriate.

Similarly, a property subject to a long-term level absolute net lease could be appraised using the ordinary (level) annuity capitalization method.

Finally, and probably the most typical, is the situation where the rental income and property value are expected to rise over the income forecast period. This period generally is shorter than the building's remaining economic life. In this situation it is necessary to adjust the capitalization rate to reflect future value increases. Each of the land residual methods used to process these three income patterns is illustrated.

In the following illustrations (Exhibits 15.3, 15.4 and 15.5), the net operating income is $72,000 and the building value is $550,000. The capitalization rates vary slightly due to different forecast income patterns over the fifty-year remaining economic life (REL) of the building.

Exhibit 15.3 begins with a 10% discount rate, and, after adding a 2% (1/50) annual recapture rate, a 12% building capitalization rate is realized. The site value results from capitalizing the $6000 residual income by the 10% site capitalization (discount) rate.

Exhibit 15.4 illustrates the handling of a long-term well secured lease by use of the Inwood coefficient, or the present worth of 1 per period factor. The principal steps begin with deducting the building income from the net operating income. Next, the residual site income is capitalized on a straight-line basis. This capitalization process presumes that the site value will be unchanged

Exhibit 15.3
Direct capitalization with straight-line recapture (declining income)

Net operating income	$72,000	
Less income to building ($550,000)(.10 + .02)	– 66,000	
NOI residual to site	$ 6,000	
Capitalized at 10% equals		$ 60,000
Plus building value		550,000
Total present worth of property		$610,000

Exhibit 15.4
Ordinary annuity capitalization (level income)*

Net operating income	$72,000	
Less income to building		
$550,000/9.914814†	− 55,473	
NOI residual to site	$16,527	
Capitalized @ 10% (in perpetuity) equals ($16,527/.10)		$165,270
Plus building value		550,000
Total present worth of property		$715,270

*Assumptions:
REL = 50 years
Discount rate = .10
$a_{\overline{n|}} = 9.914814$

†A more familiar step would be to multiply the building value by 1/9.914814 which is .1008591 and is the installment to amortize one factor.

Exhibit 15.5
Capitalization Under Rising Value (increasing income)*

Net operating income	$72,000	
Less income to building		
$550,000 (.09 + 1/50)	− 60,500	
NOI residual to site	$11,500	
Site value		
$11,500/(.09 − 2/50)		$230,000
Plus building value		550,000
Total present worth of property		$780,000

*Assumptions:
First-year NOI = $72,000
Expected changes in value
Building; −100%
Site; +200%
$p = 50$
Yield rate = 9%
$R_0 = Y - \Delta a$

More accurate value estimates result when this method is used for a shorter term forecast period.

over the remaining economic life of the building. A higher site value results from using the same discount rate (10%) as in Exhibit 15.3. The reason for this higher value is because the annuity rate has a recapture rate built into it (.100859), whereas the building capitalization rate in Exhibit 15.3 equals 12%.

A different, but quite realistic, assumption provides the basis for Exhibit 15.5. In this situation, the building value is expected to completely diminish over its REL while the site value is forecast to double in the same period. The equation used to solve this problem is shown at the bottom of Exhibit 15.5: R_0 = overall capitalization rate; Y_0 = overall property yield; a = annualizer $(1/p)$; and p = holding period, which in this case is the remaining economic life of the building.

PROBLEMS

Question: In appraising a property nearing completion, you have reached the following conclusions:

Current net operating income	$ 62,000
Construction cost upon completion	$350,000
Expected value changes over 7-year holding period:	
site + 49%	
building − 7%	
Typical yield rate 14%	

Based on this information, what is the present value of this property?

Answer:

NOI	$ 62,000
Less building income ($350,000)(.14 + .07/7)*	−52,500
Residual to site	$ 9,500
Site value $9,500/(.14 − .49/7)	$135,714
Plus building value	350,000
Indicated property value	$485,714
Rounded to	$486,000

*$R_0 = Y_0 - \Delta\, a$; Y_0 = yield, Δ = total value change over holding period, a = annualizer $(1/p)$, p = holding period

Question: A developer has requested your advice in determining if an existing retail building is optimizing the value of the underlying site. In your research, you have located the following recent sales:

Sales	*Size (s.f.)*	*Features*	*Sale date*	*Price*
1	10,000	similar	this month	$77,500
2	10,500	similar	6 months ago	78,000
3	9,200	corner site	3 years ago	53,500
4	8,000	heavy truck traffic	2 years ago	48,000

The appraised property has a 9700 square-foot site and a five-year-old building with a single tenant. Current net operating income is $35,200; investors normally would expect a 12% return on such an investment, excluding capital recovery; the expected remaining economic life of the present building is twenty-five years, and it is judged to be worth $175,000.

1. Find the present value of the site using the above site sales and land residual method, assuming a 6% annual rate of appreciation, a 15% corner influence adjustment, and an 18% traffic influence adjustment.
2. What is your conclusion as to the property's highest and best use?

Answer:

1. Value by use of site sales:

Sales	*Indicated value/s.f.*
1	$7.75 ($77,500/10,000 s.f.)
2	7.65
3	7.73
4	7.80

After considering all of the four sales, but placing the most weight on sales 1 and 2, it appears that the site is worth $7.73 a square foot.

9,700 square feet × $7.73	$74,981
Rounded to	$75,000

Value via land residual method:

Net operating income	$35,200
less income to building ($175,000 × .16) (.16 = .12 + .04)	28,000
Income available to site	$7,200
Capitalized at .12 equals site value	$60,000

2. The present unencumbered site value of $75,000 is $15,000 in excess of the value of the site encumbered by the present building. Since the highest and best use(s) produces the highest present site value, then the present building is not the highest and best use of this site. The presence of this building therefore reduces the value of the site. The maximum site value and highest and best use would be similar to those uses for which sales 1–4 were purchased.

Question: You are appraising a proposed 11,000 square-foot office building with a leaseable area of 10,300 square feet. This structure is an appropriate use of the site. It will cost $550,000 to build this structure, excluding the site price. Your appraisal will be based on an analysis of the following four recently built and sold properties:

Property	*Sale price*	*Gross building area (s.f.)*	*Construction cost*	*Leaseable area (s.f.)*	*Operating expense ratio*	*Net operating income*
1	$650,000	12,000	$525,000	11,200	.42	$78,000
2	720,000	14,200	610,000	13,400	.46	89,900
3	485,000	8,300	402,000	7,700	.40	56,300
4	565,000	10,400	437,000	9,800	.38	68,600

Properties of this type normally require a 9% risk rate and have remaining economic lives of forty years.

1. Find the value of the appraised property using an overall capitalization rate.
2. Find the property value using the land residual technique.
3. Which method produces the best indication of value? Explain.

Answer:

1. Indicated square foot rental of subject

Sales	*Square foot rental*
1	$6.96 ($78,000/$11,200 s.f.)
2	6.71
3	7.31
4	7.00

Sales 1 and 4 are most similar in size, therefore subject's NOI is judged to be $72,100 (10,300 s.f. × $7.00); the estimated square foot rental is rounded.

Indicated overall capitalization rate

Sales	*Overall cap. rate*
1	.1200 ($78,000/$650,000)
2	.1249
3	.1161
4	.1214

Range of values: $577,260 to $621,020, with sales 1 and 4 being the most comparable (based on size); therefore the indicated value is $600,800 ($72,100/.1200). The capitalization rate is expressed in rounded figures as normally would be expected for such income properties.

2. Indicated building value

Sale	*Cost/s.f.*		
1	$43.75 ($525,000/12,000 s.f.)		
2	42.96		
3	48.43		
4	42.02		
Net operating income		$72,100	
Less earnings to building ($550,000 × .1150)*		– 63,250	
NOI residual to site		$ 8,850	
Capitalized at risk rate (.09)			$ 98,333
Plus building value			550,000
Indicated value			$648,333
		Rounded	$648,300

*.0900 + .025 = .1150
(1/40)

3. Comment on similarity of property features, such as size, efficiency (ratio of leaseable to gross building area), operating expense ratio, and location. Also, note differences in construction costs. The subject property, being more expensive and presumably best equipped, probably would rent for slightly more than the sale properties.

SUMMARY

Three new terms—building capitalization rate, highest and best use, and land capitalization rate—should be reviewed and fully understood since each of these terms is used extensively in this chapter. (Highest and best use was discussed earlier in Chapter 2). The land residual technique is well adapted to appraising new buildings where their reproduction cost can be estimated accurately, and preferably where the building contributes a relatively small part of the total property value. When this method is used for old buildings, it is advisable to use the depreciated value instead of the reproduction cost-new.

The land residual technique offers a sound method for judging the highest and best use of a vacant or improved site. The highest and best use of a vacant site is found by determining a use that produces the highest present site value. By comparing the value of similar sites to the appraised improved site via the land residual method, it can be determined if the present building is underutilizing the site. That is, if similar site sales reveal a higher site value than by the residual approach, then the site is not realizing its highest and best use.

The value of a site can be estimated by use of the land residual method if the income is (1) declining, (2) level over a long period, or (3) increasing. The appraiser needs to estimate which income pattern applies to the appraised property. Each of the physical residual techniques should provide essentially the same value indication if the data are properly compiled and carefully analyzed. Importantly, certain of these techniques are more germane to particular circumstances than others.

REVIEW QUESTIONS

1. Explain how a land capitalization rate differs from a building capitalization rate.
2. List three situations where the land residual technique is appropriate.
3. How might the use of cost-new rather than the present value of a building distort value in the land residual method?
4. Is a property's highest income indicative of its highest and best use? Explain any exceptions.
5. Identify three situations where different variations of the land residual can be used.
6. Describe the appropriate capitalization method to be used with each of the income patterns covered in Question 5.

7. Explain why the values differ under the three income patterns presented in Exhibits 15.3 through 15.5.

8. State any advantages offered by the building residual technique over the land residual method.

ADDITIONAL READINGS

Goulet, Peter G. "Land Residual Technique," *Real Estate—A Value Approach* (Encino, Calif.: Glencove Publishing Co., Inc., 1979), pp. 102–106.

Lum, Y. T. "Values, Leaseholds and the Appraising of Leaseholds by the Residuals." *The Real Estate Appraiser* 29 (February 1963): 4–11.

Schmutz, George L. "The Income Approach-Land Residual Process," *The Appraisal Process* (North Hollywood, California: George L. Schmutz, 1948), Chapter XXIX.

Wall, Norbert F. "A Case Study: Land Residual Technique." *The Real Estate Appraiser* 33 (February 1967): 22–26.

MODULE VIII
Renovation Analysis

This material examines the feasibility and principles of changing the appearance and/or the structural nature of the property. Factors to be considered in renovation analysis and a feasibility methodology are discussed.

CHAPTER 16

LEARNING OBJECTIVES

When a student finishes this chapter, he or she should be able to:

- Gain an appreciation of the similarities and differences among the different types of renovation.
- Become aware of the different costs and risks associated with renovation of real property.
- Understand the methodologies that may be used in judging the financial feasibility of building renovation.
- Understand the principal advantages of older, centrally located buildings over newer, outlying buildings.
- Realize the principles that relate to renovation appraisals.

Renovation Analysis

IMPORTANT TERMS AND PHRASES

adaptive use: Converting an older, but structurally sound, building to a new use that is presumably more profitable.

modernization: An effort that involves updating a building either architecturally or functionally. Architectural modernization might involve the addition of modern building surfaces over the existing exterior walls. Functional modernization, on the other hand, includes modern substitutes for present equipment. Examples of this type of modernization are elevators, plumbing, electrical wiring, and heating and air conditioning systems.

rehabilitation: Improving a property to an acceptable level of utility or improving its appeal and marketability, but without extending its economic life. Rehabilitation is the correction of deferred maintenance, such as decorating, painting, tuckpointing mortar joints in masonry, repairing roof, floor tiles, or sanding and refinishing floors. It does not involve changing the plan or design of the building.

remodeling: Performed to improve the economic productivity of a property, often by converting it to a higher and better use. Remodeling involves changing the design or plan of a structure, such as converting a large residence to several apartments. The result of this work is to increase the income flow and extend the building's economic life.

renovation: This is the generic term that encompasses all of the terms contained in this section. Renovation involves repairs, replacements, and other changes necessary to revive a building.

restoration: Recovering the form and details of a property and its setting as it appeared in an earlier period by removal of later work or by replacement of missing earlier work. An example of restoration would be the removal of alterations that occurred to an architecturally significant building so as to reveal the former unaltered structure. Restoration can be expected to increase a property's rental income and extend its economic life.

Due to the scarcity of developable urban sites and continually rising construction costs, an increasingly important dimension of income property appraising is the feasibility analysis of proposed renovation projects. In fully understanding this concept, the student first will need to grasp the meaning of the terms covered at the beginning of this chapter. Covered herein are the advantages of using older buildings that typically are in cities, the criteria used to determine renovation feasibility, and a list of factors that should be considered in renovation analysis. Presented too is a methodology that can be used in studying the feasibility of prospective renovation.

VALUE PRINCIPLES RELEVANT TO RENOVATION FEASIBILITY ANALYSIS

Several variations of the renovation concept have been defined previously. These variations include updating a building, improving a building's appeal and marketability, altering an existing building's design, preservation of distinctive architectural features, as well as adapting outmoded space to a use or combination of more profitable uses.

Some of the advantages of using existing structures instead of new buildings are:

1. *Location.* Buildings suitable for renovation typically are well situated in central cities and have the advantage of public transportation and built-in markets due to the density of residential and office populations.
2. *Price.* Many "by-passed" buildings from another era, although partially or even entirely unused, can be very competitive with new structures. Prices for such structures generally are depressed, and even when considering the cost of renovation, they still are appealing.
3. *Structural strength.* Some older structures are capable of carrying heavy floor loads required for such uses as the installation of filing and storage cabinets and for computer installations.
4. *Linkages.* This term relates to those forces that draw and hold establishments together. Some examples of linkages found in central cities versus outlying areas are:
    a. access to specialized outside services (such as metal fabricators) that many small establishments cannot provide for themselves
    b. advanced banking facilities
    c. staff functions (such as engineering, accounting, legal counsel) that can be hired when needed
    d. police and fire protection
    e. lower insurance costs and utility rates
    f. fast delivery services, which permit maintenance of small inventories

g. large-lot buying and selling savings through common brokers and jobbers
h. favorable rates for less-than-carload transportation of supplies and finished products
i. broad and interchangeable labor market
j. public transportation for employees
k. speed of communication.[1]

5. *Design appeal.* In many cities there has been a surge of office construction, often with an uninteresting, look-alike quality. Renovation of an existing structure can add a different texture, interest, and a certain charm in a district of towering buildings. These older buildings are appealing for shops, boutiques, craft stores, restaurants, theatres, shopping malls, as well as offices and apartments.

6. *Time savings.* With the many regulatory "hoops" that developers must jump through today in launching a new development, use of an existing structure can save considerable time and expense in placing a property on the market.

Public sector participation has caused a greater awareness of building preservation, particularly for those structures having historic or job-creating potential. Under certain circumstances, tax incentives and investment tax credit are available for this work. Public agencies tend to be sympathetic toward recycling existing structures, which can encourage revitalization of urban neighborhoods. There is the availability of HUD funding, assistance by local redevelopment authorities, and federal income tax benefits available to investors.[2]

Thus far in this chapter, various types of renovation have been defined and some of the advantages of undertaking such ventures have been examined briefly. Missing is the analysis needed to detect any pitfalls as well as to determine the financial feasibility of such ventures. The balance of this chapter will consider each of the major types of renovation as well as present an analytical methodology to determine the feasibility of renovation.

CRITERIA USED TO DETERMINE THE FEASIBILITY OF RENOVATION

The underlying principles dictate whether a renovation project is feasible.

1. *Principle of balance.* Value of a property is maximized when the agents of production are in balance. For example, a property's maximum net operating income would not be realized if the operating costs were increased because it lacked storm doors and windows. Conversely, installation of excessive amounts of insulation may cost more than its contribution to the value of the property.

2. *Principle of contribution.* This principle is essential to the proper restoration of a property. It states that the value of a building component is measured by its net return to the property or by its addition to the value of the property. An example of this principle is the recapture of the cost of the equipment installed in an office building through increased rentals. Thus it is not financially feasible if the cost of remodeling a structure cannot at least be offset by increased property value.

3. *Principle of highest and best use.* A starting point in renovating property is to determine the highest and best use of the property prior to any changes. This analysis gives a basis for judging the initial value of the property. Next, the highest and best use of the property is forecast after the prospective improvements are made in order to determine the "after" value. The project is feasible if the "after" value exceeds the "before" value.

4. *Principle of conformity.* This principle states that property value is maximized when there is a reasonable degree of architectural similarity and compatible land use activity within a defined area. Within the context of renovation, this principle involves looking ahead to the finished product and judging whether the modified use is compatible with the neighboring building architecture, and if the prospective use fits in with adjoining land use activities. If it does, then the proposed renovation has a strong chance of being successful.

Key Factors Considered in Renovation Analysis

Several factors should be carefully considered in analyzing a property for prospective renovation. These factors contribute to the risk of default that is typically greater in renovation projects than in acquiring a property that already is in satisfactory condition or in building a structure anew. These differences in risk should be reflected in the equity yield and in the mortgage terms.

1. Analysis must be conducted of prospective tenants, space, design, amenities, and income and expenses. Today's unrealistically optimistic investor may be tomorrow's bankrupt former investor.

2. Operating expenses must be examined since they will change once a property has been renovated. Since the property will be more valuable, property taxes will rise. Also, increased collectible rental income will result in a higher property management fee. In all probability, the property is underutilized prior to the renovation work, and will enjoy a higher occupancy level afterwards.

3. Maintenance expenditures surely will change. These expenses ordinarily will be lower unless the property in its "before" state simply is not adequately being maintained.

4. Another change that can be expected as a result of the renovation is extension of the property's remaining economic life. This extension can cause a lower capitalization rate and in turn a higher property value.

5. Another prospective change is more favorable mortgage terms. Prior to renovation, a conservative loan-to-value ratio, comparatively short loan term, and high interest rate would be expected. These mortgage conditions would result in higher mortgage debt service, lower cash flow to equity, as well as a higher capitalization rate and reduced property value.

A fundamental question for which scant information may exist is, "Will the property be leasable at a competitive rental upon completion?" Answers to this question probably are best obtained from a careful analysis of similar situations in other markets, as well as the need for and attitude toward renovated space in the subject market. The probability of successful leasing at competitive rates also will be influenced by the extent of vacancies of competitive buildings.

The expense and time required to complete a renovation project are essential features to be analyzed in a feasibility study. In order to obtain realistic cost estimates, it is advisable to deal with an architect and contractors who are experienced in this specialized type of work. It may cost 25 to 40% more to perform this work than to undertake similar work on a new building. Many unforeseen problems may be uncovered in the structure, plumbing, and electrical service once the work begins. In addition to the actual "hard costs," the architect's, attorney's, and other consultants' fees must be added. Any rental loss during the construction phase must be accounted for, as well as discounted rental income, since it may take at least a year to complete the renovation and leasing. The length of any work delays should be estimated on a realistic basis since such delays generally are inevitable.

A RENOVATION FEASIBILITY METHODOLOGY

The financial feasibility of a real estate project can be determined by the following broad criteria; that is, a project should be feasible if any or all of the following criteria are satisfied:

Renovation is feasible if:

1.	post-renovation value	≥	pre-renovation value + renovation costs
2.	incremental income ÷ incremental equity	≥	required yield on incremental equity due to increased value of property
3.	post-renovation value (with additional yield on renovation costs)	≥	post-renovation value (without additional yield on renovation costs)

The following illustrations show how these criteria can be applied in determining the feasibility of a building. Assume the following conditions:

Pre-renovation			
Gross income			$67,500
Operating expense ratio,	55%		
Equity yield rate,	13%		
Mortgage constant,	14.92%		
(20 years, 14% interest, monthly installments, 60% loan to value)			
Investor's equity (.40 × $215,000)			86,000
Forecast remaining economic life, 30 years			
Cost of renovation			
Actual hard costs		$415,229*	
Rent loss (net)†, 18 months		45,560	
Construction loan interest		52,940	
Total			$513,729
Post-renovation			
Gross income			$160,000
Operating expense ratio,	40%		
Equity yield rate,	11%‡		
Plus 20% equity yield on renovation costs			
Mortgage constant,	13.27%		
(30 years, 13% interest, monthly installments, 75% loan to value)			
Investor's equity (.25 × $756,000)			189,000
Forecast remaining economic life, 40 years			

Pre-renovation value

Gross income	$67,500
Less operating expenses ($67,500 × .55)	− 37,125
Net operating income	$30,375

Capitalized at:

$$
\begin{aligned}
.60 \times .1492 &= .0895 \\
.40 \times .1300 &= \underline{.0520} \\
& .1415
\end{aligned}
$$

*See the first question later in this chapter under the heading "Problems" for breakdown.

†Rent loss, after deducting operating expenses.

‡The equity yield rate is lowered from the pre-renovation stage due to the reduced risks and extended economic age.

Pre-renovation value ($30,375/.1415)	$214,664	
	rounded to	$215,000
Post-renovation value		
Gross income	$160,000	
Less operating expenses ($160,000 × .40)	– 64,000	
Net operating income	$ 96,000	
Capitalized at:		
.75 × .1327 = .0995		
.25 × .1100 = .0275		
.1270		
Post renovation value	$755,906	
($96,000/.1270)	rounded to	$756,000
Total investment after renovation		
Pre-renovation value + renovation costs equals		
$215,000 + $513,729 =		$728,729

This project satisfies the first feasibility test since the post-renovation value ($756,000) is greater than the pre-renovation value plus renovation costs ($728,729).

The previous renovation method can be refined further since most investors will expect to earn a higher yield on the equity capital invested to renovate a building than on the property after it has been renovated. The following method addresses this situation first by developing a capitalization rate (*a*) based on the incremental income and the increased value resulting from the renovation. This capitalization rate (*a*) next is compared to the capitalization rate (*b*), which is the difference between the yield rate expected on the renovation capital outlay and the value of the project upon completion (e.g., 20% – 11%). If rate (*a*) is more than rate (*b*), the investor will earn sufficient income from the project to justify his investment.

Problem

Can the investor maintain an 11% return on his or her equity while obtaining a 20% yield on the renovation costs?

Solution

1. Find the incremental income necessary to give an 11% yield.

Forecast post-renovation NOI	\$96,000
less return on post-renovation investment (\$728,729 × .1270)	– 92,549
Incremental income to give 11% yield	\$ 3,451

2. Relate incremental income to incremental equity due to increased value of property.

   Δ I = \$3,451
   Δ Eq. = (\$189,000 – \$86,000)*
   = \$103,000
   Incremental income/Incremental equity = .0335

This rate may be thought of as the capitalization rate for the incremental income. The Annual Installment to Amortize One in the compound interest tables for 9% (20% – 11%) for forty years is .092960. This rate considerably exceeds the required rate of .0335, indicating that the investor cannot achieve the desired 11% yield. Thus, the investment fails to meet the second feasibility criterion since only \$3,451 incremental income is available, but \$9,575 would be needed to meet the investor's yield requirements.

Alternative Solution

An alternative solution to this investment problem is to develop an overall capitalization rate which recognizes the division in the equity rate for the renovation expense and the post-renovation value. If the capitalized value of the post-renovation net operating income is equal to or greater than the previously indicated post-renovation value (which makes no provision for the additional yield on the renovation expenditure), then the project is feasible.

Using an overall rate comprised of a split equity rate

Overall capitalization rate

$$\Sigma = \begin{cases} .75 \times .1327 = .0995 \\ .1138 \times .1100 = .0125 \\ .1362\dagger \times .2000 = .0272 \end{cases}$$

$$.1392$$

$$\underset{(NOI)}{\$96{,}000} / \underset{(R_0)}{.1392} = \underset{(V)}{\$689{,}655}$$

rounded to \$690,000

---

*Post-renovation equity (\$756,000 × .25) = \$189,000
Pre-renovation equity (\$215,000 × .40) = 86,000

†Change in equity (x) (\$189,000 – \$86,000) = \$103,000
Value after renovation (y) = \$756,000
(x)/(y) = .1362

This appraised value of $690,000 falls shy of the $756,000 value, which did not allow for the 20% equity yield. Therefore, the investment is shown to be unwarranted, and thus does not meet the third feasibility criterion. An investor ordinarily would expect to earn a higher return on the riskier renovation costs, and the feasibility analysis should reflect this difference.

PROBLEMS

Question: Your client has purchased a six-story loft building that was built sixty years ago. This client expects to renovate the structure for mixed use occupancy, ranging from small fashion shops to expensive apartments. In anticipation of this conversion, you have obtained estimates for performing the needed work. However, your client now wants you to identify each phase of the work, such as modernization, and to provide subtotals for each category based upon the following costs:

Replace broken windows	$ 926
Install modern entrance doors	8,235
Install entrance foyer carpeting	4,306
Replace galvanized iron with copper plumbing	42,319
Upgrade wiring and electric service	93,100
Exterior sandblasting, caulking, and sealer	13,163
Exterior trim painting	2,500
Repair freight elevator	15,205
Install two new passenger elevators	162,000
Repair plumbing on first floor	4,300
Decorate interior of apartments	7,000
Carpentry work on first floor renovation	9,200
Sand and refinish apartment floors	3,625
Install partitions throughout building	16,500
Repair roof	5,000
Install new plumbing fixtures	26,400
Remove sheet metal facade on front of building and repair any damage	$ 1,450
Total	$415,229

Answer:

Modernization (Students should review definitions at the beginning of the chapter.)		
Install entrance doors	$ 8,235	
Carpet installation	4,306	
Upgrade electric service	93,100	
New passenger elevators	162,000	
New plumbing fixtures	26,400	$294,041
Rehabilitation		
Replace broken windows	$ 926	
Copper plumbing	42,319	
Sandblasting and caulking	13,163	
Exterior trim painting	2,500	
Repair freight elevator	15,205	
Repair plumbing	4,300	
Decorate apartments	7,000	
Sand and refinish apartment floors	3,625	
Repair roof	5,000	94,038
Remodeling		
Carpentry work on first floor	$ 9,200	
Install partitions	16,500	25,700
Restoration		
Remove sheet metal		1,450
Total renovation costs		$415,229

Note: All of these expenditures fall under the general categories of adaptive use and renovation.

Question: You are advising a client regarding the prospects of converting an older apartment building with fifty-two units to a residential condominium. At present, the building is producing $149,760 annual income after deduction of vacancy and collection losses and all operating expenses. An appropriate overall capitalization rate for this class of apartment buildings is 13%. The investor has an option to purchase the building for $1,200,000, or $23,077 a unit.

Once the building has been converted to fifty condominiums, the units are expected to completely sell out at an average price of $65,000 within one year after conversion. How much can the investor afford to pay per condo unit to renovate this property if the holding costs and sales commissions are $453,000 and the desired profit on the sales price is 20%?

Answer:

$$\begin{aligned} PV &= \$149{,}760/.13 \\ &= \$1{,}152{,}000 \end{aligned}$$

Say, $1,150,000

Gross sales price ($65,000 × 50) =			$3,250,000
Less:			
	purchase price	$1,200,000	
	profit ($3,250,000 × .20)	650,000	
	holding costs	453,000	2,303,000
Allowable remodeling costs			$ 947,000, or $18,940/condo unit

Question: An investor is considering the purchase of a ninety-year-old partially occupied six-story building of masonry construction. This property currently is used for offices on the first three floors, storage on the fourth and fifth floors, with the sixth floor being vacant. The building appears to be structurally sound and is located in the midst of a downtown office district where several high-rise office buildings have been completed in the past four years.

Current potential gross income	$150,000
Vacancy and collection losses	30%
Operating expenses, including replacement reserves	$ 80,000
Applicable overall capitalization rate before renovation	17%
Expected renovation costs (including 35% for contingencies)	$700,000
Forecast net operating income after renovation	$168,000
Overall capitalization rate after renovation	14%

Is this investment financially feasible if the investor requires a 25% margin of profit between the purchase price (which equals the appraised value) plus renovation costs and the value after renovation?

Answer:

Value before renovation:	
Gross income	$150,000
less vacancy and collection losses @ 30%	– 45,000
Effective gross income	$105,000
less operating expenses and replacement reserves	80,000
Net operating income	$ 25,000
Present value (NOI capitalized at 17%) = $147,059; rounded to	$147,000
Value after renovation:	
Net operating income	$168,000
Capitalized at 14%	
Value after renovation	$1,200,000
Renovated value required by investor equals (pre-renovation value + renovation costs) (1 + profit margin) ($147,000 + $700,000) (1.25) =	$1,058,750
versus	
Forecast value after renovation	$1,200,000
Conclusion: renovation project is financially feasible since a profit (42%) is forecast.	

SUMMARY

The term, *renovation,* includes various other aspects of updating older properties. These processes include adaptive use, which is converting structurally sound older properties to more profitable new uses and remodeling that necessitates changing the design or plan of a structure to make it more productive.

The central location of many older structures have made their renovation especially attractive. These structures frequently are better built and less costly than new facilities and require less time to complete for prospective occupants.

Several appraisal principles govern whether a property renovation project is financially feasible. These principles are the principle of balance, contribution, highest and best use, and conformity. In addition to understanding these principles, other aspects such as pro forma income and expense analysis and mortgage financing terms also must be carefully studied.

This chapter concluded with an illustrated renovation feasibility methodology. This method showed how the pre- and post-renovation property values are derived as well as how to break the equity yield into two components—one for the yield on the renovation expense and the other on the post-renovation property value.

REVIEW QUESTIONS

1. Distinguish between modernization and remodeling.
2. How do the adaptive use and modernization processes differ?
3. List and briefly give the significance of four advantages of older central city buildings over newer outlying structures.
4. Explain how the principles of contribution and conformity govern the renovation concept.
5. What impact is renovation likely to have on mortgage finance terms?
6. Outline the steps involved in renovation feasibility analysis.
7. List three types of expenses that are associated with each of the following classes of renovation: rehabilitation, remodeling, and modernization.

ENDNOTES

1. James H. Boykin, "Industrial Potential of the Central City" (ULI Research Report 21. Washington, DC: Urban Land Institute, 1973), p. 6.
2. Thomas J. Martin and Melvin A. Gamzon, "Adaptive Reuse Gives Life to Old Buildings," *Real Estate Review* 6 (Fall 1976): 29–30.
3. A variation of this method is found in William N. Kinnard, Jr., *Income Property Valuation* (Lexington, Mass.: D.C. Heath and Co., 1971), pp. 407–409.

ADDITIONAL READINGS

Aldis, Graham. "Rating the Office Building." *The Appraisal Journal* 8 (October 1940): 325–331.

Appraisal Institute of Canada. "Rehabilitation, Remodelling and Modernization," *Real Estate Appraising in Canada* (Winnipeg, Man.: Appraisal Institute of Canada, 1973), pp. 278–286.

Barnes, McKim N. "A Strategy for Residential Rehabilitation." *Real Estate Review* 6 (Fall 1976): 40–45.

Dunham, Howard W., Jr. "Conversion of an Obsolete Railroad Station into a Modern Restaurant," *The Appraisal Journal* 44 (October 1976): 500–509.

Edgerton, William H. "Urban Rehabilitation—Some Guidelines and Costs." *The Appraisal Journal* 38 (April 1970): 314–316.

Heritage Conservation and Recreation Service. *The Secretary of the Interior's Standards for Rehabilitation and Guidelines for Rehabilitating Historic Buildings* (Washington, D.C.: U.S. Department of the Interior, 1980), 14 pp.

Johnson, Philip M. "Rehabilitation Feasibility Studies in Federally Assisted Areas." *The Appraisal Journal* 34 (April 1966): 183–195.

Johnson, Walker C. "The Recycling Phenomenon." *Real Estate Today* 12 (October 1980): 37–42.

Kinnard, William N., Jr. ''Renovation and Conversion.'' *Income Property Valuation* (Lexington, Mass.: D. C. Heath and Co., 1971), pp. 406–409.

Mace, Edward E. ''Restoration in Real Estate: The Retail 'Theme' Center.'' *Real Estate Review* 6 (Fall 1976): 34–37.

Martin, Thomas J. and Gamzon, Melvin A. ''Adaptive Reuse Gives Life to Old Buildings.'' *Real Estate Review* 6 (Fall 1976): 28–33.

Post, Edward T. ''The Appraiser and the Builder.'' *The Appraisal Journal* 14 (October 1946): 395–400.

Roddewig, Richard J. ''Building on Yesterday.'' *Real Estate Today* 12 (October 1980): 22–31.

Textbook Revision Committee. ''Rehabilitation, Modernization, and Remodeling,'' *The Appraisal of Real Estate,* 7th ed. (Chicago: American Institute of Real Estate Appraisers, 1978), pp. 497–505.

Wall, Matt R. ''Analyzing Rehabilitation Feasibility.'' *Real Estate Today* 12 (October 1980): 37–42.

MODULE IX
Final Review and Reconciliation

The purpose of this module is to estimate one figure for the value of the property using all previous indicators of value. This material covers the advantages and disadvantages of each value indicator and the factors to examine in deciding whether one value indicator should be given more weight.

CHAPTER 17

LEARNING OBJECTIVES

When a student finishes this chapter, he or she should be able to:

- Discuss the difference between the final review and reconciliation processes.
- Understand the relative merits of each of the three approaches to value.
- Explain the major factors to be considered in each approach.
- Explain the principal criteria to analyze in weighing the emphasis given to each approach.
- Discuss the errors to avoid in reaching a final estimate of value.
- Understand the nature and content of the Limiting Conditions and Certification sections of a report.

Final Review and Reconciliation

IMPORTANT TERMS AND PHRASES

certification: A concluding section in an appraisal report that assures the client that the appraiser has personally inspected the property and written the report according to professional standards.

letter of transmittal: A letter preceding the appraisal report and is addressed to the client. Ordinarily, it includes reference to the appraiser's authorization to make the appraisal, property identification, rights appraised, appraisal objective, reference to the report, value estimate, date of appraisal, and signature.

limiting conditions: A section of an appraisal report that explains the conditions under which the assignment was made and the limitations of the report.

reconciliation: A final step in an appraisal whereby the appraiser resolves several value indications into a final value conclusion or estimate; sometimes known as correlation.

value estimate: The final value reported in an appraisal and based on a comparative analysis of the several indications of value.

value indication: A value revealed by a particular appraisal approach; it is inconclusive.

This chapter focuses on the final review of the appraisal analysis and the reconciliation of the values indicated by the different value approaches. The relation and distinction between these two parts of the value conclusion are discussed. Considered as well are the comparative strengths of each approach and the points that should be carefully checked in these approaches. The "game rules" of an appraisal assignment and the limiting conditions, are explained along with the appraiser's certification, which assures the client that the report has been performed competently.

DISTINCTION BETWEEN FINAL REVIEW AND RECONCILIATION

This, the final phase of an appraisal report, is in a sense the most critical step. After having compiled and analyzed a variety of data, the appraiser has developed one or more indications of value. If there is more than one indication of value, then the appraiser obviously has not reached a final estimate of value. Too often this critical phase of the appraisal report is handled superficially with the danger of an error being uncorrected, an important concept being mishandled, or the most relevant value indicator for a particular property being incorrectly perceived.

The two final steps, review and reconciliation, are interrelated but are distinctly different. After the appraiser has arrived at independently derived indications of value, the next step is to meticulously review the material to determine if there has been an arithmetical or judgmental error. Once the accuracy and reliability of the data have proved acceptable, then the indications of value are reconciled. Reconciliation is the act of making ideas or, in this case, value indications consistent, compatible, or harmonious. Therefore it may be said that *review* involves a check for errors of any type, while *reconciliation* is an effort to resolve several different indications of value into a final value conclusion. It is important to remember that even the final reported value is not necessarily the value of the property but rather the appraiser's estimate of value.

REVIEW OF THE APPROACHES TO VALUE

It is pointless to analyze the three indications of value to arrive at a final estimate of value until the accuracy and the reliability of the separate approaches to value have been ascertained. Only after a careful review of the report can the appraiser confidently reach a final conclusion of value. A guideline in reviewing each of the approaches to value is for the appraiser to check the mathematics, assumptions, logic, relevance and appropriateness, technique, and quantity and quality of data considered. Some of the major factors to be reviewed in the three approaches follow.

Cost-Less-Depreciation Approach

This approach is best applied to new properties that have experienced minimum accrued depreciation. Also it can be used advantageously in appraising unusually designed, special-use, or institutional structures such as churches or factories. The cost approach is beneficial when there are scant data for the other two approaches. Care must be taken in accurately estimating the cost-new and the full extent of all causes of accrued depreciation.

The cost approach does not set the upper limit of value any more than any other approach. The principle of substitution holds that a person ordinarily is not justified in paying more for an existing property than that amount required to have a similar structure built without undue delay on a comparable site. However, this principle does not state that the upper limit of value should be set by the cost approach for an older property suffering from accrued depreciation.

The appraiser should carefully check:

1. The adequacy and comparability of the site sales.
2. The condition of comparable sites on the date of sale, including zoning, utilities, site preparation, and sale terms.
3. The confirmation of each site sale; if a sale has not been confirmed, then it may not be a reliable indication of the subject site's value.
4. The logic of the adjustments made between comparable sales prices and the indicated appraised site value.
5. The mathematical accuracy and reliability of the reproduction or replacement cost-new.
6. The accuracy and market support of the different elements of estimated accrued depreciation.

Direct Market Comparison Approach

This method is well adapted to properties in active real estate markets where there are a sufficient number of recent sales of similar properties. If these sales accurately gauge the market value of the appraised property, there should have been no unusual motivation by the buyer or seller in transferring the property, the properties should have similar locational characteristics, and all adjustments should be derived from the market and not from the appraiser's personal biases.

Some of the factors to be checked in reviewing this approach are:

1. Check the consistency in the units of comparison with those used by investors in such properties. Since the appraiser's responsibility is to serve as a

mirror of the marketplace, then it is improper for him or her to inject adjustment factors that are not generally used by persons dealing with such properties. To do so is to derive a value other than market value.

2. Confirm the sale price and the comparability as it relates to size, nature, location of property, and the date of sale.

3. Investigate the physical features of the property when it was conveyed. For example, if the appraiser includes as part of the sale price a section that was built after the conveyance, then the unit sale price would be decreased and also the indicated value of the appraised property would be understated.

4. Check for potential double-counting of adjustments. For example, if the sale property has a feature worth $10,000 but the appraised property lacks this feature, it would require a minus $10,000 adjustment. Had the required adjustment been a plus $10,000, then the indicated value of the appraised property would have been off by $20,000.

Income Approach

This method is best applied to an income-producing property. Essential to its proper use is sufficient rental and expense information as well as the ability of the appraiser to develop a market-derived capitalization rate that relates to the appraised property. Not only must the derived rate relate to the property, but the capitalization technique must be consistent with the nature of the property.

Some of the key factors that should be reviewed in this approach are:

1. *Comparability of the units of value.* Suppose that a comparable property is rented on the basis of the tenant paying for maintenance, but the subject is appraised on the basis of the owner paying such expenditures. If the appraiser does not detect this difference, the indicated market rent for the appraised property will be incorrect. Also, the rent suggested for the appraised property will be distorted if the square footage of the building is measured differently.

2. *Vacancy and collection losses.* It is unrealistic to assume a high occupancy rate for a new property since it will take a number of months to achieve stabilized rental occupancy. The operating expenses should be convincingly supported by operating statements of other similar age and type properties.

3. *Capitalization rates and techniques.* These items should be appropriate to the nature of the property and assignment. Capitalization rates must be developed in the market and reflect investors' attitudes. Complicated

capitalization formulas are no substitute for sound and thorough research. Capitalization rates should be based on sale-rental properties that are similar to the appraised property in their operating expense ratios. Care should be used in choosing a residual method that conforms to the age and type of property. The capitalization method should match the anticipated income pattern of the appraised property.

RECONCILIATION

After the appraiser has reviewed the report to locate and correct any errors, the different indications of value can be reconciled into a final estimate of value. The appraiser must check the value that was defined at the beginning of the report since the concluded value must correspond with the value initially defined.

The appraiser should check the purpose of the report to be certain that those approaches that best relate to the purpose of the report are given proper emphasis. Finally, a review of the rights appraised will guide the appraiser in deriving a value consistent with these appraised rights.

Importance of Each Approach

In this important and final phase of the report, the appraiser must weigh the evidence analyzed on the different approaches to determine:

1. Which approach offers the greatest volume of relevant data for analysis?
2. Which approach best reflects the attitudes of investors and tenants of such property?
3. Which approach is based on the most relevant and current data?
4. Which approach is best substantiated?
5. Which approach best fits the age and nature of the property?
6. Which approach leaves the appraiser feeling most comfortable as to the indicated value? This "comfort index" is a fundamental, but important criteria in that eventually the appraiser must feel satisfied and confident with the indicated final estimated value.
7. Which approach will appear most logical, most readily understood, reasonable, and convincing to the client?
8. Which approach most faithfully measures the value-influencing features, such as incurable functional obsolescence or unusually strong tenant appeal for the property?

Correlation is not where the appraiser "makes himself or herself look good" by shaving the highest indicated value and increasing the lowest value so as to create a tight range of indicated values.

The appraiser discredits his or her own analysis if, after having completed the report to this point, he or she then elaborates on why each approach is weak, finally concluding that the appraiser is influenced by one approach that is not quite as bad as the others. Instead, the appraiser is obliged to thoroughly research the community for comparable properties, fully and logically analyze the property via appropriate techniques, and then cite the relative merits of each approach used.

By use of clear and convincing logic, the appraiser arrives at the final estimate of value. This conclusion is not based on simple or even weighted averages since each approach is not equally applicable or reliable for a given assignment. The appraiser is obliged to judge which indication of value is most influential in reaching a conclusion. It will be found, however, that all of the approaches usually influence, to a degree, the appraiser's conclusion of value.

Once the appraiser has carefully considered the quantity, quality, and relevance of data, as well as appropriateness of an analytical method, then he or she will likely emphasize one or two approaches over the others. This is the "moment of truth." No mathematical formulas or averages of any sort can substitute for judgment. Averages in valuation are just as misleading as stating that the correct time is the average of the times shown by three different watches, with one watch not having worked for ten years.

It sometimes is claimed that in a perfect market setting, each of the approaches would reveal the same value. Such a convergency in value indications would not occur even if the market were fully efficient, because of the

Exhibit 17.1
Reconciliation of indicated value

The market value indications for this property by the three approaches are:

Depreciated Cost Approach	\$524,600
Direct Market Comparison Approach	\$536,300
Capitalized Income Approach	\$525,200

These approaches produced a range from \$524,600 to \$536,300, a difference of \$11,700. Each of these approaches was helpful in arriving at a final estimate of value. This is a new building and very reliable income and expense information was available as well as an overall capitalization rate derived from the sale of several very similar properties. Therefore, the most emphasis will be assigned to the Depreciated Cost and the Capitalized Income Approaches.

It is concluded that the market value of this property as of July 28, 1981 is:

FIVE HUNDRED TWENTY-FIVE THOUSAND DOLLARS.................(\$525,000).

appraiser's different interpretations of these data. So, there always will be differences in the indications of value. The appraiser's responsibility is to be certain that these interpretations are as accurate as possible, and the value conclusion is logically defensible and convincingly conveyed to the client. The final estimate of value should be expressed as of a particular date and rounded in terms normally expressed by persons dealing in such property. For example, it would be unusual for a property selling in the $1 million range to have an expressed value of $1,000,250.

The value conclusion may be expressed in the format shown in Exhibit 17.1. Sometimes, the total value will be allocated between the site and improvements.

LIMITING CONDITIONS

The purpose of this section is to clearly explain the conditions under which the assignment was made and the limitations of the report. These conditions may be included in the letter of transmittal or prominently set forth elsewhere in the report. Although most of the conditions normally used apply in the majority of assignments, the appraiser must be careful to use appropriate limiting conditions for each appraisal. Limiting conditions that might be used are:

1. No opinion of a legal or engineering nature is expressed or implied, nor is any responsibility assumed for matters of this nature.
2. Unless otherwise noted, the property has been appraised as though the title is unaffected by any liens or encumbrances, and the present use (specify) is responsibly and competently managed.
3. The appraiser is not required to give testimony or attendance in court by reason of this appraisal unless previously arranged.
4. Neither the employment to make the appraisal nor the compensation is contingent on the amount of the valuation reported.
5. Plans and maps contained in this report are intended to assist the reader in visualizing the property and its location. The appraiser has made no survey of the property and assumes no responsibility in connection with such matters.
6. The appraisal is to be used in the whole, not in part. No part of it is to be used by another party in making a summation appraisal.
7. Information on which this report is based has been obtained from sources customarily used and judged reliable, but cannot be guaranteed by the appraiser.

Some appraisers have found that clients fail to attentively read the Limiting Conditions or otherwise misuse the report for promotional purposes, so a separate section of the Limiting Conditions may be set forth as shown in Exhibit 17.2.

Exhibit 17.2
Restriction upon disclosure and use

Disclosure of the contents of this appraisal report is governed by the By-Laws and Regulations of the (state professional society in which membership is held).

Neither all nor any part of the contents of this report, especially any conclusions as to value; the identity of the appraiser, or any reference to [specify the society or institute in which membership is held and identify the professional designation] shall be disseminated to the public through advertising, public relations, news, or sales media or any other public means of communication without prior written consent and approval of the undersigned.

Certification

This section of an appraisal report assures the client that the appraiser has personally completed the appraisal according to professional standards. It may be set up as follows:

I, the undersigned, hereby certify that to the best of my knowledge and belief, the statements contained in this appraisal and upon which the opinions expressed herein are based are correct, subject to the limiting conditions herein set forth.

I have no present or anticipated future interest in this appraised property.

No one other than the undersigned prepared the analyses, conclusions, and opinions concerning the findings presented in this report.

This report has been inspected personally by the undersigned appraiser.

This appraisal has been made in conformity with the Professional Standards of (specify appropriate professional appraisal organization).

*Date:*__________________ *Signature:*__________________

SUMMARY

The final review and reconciliation is a critical phase in the appraisal process. Once the relevant data have been compiled and analyzed, a conclusion is reached. The review step involves a careful checking of the appraisal report for any arithmetical or judgmental errors. Once the appraiser is satisfied that there are no errors, or that they have been corrected, the different indications of value are reconciled into a single value estimate.

The review process requires that each approach to value be checked as to its accuracy and relevance to the appraisal assignment. Finally, a final value is reached in the value reconciliation and is greatly influenced by the best, substantiated, and convincing approach.

The "limiting conditions" must fit each appraised property so that the client clearly understands the limits of the appraiser's responsibility. Usually, the next part of the appraisal is the "Certification" where the appraiser guarantees that he or she personally inspected the property, wrote the report, and adhered to professional appraisal standards in completing the assignment.

REVIEW QUESTIONS

1. Distinguish between the terms final review and reconciliation.
2. List the types of properties for which each approach to value is best adapted.
3. What are the principal factors that should be considered in reviewing each approach?
4. Why might the reconciliation phase of an appraisal be thought of as "the moment of truth"?
5. Add three limiting conditions to the list in the chapter that you judge to be necessary for an appraisal. Give the reasoning for your selection.
6. Explain the difference between a value indication and value estimate.

ADDITIONAL READINGS

Bloom, George F., and Harrison, Henry S. "Reconciliation and Final Value Estimate," *Appraising the Single Family Residence* (Chicago: American Institute of Real Estate Appraisers, 1978), pp. 278–295.

Featherston, J. B. "Correlation and Final Value Estimation." *The Real Estate Appraiser* 34 (January–February 1968): 40–46.

Kahn, Sanders A.; Case, Frederick E.; and Schimmel, Alfred. "Correlating the Approaches," *Real Estate Appraisal and Investment,* 2nd ed. (New York: The Ronald Press Company, 1977), pp. 211–215.

Kinnard, William N., Jr. "Final Value Estimation and Income Property Report Writing," *Income Property Valuation* (Lexington, Mass.: Heath Lexington Books, 1971), pp. 441–452.

Schmutz, George L. "Correlation of the Value Estimates," *The Appraisal Process* (North Hollywood, California: George L. Schmutz, 1941), pp. 155–158.

Smith, Halbert C. "Reconciliation," *Real Estate Appraisal* (Columbus, Ohio: Grid, Inc., 1976), pp. 177–178.

Textbook Revision Subcommittee. ''Reconciliation of Value Indication,'' *The Appraisal of Real Estate,* 7th ed. (Chicago: American Institute of Real Estate Appraisers, 1978), pp. 506–509.

Ventolo, William L., Jr., and Williams, Martha L. ''Reconciliation and the Appraisal Report,'' *Fundamentals of Real Estate Appraisal,* 2nd ed. (Chicago: Real Estate Education Company, 1980), pp. 179–226.

Yasumoto, Harry. ''Reconciliation.'' *The Appraisal Journal* 44 (October 1976): 612–614.

MODULE X
Special Cases

This material covers special cases that the appraiser often encounters in the business. Examples include assignments where the lender is participating in the income or equity of the business, partial interest ownership, sale-leasebacks, and air rights. The discussion includes examples of each. One chapter covers condemnation exclusively. Since many assignments include valuation for condemnation purposes, the student should have a beginning knowledge of pertinent definitions and techniques.

CHAPTER 18

LEARNING OBJECTIVES

When a student finishes this chapter, he or she should be able to:

- Understand how equity and income participations evolved and how property financed in this manner can be appraised.
- Explain the air rights concept and an appraisal methodology that may be used in evaluating these rights.
- Explain how leased fee and leasehold values relate to each other and to fee simple value.
- Appraise sandwich leaseholds.
- Estimate the present worth of properties subject to sale-leasebacks and also provide an estimate of the reversionary value needed to produce a desired yield rate.

Lender Participations, Partial Interests, and Sale-Leasebacks

IMPORTANT TERMS AND PHRASES

absolute net lease: Requires that the tenant pay all or part of the real estate taxes, insurance, and maintenance expenses.

air rights: A partial interest in real property, giving the possessor the right to undisturbed use and control of a designated space, either at, above, or below the surface.

discount rate: This term has two meanings: (1) in direct capitalization it refers to a return on an investment and can be used as a site capitalization rate, (2) in annuity capitalization, it is used to discount future income to a present value and includes a provision for return on and of value.

expense stop: A lease provision that requires the lessee to pay certain increases in expenses; also known as an escalation clause.

fee simple: An absolute estate without any limitations or constraints except eminent domain, escheat, police power, and taxation.

leased fee estate: An interest in real property held by a lessor; the right of use and occupancy being conveyed under a lease to another party with the right of repossession retained by the lessor at the expiration of the lease.

leasehold: An interest in real property created by a lease entitling the lessee to the right of occupancy and use of the premises for a specified period under certain conditions.

lender participation: A means used by mortgage lenders to increase their yield by sharing in the profitability of a secured property through equity ownership or income participation, or both.

mortgaged out: A 100% loan. For a newly built project, it generally would cover the acquisition cost of the site plus the development cost rather than the full value of the project.

sale-leaseback: A real property transaction where simultaneous agreements are made to convey property to an investor who enters into a long-term lease with the seller who becomes the lessee and the investor, the lessor.

This chapter presents to the reader two sophisticated means of financing real estate and an insight into partial interests in real estate. Departing from the notion in earlier times where the effect of debt financing on property value was disregarded, this chapter covers situations where a lender shares in a property's income and value. The different partial interests (rights) in real property are discussed. These rights include air rights, the leased fee and leasehold estate, and a discussion of how these rights are appraised. This chapter concludes with an explanation of how to appraise a sale-leaseback.

LENDER PARTICIPATIONS

Until fairly recently, a paradox existed in the appraisal of income property. The appraiser often was obliged to consider the appraised property as if it were free of any debt; that is, the property was viewed as if the purchaser paid and the seller received all cash when the property was transferred. However, real property is seldom purchased without considerable debt financing. In fact, one motivation in acquiring income property is the use of a minimum of equity capital through use of borrowed capital. Although property was assumed to be "free and clear," it was common practice to develop a discount rate by considering typical available loan terms. The following example illustrates this point by use of the band of investment approach to developing a discount rate that was discussed in Chapter 7.

Loan and equity ratios	Rates*	*Weighted rates*
.75	× .12	= .090
.25	× .10	= .025
Discount rate		.115

*Mortgage interest rate.

Carrying this example a step further, an overall capitalization rate can be developed by inserting the annual constant rate. Also considered is the equity dividend rate expected by the equity investor, after deducting annual debt service from the net operating income. A brief example of developing an overall capitalization rate is illustrated here for a 75% loan-to-value mortgage, a 12% interest rate, monthly installments, and a twenty-five-year loan term.

Loan and equity ratios	Rates	*Weighted rates*
.75	× .1264*	= .0948
.25	× .08	= .0200
Overall rate		.1148

*Annual mortgage constant (R_M).

From this example it can be seen that the mortgage terms are a valid consideration in appraising real property. Carrying this logic further, we arrive at mortgage-equity capitalization (see Chapter 9), which is a marked improvement over the "free and clear" method of appraising. Under the mortgage-equity concept, property is analyzed on the basis of typical debt financing. Instead of considering the remaining economic life of the improvement, a shorter holding period typically anticipated by investors is used. This technique provides for anticipated change in the property value during the holding period and includes a return on the equity investment rather than the price of the entire property.

Use of the mortgage-equity concept and the Ellwood technique with preprinted tables adds a note of realism to the appraisal of income property. Appraisal techniques should reflect changing investors' attitudes and financing methods. For example, a significant change in mortgage financing occurred beginning with the 1967–1968 "credit crunch." A growing "lender's market" favored mortgage lenders demanding payments over and above the fixed-rate, fixed-term mortgage agreement. For years, the return received by lenders of debt capital in real property had lagged the yields realized by equity investors, even though equity investors typically invested relatively little capital. Sometimes equity investors "mortgaged out," and put none of their capital in a project.

Although numerous variations of mortgagee (lender) participation arrangements may be negotiated, there are two basic categories. These arrangements are known as *income participation* and *equity participation.* A lender can participate in project income at the gross income, net operating income, or cash flow stages in addition to scheduled mortgage interest payments. Participation in cash flow may be either before or after income taxes. This form of lender participation ordinarily ends when a property is sold.

Equity participation is not as restricted as income participation since the mortgagee may participate in the earnings of the property after it has been sold by the borrower. Also, a lender may participate in net sale proceeds, refinancing, income-tax shelter, and even in specified project income.

Examples

This section deals with the evaluation of the total interest in real property comprised of the mortgagors' (borrowers') and morgagees' (lenders') shares. Additionally, the following mortgage-equity technique shows how mortgagee income and equity participation can affect property value. Before estimating the value of a property, it is necessary to (1) determine the interests held by the parties involved in a participation mortgage loan, and (2) ascertain the amount and timing of income flows receivable by the respective parties. The balance of this section contains three applications of mortgage-equity analysis of participation mortgage loans subject to the following conditions.[1] The first example (Fig. 18.1) is a mortgage loan without any lender participation in the property

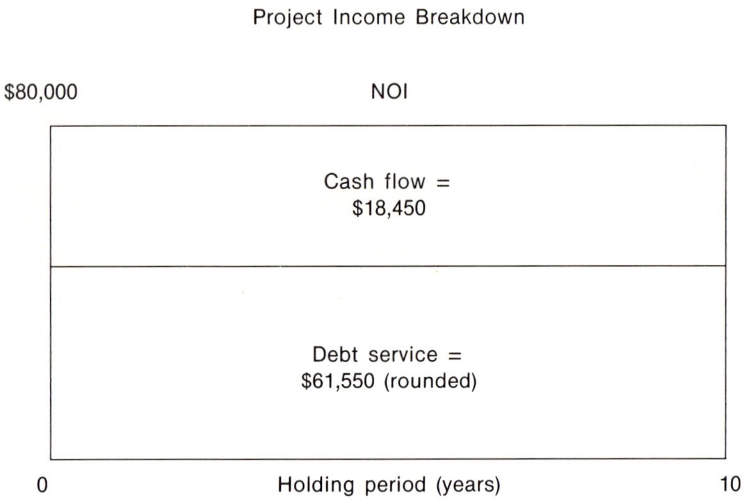

Fig. 18.1 Conventional mortgage terms (no participation) assume an equity yield rate of 16%

income or value. The remaining three figures show different forms of lender participation and the effect of such financing on the borrower's interests in real property.

As the lender increasingly shares in the ownership benefits of the property, the equity owner's interest is eroded. Consequently, a higher equity yield rate is used to reflect this changing relationship. This rate increases from 16% to 18% between Exhibits 18-1 and 18-3.

Mortgage, Income and Sales Conditions*

Mortgage loan terms:	
Original loan amount	$487,000
Loan balance at the end of 10 years	$427,374
75% loan-to-value ratio	
25-year term	
Monthly installments	
Level payments	
12% interest rate	
1.30 debt coverage ratio (actual, 1.2998)	
Income and Sale Conditions:	
Forecast annual net operating income	$ 80,000
Forecast gross sales price at end of tenth year	$800,000
Borrower's sales expenses at end of tenth year	$ 50,000

*The effect of lender requirements also is covered in Chapter 12.

The lender's share in the value of the mortgage property increases in each successive exhibit. The mortgagee does not participate in the property value in this first example, but only receives interest payments on the $487,000 mortgage at 12% for twenty-five years. (The effect of lender requirements also is covered in Chapter 12.)

Present value of lender's interest			
Initial amount of loan			$487,000
Present value of borrower's equity interest			
PV of annual cash flow			
$18,450 × 4.833226		$89,173	
($80,000 − $61,550)($a_{\overline{n}\rvert}$ factor for 10 yrs., 16%)			
plus PV of sale proceeds to borrower	$750,000		
($800,000 − $50,000)			
less loan balance			
($487,000) (83.321664/94.946551)	− 427,374*		
($a_{\overline{n}\rvert}$, 12%, 15 yrs.)($a_{\overline{n}\rvert}$, 12%, 25 yrs.)			
Net cash reversion to borrower	$322,626		
(V^n factor for 16%, 10 yrs.)	× .226684	+ 73,134	
Total present value of borrower's interest			$162,307
Total present value of property			$649,307

*Alternatively, this loan balance could have been computed using the monthly mortgage debt service and present value of $1 per period factor at 12% for fifteen years, as follows: ($61,550/12)(83.321664) = $427,371.

The borrower's $18,450 cash flow in Fig. 18.1 is reduced by $4,800 in Fig. 18.2 since the lender receives $61,550 annual debt service as well as 6% of the net operating income ($80,000). The decreased share in the net operating income by the borrower reduces its ownership share from $162,307 to $123,907. In turn, the lender's interest in the property has increased (from $487,000 to $524,647).

Assume: an equity yield rate of 17%

lender participates in 6% of NOI for 25 years in addition to loan interest payments

lender's discount rate is 12%

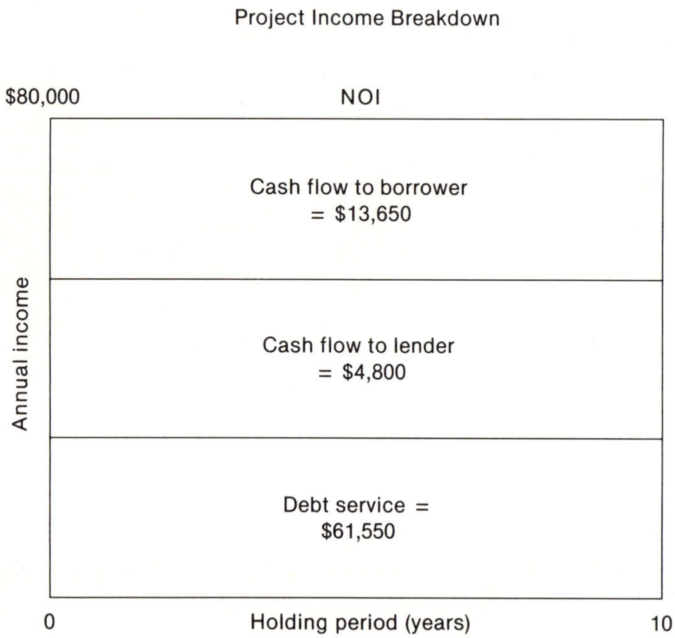

Fig. 18.2 Lender participation in net operating income

Present value of lender's interest:			
Initial loan amount		$487,000	
Present value of cash flow to lender ($4,800)(7.843139)		+ 37,647	$524,647
($a_{\overline{n}|}$ factor for 12%, 25 yrs.)			
Plus present worth of borrower's interest:			
PV of cash flow to borrower ($13,650)(4.658604)		$ 63,590	
($a_{\overline{n}|}$ factor for 17%, 10 yrs.)			
PV of net cash reversion to borrower	$322,626		
Lender's interest at end of tenth year ($4,800)(6.810864)	− 32,692		
($a_{\overline{n}|}$ factor for 12%, 15 yrs.)*			
Cash reversion to borrower	$289,934		
Reversion factor (17%, 10 yrs.)	× .208037	+ 60,317	
Total present value of borrower's interest			$123,907
Total present value of property			$648,554

*This deduction is necessary to recognize the lender's interest in the property income for fifteen years beyond the anticipated holding period.

The borrower's interest in the property earnings decreases even more as the lender participates in the annual cash flow plus the reversionary value of the property when it is sold. Figure 18.3 shows that the lender participates in 25% of the cash flow ($18,450), which is $4,612 or slightly more than under the plan shown in Fig. 18.4. However, once the present value of the net cash reversion ($31,096) is added to the lender's benefits, the borrower's ownership share is reduced to $108,421.

This example is similar to the previous example except the lender participates in both the income and reversionary property value.

Assume: lender shares in 25% of cash flow and net cash reversion in addition to loan interest payments

lender's discount rate is 10% (lower than in previous examples due to greater benefits received)

borrower's equity yield rate is 18%

net cash reversion to lender is $322,626 ($750,000 − $427,374)

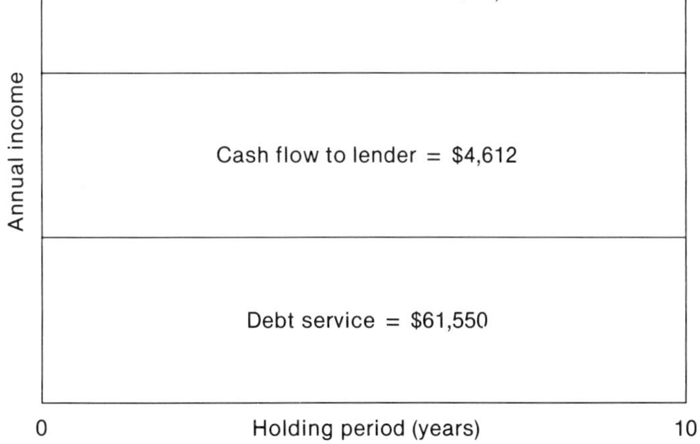

Fig. 18.3 Lender participation in annual cash flow and reversion

Increasing use of seller financing has occurred in recent years as institutional sources of mortgage funds have become scarce and more expensive. Owners have filled this breach by providing financing, often with a balloon mortgage. Sellers can improve their yield by requiring a share of the property income. If, as in this example, the seller participates in the cash flow, the purchaser is assured of having covered the operating expenses and mortgage debt service before the lender's participation begins.

Assume: seller participates in 20% of cash flow
($487,000 loan, 12% interest, 25-year term, level monthly installments)
seller-lender's discount rate on loan is 12%
buyer-borrower's equity yield is 17%
seller-lender's discount rate on cash flow participation is 15%

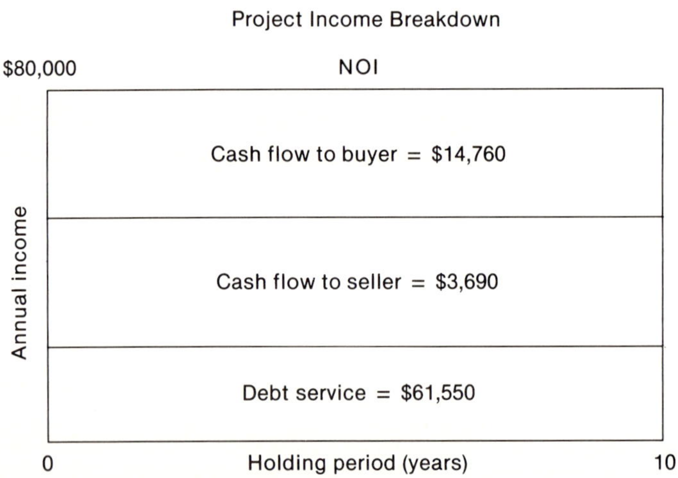

Fig. 18.4 Lender participation in cash flow, using installment sale financing

---

Present value of lender's interest:		
Initial loan amount	$487,000	
PV of cash flow to lender ($4,612)(6.144567)	+ 28,339	
($a_{\overline{n}|}$ factor for 10%, 10 yrs.)		
Present value of net cash reversion to lender ($322,626 × .25)(.385543)	+ 31,096	
(V^n factor for 10%, 10 yrs.)		
Total present value of lender's interest		$546,435

(continued)

Present value of borrower's interest:			
PV of cash flow to borrower			
($13,838)(4.494086)		$ 62,189	
($a_{\overline{n}|}$ factor for 18%, 10 yrs.)			
Present value of net cash reversion to borrower			
($322,626 × .75)(.191064)		+ 46,232	
(V^n factor for 18%, 10 yrs.)			
Total present value of borrower's interest			$108,421
Total present value of property			$654,856

The type of mortgage financing discussed in Fig. 18.4 involves debt financing provided by a seller. A participation in cash flow is sometimes required in order to secure seller financing. In this example, the seller-lender requires 20% of the cash flow (.20 × $18,450). This participation in the cash flow generates an additional $23,853 interest in the property for the seller.

Present value of seller's interest:			
(PV of annual debt service			
($61,550)(7.843139)		$482,745	
($a_{\overline{n}|}$ factor for 12%, 25 yrs.)			
Present value of cash flow to seller			
($3,690)(6.464149)			
($a_{\overline{n}|}$ factor for 15%, 25 yrs.)		23,853	
Present value of seller's interest			$506,598
Present value of buyer's interest:			
PV of cash flow to buyer			
($14,760)(5.766232)			
(V^n factor for 17%, 25 yrs.)		$ 85,110	
Present value of cash reversion to buyer			
Expected net sale proceeds	$750,000		
Balance of purchase money mortgage			
($487,000)(.877564)*	− 427,374		
Value of seller's income participation			
($3,690)(6.464149)			
($a_{\overline{n}|}$ factor for 15%, 25 yrs.)	− 23,853		
	$298,773		
Discounted @ 17% for 10 years	× .208037		
		$ 62,156	
Present value of buyer's interest			+ 147,266
Present value of property			$653,864

*See page 376.

As the present value of the borrower's interest in the property diminishes from Fig. 18.2 to Fig. 18.3, a higher yield rate is justified. Conversely, the lender's discount rate declines as its participation in the ownership of the property increases.

PARTIAL INTERESTS IN REAL PROPERTY

A basic trait of real property that is recognized by appraisers is its divisibility into multiple interests or rights. Often appraisal assignments require that the appraiser estimate the value of one or more of these interests in real property. Two of these possibilities are discussed in the following sections. These sections will cover the nature and appraisal of air rights and leased fee and leasehold interests.

Air Rights

Air rights may be defined as a partial interest in real property which gives the possessor the right to undisturbed use and control of a designated space, either at, above, or below the surface. Air space, on the other hand, is a separate parcel and legally described area under or above another structure. Some examples of the use of air rights are public parks over depressed railroad right-of-ways, buildings over expressways, elevated expressways over private property, buildings over parking lots, and buildings that extend over municipally-owned sidewalks. Variations of this concept are covered in Chapter 19.

Some early examples of the use of air rights are the *Chicago Daily News,* which was leased by the Chicago Union Terminal over its tracks, and the Waldorf Astoria Hotel, which was built over the New York Central Railway in New York City. These developments occurred in 1927 and 1930, respectively. At about the same time, Chicago's Merchandise Mart, containing 4.2 million square feet, was built over a railroad right-of-way. More recent examples of this type of development are the George Washington Bridge Apartments over New York's George Washington Bridge approach, the United Nations Building over the F.D.R. Drive in New York City, and Prudential Center over the Massachusetts Turnpike in Boston.

Unquestionably, air rights, or as it sometimes is called, "platform development," is more expensive than development on land. Therefore why would this more expensive-type development be used? Its use is justified when the cost of land in highly developed urban areas becomes so high that it is less expensive to use air rights development. Also, it may be used when an especially attractive location would otherwise be undeveloped; it allows land assemblage by tying together land on either side of a right-of-way with development above the right-of-way. Offsetting these advantages are the disadvantages of higher foundation and construction costs, design problems, and the necessity of removing exhaust fumes from vehicles passing beneath the platform.

The air rights lease is used essentially for two purposes. The first is to permit construction of a building over property belonging to another party. The second is to maintain site prominence, view, or unencumbered flow of light and air to a building. To preserve these advantages, an office building owner may lease the unused development rights above an adjoining smaller building, thus prohibiting future development. This use of air rights is similar to the transfer of development rights (TDR) concept, which was popularized in Chicago and New York City. Essentially the TDR scheme permitted the maintenance of an architecturally significant building by selling its unused development rights to another property owner who then would intensify development to the extent of the acquired development rights.

Air Rights Appraisal Methodology The value of air rights will be considerably less than that of the fee site value since these rights are less than full fee rights. Moreover, the value of these rights are lessened by construction problems and costs. The Illinois Central Railroad, in judging the price for air rights over right-of-ways in Chicago, uses the following technique and is illustrated in Exhibit 18.1:

Exhibit 18.1
Air rights valuation

1. Unencumbered land value	$900,000
2. Plus plottage value	+ 100,000
	$1,000,000
3. Maximum number of floors allowed	30
4. Deduct space for air rights	6
5. [(4)/(3)][(1) + (2)], or (6/30)($1,000,000)	$200,000

1. Determine the fee value of the unencumbered land.
2. Add a value for assembly of a large parcel.
3. Determine the maximum number of floors permitted by zoning floor area ratio.

4. Deduct the space retained by the railroad in terms of the number of floors from the maximum floors allowed by zoning to obtain the remaining floors.
5. Multiply the ratio of floors occupied by the right-of-way to total floors permitted by zoning by the total fee value to equal the value of the airspace.[2]

A formula that may be used for valuing tunnel easements states that $V - A = R$, with:

V = value of the land before taking of air rights,

A = value of air rights after taking of air rights,

R = remaining interest in the property.

A different and more complex equation, used in appraising the George Washington Bridge approach follows along with an illustration in Exhibit 18.2.

$$R = V^c - A, \text{ or } V^c - [X + (C - D)] - I = A$$

where

A = air rights value

V^c = land value by comparison in fee simple, vacant but improved with all utilities at lot line,

X = loss of residual value from functional or economic obsolescence arising from creation of the air rights,

C = added capital improvement costs to air rights purchaser or lessee in construction of building,

Exhibit 18.2
Air rights valuation

$A = V^c - [X + (C - D)] - I$, with

$$\begin{aligned} A &= \$1{,}000{,}000 - [\$50{,}000 + (\$750{,}000 - \$100{,}000)] - \$100{,}000 \\ &= \$1{,}000{,}000 - \$50{,}000 - \$650{,}000 - \$100{,}000 \\ &= \underline{\underline{\$200{,}000}} \end{aligned}$$

$$\begin{aligned} R &= V^c - A \\ &= \$1{,}000{,}000 - \$200{,}000 \\ &= \underline{\underline{\$800{,}000}} \end{aligned}$$

D = savings to air rights purchaser or lessee in excavation and foundation costs, demolition, tenant relocation, and income losses during relocation and demolition,

I = added interest and carrying charges as a result of added capital improvement costs in C,

R = residual value of fee interest.[3]

Leased Fee and Leasehold Estates

The overall value of a property unencumbered is fee simple value. In estimating the value of an income property, the logical starting point is the lease, if one exists. A *lease* is a legal document that conveys certain interests in real property to a lessee (tenant) from the lessor (owner) for a specified period and under certain conditions, including periodic payment of rent. A competent appraisal is not possible without the appraiser understanding the lease. He or she should ascertain the significance of future payment provisions, expense stops, and accurately identify the size of space leased to the tenant(s).

Leases may specify different rental levels for similar buildings. Such differences in rentals may be caused by different financial strength of tenants. Generally, strong tenants cause relatively favorable mortgage terms. The resulting mortgage terms and lower-risk tenants ordinarily produce lower capitalization rates and higher property values.

The total property value is equated with the fee simple interest, which is called the *freehold.* The value of the fee simple interest is made up of the leased fee (lessor's) interest and the leasehold (lessee's) interest. The total of these two partial interests cannot exceed the value of the fee simple interest.

Leased fee estate This interest is held by the lessor. The lessor has the right to rent the property to another party, receive rental payments, and usually repossess the property at the end of the lease. It follows that the value of a lease interest is (1) the present worth of the rental specified in the lease (contract rent) during the lease term(s), plus (2) the present worth of the reversionary value of the property at the expiration of the lease.

For example, suppose that a property owner has just negotiated a twenty-year absolute net lease for $30,000 a year, with the rent being paid at the beginning of each month. The property is now worth $275,000, is expected to increase annually at 6%, and will revert to the lessor at the end of the lease. The present worth of the leased fee interest in this property, assuming an 11% discount rate, is found by the following procedure:

	PV of rental income =	
	(\$30,000/12) (96.881538 × 1.0091667)*	\$244,424
	(monthly rental) (PV of 1 per period × 1 + .11/12)	
plus	(\$275,000) (.124034 × 3.207135)†	109,393
	(PV) (PV of 1 × FV of 1 at 6% annually)	
Total present worth of leased fee		\$353,817

*Adjusted to beginning of month payments (also shown in Chapter 6). This calculation can be handled two ways. One method is to multiply the appropriate EOP factor by a BOP adjustment factor, as the preceding shows. A second method is to not discount the first month's payment (\$2,500) and discount the remaining payments as if they were received at the EOP for nineteen years and eleven months. The first step is to compute V^n for nineteen years, eleven months. This is done as follows:

$$.124870 \times .904499 = .112945$$
$$(V^n\text{, 19 years})(V^n\text{, 11 months})$$

Substitute in the formula for $a_{\overline{n}|}$

$$a_{\overline{n}|} = \frac{1 - V^n}{i}\text{, with } i = .11/12,$$

therefore,

$$a_{\overline{n}|} = \frac{1 - .112945}{.00916667} = 96.769601.$$

PV of rental income at BOP =	\$ 2,500
+ (96.769601)(\$2,500)	241,924
	\$244,424

†Discounted at 11% annually and reflecting 6% annual compounded rate of appreciation. The monthly 11% reversion factor .111919 may be used in place of .124034. However, an annual reversion rate is preferable.

If the value of the leased fee estate is less than the value of the entire property, a positive leasehold interest exists. Conversely, a negative leasehold interest exists when the value of the leased fee estate exceeds the value of the fee simple interest, or total property value.

Leasehold estate When a property is leased to a second party (lessee), part of the fee owner's rights are "sold" during the term of the lease for rental payments. Ordinarily, the lessee will have no financial interest in the property when the lease is initially signed. This lack of interest is because the rent specified in the lease generally equals the prevailing rental for the property (often called market rent). If there are no lease provisions, such as expense stops, step-up payment clauses, or rent indexing, the economic rental may be expected to rise above the contract rental. In such cases, the tenant acquires a financial benefit from the lease known as a leasehold interest. If the appeal of the property declines and in turn rental demand weakens, the tenant may find that the lease payments exceed the rental that the property could bring in the open market. Consequently, the tenant has a negative financial interest in the property. An important point is that the total of the leased fee and leasehold interests can never be greater than the fee simple property value.

A key in deciding whether a lessee has a positive interest in a property where the prevailing market rent exceeds the contractual rental is the lease terms. If the lease permits subleasing, there could be a leasehold interest enjoyed by the tenant. If subleasing is prohibited, it is doubtful that the higher market rental would benefit the tenant.

A positive leasehold interest is shown in the following illustration, which builds on the previous example. Everything remains the same except that the property currently can rent for $36,000 net annually instead of the $30,000 specified in the lease; the lessor's interest is valued to yield 12%.

Value of leasehold interest =
[($36,000 − $30,000)/12] (90.819416 × 1.01) =
[(net monthly leasehold income) (PV of 1 per period × 1 + .12/12)]
($500) (91.727610) =
$45,864

Sandwich lease In a situation where the market rent is greater than the contract rent, and if not prohibited by the lease, the lessee can sublease the property at a profit. The lessee's interest extends only until the prime lease is terminated.

The initial step in estimating the value of the sandwich leasehold is to judge the value of the property based on its market rental. Next, the value of the leased fee is estimated, followed by an estimate of the leasehold, which is the unencumbered property value less the value of the leased fee. This procedure is outlined in Exhibit 18.3.

Sale-Leaseback

The sale-leaseback, sometimes called purchase-leaseback, concept dates back to England nearly 150 years ago. However, it has been used in this country on a wide-scale basis for less than 40 years.

A sale-leaseback involves a real property transaction where simultaneous agreements are made to convey property to an investor who enters into a long-term lease with the seller. The seller becomes the lessee, and the investor becomes the lessor.

Evaluating Sale-Leasebacks

In dealing with a sale-leaseback, it should be noted that most compound interest tables are set up on the basis of payments being received at the end of a period. *Traditionally, lease payments are paid at the beginning of a period.* It is relatively simple to convert a rate from end of period to beginning of period (as shown in Chapter 6 and below). The end-of-period rate is multiplied by the

Exhibit 18.3
Sandwich leasehold

Facts:

The present value of property is $600,000 with the building contributing $100,000. The building is expected to have no value at the end of the present ten-year lease, and the land value will be unchanged. The net income to lessor, payable at the beginning of the month, is $4500; the lessor expects a 10% return.

The appropriate PV factors for 10% monthly are:

$V^n =$ .369406
base = 1.0083333
(1 + .10/12)
$a_{\overline{n}|} =$ 75.671163

The lessee has subleased the property at $6000 a month, with the rent payable at the beginning of the month. The appropriate discount rate for a sandwich lease is thought to be 12%. The corresponding PV factors are:

$a_{\overline{n}|} =$ 69.700522
base = 1.010

(a) Value of leased fee:

$4500 × 75.671163 × 1.0083333		$343,358
plus reversion	$100,000 × .369406	36,941
		$380,299

(b) Value of sandwich leasehold:

Market rent	$6000	
less contract rent	4500	
	$1500 × 69.700522 × 1.01 =	$105,596

(c) Value of sublessee's interest:

Market value of property		$600,000
less value of leased fee	$380,299	
less value of sandwich leasehold	105,596	485,895
		$114,105

base for that rate and installment frequency, as shown in the following example, which begins with monthly end-of-period installments ($1/a_n$) for forty years at 12%, or 0.010084.

Adjusting End of Period to Beginning of Period Installments

$$\text{Base} = 1 + .12/12, \text{ or } 1.01$$

$$\text{Capitalization Rate} = \left(\frac{.010084}{1.01}\right) \times 12 = .119810$$

The amount of an offer for a property producing $1000 a month net rental income would be $100,159 ($12,000/.119810), rounded to $100,000.

Exhibit 18.4
Value of sublessee's interest

Assume now that the property is worth \$388,000 rather than the previous \$600,000, but the leased fee is still worth \$343,000 (rounded from previous example), leaving a value for the two leasehold positions of \$45,000. The annual amount charged by the lessee to the sublessee is \$35,000. This amount compares to \$30,000 charged the lessee and \$36,000 that is the market rent.

The twenty-year annuity factor developed by comparing the value and income available to the combined leasehold positions is:

$$\frac{\$45{,}000}{\$36{,}000 - \$30{,}000} = 7.50$$

This twenty-year annual annuity factor approximates that for the 12% rate (7.469444). A rate of 12% then is the appropriate discount rate for the combined leasehold positions.

Using a judgmentally-derived discount rate of 13% to reflect a slightly higher degree of risk for the sublessee's position, the value of the sandwich lease is computed as follows:

\$35,000 − \$30,000 = \$5,000 (rent difference)

PV of \$5,000 for 20 years @ 13% =
\$5,000 × 7.024749 × 1.13*
(PV of 1 per period)

Value of sandwich lease	\$39,690
Thus, the value of the sublessee's interest is: \$45,000 − \$39,690 =	
Value of sublessee's interest	\$5,310

*This example uses an annual base (1 = .13/1); a monthly base and discount factor would be acceptable.

Exhibit 18.5
Purchase-leaseback investment yield characteristics, lease term 15 years

Interest rate	.0700		.0725		**.0750**		.0775	
Annual rent	.1072		.1089		.1106		.1122	
	Yield	Reversion	Yield	Reversion	Yield	Reversion	Yield	Reversion
	.0750	.0920	.0775	.0948	.0800	.0977	.0825	.1007
	.0800	.1940	.0825	.1999	.0850	.2060	.0875	.2123
	.0850	.3067	.0875	.3161	.0900	.3258	.0925	.3357
	.0900	.4311	.0925	.4444	.0950	.4580	.0975	.4720
	.0950	.5683	.0975	.5857	**.1000**	**.6037**	.1025	.6222
	.1000	.7192	.1025	.7414	.1050	.7642	.1075	.7877
	.1050	.8852	.1075	.9125	.1100	.9407	.1125	.9697
	.1100	1.0675	.1125	1.1005	.1150	1.1346	.1175	1.1696
	.1150	1.2675	.1175	1.3068	.1200	1.3473	.1225	1.3890
	.1200	1.4868	.1225	1.5330	.1250	1.5806	.1275	1.6296

Source: Reprinted from *Ellwood Tables for Real Estate Appraising and Financing,* 4th ed.

A purchaser, involved with a purchase-leaseback, generally expects to recover the equity during the lease period, plus a return over and above the investment recaptured. Any value remaining in the property at the expiration of the lease enhances the investor's yield. Several problems follow to illustrate this investment rationale. These problems may be solved by using compound interest tables, or Table IV "Purchase-Leaseback Rent Factors and Capitalization Rates" found in the *Ellwood Tables.*

A different type of sale-leaseback problem occurs when an investor wants a particular yield rate. For example, by use of Exhibit 18.5, it can be seen that for an investor seeking to recapture an investment of \$500,000 at 7 1/2% interest rate over fifteen years, and expecting a 10% yield rate on the sale price, should charge \$301,850 (.6037 × \$500,000).

PROBLEMS

Question: A warehouse has been leased by the owner on an absolute net basis to a regional supplier for six years. The original lease specified an initial term of twenty-five years, with three- to five-year renewals. Monthly rental is \$15,400, payable in advance.

The owner of this property has a loan balance of \$1,100,000; the prepayment penalty period has expired. Since the accelerated depreciation tax benefits have been greatly reduced and the tax-deductible mortgage interest lessened somewhat, the owner is interested in either selling, refinancing, or using another advantageous method to improve the owner's income tax situation. A better investment cannot be found; therefore, the owner does not want to sell the property and is not interested in refinancing it, so it is decided to use a sale-leaseback arrangement, as follows.

A pension fund offers to buy the property at its present market value, based on a 10% return, with the present lease remaining intact, and the property value being completely recovered over the remainder of the initial lease period. (The 10%, nineteen-year amortization installment rate for end-of-period payments is .009812). Compute the amount of the offer.

Answer:

Capitalization rate $= \left(\dfrac{.009812}{(.10/12) + 1}\right) \times 12 = .116771^*$

Annual NOI = \$15,400 × 12, or \$184,800

Amount of offer = \$184,800/.116771

= \$1,582,585; say \$1,580,000

*Also see L. W. Ellwood, *Ellwood Tables for Real Estate Appraising and Financing,* 4th ed. (Cambridge, Mass.: Ballinger Publishing Company, 1977), p. 617.

Question: Determine the annual rental payments necessary for a sale-leaseback if a supermarket chain is to secure financing of $50,000,000 to expand its outlets into several new markets. The investor seeks a 9% return via prepaid quarterly installments with the above investment being completely repaid at the end of twenty-two years. The quarterly end-of-period amortization factor at 9% for twenty-two years is 0.026197.

Answer: $$\text{Annual rental payments} = (\$50{,}000{,}000)\left(\frac{.026197}{(.09/4) + 1}\right)(4)$$

$$\text{Annual rental payments} = (\$50{,}000{,}000)\,(.102482)$$
$$\text{Annual rental payments} = \$5{,}124{,}108$$

Question: Another investment consideration involving a sale-leaseback is where an investor wants to estimate the reversionary value of a property at the expiration of the lease necessary to produce a desired yield. Alternatively, in negotiating the repurchase of an option to renew the lease, an investor may begin with the lease terms, rental payments, and probable reversion. The question, then, is what yield can be anticipated under such conditions. To solve these problems, use of the "Purchase-Leaseback Investment Yield Characteristics" table found on pages 623–636 of the fourth edition of the *Ellwood Tables* is recommended (or Exhibit 18.5). The following problems use excerpts from these tables.

An investor expects to purchase a retail property with an investment of $2,000,000. This property will be acquired subject to a fifteen-year lease that produces a 7% return; rent is payable at the beginning of the month. What sale price would be required at the end of the lease to give the investor a 12% yield?

Answer:

$$\text{Required sale price} = \$2{,}000{,}000 \times 1.4868$$
$$= \underline{\underline{\$2{,}973{,}600}}$$

Question: Advise your client of an appropriate repurchase price to charge for an office building under the following circumstances:

Property is subject to an absolute net lease that will amortize the value of the investment (purchase price) at 7 1/4% over fifteen years. Your client, the present owner, is agreeable to selling the property back to the former owner on the basis of a 12% yield. The original purchase price was $700,000.

Answer: A glance at Exhibit 18.5 shows that in the .0725 interest rate column 12% falls between yields of 11.75% and 12.25%. By visual inspection, the reversion factor between these two yield rates is seen to be one-half the difference of the reversion factors 1.3068 and 1.5330, or 1.4199. When multiplied by $700,000 the recommended sale price is $994,000 (rounded from $993,930).

If the fractions become more complicated, the following method can be used to interpolate for an exact figure.

$$\begin{array}{r} .1225 \\ -\ .1200 \\ \hline .0025 \end{array} \qquad \begin{array}{r} .1225 \\ -\ .1175 \\ \hline .0050 \end{array} \qquad \begin{array}{r} 1.5330 \\ -\ 1.3068 \\ \hline 0.2262 \end{array}$$

$$\begin{aligned} \text{Sale Price} &= [1.3068 + (.0025/.0050)\,(0.2262)]\,(\$700{,}000) \\ &= (1.3068 + 0.1131)(\$700{,}000) \\ &= \underline{\underline{\$993{,}930}} \end{aligned}$$

Question: A property has been purchased for $1,500,000 and simultaneously leased to the seller with the understanding that the seller can repurchase the property at the expiration of the lease. The lease period is eighteen years, with a monthly rent of $10,000 (BOP). Advise the involved parties of the repurchase price that will give the present owner a yield of 10%. (Use the formula given below.) The desired reversion for any investment yield can be found by using the following formula:

$$\text{Reversion} = V[(1 + i)^n - d(1 + i)S_{\overline{n|}}]$$

where

V = purchase price,

$(1 + i)$ = base; i.e., 1 + effective interest rate, which is the nominal interest rate divided by the number of installments,

n = number of rent installments in the lease,

d = periodic rent per dollar of purchase price (beginning of period, BOP),

$S_{\overline{n|}}$ = future worth of one per period at rate i for n periods.[4]

Answer:

$$\begin{aligned} d &= \$10{,}000/\$1{,}500{,}000 \\ &= 0.006667 \\ \text{Reversion (repurchase price)} &= V[(1 + i)^n - d(1 + i)S_{\overline{n|}}] \\ &= \$1{,}500{,}000[6.004693 - (.006667) \\ &\quad (1.008333)(600.563212)] \\ &= \$1{,}500{,}000[6.004693 - 4.037320] \\ &= \$1{,}500{,}000 \times 1.967373 \\ &= \$2{,}951{,}060 \\ \text{Rounded to } &\underline{\underline{\$2{,}950{,}000}} \end{aligned}$$

SUMMARY

To appraise any real property correctly requires that the appraiser consider those factors that influence value. A major influence on income property value is mortgage financing. This influence extends beyond the repayment of the loan at a fixed interest rate over a specified term. As the lender participates more in a mortgage property's income and its value, the value of the equity owner's share decreases.

One real property right is known as air rights. Three methods were suggested for appraising these rights. One of these methods required that (1) the value of the unaffected property be estimated, and (2) a ratio of floors lost to the total number of floors allowed by zoning be set. The value of the air rights was (1) multiplied by (2).

The value of the fee simple interest consists of the leased fee (lessor's) interest and the leasehold (lessee's) interest. A lessee will have a positive interest in the property where the current market rent exceeds the rent specified in the lease. A sandwich leasehold exists when the original lessee subleases the premises to another party.

A sale-leaseback exists when simultaneous agreements convey a property to an investor who enters into a long-term lease with the seller. The amount of an offer in a sale-leaseback can be determined by developing a beginning of period capitalization rate and then capitalizing the rental income.

REVIEW QUESTIONS

1. Explain why it is sometimes appropriate for the appraiser to consider lender income or equity participation in appraising real property.
2. What two steps should precede the value estimate of a property subject to participation mortgage financing?
3. How does the appraisal of air rights relate to the bundle-of-rights concept?
4. Brieftly summarize the Illinois Central Railroad air rights appraisal methodology.
5. Using the following information, estimate the leased fee value of the property.

   Net rent specified in lease: \$1000 a month, due at beginning of month

   Prevailing net rental rate: \$1200 a month, due at beginning of month

   Value of property at end of fifteen-year lease: \$300,000

   12% discount rate used

   reversion factor = .166783; $a_{\overline{n}|}$

   factor = 83.321664 (end of month)

6. Compute the annual rent required with a sale-leaseback to finance $1,500,000 under the following conditions: The investor desires a 10% return on annual installments over twenty years (end-of-year amortization factor = .117460).

ENDNOTES

1. The four examples were influenced by an article by Jerome J. Dasso, William N. Kinnard, Jr., and Stephen D. Messner, "Lender Participation Financing: Case Applications in Appraising Participation-Financed Properties," *The Real Estate Appraiser* 37 (May–June 1971): 11–25.
2. Lawrence E. Williams, Jr., and Daniel J. McNichol, "Valuation of Airspace," *The Appraisal Journal* 41 (April 1973): 243, citing Robert R. Wright, *The Law of Airspace* (New York: Bobbs-Merrill Company, Inc., 1968), pp. 323–324.
3. Williams and McNichol, pp. 241–242, citing Walter R. Kuehnle, "Valuation of Vertical Highway Tunnel Easements for Right-of-Way," and John R. White, "George Washington Bridge Approach Case Study," in American Institute of Real Estate Appraisers' *Case Studies in Air Rights and Subsurface Tunnel Road Easements,* Chicago, 1964.
4. L. W. Ellwood, *Ellwood Tables for Real Estate Appraising and Financing,* 4th ed. (Cambridge, Mass.: Ballinger Publishing Company, 1977), pp. 133–134.

ADDITIONAL READINGS

Boykin, James H. "Purchase-Leaseback," *Financing Real Estate,* 3rd printing (Lexington, Mass.: D. C. Heath and Company, 1979), pp. 513–520.

Dasso, Jerome J.; Kinnard, William N., Jr.; and Messner, Stephen D. "Lender Participation Financing: Its Nature and Significance to Appraisers." *The Real Estate Appraiser* 37 (March–April 1971): 13–19.

Dasso, Jerome J.; Kinnard, William N., Jr.; and Messner, Stephen D. "Lender Participation Financing: Case Applications in Appraising Participation-Financed Properties." *The Real Estate Appraiser* 37 (May–June 1971): 11–25.

Dasso, Jerome J.; Kinnard, William N., Jr.; and Messner, Stephen D. "Lender Participation Financing: Applications of Sensitivity and Investment Analyses." *The Real Estate Appraiser* 37 (July–August 1971): 33–40.

Ellwood, L. W. "The Purchase and Leaseback Tables," *Ellwood Tables for Real Estate Appraising and Financing,* 4th ed. (Cambridge, Mass.: Ballinger Publishing Company, 1977), pp. 121–134, 601–636.

Miller, R. A. Stuart, and Kafes, James C. "Mortgagee Participation: Effects on Real Estate Investments." *The Appraisal Journal* 39 (April 1971): 178–193.

Williams, Lawrence E., Jr., and McNichol, Daniel J. "Valuation of Airspace." *The Appraisal Journal* 41 (April 1973): 234–253.

CHAPTER 19

LEARNING OBJECTIVES

When a student finishes this chapter, he or she should be able to:

- Discuss the difference between eminent domain and police powers, especially with regard to just compensation to property owners.
- Understand the larger parcel concept and its significance in condemnation appraising.
- Understand the several fundamental types of partial takings, possible compensable damages to remainders, and how to evaluate such situations.
- Explain the principal types of easements and how they can be appraised.

Condemnation and Easement Appraisals

IMPORTANT TERMS AND PHRASES:

condemnation: The judicial or administrative process used by government in the exercise of its power of eminent domain.

easement: A nonpossessing (no transfer of ownership) interest in a property owned by another party; it may be underground, surface, or overhead.

eminent domain: A sovereign right of government to acquire private property for public use, providing just compensation is paid to the owner.

just compensation: That sum of money required to be paid to a property owner as full payment for property taken or damaged by a public body in condemnation proceedings.

larger parcel: A parcel whose size generally is determined by unity of ownership, contiguity, and unity of use criteria. It is an important concept in establishing the extent of severance damages.

right of way: The privilege of one or more parties passing over the lands of another party within a defined zone or route, such as a highway.

Condemnation and easement appraising is a specialized field within real estate appraising. This chapter covers these two topics by initially explaining the concept of just compensation, which is an essential part of condemnation and easement appraising. The various ways in which property rights may be acquired by a condemning agency are also discussed. Covered as well is the topic of how compensation is estimated when part of a person's property is taken by a public body.

The section on condemnation is followed by an examination of how the different classes of easements are appraised.

CONDEMNATION APPRAISAL

This is a specialized type of appraisal. If it is to be performed properly, then the appraiser must be familiar with all physical, engineering, legal, and economic factors necessary to judge the value of parcels subject to condemnation. These relevant factors are discussed and illustrated in this section.

Eminent Domain and Condemnation

The term *eminent domain* was initially used around 1665. Frequently the terms *eminent domain* and *condemnation* are used interchangeably. Eminent domain is the sovereign right of government to acquire private property for public use, providing there is just compensation paid to the owner. Condemnation is the judicial or administrative method used by government to exercise the right of eminent domain. Under the administrative method of condemnation, the governmental body passes a resolution or adopts an ordinance designating certain property as necessary for acquisition. The adopted resolutional ordinance generally is filed with the register of deeds or clerk of the county or municipal court where the land is located. The landowner is notified of the filing of the resolutional ordinance and then allowed a certain time to seek a higher award from a jury or other impartial tribunal if dissatisfied with the offer. Under the judicial method, which is more commonly used, a governmental agency empowered with the right of eminent domain initiates a suit against a party who owns land that is to be acquired. Once the affected landowners are given notice of the proceedings, they are allowed to appear before the court to defend their interest.

Just Compensation

The Fifth Amendment of the U.S. Constitution states "...nor shall private property be taken for public use, without just compensation...." This phrase pertains to the federal government acquisition of private property. However, the Fourteenth Amendment extends the "due-process-of-law" clause of the Fifth Amendment to the states, which has been judicially contrued to involve the obligation of a condemnor (the agency taking the property) to pay compensation. Through judicial interpretation, the term "just compensation" has been interpreted to mean "just payment." Therefore, just compensation might be thought of as payment to the owner for loss of one's property, which was further clarified in the famous statement by Justice Holmes, "The question is what has the owner lost, not what has the taker gained."[1]

Just compensation implies payment of a sum of money to a property owner for property acquired or damaged in order to make him or her whole. This term implies that there will be full and complete payment for any loss sustained by an owner whose land has been taken or damaged. "Just" implies that both the condemnor and condemnee (the property owner) are treated properly. The appraiser should note that just compensation is not necessarily synonymous with market value. Market value is a consideration in arriving at just compensation. Just compensation does not always imply full payment to the owner since full indemnity can be made only in view of those elements of value or damage that are legally permissible. In order to adequately arrive at just compensation in an appraisal, the appraiser may need legal counsel to assist in determining what elements of value should be considered.

Eminent Domain versus Police Power

There are certain similarities between eminent domain and police power, but it is essential for the professional appraiser to be able to distinguish between these terms. Sometimes in public right-of-way construction there are elements of both. Police power regulates the use of private property to curtail some aspect of the property or surrounding area that is judged harmful to the public. Eminent domain requires payment of compensation because the property taken benefits the public. Police power is designed to promote the health, welfare, and safety of the public. Examples of exercise of the police power would be the imposition of: (1) zoning laws to protect property values and prevent incompatible land use activities, or (2) building codes to maintain certain minimum building standards to protect the health and safety of the occupants. The public safety may be protected by construction of a concrete divider strip that will reduce access of traffic to a property adjoining a highway, which in turn could reduce the business volume and the value of the business.

A fundamental question that defies precise definition is where does the police power end and the power of eminent domain begin? A good guideline would be that it terminates when the injury to the property owner for not being paid exceeds the injury to the public in having to pay for the property. Supreme Court Justice Holmes once said that if regulation goes too far, then it will be recognized as a taking.

A distinction between eminent domain and police power is that the power of eminent domain is invoked when there is a physical taking of the property or property rights, and police power may be exercised with no actual taking of such property rights. Both, however, could result in a diminution in property values. In order to distinguish which of these public powers has been used, it may be necessary for the appraiser to seek legal counsel.

Whole taking Sometimes an entire property is acquired for public use. The appraisal in these cases is virtually no different than any other market value appraisal where only one appraisal is necessary to reveal the value of the entire property. Since there is no remainder, there is no need to consider either enhancement or damages to the property retained by the property owner after the taking.

Partial taking A fundamental part of appraising a property where part of it will be acquired by a condemnor, leaving a remainder, is to determine the size of the larger parcel.

Larger parcel concept A first step in partial taking appraisals for condemnation purposes is to establish the boundaries of the greater parcel. The greater parcel is a parcel that belongs to the same party who owns the part taken; it is contiguous to the part taken and is used for a common purpose. This concept is important in that it establishes the size of the remainder to which any damages or benefits are applied.

Individual state and federal laws differ on the criteria used in establishing a larger parcel. The three basic criteria normally used in setting the size of a larger parcel are:

1. *Unity of ownership.* Several parcels placed to the same use may not meet the unity of ownership test if they are in different ownership or if one parcel is owned jointly and another parcel owned individually. This test is not universally applicable.
2. *Contiguity.* Contiguity implies a physical connection of lands. Therefore, a noncontiguous parcel is generally not part of a larger parcel. For example, if two parcels in the same ownership are separated by a street, then it is unlikely that the property not subject to condemnation would experience damages.
3. *Unity of use.* There may be differences in state and federal laws regarding this larger parcel criteria. The unity of use criteria holds that parcels must be used in connection with each other rather than simply devoted to the same use. Also, highest and best use of parcels is a factor looked at to determine the larger parcel. Another test of this criteria is that the tract in question must be considered as one integrated use. For example, if the lands are placed to the same use, for a large industrial complex, even though occasionally separated by streets, it would probably be viewed as a

larger parcel. On the other hand, if two tracts such as a subdivision and retail parcel are owned by the same party, the larger parcel likely would be limited to only one of the parcels since there is not unity of use between the parcels.

Another factor, related to the preceding criteria and helpful in judging the scope of a larger parcel, is zoning. Zoning is a condition that should be considered in judging whether separate parcels are parts of a larger parcel. Differences in zoning do not preclude parcels from being part of a larger parcel. However, it is important to judge the probability of rezoning when zoning differs.

General Damages

General damages are viewed as damages common to all property within a neighborhood or suffered by a considerable number of the public. An example would be building a beltway around a community, which would divert traffic from the subject property. Any damages stemming from this rerouted traffic are noncompensable.

Consequential damages This form of damages occur when there is no taking of a part of the property. It would occur when a road grade is changed or even when traffic is diverted away from a commercial property via a bypass. Other examples might be noise and fumes from a traffic artery for which there is no compensation due the owner.

Compensable Damages

There are several different types of damages that the appraiser should be aware of in estimating the value lost to a remainder and, in turn, the total just compensation due a property owner. These different types of damages will be discussed in the following paragraphs. Initially, compensable damages will be discussed.

Severance damage Severance damage is a loss in value to the remainder property after a part of the property has been acquired for right-of-way purposes. This type of damage only applies to situations where there is a partial taking of a larger parcel.

Proximity damages This loss in value to a remainder property results from nearness of a highway or other public improvement to a building(s). The value loss usually is greater when proximity of the public improvement to the building is accompanied with a grade change, especially an elevation. Imagine, for example, that residential properties in a neighborhood typically are worth $60,000; front-yard setback of the dwellings generally is seventy-five feet; and the sites are even at road grade. The appraised property's building adds $40,000 to the total value. After the taking, the front-yard setback is reduced to forty feet, which is judged to reduce the value of the dwelling to $35,000. The value of the site acquired was $4,000; therefore, the total just compensation to the landowner is $9,000 ($40,000 – $35,000 + $4,000).

Limited access Many modern highway systems are of limited-access design in order to reduce potential traffic accidents caused by multiple points of access onto a roadway. Since a property owner did not have the right of access to a limited access highway prior to construction, then he or she would not enjoy this right after construction of the improvement. Hence, the abutting landowner would not be eligible for any damages afterwards.

Loss of access A severed property could have impaired access or even complete loss of access if the remaining parcels became landlocked. In the case of a landlocked parcel, the appraiser must ascertain the highest and best use of and market for the remaining parcels. It may be that the only use for a landlocked parcel is to the adjoining owner(s). If so, the value would decline sharply from its former value. A good approach is to locate similar landlocked sites that have sold recently.

Excess capacity It is possible for a property, such as a dairy farm, to be bisected by a limited-access highway. The barns could be on one side of the right-of-way and the pastures on the other side. If there were no reasonable way to provide access (such as a cattle tunnel) under the right-of-way, then the buildings would be excessively large for the pasture on that side of the right-of-way. Hence, one method of judging the functional obsolescence is to determine whether a proper ratio of building size to acreage existed prior to the taking. If so, the damages to the remaining buildings would be in relation to their surplus capacity for the land remaining on that side of the right-of-way.

Change of grade An appraiser should be especially careful in considering the impact of change of road grade upon abutting property values. In some states, owners are subject to compensation for this construction feature, while in other states they are not eligible. The appraiser should first determine if compensation is permitted for this aspect of a partial taking. If it is, then care should be taken in studying the construction plans to determine the extent of the grade change and its probable impact on the remaining property use.

Impaired access An owner of property abutting a highway has a right of reasonable ingress and egress to and from the property. Thus the denial of this right of ingress and egress to land is compensable. Helpful in determining the amount of compensation due to reduced access is the judged highest and best uses of the property prior to and after the taking. For example, a modern, three-bay service station may require 200 feet of road frontage. If, for example, 100 feet of the frontage were taken for a public improvement, then the highest and best use and value afterwards ordinarily would be reduced. In this case, the highest and best use may decline from a service station to tire repair shop use.

Noncompensable Damages

In addition to recognizing damages for which a land owner is entitled compensation, it is important to understand situations where no compensation is due an owner. The appraiser must take the appropriate steps to ascertain the precise extent that compensation is due an owner in each particular situation. The following examples depict some instances where the property owner is not entitled to compensation.

Damages during construction A decrease in the volume of business during construction of a public improvement generally is viewed as being temporary and not compensable. The same rule applies to other types of inconvenience experienced during the construction period.

Traffic regulations Imposition of traffic regulations is an example of government's exercise of its police powers and is not compensable. For example, an abutting property owner would not be compensated for the construction of a concrete median strip in front of the property, nor for diverted or rerouted traffic or no-parking regulations.

Circuitry of travel As long as a party has reasonable access to and from his or her property, compensation to the property owner does not need to be paid by the condemning authority. Thus a landowner would not be entitled to compensation even if his or her property was located on a through street before the taking, but afterwards on a dead-end street, cul-de-sac, or frontage road. However, there is no universal agreement on whether compensation should be paid to an owner where there formerly was uninterrupted access to the site but later construction of a limited-access highway resulted in circuitous routing to the property.

Diversion of traffic It generally has been ruled that no person has a vested interest in a highway continuing to be located in a particular place. That is, the public has no responsibility to deliver traffic to a given party's door. Thus, if a beltway caused traffic to be diverted from a property, there would be no need for payment by the condemnor.

Future development plans Compensation would be payable in condemnation to a landowner for present development, but the owner probably would not be entitled to compensation for the frustration of future development plans. Also, courts generally hold against damages being awarded for remote and speculative future development of a property. Even if compensation is allowed for a development currently underway, the accompanying expenses must be deducted from the gross sales revenue, and the net sales revenue discounted to a present value.

Loss of business A property owner generally is not entitled to compensation for the interruption or loss of business or goodwill. Loss of profits, present or future, are viewed in most states as noncompensable. (This was brought out by the court in the case of United States v. General Motors Corp., 323 U.S. 373, 65 Sup. Ct. 357, 89 L.Ed. 311 in 1945.)[2]

Remainder Parcel Appraisal

There are two principal methods used in appraising properties involved in partial takings. One method involves the following steps:

1. Value the entire property before the taking.
2. Value the part taken as part of the whole property.
3. Value the remainder as part of the whole property.
4. Value the remainder considering any enhancement or damages.

The result of these calculations is the total just compensation to which the landowner is entitled. Variations of this method are generally used in the individual states in partial takings:

1. Before value less after value, considering all benefits from the project.
2. Before value less after value, considering special benefits to the remainder.
3. Value of the land and improvements taken plus damages to the remainder with benefits to the remainder subtracted from damages to the remainder.
4. Value of the land and improvements taken plus damages to the remainder with special benefits only to the remainder subtracted only from damages to the remainder.[3]

Another method is known as the *before-and-after rule,* which also is the *federal rule.* The steps involved in seeking just compensation under this method are:

1. Estimate the value of the whole property prior to taking.
2. Estimate the value of the property after the taking, considering any enhancement or damages to the remainder.

In some jurisdictions, the benefit set-off rule is permitted; thus, it would be possible for a right-of-way to be built upon one's property with no compensation being paid. This situation might occur where an interstate interchange is located on a property; land formerly suitable for agricultural purposes and worth perhaps $500 an acre rises in value to several thousand dollars per acre, more than offsetting the value of the part taken and any damages. Any enhancement in value in the before value due to the proposed project should not be considered by the appraiser.

Damages—Cost-to-Cure

In some instances, the extent of damages can be mitigated by use of the cost-to-cure method. For example, this method can be used where a well needs to be replaced in order to make a residential property habitable, a driveway needs to be replaced to retain the utility of a garage, an entrance to a building requires relocation, or construction of a cattle tunnel beneath an interstate highway is necessary. The cost-to-cure is the current cost of making the necessary adaptation. Ordinarily, the appraiser would appraise the property using before-and-after value estimates. If, for example, the damages prior to estimating the cost to cure is $10,000 and the cost-to-cure is $4000, then the latter approach should be used with the estimated damages amounting to $4,000.

In a situation where there is a frontage taking of an income-producing property, the entrance may need to be relocated to the side to make the building usable. Then, a before-and-after value analysis can be used to judge the value lost, if any, due to the relocation of the entrance.

Illustration of Partial Taking—Damages to Remaining Home Sites

This illustration involves 5.50 acres containing six platted home sites, as shown in Fig. 19.1. The sizes of these lots are: 0.76 acre (#1), 0.82 acre (#2), 0.88 acre (#3), 1.26 acres (#4), 0.95 acre (#5), and 0.83 acre (#6). These sites make up one section of a partially developed subdivision of forty home sites. Demand is reasonably strong for sites in this outlying neighborhood of a small community. Homes in the subject subdivision sell from $50,000 to $80,000.

The purpose of the appraisal is to estimate the current market value of the fee interest of the six sites and to estimate the just compensation due the owner from the widening of a nonlimited access highway. Five recent site sales were analyzed (as summarized next) to arrive at the value of base lot #5. Subsequent analysis of the sales and differences between the base site and the other five sites produced value indications for these sites.

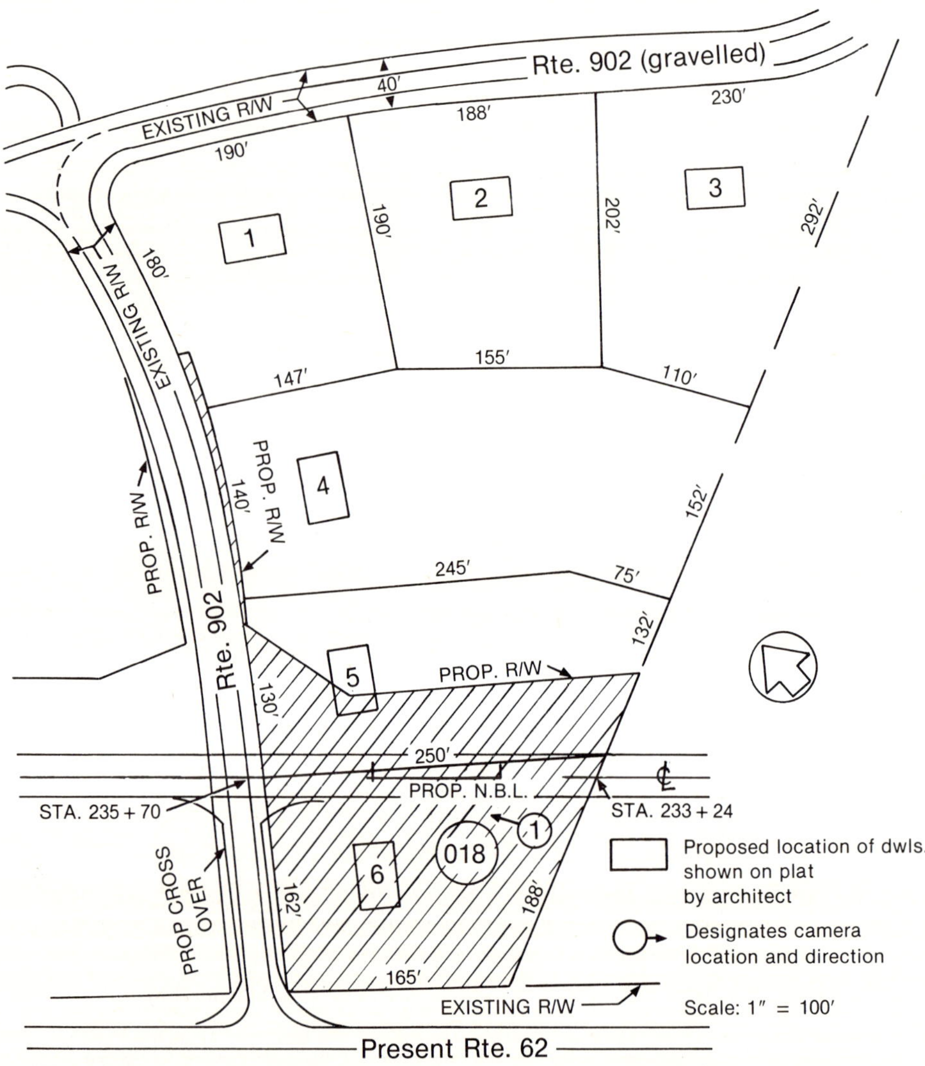

Parcel No.	018
Whole Area	5.50 Ac.
Take Area	1.20 Ac.
Remainder	4.30 Ac.

Fig. 19.1

Base lot—lot 5					
Sale no.	1	2	3	4	5
Sale price	$12,000	$ 9,000	$8,500	$13,500	$ 7,500
Size	−3,000	—	—	−1,000	+1,500
Water frontage	—	—	—	−3,500	—
Location	−1,000	−500	−1,500	—	+1,000
Trees and terrain	—	+1,000	+1,000	—	—
	+18%	+12%	+21%	+5%	
Sale date	(+2,160)	(+1,080)	(+1,785)	(+675)	—
Indicated value	$10,160	$10,580	$9,785	$ 9,675	$10,000
Value of whole property					$61,500

Allocated thusly:

	Size	*Value*
Lot 1	0.76 acre	$11,750
Lot 2	0.82 "	10,500
Lot 3	0.88 "	10,500
Lot 4	1.26 "	10,250
Lot 5*	0.95 "	10,000
Lot 6	0.83 "	8,500
Totals	5.50 acres	$61,500

Value of the part taken:

No improvements are being taken but 1.20 acre of land will be acquired, distributed as follows: lot 1, 0.01 acre; lot 4, 0.03 acre; lot 5, 0.33 acre; lot 6, 0.83 acre.

Lot value	*Lot size*	*Value per acre*	*Amount taken*	*Value*	
Lot 1; $11,750	.76 ac.	= $15,460 ×	.01 =	$ 155	
Lot 4; $10,250	1.26	= 8,135 ×	.03 =	244	
Lot 5; $10,000	.95	= 10,526 ×	.33 =	3,474	
Lot 6; (whole taking)			.83 =	8,500	12,373
Value of remainder as part of whole property: ($61,500–$12,373)					$49,127

*Base lot; the value of the other lots in the appraised subdivision were adjusted based on size, frontage, and shape. The computations are not shown in this illustration for the sake of simplicity.

Value of Remainder after the Taking

After the taking, the property will contain 4.30 acres (see Fig. 19.2). There will be no appreciable change in road grade; it will vary from existing grade to a cut of about four feet. There will be a storage lane for vehicles turning onto Route 902 from the north bound lane—an improvement over the former dual lane road. The overhead transmission lines will be relocated to the opposite side of Route 62, improving the appearance of the remaining sites.

If lots 1, 2, and 3 are extended an additional fifty feet toward Route 62, the additional size will offset the closer proximity to the highway. These sites will be damaged to the extent of re-survey charges of $150 per site.

The elongated remainder of lot 5 has no value as a building site itself. However, when combined with lot 4 (as shown on revised plat) it becomes a usable building site.

An analysis of comparable sales (this part should be fully documented in an appraisal report) reveals the following values:

Lot	*Size*	*Value*	
1	0.92 acre	$11,750	
2	1.00	10,500	
3	1.00	10,500	
4–5	1.38	10,250	
	4.30 acres		
Total value		$43,000	
less re-survey fee		600	$42,400
Damages to remainder ($49,127 – $42,400)			$ 6,727
Total just compensation			
Value of part taken		$12,373	
Damages to remainder		6,727	$19,100

EASEMENTS

An easement is a nonpossessing interest in a property owned by another party; there is no transfer of ownership. The grantee is permitted to perform certain acts within the easement boundaries and receives those property rights necessary to perform these functions. The grantor retains the residual rights in the easement area and is entitled to enjoy the use of the balance of the property not restricted by the easement.

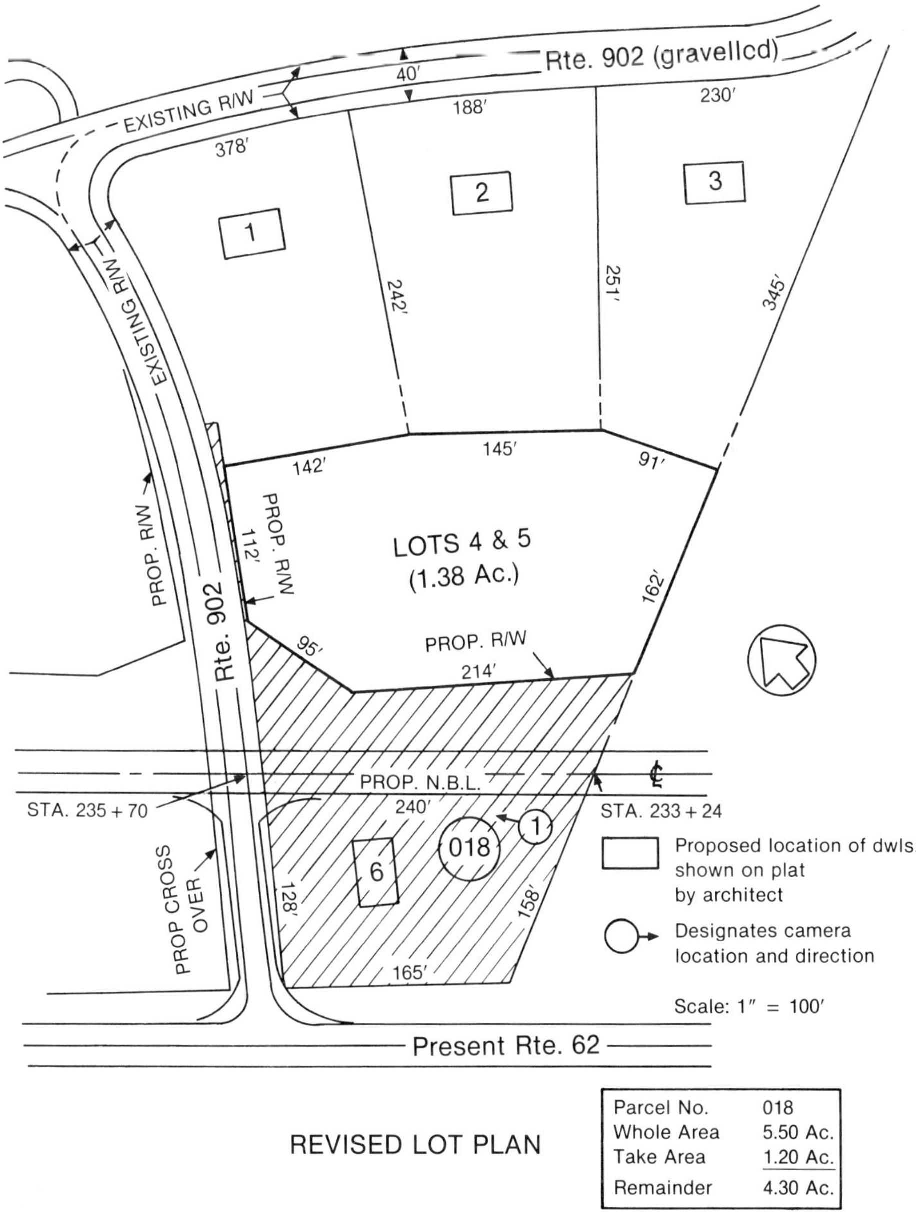

Rte. 902 (gravellcd)
40′
EXISTING R/W
188′
230′
378′
1
2
3
242′
251′
345′
EXISTING R/W
142′
145′
91′
PROP. R/W
112′
PROP. R/W
LOTS 4 & 5
(1.38 Ac.)
162′
Rte. 902
95′
PROP. R/W
214′
PROP. N.B.L.
STA. 235 + 70
240′
STA. 233 + 24
1
018
6
PROP CROSS OVER
128′
158′
165′
Proposed location of dwls. shown on plat by architect
Designates camera location and direction
Scale: 1″ = 100′
Present Rte. 62
REVISED LOT PLAN
Parcel No. 018
Whole Area 5.50 Ac.
Take Area 1.20 Ac.
Remainder 4.30 Ac.

Fig. 19.2

Classes of Easements

There are three basic types of easements: underground, surface, and overhead. Underground easements may be used for water and gas lines, sanitary sewers, and storm drains. Surface easements include railroad rights-of-way, canals, and flowage easements. Overhead easements may provide for distribution and transmission electric line installations, avigation easements, and air rights development. A brief description of these and other easements follows:

Underground easement This involves the right to use ownership rights under another party's real property. It may be for the purpose of installing sewer or water lines, tunnels for transportation of pedestrians or motor vehicles, or even for transmission of electricity, gas, and steam.

Flowage easement This type of easement may be acquired by a government agency to periodically flood an area as part of a reservoir function. It can impair the continuous use of the land, as well as subject crops to the risk of periodic flooding.

Clearance easement This form of easement deprives the fee owner of full enjoyment of the space over his or her lands. It often relates to adjacent airport operations and may give the grantee the perpetual right to cut and remove trees and underbrush to a specified height, as well as the right to remove any structures within a defined plane. Also, the construction of structures is limited to a certain height. A clearance easement does not permit the flight of aircraft over a given property, but only protects from obstruction.

Avigation easement This is a right granted by a property owner to an airport to use defined air space above the property owner's land for the flight of aircraft. The degree of restriction varies according to the distance of the property from the airport and the glide angle necessary to accommodate the aircraft. The owner is prohibited from having structures and trees above a certain height that would intrude into the glide path.

Construction easement This is a temporary right granted by a property owner to another party for temporary use in construction of facilities such as a highway.

Slope easement This is a right given to another party, generally a public body, to slope the land from the improvement onto the landowner's property. It may or may not be a permanent easement and should set forth the extent, if any, of use restrictions on the owner of that portion of the property.

Scenic easement This easement is created in order to maintain a particular view of a significant natural phenomenon or significant man-made structure. The fee owner retains ownership of the property and can use it to the extent of not violating the restrictions.

Facade easement This type of easement is often used to preserve historic or architecturally significant properties whereby the owner is prohibited from making exterior changes.

Problems Illustrating Different Types of Easements

Construction easement A construction easement is a temporary easement that is used in the construction of an adjoining facility, such as a pipeline. It gives the grantee (buyer) an opportunity to store dirt and other materials and equipment, as well as to maneuver equipment necessary to the construction of the facility.

The steps that might be followed in estimating the compensation due the fee owner are as follows:

1. Estimate the location and extent of the construction easement.
2. Estimate the use period to the easement. The appraiser must be careful to allow for all probable delays in completion of this phase of the project so that the owner will be compensated for the full period of use.
3. Estimate the unencumbered value of the land affected by the easement.
4. Derive the appropriate rent for the use period. This rent may be set at a percentage of the land value, such as 10%, but it should be in line with rent expected for similar parcels. Rural properties generally rent for so much annually per acre.
5. Arrive at the full amount of compensation due the owner—assuming no physical damages done to the property. If there are physical damages, then additional compensation would be necessary.

These steps are further illustrated in Exhibit 19.1.

Pipeline easement A transmission pipeline may be located in either an easement or in a right-of-way where title to land is conveyed to the pipeline company. An advantage of using an easement is that the fee owner's property remains undivided. The value of the easement acquisition may be judged by examining the extent of the impaired utility caused by the underground construction. Proof of any loss in utility should be based on sales of other similar properties affected by pipelines carrying products of relative physical proper-

Exhibit 19.1
Construction easement appraisal

Value of whole property (no improvements)	
20 acres @ $5,000	$100,000
Value of part taken	
5 acres in fee @ $5,000	25,000
Value of remainder before damages (if any)	75,000
Value of remainder after take	
15 acres @ 5,000	75,000
Damages	0
Total just compensation	
Value of part taken	$ 25,000
Value of temporary construction easement	
(1.5 years) (1 acre) ($5,000) (10% rent)	750
Damages	0
Total just compensation	$ 25,750

ties, e.g., natural gas. Suppose, for example, that buyers typically pay 50% of the full market value due to the encumbrance. Then, the market value of the unencumbered land first would be estimated. Next, the percentage of unencumbered value (e.g., 50%) times that value would equal the value of the easement. The difference between this figure and the unencumbered fee value would be an indication of the compensation due the owner.

Another method of judging the compensation due an owner whose land is traversed by a pipeline easement is to first estimate the unencumbered value of the land. Next, the value of the encumbered easement would be estimated and then deducted from the fee value. This would indicate the compensation due the fee owner.

Overhead transmission line easement An electrical utility easement may be for distribution of electricity to dwellings and businesses. A distribution easement generally is viewed as an asset to a property since it is accompanied with electric service to the structure, without which the property would lack electricity for heat, lighting, and equipment. The other type of easement is the transmission line easement, which usually involves large towers. The width of these easements may be one hundred feet or more. With these easements, the grantor conveys those property rights that are necessary to construct, maintain, operate, inspect, and repair the improvements within the designated easement area.

Prior to actually evaluating an easement, the appraiser must fully grasp the extent of property rights controlled by the fee owner and also which of those rights are conveyed to the grantee. The difference between the rights owned and conveyed equals the remaining rights, which establishes the value remaining to the fee owner once these rights have been conveyed to the utility company. Importantly, both the allowable damages and benefits to the remainder should be considered.

Remaining value of land within easement Sometimes it is necessary to assign a percentage value to the owner's land within an easement. Nevertheless, there are preferred methods for arriving at this value conclusion. Perhaps the optimum method is to find conveyances of similar easements to adjoining owners. This approach reveals the value of easements, and, when compared to the present value of unaffected similar land, can indicate a percentage value loss. This percentage should be derived from similar properties with the same highest and best use encumbered by easements. These easements generally are put to extensive uses or passive uses, such as lawns, landscaping, vegetable gardens, open space buffer zones, driveways, play fields, and tennis courts.

Damages to remainder The strongest evidence of the value of land adjoining a transmission line easement is sales of similarly affected property. An easement will damage a remainder if it physically disrupts a land use or development plan. An example of this would be where a transmission line easement traverses a property zoned for and having a highest and best use as single-family residences. Some home sites could be lost, as well as the necessity for other sites being redesigned, adding to the cost of development. While damages may appear to be caused by the unsightliness of overhead wires and steel towers, interference with television and radio reception and fear of danger from these facilities, damages are most convincingly proven by transfers of similar properties. Crop loss is a consideration for damages of agricultural lands.

Exhibit 19.2 illustrates how a property subject to an electric transmission line easement might be appraised.

Avigation easements An avigation easement is the right of flight over land within a certain defined space, and the right to cause noise and dust. This right permits the clearing of obstructions and agreement to enter the property to enforce the rights acquired. There are two basic reasons for the establishment of avigation easements. One reason is to assure the safe operation of aircraft in and out of airports. The second reason is to minimize the likelihood of complaints and even lawsuits due to noise generated by jet aircraft using airports. The bottom of the easement is called the "glide angle plane," which, as a rule, prohibits obstructions more than two to three feet high to each one hundred feet of vertical extension away from the airport runway (see Fig. 19.3). Usually, avigation easements are appraised on a before-and-after basis; that is, the unencumbered value of the property is estimated. Deducted from that is the value as encumbered by the easement, thus leaving the value of the ease-

Exhibit 19.2
Electric transmission line easement appraisal

Before fee value of larger parcel*		
50 acres @ $2,000		$100,000
Before fee value of 5-acre easement		
5 acres @ $2,000	$10,000	– 10,000
Remaining value of 5-acre easement to fee owner (supported by market evidence)	– 6,000	
Market value of easement rights to be acquired	$ 4,000	
Value of remainder as part of the larger parcel prior to taking		$ 90,000
Value of remainder after the taking, considering effects of easement		
43 acres @ $2,000	$86,000	
2 acres @ $ 500†	+ 1,000	– $ 87,000
Damages accruing to remainder		$ 3,000
Plus value of easements rights to be acquired		+ 4,000
Total just compensation to landowner		$ 7,000

*A larger parcel; a property under one ownership that is contiguous with the part taken and used for a common purpose.

†The value of this 2-acre parcel has been reduced due to its irregular shape which will be difficult to develop and its isolation from the balance of the prospective subdivision land.

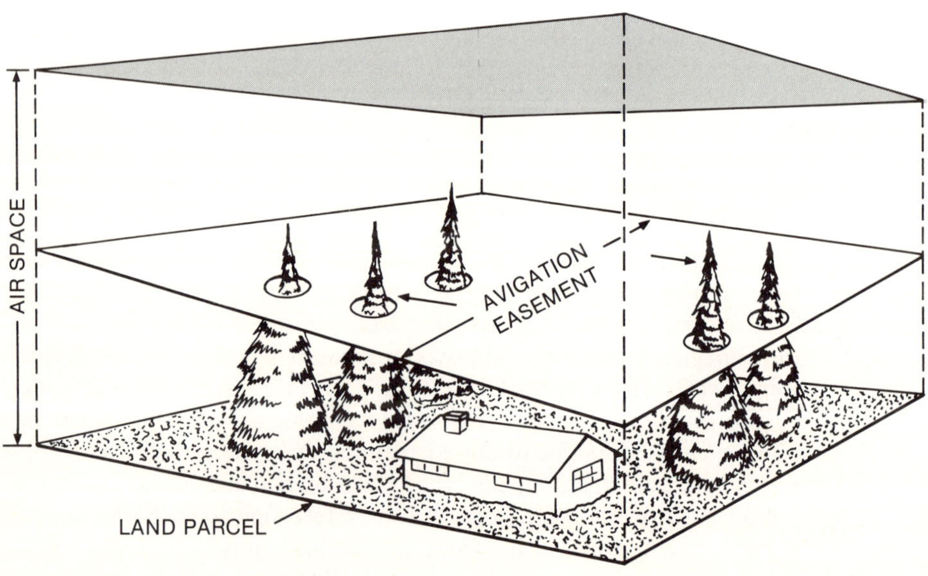

Fig. 19.3 Avigation easement valuation
Source: Greer A. Allen, Jr., A.S.A. Land Acquisition Specialist, Seattle, Washington.

ment or compensation to the underlying fee property owner. Proximity of the property to the end of the runway and the elevation of the glide angle of the plane above the appraised property probably are most significant in judging the impact of an easement on a particular property.

Usually, appraisers are not concerned with space above 1000 feet, which courts regard as navigable airspace. Another point to remember in judging the extent, if any, of intrusion into the fee owner's airspace is the nature of the permitted use of that land. Existing zoning ordinances may already prohibit certain probable uses as well as place height limitations on buildings. Land placed to certain uses have actually enjoyed a rise in value, not because of the noise or intrusion created by overflying aircraft, but due to the compatibility of that land use with the airport. Hence, the close proximity to the airport lends to its value. Conversely, residential properties and schools are generally viewed as being incompatible with close proximity to airports.

Where authorized by state law, benefits should be offset against the value of the part taken and/or damages to the remainder. In the after-value appraisal, there should be no consideration of damages that are not compensable or benefits not allowable under state law.

Appraisal of the after value Prior to considering market data, the appraiser should carefully examine the easement document to determine the extent of the limitations placed on use of the property and how these restrictions affect highest and best use as well as value. The appraisal of the after-value should be supported to the same extent as the appraisal of the before-value. This support can be provided by one or more of the following methods, going from most convincing to least convincing. Percentage computations should be avoided unless there is convincing proof that avigation easements values bear a percentage relationship to fee values and increase or decrease in direct proportion to the fee value.[4]

1. Sales comparable to the remainder property
2. Sale of comparable properties from which there have been similar acquisitions or takings for like usages, such as clearance easements, scenic easements, air rights easements, or power line easements
3. Development of the income approach for properties that show economic loss or gain as a result of similar acquisitions or takings for like usages
4. Public sales of comparable lands by the state or other public agencies.

PROBLEMS

Question: You have accepted an assignment to appraise the vacant parcel identified on the following plat (Fig. 19.4). Key facts pertaining to this property are: whole area is 5.12 acres, area being taken is 1.52 acres; and site is

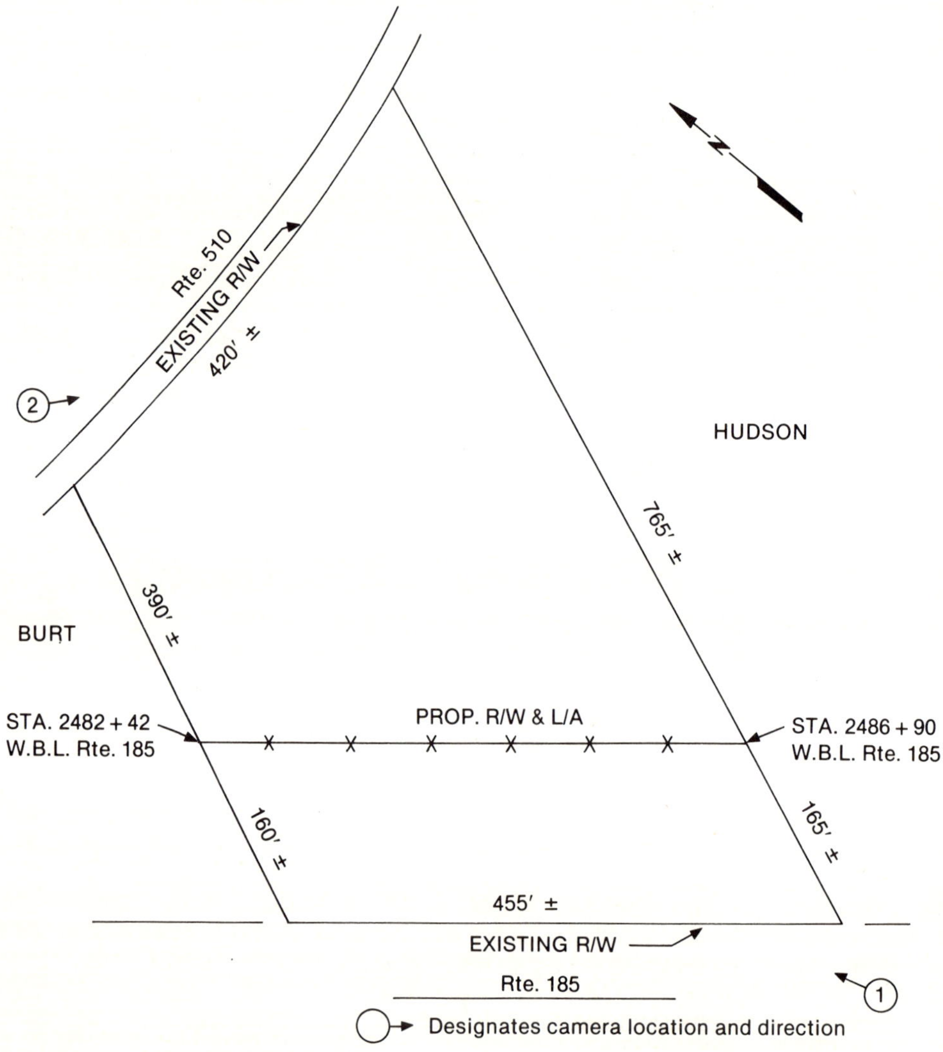

Project	0064-068-101, R/W 205	Whole Area	5.12 ac.
Owner	Hugh L. Dowling	Take Area	1.52
Parcel No.	036	Remainder	3.60 ac.
Scale	Not to scale		

Fig. 19.4

about four to five feet above road grade along Route 861 and is generally at grade on Route 280. The land is zoned and used for agricultural purposes, but its highest and best use due to nearby development is for residential "farmettes" or homesites.

Estimate the value of the (1) whole property, (2) part taken, (3) remainder, (4) damages or benefits, and (5) total just compensation.

The whole site value is reflected by the following two recent sales.

Features	*Sale 1*	*Sale 2*
Sale price	\$15,000	\$8,700
Size	4.9 acres	3.21 acres
Location	10% superior to subject	—
Terrain	equal	5% superior to subject
Access	equal (dual frontage)	15% inferior (single frontage)
Sale date	+ 8%	—

Answer:

1. Value of whole property

Indicated value per acre
Sale 1 \$3,000
Sale 2 2,981
5.12 acres @ \$3,000 — \$15,360

2. Value of part taken

1.52 acre @ \$3,000 — − 4,560

3. Value of remainder as part of whole property — \$10,800

4. Value of remainder after the taking
(5.12 ac. − 1.52 ac. = 3.60 ac.)
3.60 acres @ (\$3,000 × .85)* — − \$ 9,180

5. Damages
(\$10,800 − \$9,180) — \$ 1,620

6. Total just compensation
Value of part taken \$4,560
Damages + 1,620 — \$ 6,180

*Note Sale 2's adjustment for single-road frontage.

SUMMARY

"Eminent domain" forms the basis for condemnation appraising since it is the sovereign right of government to acquire private property for public use. Prior to private property being acquired by government, just compensation must be paid to the landowner. The real estate appraiser plays an important role in estimating the amount of this compensation. In doing so, he or she must understand whether the public action affecting private property is an exercise of the eminent domain or the police powers. A property owner is not entitled to compensation when the government's police powers are invoked. Ordinarily, a property owner may expect compensation from the condemnor under eminent domain. An owner would be paid by government if all his or her property was taken or if part of the property was taken and the balance lost its value for reasons such as loss of access. The larger parcel concept provides a basis for determining the extent of damages that a remainder parcel may suffer.

Sometimes a property loses value as the result of a public project being constructed. However, in such cases as when traffic is diverted or future development plans are frustrated, the owner is not entitled to compensation from the public agency causing the loss in value.

An easement is a means for one party to obtain use of another party's property without actually acquiring the property. There are underground, flowage, clearance, avigation, construction, slope, scenic, and facade easements. The amount of payment a property owner is due usually depends on the extent that the easement impairs the use of property in and adjacent to the easement.

REVIEW QUESTIONS

1. Is market value equal to just compensation? Discuss.
2. Explain the importance in condemnation appraising of accurately identifying the larger parcel.
3. What is the fundamental difference between eminent domain and police powers with regard to appraising?
4. Discuss how partial takings differ from whole takings, pointing out the major appraisal considerations under each.
5. List four types of compensable damages, and briefly discuss how each can be estimated.
6. Outline the steps involved in appraising property subject to a partial taking under the two major methods presented in this chapter.

7. How does a construction easement differ from most other types of easements?

8. Give the basic difference between a clearance easement and an avigation easement.

ENDNOTES

1. Boston Chamber of Commerce v. Boston, 217 U.S. 189 at 195 (1910). *Compensable versus Noncompensable Damages.*
2. American Association of State Highway Officials, *Acquisition For Right-Of-Way* (Washington, D.C.: Association Committee on Right-of-Way, 1962), p. 48.
3. O. R. Colan Associates, Inc., *Appraisal Review on Federal-Aid Highway and Related Programs Training Course* (Washington D.C.: Federal Highway Administration, 1978), p. 99.
4. Greer A. Allen, Jr., "Avigation Easement Valuation" (Seattle: Federal Aviation Administration, n.d.), p. 11. (mimeographed)

ADDITIONAL READINGS

American Association of State Highway Officials. *Acquisition for Right-of-Way* (Washington, D.C.: American Association of State Highway Officials Committee on Right-of-Way, 1962).

Angers, Allen J. "Valuation of Pipeline Servitudes." *The Appraisal Journal* 40 (January 1972): 114–122.

Barnes, William C. "Considerations in Value Findings for Avigation Easements." *The Appraisal Journal* 42 (July 1974): 441–447.

Boettcher, Lloyd D. "Appraisal of a Flowage Easement." *The Appraisal Journal* 25 (January 1957): 35–38.

Crawford, Claude O. "Appraising Damages to Land From Power Line Easements." *The Appraisal Journal* 23 (July 1955): 367–378.

Hall, Thomas H., III. "Easement Valuation." *The Appraisal Journal* 39 (April 1971): 254–263.

Kinnard, William N., Jr. "Tower Lines and Residential Property Values." *The Appraisal Journal* 35 (April 1967): 269–284.

National Education Committee (ed.). *Selected Readings in Right-of-Way* (Los Angeles: American Right-of-Way Association, Inc., 1968).

Schmutz, George L. (revised by Edwin M. Rams). *Condemnation Appraisal Handbook* (Englewood Cliffs, N.J.: Prentice-Hall, Inc., 1963).

Smith, Walstein, Jr. "Some Enchanting Easements." *The Appraisal Journal* 48 (October 1980): 527–539.

Special Technical Committee of the Education Committee. *Condemnation Appraisal Practice,* 2nd printing (Chicago: American Institute of Real Estate Appraisers, 1963).

U.S. Department of Transportation, Federal Aviation Administration. "Appraisal and Appraisal Review." *Land Acquisition and Relocation Assistance Under the Airport Development Aid Program* (February 10, 1975): 9–16.

Williams, Howard L., and Davis, W. D. "Effect of Scenic Easements on the Market Value of Real Property." *The Appraisal Journal* 36 (January 1968): 15–24.

Williams, Lawrence E., Jr., and McNichol, Daniel J. "Valuation of Airspace." *The Appraisal Journal* 41 (April 1973): 234–253.

MODULE XI
Illustrated Narrative Appraisal

This module contains an income property narrative appraisal to illustrate a complete appraisal report from beginning to end. Comments are made periodically to emphasize important appraisal methodology.

MARKET VALUE APPRAISAL
of
The La Plaza Office Building
8026 Vantage Drive
San Antonio, Texas 78230

Prepared for:

Mr. William B. Stevenson
Acquisition Manager
Sierra Real Estate Equity Trust
300 Montgomery Street, Suite 525
San Francisco, California 94104

Prepared by:

LOVE AND DUGGER
Real Estate Consultants and Appraisers
802 Main Plaza Building
San Antonio, Texas 78205

In addition to including the type of property, the client's name, and the name and address of the appraiser, the title page should include the date of the appraisal.

March 10, 1981

Mr. William B. Stevenson
Acquisition Manager
Sierra Real Estate Equity Trust
300 Montgomery Street, Suite 525
San Francisco, California 94104

Dear Mr. Stevenson:

As requested in your letter dated February 27, 1981, we have made a Market Value appraisal of The La Plaza Office Building located at 8026 Vantage Drive in the City of San Antonio, Texas.

Reprinted with permission.

The objective of this appraisal was to estimate the Market Value of the property as of the current date, March 1, 1981, subject to the existing office space leases and subject to a first lien mortgage loan payable to Baltimore Life Insurance Company. Your letter specifically requested that this report include "market data of comparable buildings in the market area, proposed new construction, comparable sales data, raw land prices, replacement cost, office space demand and projected absorption rates." These items have been covered in the attached report. The value reported in this report includes the value of the real property and the value of the existing favorable mortgage financing.

In estimating the Market Value, your consultant has utilized the three traditional approaches to Market Value; the Cost Approach, the Market Data Approach and the Income Approach.

As a result of our analysis, the concluded Market Value or most likely selling price of the Leased Fee Estate of the appraised property as of March 1, 1981 was:

ONE MILLION FIVE HUNDRED THOUSAND DOLLARS ($1,500,000.00).

We trust this information serves your purpose at this time. Please contact our firm if there are any additional questions regarding the appraised property or the analysis made.

Respectfully submitted,
SCRUGGS LOVE, JR., M.A.I.

> Refer to the person and date the appraisal was authorized.
>
> Set forth the objective of the assignment, and any special instructions by the client.
>
> It is generally advisable to refer to the report, of which the letter of transmittal is a part, and the number of pages contained in the report.
>
> Use leaders to assist reader in coupling sections with the corresponding page numbers.
>
> Generally, only the main section headings are required, especially if the report has a large number of subsections.
>
> It is helpful, but not necessary, to continue pagination throughout the report. Certainly, each page in the body of the report should be numbered to aid the appraiser in conferring with the client, in presenting court testimony or reviewing the report by another party.

TABLE OF CONTENTS

> This section is extremely valuable to a busy executive who can quickly digest the essentials of a long appraisal report. This summary should highlight items of importance to the client. Technical terms, such as "efficiency," should be defined briefly if the client is not familiar with such terminology.

SUMMARY OF SALIENT FACTS AND CONCLUSIONS

Property Appraised:	Two-story La Plaza office building containing 29,835 square feet GBA and 24,389 square feet NLA; 82% efficiency.
Location:	8026 Vantage Drive in the northwest section of San Antonio, Texas near IH-10 (West) and Callaghan Road.
Objective of the Appraisal:	To estimate the Market Value as of the current date, March 1, 1981. The appraisal is to be utilized to assist in making a decision regarding the purchase of the property.
Property Rights Appraised:	Leased Fee Estate subject to 15 tenant office leases varying in length from one month to four and one-half years. Also subject to a non-exclusive ingress and egress easement recorded in Volume 1278, Page 1 of the Deed Records of Bexar County. Also subject to a mortgage loan payable to Baltimore Life Insurance Company with a current balance of approximately $546,700.00, payable monthly in the amount of $5,354.00, including 9-1/4 percent annual interest; 16.79 years remaining term.
Zoning:	"B-2" Business District, which allows for general retail and office development.
Highest and Best Use:	It is concluded that the highest and best use of the property is its present use as a garden office building.
Site:	378.31 feet frontage on the west boundary along Cherry Ridge; 182.08 feet on the north boundary along Vantage; 370.0 feet on the east boundary; and 204.0 feet on the south boundary. The site contains 1.71 acres or 74,488 square feet, more or less.

Improvements: Two-story precast concrete and steel frame office building, concrete pier and beam foundation, built-up tar and gravel roof covering. Building height 26.0 feet. Exterior walls precast 6″ concrete panels. Interior walls 5/8″ vinyl covered, gypsum board and paneling, walls and ceilings full batt insulation. Flooring 3″ concrete with vinyl and carpet covering. Acoustical ceilings; two (2) mens' and two (2) womens' restrooms; central heat and air-conditioning system.

Site Value: 74,488 SF @ $4.15/SF Rd. $ 309,000
Estimated Replacement Cost New: 29,835 SF @$41.40/SF Rd. $1,235,054*
Market Value of Fee Simple Title Subject to Existing Mortgage:

The Value Indicated by the Cost Approach: $1,670,000
The Value Indicated by the Market Data Approach: $1,544,000 to $1,561,000
The Value Indicated by the Income Approach: $1,541,800 to $1,566,500
Final Estimate of Value of the Fee Simple Title Subject to the Existing Mortgage $1,560,000
Market Value of Leased Fee Estate: $1,500,000
Allocated:
Land $ 309,000
Improvements $1,191,000

It is recommended that the deed book reference to the legal description be provided at this point.

IDENTIFICATION OF THE PROPERTY

The appraised property is known as The La Plaza Office Building and is located at 8026 Vantage Drive in the northwest section of the City of San Antonio near the southeast corner of the intersection of Vantage Drive and IH-10. The property is located at the southeast corner of the intersection of Cherry Ridge and Vantage Drive. The property is legally described as follows:

> 1.71-acre tract of land, more or less, out of Lots 2 and 3, Block 23, New City Block 13627, Greenbriar, UNIT 12, City of San Antonio, Bexar County, Texas, recorded in Volume 5870, Page 201, Deed and Plat Records, Bexar County, Texas, described as follows:

*See page 453 for exact development of this figure.

BEGINNING for reference at the point of intersection of the South line of Callaghan Road with the West line of Pinebrook Drive;

THENCE in a Southeasterly direction along the West line of said Pinebrook Drive, 492.43 feet;

THENCE S 41°10′8″ W, 194.70 feet along the Southeast line of Vantage Drive to an iron pin set for the POINT OF BEGINNING of the tract herein described:

THENCE S 48°49′52″ E, 370.00 feet to an iron pin set for the most Easterly corner of the tract herein described;

THENCE S 41°10′08″ W, 204.00 feet to an iron pin set for the most Southerly corner of the tract herein described;

THENCE N 48°49′52″ W, 244.00 feet to an iron pin;

THENCE N 42°23′11″ W, 50.19 feet;

THENCE N 37°25′50″ W, 84.12 feet to a point in the curve having a central angle of 09°50′18″, a radius of 430.00 feet and a tangent of 37.01 feet;

THENCE Northeasterly along said curve and to the left and along the Southeast line of Vantage Drive 73.84 feet to an iron pin set for the P.T. of said curve;

THENCE N 41°10′08″ E, 108.24 feet to the POINT OF BEGINNING.

There is also a non-exclusive easement for ingress and egress over and across a property described in Volume 1278 at Page 2 of the Deed Records of Bexar County. This ingress and egress easement is 51 feet wide being described out of Lot 3, Block 23, New City Block 13627, Greenbriar Unit 12, City of San Antonio, Bexar County, Texas according to the plat records in Volume 5870, Page 201 of the Deed and Plat Records of Bexar County, Texas. This ingress and egress easement provides for access from the appraised property to IH-10, which is located one block to the West of the appraised property.

> If a survey was not made especially for the purpose of the appraisal assignment, then reference to the source containing the dimensions and area should be presented.

Your consultant was not furnished with a survey of the appraised site. For purposes of this report, the land area is estimated to be approximately 74,488 square feet or 1.71 acres, more or less described by the metes and bounds description above and as shown in Volume 1278 at Page 2 of the Deed Records of Bexar County.

> It is essential that both the appraiser and client agree on the objective of the appraisal. This objective influences the manner in which the appraiser conducts his or her research and which points are emphasized in the appraisal.

OBJECTIVE OF THE APPRAISAL

The objective of this appraisal is to estimate the Market Value of the La Plaza Office Building property as of the current date, March 1, 1981. This was the date of the last inspection of the appraised property. It is my understanding that this appraisal is to be utilized by you to assist in making a decision regarding the contemplated purchase of the property.

> A straight-forward definition of the value estimated in the report should be presented near the beginning of the report.

DEFINITION OF MARKET VALUE

For purposes of this report, Market Value is described as "the highest price in terms of money that a property would bring in a competitive and open market under all conditions requisite to a fair sale, the buyer and seller each acting prudently and knowledgeably and assuming the price is not affected by undue stimulus." It is the price a willing seller would sell and a willing buyer would buy, neither being under abnormal pressure and both being fully informed.

> Considerable care must be taken to clearly state the property rights appraised since the failure to do so may cause the client to become dissatisfied with the estimated value.

PROPERTY RIGHTS APPRAISED

The property rights appraised are those constituting the mortgaged Leased Fee Estate to the appraised property subject to the lessee's interest in the various leases and subject to the payment of a certain first lien note in the original principal amount of $675,000.00, payable to the Baltimore Life Insurance Company by instrument dated December 27, 1972, recorded in Volume 6994, Page 24, Deed and Trust Records, Bexar County, Texas. The value reported includes the sum of the value of the real property and the value of the existing favorable financing.

> Regional and city data should be included only if it assists the appraiser in arriving at a reliable estimate of the property's (1) highest and best use, and (2) defined value. Included in these data would be key land use activity trends in the subject neighborhood.

CITY, NEIGHBORHOOD AND LOCATION DATA

The city of San Antonio is located in south central Texas, 150 miles north of Nueva Laredo, Mexico; 190 miles west of Houston; and 75 miles south of Austin, the State Capital. San Antonio is the oldest city in Texas, having been founded as a military garrison in 1718 by the Viceroy of Spain. It is also the tenth largest city in the United States and the third largest in Texas. San Antonio is the County Seat of Bexar County and the City occupies an area of 317 square miles. The total area of Bexar County is 1,246 square miles. San Antonio is part of a standard metropolitan statistical area of 2,527 square miles which includes the Counties of Comal and Guadalupe as well as Bexar.

The local economy is based on manufacturing, commercial trade, mineral production, medical facilities, agriculture, government employment and tourism. While the population growth of San Antonio has not been as spectacular as some other major Texas cities, the growth was 43.9 percent from 1950 to 1960, 11.3 percent from 1960 to 1970 and has been approximately two percent from 1970 to the present time. The City has not received the final census count from the census bureau.

In general, the outlook for the local economy for the foreseeable future is excellent. The oil and gas industry in south Texas is "booming" with the current shortage of oil and gas and the increased demand. The Reagan Administration's emphasis on national defense spending should further reinforce the local economy as San Antonio has five major military installations.

San Antonio is also fortunate to be in the "sunbelt," and as such, should continue to experience a population and business growth in the foreseeable future. The appraised property is located in the northwest quarter of the City in one of the most rapidly growing areas along the corridor of IH-10 West to El Paso. Your consultant can see no reason why this trend should not continue in the foreseeable future.

The location of the South Texas Medical Center, approximately one mile west of the appraised property; the location of the United Services Automobile Association Headquarters at the intersection of Fredericksburg Road and IH-10 (the State's largest office building complex); and the selection of the northwest quarter of the City as a site for the University of Texas at San Antonio are further evidence of the stability and growth of the northwest quarter of the City. Recently, Datapoint Corporation, one of the largest employers in the City, has acquired approximately 120 acres of land for their new headquarters complex to be located on the west side of IH-10 between DeZavala Road and Hausman Road. Further, announcements have been made in recent months of two proposed regional malls to be located in this quadrant of the City. One is planned at the intersection of IH-10 and DeZavala Road, and the other at F.M. 1604 and IH-10.

> At the end of this section, the appraiser should summarize the implications of the material covered with regard to the state of the local economy, appeal of the immediate neighborhood, and, finally, how all of these factors influence property value.

OFFICE BUILDING MARKET

> Although it is not always possible to obtain such detailed and current information as presented in this section, the appraiser is obliged to thoroughly analyze the local area to ascertain construction, vacancy, rental rate, and other trends pertinent to the appraisal of a particular property.

The late 1960's and the first half of the 1970's featured a departure of several hundred thousand square feet of tenant space out of the downtown area to the northern sectors of the City along Interstate Loop 410.

From 1973 through 1975, several trends developed which adversely affected office buildings in San Antonio. This was a time when there was little demand for suburban office space and the local and national real estate economy was in a period of recession. Also, interest rates reached historical highs that only recently have been surpassed. To further complicate this situation, utility rates increased dramatically. Several major suburban office buildings underwent severe economic duress.

There were very few office buildings constructed in 1976 and 1977. The recovery of the City's office market began quietly in 1977 with a prevailing mood of confidence and a sense that the worst was over, rather than with significant hard evidence of improved conditions. Space was being leased at an increasing ratio and rentals began trending upward.

Then, in 1978, hard evidence revealed a dramatically improved office market. San Antonio enjoyed a heightened economic viability by virtue of its location in the rapidly expanding southern sunbelt region. General economic conditions were on the upswing, and local owners became expansion-minded. A recent survey completed by your consultant indicates that approximately 1,196,024 square feet of net leasable area in 15 office buildings is currently under construction in the northern part of the City.

In addition to this, in the central business district of the City, there are three office buildings currently under construction containing 688,000 square feet of net leasable area. In the office market study, 127 major office buildings that are either existing or under construction were analyzed and classified into categories for analytical purposes. The buildings were graded on the basis of categories "A" through "D" depending on tenant profile, location, age and condition.

The category for individual buildings was not identified in this study. In the Northwest Sector of the City, 29 office buildings were analyzed in categories "A" through "C", there being no category "D" buildings in this sector of the City. The La Plaza Office Building (Category "B") has 24,389 square feet of net leasable area and no vacancies at the present time. The average rental rate is $7.64 per square foot per year or $0.64 per square foot per month. The gross building and net leasable area reported in the rental survey are slightly different from those shown in this report.

A summary of the findings of the rental survey for the Northwest Sector of the City is shown in the following chart:

EXISTING OFFICE BUILDINGS
NORTHWEST SECTOR

Type of building	*Number of buildings*	*Sq. ft. N.L.A.*	*Sq. ft. owner occupied*	*Percent of N.L.A.*	*Sq. ft. vacant/ percent*	*Rental rate per sq. ft.*
Category A	3	342,248	57,535	19	0	$.70–$1.10
Category B	18	1,226,014	60,065	68	12,428/1%	$.70–$1.25
Category C	8	233,353	2,813	13	2,150/2.2%	$.65–$0.80
	29	1,801,615	120,413	100	17,678/1%	

For purposes of analysis, the Northwest Sector is located West of Vance Jackson and North of the central business district.

> If data presented in the report were not prepared by the appraiser, the source should be identified. For example, a certain population forecast may have been used and the client can check the original source if he or she chooses, providing the source is shown.
>
> In business report writing, the writer should write in a simple, straight-forward manner. Avoid stilted language. Remember, you should write to *express,* not to *impress.*

There are virtually no vacancies in the existing office buildings in the northwest section of the City at the present time. However, your consultant knows of an additional 479,574 square feet of net leasable area in eight office buildings that are currently under construction in this section of the City. This will increase the tenant space from 1,681,202 square feet by 425,697 square feet or an increase of approximately 25 percent. Also, announcements have been made on an additional 492,708 square feet of net leasable area proposed in this sector which, if built, would further increase the tenant space by approximately an additional 25 percent.

In your consultant's opinion, it is doubtful that the buildings currently under construction, or proposed, will have a material affect on the occupancy of The La Plaza Office Building because the tenants in the subject office building are well established and paying rentals well below those required by the newer office buildings. However, it does appear that if the proposed buildings are constructed as announced, the buildings under construction, and proposed, will experience lease-up periods in excess of 18 months. A chart summarizing the existing and proposed office buildings is shown on the following two pages of this report. The most comparable office buildings to the appraised property are the Canavan Center, Conroy Square and Exchange Plaza.

Existing and Proposed Office Buildings

Northwest Sector
March, 1981

Name of building and address	*No. of flrs./ buildings*	*G.B.A.*	*N.L.A.*	*Area occupied by owner*	*Tenant space*	*Sq. ft. vacant*	*3/1/81 Quoted Mo. Rent per sq. ft.*	*Age/ Cond.*	*Remarks*
Existing:									
Babcock Plaza 104 Babcock	1	12,000	10,500	0	10,500	0	$0.60	1981*	*Remodeled in 1981.
Canavan Center 8647 Wurzbach	2 & 3 19	unknown	36,000	0	36,000	3,340 9%	$0.70–$0.80	1973–79 Good	$0.80 rental includes utility; $0.70 rent rate, tenant pays utilities. Recent expansion and remodeling.
Colonies North Professional Bldg. 3740 Colony Drive	3	unknown	22,000	0	22,000	0	$0.70	1968 Good	
Computer Building 9502 Computer Dr.	2	unknown	31,000	0	31,000	0	0	1980 Excellent	Datapoint Corporation occupies 100% of the building.
Conroy Square 3355 Cherry Ridge	2	41,403	41,403	0	41,403	0	$0.80	1973 Fair	

Name of building and address	*No. of flrs./ buildings*	*G.B.A.*	*N.L.A.*	*Area occupied by owner*	*Tenant space*	*Sq. ft. vacant*	*3/1/81 Quoted Mo. Rent per sq. ft.*	*Age/ Cond.*	*Remarks*
Console Building 9501 Console Drive	2	unknown	31,000	0	31,000	0	0	1980 Excellent	Valero Energy Corporation occupies 100% of the building.
Corporate Center 4803 N.W. Loop 410	1	unknown	33,722	0	33,722	0	\$0.85–\$1.00	1977 Good	In higher rentals, lessor pays utilities.
Corporate Square 4803 N.W. Loop 410	2	unknown	66,394	30,000	36,394	2,592 24%	\$0.90	1980 Good	Hartford Insurance Company is the largest tenant.
Exchange Plaza Vantage Drive	2 & 3	21,008	16,585	0	16,585	0	\$0.70	1975 Fair	
Fairway Executive Tower 4204 Gardendale	3	unknown	41,811	0	41,811	836 2%	\$0.85	1975 Good	
5555 Fredericks-burg	2	13,300	12,000	6,000	6,000	0	\$0.95	1980 Good	A new building is under construction.

First National Bank Building 6243 N.W. Expressway	10	160,000	103,302	458	102,844	0	$0.70	1975 Good	First National Bank occupies the first two floors.
410 Place 6322 Sovereign	2	60,000	55,000	0	55,000	1,500 3%	$0.78	1974 Good	
G.E.C.U. Building 6061 N.W. Expressway	7	112,329	99,946	57,077	42,869	0	$0.95	1976 Good	
G.I.C. Insurance 9100 IH 10	3	29,000	23,500	16,000	7,500	0	$1.00	1979 Good	Datapoint Corporation occupies the 7,500 tenant space.
Highpoint Executive 1603 Babcock	2	57,000	55,788	0	55,788	9,000 16%	$0.90	1980 Good	This unique construction has a central courtyard.
Koger Executive Center 4500 N.W. Loop 410	3 & 4 20	unknown	500,000	0	500,000	0	$0.75	1975 Good	
Knoll 7900 Callaghan Rd.	2 & 3	39,600	35,141	0	35,141	0	$0.85	1976 Good	
The La Plaza Office Building 8026 Vantage Drive	2	29,475	24,475	613	23,862	0	$0.80	1973 Good	
MLR Building 5710 N.W. Expressway	2	13,000	12,400	2,200	10,200	0	$0.60	1974 Fair	

Name of building and address	*No. of flrs./ buildings*	*G.B.A.*	*N.L.A.*	*Area occupied by owner*	*Tenant space*	*Sq. ft. vacant*	*3/1/81 Quoted Mo. Rent per sq. ft.*	*Age/ Cond.*	*Remarks*
Metropolitan Life Building 6061 N.W. Loop 410	2	unknown	12,000	0	12,000	0	$0.80	1974 Fair	
Oak Hills Tower 5430 Fredericks-burg	6	97,344	82,832	0	82,832	0	$0.80–$0.85	1975 Good	
One Park Ten 6800 Park Ten Blvd.	2/ 4	170,000	159,725	0	159,725	0	$0.95	1973 Good	The four buildings are joined by atriums.
Stewart Title 2961 Mossrock	2	15,976	13,693	6,864	6,829	0	$0.75	1971 Fair	Remodeling is underway.
Summit Tower I 5825 Callaghan	6	80,000	69,000	0	69,000	0	$0.85	1974 Good	
Summit Tower II 5815 Callaghan	1	15,000	13,000	0	13,000	0	$0.85	1978 Good	
Summit Tower III 5825 Callaghan	2	26,000	24,000	0	24,000	0	$0.85	1980 Good	
222 Building 222 N.W. Expressway	2	25,000	20,837	0	20,837	410 2%	$0.65	1970 Fair	

Turtle Creek Tower I 8415 Data Point Dr.	10	160,000	139,000	0	139,000	0	$1.10	1980 Excellent	Twin tower under construction.
The Vineyard 7475 Callaghan	3	unknown	15,561	1,201	14,360	0	$0.85	1977 Good	
TOTALS:			1,801,615	120,413	1,681,202	17,678			
Under construction:									
Cherry Ridge Plaza 3311 Cherry Ridge Dr.	1	112,000	106,400	0	106,400	100% pre-leased	0	June 1981	
Citizens National Bank Building Loop 410 & Fredericksburg	5	59,498	54,114	35,226	18,888		$1.13	July 1981	
Colonial National Bank Building IH 10 & Wurzbach Rd.	4	52,965	49,744	17,451	32,293	50% pre-leased	$1.09–$1.17	1981	
Condo Offices Mossrock	1	16,000	14,100	1,200	12,900		$0.85	June 1981	
5555 Fredericksburg	2	13,300	12,000	0	12,000		$1.00		

Name of building and address	*No. of flrs./ buildings*	*G.B.A.*	*N.L.A.*	*Area occupied by owner*	*Tenant space*	*Sq. ft. vacant*	*3/1/81 Quoted Mo. Rent per sq. ft.*	*Age/ Cond.*	*Remarks*
5555 Fredericksburg									
Mockingbird Plaza Mockingbird Plaza & Fredericksburg	1–3 7	unknown	60,250	0	60,250		$1.10	May 1981	
Mossrock Garden Offices Mossrock	2	50,000	43,966	0	43,966		$0.95	May 1981	
Turtle Creek Tower 8415 Data Point Dr.	10	160,000	139,000	0	139,000		$1.10+		73,000 sq. ft. occupied by Datapoint Corporation.
Totals:			479,574	53,877	425,697				
Proposed:									
Lincoln Center Office Tower Westside IH 10 & North Loop 410	8	160,758	156,725	2,500	154,225				Early planning stages.

Kelly National Bank Building Bandera & Wurzbach	8	151,384	135,445	41,116	94,329	$1.10	Bank will occupy basement, 1st floor and one-half of 2nd floor. Completion summer of 1982.
Santiko's, Inc. IH 10 & Loop 410	12	175,400	162,000	10,000	152,000		Proposed for summer of 1982.
Greatview Building Callaghan & IH10	4	47,738	38,538	3,000	35,538		Proposed for January 1982.
Totals:			492,708	56,616	436,092		

TAXES AND ASSESSED VALUE

The taxes and assessed value for the current year for the various taxing agencies are shown below:

Taxing agency	*Assessed values* Land	Improvements	Total	*Tax rate per $100*	*Annual taxes*
City of San Antonio	$74,490	$502,480	$576,970	$0.44	$ 2,538.67
NE Inde. School Dist.	$82,080	$372,230	$454,310	$1.51	$ 6,865.00
Bexar Country - State of Texas	$74,490	$502,480	$576,970	$0.77	$ 4,451.33
				Total annual taxes	$13,855.00

In accordance with a recently passed State law, Bexar County is currently being reappraised for ad valorem tax purposes. Effective January 1, 1982, all properties in Bexar County are to be appraised for tax purposes on the basis of their 100 percent market value. At the present time, the City of San Antonio and Bexar County's values for tax purposes are based on a "1972 valuation." The new valuations are not known at the present time, as the reappraisal has not been completed.

> Emphasis in this section should be given to recent tax levy trends and the probable short-term future real estate tax burden in view of planned municipal revenue needs. If the tax burden is significantly out of line with surrounding communities, then this fact should be mentioned.

Recent announcements by the Bexar County Tax Assessor/Collector indicate that it is doubtful that the new reappraisals will be completed in accordance with the current State law by the target date of January 1, 1982 and will, in all probability, not be completed prior to January 1, 1983. Section 26.4 of the Texas Property Tax Laws provides that after the Board of Equalization has approved and certified the tax rate, the tax assessor calculates the tax rate so as to produce the same amount of tax revenue as 1980. This rate, as established by the tax assessor, cannot be increased more than three percent until governing body gives legal notice to the tax payer and holds public hearings on the proposed increase. While the ad valorem taxes on the appraised property will, in all probability, be increased in the future, there should be adequate notice as to these increases.

> There should be a "Zoning" section between the "Neighborhood Analysis" and "Description of the Site" sections. This section should identify and describe the zoning for the appraised property, as well as list the major uses permitted under the appropriate section of the zoning ordinance.

DESCRIPTION OF THE SITE

The appraised site is located one block east of the intersection of IH-10 and Vantage Drive on the southeast corner of the intersection of Cherry Ridge Drive and Vantage Drive.

The Warranty Deed recorded in Volume 1278 at Page 1 of the Deed Records of Bexar County describes the site as containing 1.71 acres, more or less, or approximately 74,488 square feet of land area. The site has a frontage of 182.08 feet on the southeast side of Vantage Drive; 378.31 feet on the northeast side of Cherry Ridge Drive; 204 feet on the southwest boundary; and 370 feet on the northeast boundary. Please refer to the site plan in the Addendum portion of this report.

The property is slightly above street grade along Cherry Ridge and slopes upward three to four feet to a high point in the northeast corner. All city utilities are available and connected to the site. The property has good access to all parts of the City via IH-10 and Interstate Loop 410, approximately one mile South of the appraised property. Vantage Drive and Cherry Ridge Drive are secondary access arteries, having two-way traffic with concrete curbs, asphalt-paved streets and no crosswalks. There is a 51-foot wide ingress and egress easement providing access from the appraised property to IH-10. The drainage appears to be adequate.

> A plat of the appraised site would appropriately be located at this point as well as photographs, if the site were vacant.

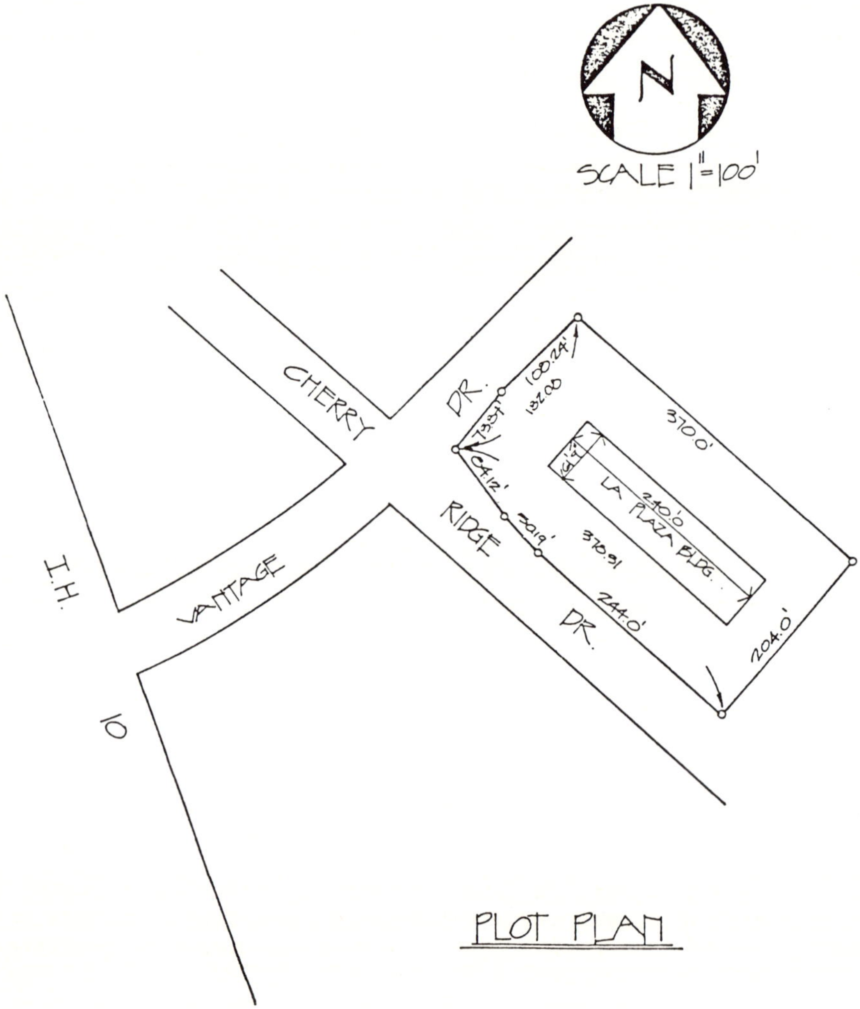

The soil and subsoil conditions in this area are desirable for the construction of most commercial improvements including office buildings.

From the site, it is approximately a seven-minute drive to the San Antonio International Airport, via IH-10 and Interstate Loop 410 (East); ten minutes to the central business district of the City, via IH-10; four minutes to the South Texas Medical Center, via Callaghan Road and Fredericksburg Road; and five minutes to the University of Texas at San Antonio, via IH-10 and UTSA Boulevard.

The immediate area surrounding the appraised site has numerous new developments including the Cherry Ridge Plaza office building complex, immediately South of the appraised property; the Hometel development close to the northeast corner of the intersection of IH-10 and Interstate Loop 410; the Northwest Six Theatres, North of Interstate Loop 410 on the west side of IH-10; a recently constructed shopping center at the northeast corner of the intersection of Callaghan Road and IH-10; and the current development of the 168-acre Strauder Nelson Estate property on the northwest corner of the intersection of IH-10 and Callaghan Road. A plat of the land is attached in the Addendum section of this report.

> This section, often overlooked, should indicate when the building(s) was constructed, sections added to the building, recent sale prices for the property, date of sale, parties involved, and a statement of whether the sales price represented market value.

HISTORY OF THE APPRAISED PROPERTY

The appraised property was constructed by the Quincy Lee Company in late 1972 and 1973. Quincy Lee is one of the most successful developers of office parks, industrial properties and apartment projects in the City of San Antonio. The subject property was transferred from Quincy Lee, et al to La Plaza Associates, A Partnership, on September 7, 1978 as recorded in Volume 1278 at Page 1 of the Deed Records of Bexar County. The La Plaza Associates have operated the property since their acquisition and are the current owners of record for The La Plaza Office Building.

> In order to insure that the client understands the nature of this section, it should begin with a brief definition of highest and best use.

HIGHEST AND BEST USE ANALYSIS

According to the City of San Antonio, the appraised property is zoned "B-2" Business District. This is a general, commercial zoning classification which allows for both general retail and office development. The present improvements are conforming under this zoning.

The appraised property is located in an area that has both general retail, such as restaurants, service stations and retail stores as well as office buildings. The subject site is not located on a major traffic artery such as IH-10 or Callaghan Road and, as such, is probably better suited for office use than retail use. The existing improvements were designed for garden office usage, and the appraised property has an eight-year history of successful application to this use. Additionally, the demand for office buildings in the subject property neighborhood is well established. The design and placement of the appraised property improvements on the site is in keeping with the neighborhood and in conformity with the surrounding land usages. Considering these facts, it is the judgment of your consultant that the highest and best use for the appraised property is for its present use as a garden office building.

It is noted that the existing combination of land and improvements do not create value over the value of the site as if vacant and the cost new of the improvements less physical deterioration. Thus, no allowance for developers' or entrepreneurial risk and profit is indicated. This tends to indicate that the existing improvements may not represent the highest and best use of the site as if vacant.

> This section is a culmination of regional, city, neighborhood, site and possibly building analysis. It should never be limited to a simplistic "statement of highest and best use."

> In compiling construction costs, the appraiser must be certain to include the developer's risk and profit or such costs will be understated.

DESCRIPTION OF THE IMPROVEMENTS

> A floor plan and photographs of the improvements would either be at this point of the report or referred to in the Addenda.

The appraised site is improved with a two-story, garden office building containing 29,835 square feet of gross building area and 24,389 square feet of net leasable area, having an 82 percent efficiency. The improvements are logically situated on the site, and there are approximately 140 to 150 parking spaces available for the tenants and guests of the building.

The building fronts to the northwest, facing Cherry Ridge Drive. Your consultant was furnished with the plans prepared by Charles H. Randall, architect, as Project No. C70-2N in January, 1971 with revisions on February 23, 1971. The consultants utilized in the preparation of these plans were Feigenspan and Pinnell, Structural Engineers and K. M. Ng & Associates, Mechanical Engineers. The plans are considered to be an attachment to, and a part of this appraisal, and this report is accordingly so premised. No specifications for the subject improvements were available.

The building has a concrete pier and beam foundation, is two stories in height, being approximately 26 feet, has precast six-inch concrete panelled walls and a built-up tar and gravel roof. The interior walls are vinyl gypsum board and panelling. Both the walls and ceilings have full batt insulation. The flooring is lightweight aggregate three-inch concrete with vinyl tile and carpet floor covering. The ceilings are acoustical tile with recessed fluorescent lighting fixtures. There are two 21′ × 20′ penthouses on the roof, housing the heating and air conditioning equipment with three condensing units located between the penthouses installed on the roof. The central heat and air conditioning system is natural gas and includes three 30 HP condensing units, two 50 HP air handlers and 16 strip heaters. There is also a natural gas fired boiler located in penthouse number two. The building has a porcelain enamel facia running along the roof line. There are three interior metal and concrete stairwells and one Otis elevator.

> Some appraisers find it easier to communicate with their clients by using the following format:
>
> FOUNDATION: Concrete pier and beam
> EXTERIOR WALLS: Precast six-inch concrete panels, 26 feet high etc.

Each floor has a mens' and womens' restroom. In the mens' restroom, there are three commodes, two urinals and two wall lavatories and in the womens' restroom, there are three commodes and two wall lavatories. There is a snack bar for the convenience of the building occupants, located on the first floor off the entry lobby. The wall and roof framing of the building is steel joist. The construction is average for garden office buildings in this area and the design and layout is good. The overall condition of the improvements is average for an eight-year-old building.

On-site improvements include 2,423 square feet of concrete sidewalks, approximately 55,622 square feet of asphalt paving, eight concrete planters, one marquee and 250 linear feet of six-foot wood privacy fencing. All of the on-site improvements are in average-to-good condition.

SITE VALUATION

Your consultant made a search of the records of a title company and of the Bexar County Courthouse to find comparable land transfers which would be of assistance in estimating the Market Value of the subject site as if vacant as of the current date.

Each of the comparable land transfers found was confirmed with the broker or one of the parties involved in the transaction. A summary of the most persuasive sales follows. These sales are spotted on the comparable sales map found in the Addendum portion of this report.

> It may be helpful to use an adjustment grid to assist the reader in visualizing the similarities and differences between the sale sites and the appraised sites as well as the type and size of adjustments made by the appraiser.

Sale No. One: An unimproved tract of land located at the southwest corner of the intersection of Wurzbach Road and Lockhill-Selma Road transferred on March 24, 1980 from L. A. Denton, Trustee, to the Gulf Oil Company as recorded in Volume 1882 at Page 52 of the Deed Records of Bexar County. The property sold for $215,620.00 or on the basis of $5.00 per square foot of land area for 43,124 square feet. The property is located near the entrance to the Whispering Oaks subdivision, having 193.29 feet of frontage on the south side of Wurzbach Road and 170.74 feet on the west side of Lockhill-Selma Road and is irregularly shaped. The site is heavily wooded with native oak trees and slopes downward from a high on the northeast corner to a low on the southwest corner of approximately 16 feet. There is a drainage easement running through the northwesterly portion of the property.

The sale property's location is better for most commercial retail purposes than the subject property's location because the sale property is located at the corner of two major traffic arteries. However, from the standpoint of drainage and topography, the subject property is much better than the sale property. Also, there has been a slight increase in land prices in this area during the past year. Considering these facts, it is the judgment of your consultant that this transfer tends to indicate the value of the subject property to be between $4.00 and $4.25 per square foot of land area as of the current date.

> It may be easier for the reader to grasp the essence of each sale if the key facts are stated at the beginning of each sale, for example:
> *Sale No. Two:* Sale price, $192,861; size, 55,103 square feet; price per square foot, $3.50.

Sale No. Two: A property located approximately three miles Northwest of the subject site around the northeast corner of the intersection of Huebner Road and IH-10 transferred from Shewgai Lim to Sewell Properties on November 1, 1979 as recorded in Volume 1748 at Page 53 of the Deed Records of Bexar County. The site contains 1.265 acres or approximately 55,103 square feet of land area. It is reported that the property transferred for $192,861.00 or on the basis of $3.50 per square foot of land area. The sale property is rectangularly shaped and has 77.45 feet of frontage on the northeast side of Huebner Road and 342.1 feet of frontage on the northeast side of IH-10. The site is level and is part of a block-up purchase of a larger tract of land to be utilized as the site of a new Cadillac automotive dealership. However, the price paid for this site in November, 1979 was in line with prevailing prices paid in this area for IH-10 frontage.

Considering the secondary location of the subject property and the increase in land prices in this area over the last one and one-third years, it is the considered judgment of your consultant that this transfer tends to indicate the value of the subject site as of the current date to be approximately $4.00 per square foot of land area.

> It always is a good policy to have another person proofread your report in addition to yourself, especially the calculations.

Sale No. Three: The property located approximately two miles Northwest of the subject property on the southwest side of IH-10, extending back to Bluemel Road transferred from H. Hahn, Jr. to National City Lines, Inc. on September 24, 1979 as recorded in Volume 1697 at Page 636 of the Deed Records of Bexar County. The site contains 4.995 acres or 217,582 square feet of land area and transferred for a reported $750,658.00, or for approximately $3.45 per square foot of land area. The property is irregularly shaped, having a frontage of 402.75 feet on IH-10 and 404.91 feet on Bluemel Road. The site is well elevated, is fairly level and has good topography. The property adjoins the Colonial National Bank and has good exposure from IH-10. Considering the increase in land prices since the date of this sale (approximately 1.4 years ago), the larger size of the sale property and the better location of the sale property with frontage on IH-10, it is the considered judgment of your consultant that this transfer tends to indicate the value of the subject site as if vacant to be between $4.10 and $4.20 per square foot of land area.

Sale No. Four: The property located approximately one and one-half miles Northwest of the subject property around the northeast corner of Wurzbach and Fredericksburg Road transferred from Marco Investments to Mel McDougal on June 18, 1980 as recorded in Volume 2002 at Page 993 of the Deed Records of Bexar County for 4.015 acres or 174,893 square feet of land area. This property was involved in a trade for Popeye's Chicken outlets based on a price of $5.00 per square foot of land area. The site is unimproved and is well elevated with excellent views. The property surrounds the Wolf's Inn Restaurant and is close to the entrance to the South Texas Medical Center.

Considering the slight increase in land prices in this area since the date of this sale, the better location of the sale property on two major traffic arteries, and the slight increase in land prices in this area since June of 1980, it is the considered judgment of your consultant that this transfer tends to indicate the value of the subject property to be in the range of $4.00 to $4.25 per square foot of land area.

Each of the comparable sales analyzed tends to indicate that the value of the subject site, as if vacant, as of the current date is in the range of $4.00 per square foot to $4.25 per square foot of land area.

Sale No. Three tends to indicate that the value of the appraised site is in the range of $4.10 to $4.20 per square foot of land area. After careful consideration of the values indicated by each of the comparable land sales analyzed, it is the judgment of your consultant that the indicated market value of the subject site, as if vacant, as of the current date is $4.15 per square foot of land area, which when multiplied times the 74,488 square feet and rounded, is $309,000.00.

VALUATION OF FEE SIMPLE TITLE SUBJECT TO EXISTING MORTGAGE

For purposes of this analysis, the property has been appraised first on the basis of fee simple title subject to the existing favorable mortgage. The value of the Leased Fee Estate is discussed in another section of this report.

VALUE INDICATED BY THE COST APPROACH

> Refer to the sources used in arriving at the cost-new. If possible, the appraiser should temper the cost data presented in national cost services with locally developed cost estimates.

The first step in the Cost Approach is to estimate the reproduction cost new and/or replacement new of the improvements using today's cost of labor and materials. Next, the accrued depreciation from all causes, including physical deterioration, functional obsolescence and economic obsolescence is deducted from the replacement cost new. The value of the site, as if vacant, is added to arrive at an indication of value by the Cost Approach.

In this report, the replacement cost new has been estimated by using the Marshall & Swift Segregated Cost Method. The replacement cost new has been checked with known costs of similar office buildings in this area. The appraised property building has been classified as a Class "C" masonry structure with an effective age of eight years, having a cost rank of two average.

These national costs have been adjusted to reflect the current cost of labor and materials in the San Antonio area. A summary of the Cost Approach follows this section of the report. The estimated replacement cost new of the building is calculated to be $41.40 per square foot of gross building area for 29,835 square feet or $1,235,054.00. The site improvements are estimated to have a replacement cost new of $32,626.00. The total replacement cost new is estimated to be $1,267,680.00.

No prudent developer would develop the subject office building without anticipating that the market value of the project will be in excess of the cost of the land, the improvements and the other costs necessary to develop the project. Local developers contacted indicated that they would anticipate 10 percent to 15 percent profit on all direct and indirect costs including the land. The value of the site, as if vacant, is estimated to be $309,000.00. Thus, the total is ($1,267,680.00 plus $309,000.00) $1,576,680.00. The total entrepreneurial risk and profit is estimated to be $236,502.00 to $315,336.00, say $275,000.00.

> See replacement cost breakdown on pages 452–453. What replacement cost estimating method has been used? How do replacement and reproduction costs differ?

> Usually, it is not necessary to include cents, such as $275,000.00.

> How was the $275,000 figure derived? Do you agree with the derivation of this figure?

VALUE OF THE FAVORABLE MORTGAGE

> It is imperative that any value-influencing factors considered in one approach must also be included in the other approaches. Otherwise, different value estimates will be revealed.

Because the La Plaza Office Building project has been appraised subject to the existing mortgage, consideration of this item is necessary in all three approaches to value. In the Market Data Approach, this influence is reflected in the comparable sales which also have favorable mortgages. In the Income Approach, the influence is reflected in the capitalization rates abstracted from the sales. However, in the Cost Approach, it must be measured directly.

The subject mortgage loan has a balance of approximately $546,700. The monthly debt service is $5,354, the nominal interest rate is 9-1/4% per year, and the remaining term is approximately 16.79 years or 202 months. The current market rate for mortgage loans available for the subject property is 13-1/2% interest with a 30-year amortization and a five-year call. This results in a mortgage constant of 13.75%. With a $546,700 loan, the payments would be $6,264 per month.

A survey of investors and real estate brokers in San Antonio was conducted to estimate the premium a typical buyer would pay for this favorable loan. All agreed that if the mortgage can be assumed, the property would sell for more because of the favorable terms to the borrower. Two commercial brokers contacted thought that the property would sell for $60,000 to $70,000 more for this reason.

	9-1/4% interest 16.79 yrs.	*13-1/2% interest 30 yrs.*		*Difference*
Monthly debt service	$5,354	− $6,264	=	($910 × 12) $10,920
Amount amortized in five yrs.	$86,540	− $9,513	=	$77,027

Estimated Value of Premium for Favorable Mortgage:

		17% PVF		*Present value*
Annual debt service	$10,920	3.199346		$34,937
Amount amortized in five yrs.	$77,027	.456111		$35,133
			Total:	$70,070

		20% PVF		Present value
Annual debt service	$10,920	2.990612		$32,657
Amount amortized in five yrs.	$77,027	.401878		$30,955
			Total:	$63,612

Estimated at $65,000

> The value adjustment accounts for the premium that an investor might pay for this property in view of its favorable loan. The amount of the premium is derived by finding the total of the present value of: (1) the difference between the 9 1/4% and the 13 1/2% mortgages, discounted at 17% and 20%; and (2) the difference between the amount amortized under the two mortgages over a five-year period.

A summary of the Cost Approach follows:

Summary of Replacement Cost New Estimate
(without Developer's Profit)

Class: C Masonry	Cost Rank: 2.0 Average
Effective Age: 8 years	Condition: 3.0 Average
Number of Stories: 2.0	Average Story Height: 12.0
Floor Area: 29.835	Cost as of: 3/81

Component	*Units(SF)*	*Cost*	*Replacement New*
Excavation and site preparation:			
Site preparation	72,963	$0.12	$8,756
Foundation:			
Concrete, bearing walls	29,835	1.02	30,432
Frame:			
Steel	29,835	2.98	88,908
Floor structure:			
Concrete on ground	14,918	1.52	22,675
Steel joists and deck, concrete	14,918	4.79	71,455
Waterproofing	14,918	0.22	3,282
Subtotal:			97,412
Floor cover:			
Carpet and pad	28,343	1.65	46,766
Tile, ceramic	1,492	4.13	6,161
Subtotal:			52,927
Ceiling:			
Fiber tile	29,835	0.81	24,166
Suspended ceiling	29,835	0.68	20,288
Subtotal:			44,454
Interior construction:			
Interior construction, frame	29,835	8.23	245,542
Plumbing:			
Plumbing	29,835	1.75	52,211
Heating and ventilating:			
Warm and cooled air	29,835	4.35	129,782
Electrical:			
Electrical	29,835	3.30	98,455
Exterior wall:			
Tilt-up concrete	8,723	6.66	58,095
Metal and glass panels	5,815	12.57	73,095
Subtotal:			131,190
Roof structure:			
Steel joists, steel deck	29,835	4.32	128,887

Component	*Units(SF)*	*Cost*	*Replacement New*
Roof cover:			
Tar and gravel	29,835	0.75	22,376
Elevators:			
Elevator	29,835	0.95	28,343
Total			1,159,675
Architect's fees	6.5%		75,379
Replacement cost new	29,835	$41.40	$1,235,054
Additions:			
Site improvements			
Concrete sidewalks	2,423	1.20	2,908
Asphalt paving	55,622	0.45	25,030
Concrete planters	8	250	2,000
Marquee (unit)	1	1,500	1,500
Wood privacy fence (LF)	250	4.75	1,188
Total cost:			$1,267,680

Summary of cost approach

Estimated replacement cost new of the building	$1,235,054.00
Estimated replacement cost new of the site improvements	32,626.00
Total estimated replacement cost new of the improvements	$1,267,680.00
Estimated entrepreneurial risk and profit	275,000.00
Total estimated replacement cost new plus developers' profit	$1,542,680.00
Less Accrued Depreciation:	
$\frac{\text{Effective Age 8 yrs.}}{\text{Effective age 8 yrs. plus 42 yrs. Remaining Economic Life}} = 16\%$	$247,000.00
Estimated depreciated reproduction cost new of the improvements	$1,295,680.00
Estimated value of the site 74,488 S.F. @$4.15 S.F. Rd.	309,000.00
The value indicated by the cost approach without consideration of the favorable mortgage	$1,604,680.00
Estimated value of premium for favorable mortgage	65,000.00
The value indicated by the cost approach including consideration of the favorable mortgage	$1,669,680.00
Rounded to:	$1,670,000.00

> This single calculation technique frequently is used to estimate accrued depreciation. More elaborate methods are covered in Chapter 5 "Cost Approach to Value."

The actual and effective age of the improvements is estimated to be eight years. The total economic life is estimated to be 50 years. The accrued depreciation has been estimated by the ratio of effective age to the ratio of effective age plus remaining economic life. All of the depreciation noted is either physical or functional in nature and arises from the age and condition of the improvements. There are no outside influences which have an adverse affect on the value of the property at the present time.

VALUE INDICATED BY THE MARKET DATA APPROACH

The Market Data Approach is the process of analyzing improved property transfers and comparing these transfers to the appraised property in order to arrive at an indication of the value by the approach.

> There is a tendency for appraisers to overuse the introduction "Your appraiser" or "Your consultant." This sentence would be more direct if rephrased: "The transfers of similar office buildings in the northern quadrant of the City of San Antonio were researched to assist . . . approach to value."

Your consultant has researched the transfers of similar office buildings in the northern quadrant of the City of Antonio to assist in estimating the Market Value of the subject property by this approach to value. Several comparable sales were found which could be compared to the appraised property. Each of these properties was inspected, analyzed as to the terms and conditions of the transfer, and compared to the La Plaza Office Building property. A chart showing a summary of the three most persuasive improved property sales analyzed is on the following page of this report.

> Use of a comparison grid can facilitate the appraiser's analysis and the client's comprehension of this analysis.

Summary of Improved Sales

Sale no.	5*	6	7
Location	IH 10 and Callaghan Area San Antonio	IH 10 and Wurzbach Area San Antonio	IH 10 and Wurzbach Area San Antonio
Address	8000 Vantage Drive 7835–7839 IH 10 and 3434 Cherry Ridge	4203–11 Gardendale	4204 Gardendale
Name of development	Exchange Plaza	Corporate Center	Fairway Executive Towers
Sales price	$1,550,000	$2,190,000	$2,635,000
Date of sale and recording	March 1981—contract	March 31, 1980 vol. 1896, page 965	March 31, 1980 vol. 1896, page 975
Legal description	Tracts 1, 2, 3, and 5 and ingress easement being Tract 4 out of Lot 7, NCB 13627	Lot 13, NCB 13662 University Estates Unit 19A	Lot 9, Block 1, NCB 14281 University Estates
Land area	121,576 sq. ft. or 2.791 acres	113,256 sq. ft. or 2.60 acres	102,497 sq. ft. or 2.35 acres
Date of construction	1974	1974	1974
Building size—GBA and NLA	GBA 40,488 NLA 34,309 sq. ft. 85% efficiency	GBA 42,000 sq. ft. NLA 33,838 sq. ft. 81% efficiency	GBA 47,000 sq. ft. NLA 41,811 sq. ft. 89% efficiency
Layout and construction	1–2 story and 2–1 story masonry	3–1 story steel frame brick veneer	3 story steel frame stucco and glass

*Sale No. 5: Building containing 4,200 sq. ft. under lease to Photogenesis Company for $1,922.13 per month plus $50.00 maintenance charge expiring September 30, 1997. All taxes, insurance and interior maintenance paid by tenant. Other three buildings containing 30,109 sq. ft. NLA currently renting for an average of $0.67 per sq. ft. per month on various short term leases, the longest being four years. Sales price was adversely affected by Photogenesis Company lease, therefore a plus adjustment of $300,000 was made. This adjustment sales price produces different overall and equity rates on pages 456 and 466.

Summary of Improved Sales (continued)

Mortgage balance:	$985,000	$1,130,000	1st lien : $1,052,483 2nd lien: $ 295,202 Total: $1,347,685
Debt service	$124,491—12% interest 25 years ± remaining, 13 years ± call	$117,300—9 5/8% interest 27.33 years remaining	1st lien : $108,788—8-3/4% int. 2nd lien: $ 36,220—11% int. Total: $145,008 1st lien : 21.50 years remaining 2nd lien: 8.43 years remaining Balloon: $243,547
Cash down payment	$565,000	$1,060,000	$1,287,315
Gross market income	$265,438 (E.G.I. $7.74/S.F. NLA includes long-term lease) Estd. $308,781	$315,100 (effective gross income, Estd.) 9.60 sq. ft. NLA 97.7% occupancy	$389,344 (effective gross income) 9.60 sq. ft. NLA 97% occupancy
Operating expenses	$109,789—est. $3.20 sq. ft. NLA	$108,282—$3.20 sq. ft. NLA	$133,795—$3.20 sq. ft. NLA
Net operating income	Actual $155,649 Estd. $189,729	Estd. $206,818	$206,477 Estd. $255,549
Cash flow to equity	Actual $ 30,772 Estd. $ 65,238	Estd. $ 89,518	$ 61,469 Estd. $110,541
Sales price per sq. ft. NLA	$45.18	$64.72	$63.02
Sales price per sq. ft. GBA	$38.28	$52.14	$56.06
Gross income multiplier	5.84 E.G.I.M.	6.95 E.G.I.M.	6.77 E.G.I.M..
Overall capitalization rate (R_0)	.1224	.094	.097
Mortgage constant (R_M)	.1264	.1038	1st lien .1034; 2nd lien .1227
Cash flow to equity (R_E)	.1155	.084	.086

Inclusion of a photograph and reference to a Sales Location Map assist the reader in visualizing the property.

Sale No. Five is a transfer this month of the office complex located directly across Cherry Ridge from the subject property. This complex, known as Exchange Plaza, transferred on the basis of $1,550,000.00. The building has a net leasable area of 34,309 square feet, which indicates the sale price per square foot of net leasable area to be $45.18. The actual effective gross income for the sale property at the time of the sale was $0.64 per square foot per month for the 34,309 square feet of net leasable area or $265,438.00 per year. The vacancy and collection losses for this property were nil. Thus, the effective gross income multiplier indicated by this sale is 5.84.

The existing leases, debt financing, and conditions of sale must be fully analyzed by the appraiser if an informed value conclusion is to be reached.

The gross income, vacancy and collection losses, and sales price were influenced as a result of a long-term lease on one of the three buildings in the Exchange Plaza complex containing 4,200 square feet of net leasable area. This building is under lease to September 30, 1997 at a rental below the prevailing market rental for the building. The other leases in the remaining two buildings, containing 30,109 square feet of net leasable area, are short term in nature, with the longest being four years.

The assumption of a 12 percent interest $985,000.00 mortgage with a 13-year call was considered by the buyers to be desirable and slightly better than they could do on the mortgage market at the present time. However, this slight advantage was more than offset by the unfavorable lease.

> The intricacies of the market approach to value are covered in detail in Chapter 4.

The buyers estimated that the purchase price was adjusted downward approximately $300,000.00 because of the existing leases. This transfer is analyzed as follows:

Gross Market Income 34,309 S.F. NLA @ $0.75 per S.F. × 12 =	$308,781.00
Less Vacancy and Collection Losses 3%	9,263.00
Effective Gross Income	$299,518.00

Effective Gross Income Multiplier:

$$\frac{\text{Adjusted Sales Price}}{\text{Effective Gross Income}} \quad \frac{\$1{,}850{,}000.00}{\$\ 299{,}518.00} = \text{E.G.I.M. } 6.18$$

Sales Price Per Square Foot Net Leasable Area:

$$\frac{\text{Adjusted Sales Price}}{\text{Square Foot NLA}} \quad \frac{\$1{,}850{,}000.00}{34{,}309.00} = \$53.92 \text{ per square foot NLA}$$

Sale No. Six is the transfer in March one year ago of an office complex located in the IH-10 and Wurzbach area approximately one and one-half miles Northwest of the subject property.

The estimated economic rental for the sale property at the time of the transfer for 33,838 square feet of net leasable area is $0.80 per square foot per month or $324,845.00 per year. The typical vacancy and collection losses are estimated to be three percent of the gross income or $9,745.00, leaving an effective gross income of $315,100.00. When this divided into the sales price of $2,190,000.00, the resulting effective gross income multiplier is 6.95. When the net leasable area of 33,838 square feet is divided into the sales price, the resulting sales price per square foot of net leasable area is $64.72. The buyers of this property were influenced by the favorable mortgage terms.

The $1,130,000.00 mortgage balance, payable at $9.775 per month at 9-5/8 percent interest for 27.333 years was assumable by the buyers. They did not actually calculate how much more was paid for the property for this reason.

Sale No. Seven is the transfer of the three-story garden office building approximately one and one-half miles Northwest of the subject property one year ago for $2,635,000.00.

The estimated economic income for the sale property at the time of the transfer is $0.80 per square foot per month for 41,811 square feet or $401,386.00 per year. The typical vacancy and collection losses are estimated to be three percent of the gross income or $12,042.00, leaving an effective gross income of $389,344.00. When the effective gross income is divided into the sales price of $2,635,000.00, the resulting effective gross income multiplier is 6.77. If the net leasable area of 41,811 square feet is divided into the sales price, the resulting sales price per square foot of net leasable area is $63.02. The first lien terms of 8-3/4 percent interest, 21.5 years terms and a mortgage balance of $1,052,483.00 are very desirable in today's market.

The second lien balance of $295,202.00, payable at 11 percent for 8.43 years remaining is also below the market. The broker stated that the price was influenced by the terms of the financing.

> After having thoroughly analyzed each sale, the appraiser explains the reasons for placing more emphasis on one or more sales than the other sales. Then, a value is chosen on the basis of the best information considered in this approach.

Sales Nos. Six and Seven are considered to be more persuasive indications of the value of the subject property because Sale No. Five, while extremely current, was adversely influenced by the long-term lease on 4,200 square feet of the net leasable area.

All three office building complexes are extremely comparable to the subject property from the standpoint of quality of construction, location, tenant mix and size, duration of office leases (with the exception of the Photogenesis lease), and age and condition. The effective gross income multiplier indicated for the subject property by Sale No. Six is 6.95, and for Sale No. Seven, 6.77.

Given equal weight, it is concluded that the proper gross income multiplier for the subject property is 6.8, which when multiplied times the effective gross income of the appraised property of $227,110.00, is $1,544,348.00 which is rounded to $1,544,000.00. The sale price per square foot of net leasable area indicated by Sale No. Six is $64.72 per square foot, and for Sale No. Seven, $63.02 per square foot of net leasable area. Giving equal weight to both sales, it is concluded that the indicated sales price per square foot of net leasable area for the subject property is $64.00, which when multiplied times the net leasable area in the appraised property of 24,389 square feet, indicates $1,560,896.00 which is rounded to $1,561,000.00.

After careful consideration, it is the judgment of your consultant that the indicated value of the subject property by the Market Data Approach with consideration of the favorable financing on the subject property is a range of $1,544,000.00 to $1,561,000.00.

VALUE INDICATED BY THE INCOME APPROACH

The Income Approach is a procedure for converting the net operating income from a property into an indication of capital value by a process called capitalization. In this instance, your consultant has utilized market capitalization.

The first step in the Income Approach is to estimate the gross economic rental or prevailing market rental for the appraised property. A summary of the actual rentals received for the subject property is shown on the following page:

A systematic display of the germane features of the appraised property's leases can assist the appraiser in his or her analysis. The square footage, utility expenditure, and lease expiration date are especially helpful in this regard.

This lease analysis is continued on page 462 to derive an estimate of the leased fee estate.

Rent Schedule

Office Number	*Tenant*	*Square Footage*	*Base Rent*	*Utility Base*	*Other Rent for Utility Base*	*Lease Expiration*	*Base Rent/ SF/mo.*
100	Chevron	4,967	$3,079.54	$0.10	0	1-31-82	$.62
101	Ray Rendon Insurance	303	196.95	.10	0	6-30-83	.65
103	Texas Medical Foundation	277	207.74	.10	0	12-31-81	.75
111	Standard Register	296	168.72	.05	$14.80	1-31-82	.57
120	R. C. Bender & Associates	2,087	1,565.00	.10	0	12-31-81	.75
123	Associated Beauty	219	142.35	.10	0	4-30-81	.65
131	Gene Wilson Appraiser	250	200.00	.10	0	2-1-82	.80
133–136	Dictaphone Corporation	3,009	1,652.68	2129 @ .05 880 @ .10	$106.45	6-30-81 2-yr. option	.55
135F	Neil Johnson	300	195.00	.10	0	3-1-81	.65
202	4-6's, Tim Collins, Bio-Nu, La Plaza, Wye, U.C. Ea.	633	411.25	.10	0	monthly	.65
203	Tribble and Stephens	1,848	1,201.20	.10	0	5-31-81	.65

205	Bill Shannon, Inc.	462	$ 300.30	$0.10	0	5-14-81	$.65
210	W.F. Lackey & Associates	450	360.00	.10	0		.80
212	Marriage License Lab	300	195.00	.10	0	5-31-81	.65
215	Mohawk Data	1,927	1,217.06	.10	0	3-31-83	.63
230	McCarty, Thompson	5,450	2,997.50	.065	190.75	9-30-82 3-yr. option	.55
219	Ezequiel Garcia, CPA	611	415.48	.10	0	7-31-83	.68
216	Harvey Olsen	1,000	700.00	.10	Esc. 0	11-30-82	.70
	TOTALS	24,389	$15,205.77		$312.00		$.62

Summary of Actual Rental Income:

Base Rent	$ 15,205.77 per month
Other Rent for Utility Base	312.00 per month
TOTAL	$ 15,517.77 per month × 12
	$186,213.00 per year divided by 24,389 SF NLA
	$7.64 per SF per year or $0.64 per SF per month

Recent rentals for comparable space, similar to the subject property building, is renting on the basis of $0.80 per square foot per month or $9.60 per square foot per year of net leasable area.

Income and expense analysis is covered in detail in Chapter 8.

Only two leases in the subject property building are currently rented for this amount, and they are both relatively small office areas. However, 5,962 square feet of net leasable area in the Exchange Plaza office complex, located across Cherry Ridge from the subject property, was recently rented on the basis of $0.80 per square foot per month. Also, the rentals quoted for the Conroy Square office building at 3355 Cherry Ridge is $0.80 per square foot per month and in other comparable existing office buildings in the northwest quarter of the City are currently quoting rents of $0.80 per square foot per month. This is also supported by the Canavan Center and many other building rentals analyzed. Thus, it is concluded that $0.80 per square foot per month is the prevailing market rental for the subject property.

After estimating the economic or prevailing rental for the subject property, the next step in the Income Approach is to estimate the typical vacancy and collection losses. This is a lump sum deduction usually made by investors, as properties very seldom live up to 100 percent of their expectations. Although the current vacancy in the appraised property is nil, and the vacancy experienced by 29 buildings in the northwest sector of the City is approximately one percent, it is estimated that a typical prudent investor would probably estimate that a reasonable expectation of vacancy and collection losses for the subject building is three percent, when considering the buildings under construction and the proposed office buildings in this area.

Thus the estimated economic rental for the subject property is $0.80 per square foot per month, which when multiplied times 24,389 square feet, is $234,134.00 per year. The vacancy and collection losses are estimated to be three percent of the gross income or $7,024 per year, leaving an effective gross income of $227,110.00.

The operating expenses have been estimated as typical based on an analysis of the past 12-month operating history of the appraised property as well as other known operating expenses for similar office buildings in this area in the files of your consultant. The taxes and insurance have been estimated as actual to be $14,864.00.

An explanation of how the income and expenses are developed, such as presented here, makes the appraisal report more convincing than it would be otherwise.

Professional management is typically five percent of the effective gross income for similar office buildings in this area. Maintenance is estimated to be $6,341.00 or approximately $0.26 per square foot per year per net leasable area. Cleaning and supplies are estimated to be $0.54 per square foot per year per net leasable area or $13,170.00. Utilities were estimated to be $1.15 per square foot per year per net leasable area or $28,047.00. Trash collection is $1,295.00; elevator contract, $565.00; air-conditioning maintenance, $1,452.00; and miscellaneous, $1,200.00 for a total operating expense of $78,290.00. This is $3.21 per square foot of net leasable area for 24,389 square feet. The previous 12-month ownership expenses were actually $78,138.00. When the total operating expenses are deducted from the effective gross income, the resulting net operating income is $148,820.00.

The appraised property has an existing mortgage loan with an approximate balance of $546,700.00, payable monthly in the amount of $5,354.00 including 9-1/4 percent annual interest for a remaining term of 16.79 years. This financing is extremely favorable in the current mortgage market. It is believed that a typical, prudent investor would take advantage of this favorable financing and purchase the property under the terms of the note subject to the outstanding balance. Thus, by utilizing a mortgage equity residual technique, the annual debt service of $64,248.00 is deducted from the net operating income of $148,820.00, resulting in a cash flow to equity amounting to $84,572.00.

ANALYSIS OF MARKET DERIVED CAPITALIZATION RATES

Your consultant has analyzed Comparable Sale Nos. Five, Six and Seven to develop overall capitalization rates and equity dividend rates indicated by these transfers. A summary of the calculations made is as follows:

Sale no. five:

Gross market income 34,309 SF NLA @ \$0.75 per SF × 12 =	\$308,781.00
Less vacancy and collection losses 3.0 percent	9,263.00
Effective gross income	\$299,518.00
Operating expenses 34,309 SF NLA @ \$3.20 per SF	109,789.00
Net operating income	\$189,729.00

Overall capitalization rate: (R_o)

$$\frac{\text{N.O.I.} \quad \$\ 189{,}729.00}{\text{Adjusted sales price} \quad \$1{,}850{,}000.00} = R_0\ .103$$

Equity dividend rate: (R_E)

$$\frac{\text{Cash flow to equity} \quad \$\ \ 65{,}238.00}{\text{Adjusted equity} \quad \$\ 865{,}000.00} = .075\ R_E$$

Investment

See page 456 for a summary of the annual debt service of each of the three sale-rental comparables. Do you agree with the above equity rate?

Cash flow to equity for Sale No. 5 is as follows:

	NOI	\$189,729
less	DS	124,491
=	CF	\$65,238

Note: 4,200 square feet is under lease with 16.59 years remaining at \$0.47 per square foot per month or \$5.64 per year; 30,109 square feet has an estimated economic rental of \$0.75 per square foot per month or \$9.00 per square foot per year. This is an average of \$8.58 per square foot per year or \$0.71 per square foot per month. The price paid was probably slightly influenced by a 12% interest mortgage with a balance of \$985,000.00 and a 13-year call having a balloon payment of \$789,866.00. However, the buyer's major concern was the lease terms.

If no adjustments are made for condition of sale, the indicated overall rate is 12.2% and the equity dividend rate is 11.5% based on market rental of \$0.75 per square foot per month. Considering the long term lease on the 4,200 square feet and using a contract rental of \$0.71 per square foot per month, the overall rate indicated is 10.0% and the equity dividend rate is 5.4%.

Sale no. six:

Gross market income 33,838 SF NLA @ \$0.80 per SF × 12 =	\$324,845.00
Less vacancy and collection losses 3 percent	9,745.00
Effective gross income	315,100.00
Operating expenses (33,838 SF NLA @ \$3.20 per SF)	108,282.00
Net operating income	\$206,818.00

Overall capitalization rate: (R_0)

$$\frac{\text{N.O.I.}}{\text{S.P.}} \quad \frac{\$\ 206{,}818.00}{\$2{,}190{,}000.00} = .094\ R_0$$

Equity dividend rate (R_E)

$$\frac{\text{Cash flow to equity}}{\text{Equity investment}} \quad \frac{\$\ \ 89{,}518.00}{\$1{,}060{,}000.00} = .084\ R_E$$

Sale no. seven:

Gross market income 41,811 SF NLA @ \$0.80 per SF × 12	\$401,386.00
Less vacancy and collection losses 3 percent	12,042.00
Effective gross income	389,344.00
Operating expenses 41,811 per SF NLA @ \$3.20 per SF	133,795.00
Net operating income	\$255,549.00

Overall capitalization rate: (R_0)

$$\frac{\text{N.O.I.}}{\text{S.P.}} \quad \frac{\$\ 255{,}549.00}{\$2{,}635{,}000.00} = .097\ R_0$$

Equity dividend rate (R_E)

$$\frac{\text{Cash flow to equity}}{\text{Equity investment}} \quad \frac{\$\ 110{,}541.00}{\$1{,}287{,}315.00} = .086\ R_E$$

Sale Nos. Five, Six, and Seven indicate a very tight pattern of equity dividend rates of 7.5 percent, 8.4 percent and 8.6 percent. Less weight is given Sale No. Five because of the necessity of adjusting for condition of the sale. It is concluded that a reasonable estimate of the equity dividend rate for the subject property is 8.5 percent. An analysis of the sales indicated overall capitalization rates of 10.3 percent, 9.4 percent and 9.7 percent. For the same reasons, it is concluded that a reasonable estimate of the overall capitalization rate for the subject property is 9.5 percent. Thus, cash flow to the equity position of \$84,572.00 is capitalized at the equity dividend rate of 8.5 percent. The resulting indication of value for the equity is $994,965.00. When the mortgage loan balance of $546,700.00 is added to the value of the equity, the resulting value is $1,541,700.00 when rounded.

> Capitalization rates and resulting values cannot be convincingly developed without evidence from such analysis as shown on pages 465–467. This is not to say that there are not other means of developing capitalization rates. (See, for example, Chapters 9–12.) It is inexcusable for an appraiser to use an unsubstantiated capitalization rate.

If the net operating income of $148,820.00 is capitalized at the overall capitalization rate of 9.5 percent, the resulting indication of value for the subject property is $1,566,000.00 when rounded.

The range in value indicated by the Income Approach using direct capitalization is from $1,541,665.00 which is rounded to $1,541,700.00 to $1,566,526.00 which is rounded to $1,566,500.00. A summary of the calculations utilizing direct capitalization follows:

Gross income:	
NLA 24,389 sq. ft. @ $0.80 per sq. ft. × 12 mos.	$ 234,134
Less vacancy and collection losses (3%)	7,024
Effective gross income	$ 227,110

> Expressing operating expenses on the basis of cost per net leasable area provides a convenient means to compare these expenses to published expenses for similar properties.

> DISCUSS IN CLASS: What are the relative merits of including or excluding replacement reserves as part of the operating expenses?

Operating expenses:		
Fixed expenses—		
Taxes ($0.57 NLA)	$13,855	
Insurance ($0.04 NLA)	1,009	
		$14,864

Variable expenses—			
Management (5%)	$11,356		
Maintenance ($0.26 NLA)	6,341		
Cleaning & supplies ($0.54 NLA)	13,170		
Utilities ($1.15 NLA)	28,047		
Trash Collection ($0.053 NLA)	1,295		
Elevator ($0.023 NLA)	565		
Air conditioning maintenance ($0.06 NLA)	1,452		
Miscellaneous ($0.049 NLA)	1,200		
		$63,426	
Total operating expenses ($3.21 per sq. ft. NLA)			78,290
Net operating income			$ 148,820
Value Subject to Existing Mortgage:			
Mortgage balance $546,700 @ .1175 R_m			64,237
Cash flow to equity			$ 84,583
Capitalized @ 0.085 R_E			995,091
Add mortgage balance			546,700
The value indicated by the income approach subject to the existing mortgage			$1,541,791
		Rounded to:	$1,541,800
Net Operating Income capitalized @ 0.095			$148,820
The value indicated by the income approach using direct capitalization			$1,566,526
		Rounded to:	$1,566,500

What is your opinion of the influence of existing financing on the value of the appraised property?

RECONCILIATION OF VALUE INDICATIONS FEE SIMPLE TITLE SUBJECT TO EXISTING FINANCING

What is the purpose of the "Reconciliation of Value Indications" section?

Is this purpose adequately handled in this appraisal report? Justify your answer based on Chapter 19.

The value indicated by each of the approaches used for the mortgaged fee simple title to The La Plaza Office Building property is as follows:

The Value Indicated by the Cost Approach	$1,670,000.00
The Value Indicated by the Market Data Approach	$1,544,000.00 to $1,561,000.00
The Value Indicated by the Income Approach	$1,541,800.00 to $1,566,500.00

Two of the three approaches to value indicate a very narrow value range for the appraised property, between $1,544,000.00 and $1,566,500.00.

The Cost Approach is considered to be persuasive because the improvements are only eight years old and are in average to good condition. There is very little deferred maintenance indicated, little functional and no economic obsolescence present. Also, there is very good support for the estimate of the value of the site as if vacant. However, the estimate of developer's profit does not tend to be well supported by the market as evidenced by an analysis of the comparable sales. Also, in the Cost Approach, the premium for the favorable mortgage must be estimated directly. In the other two approaches, the value of the favorable mortgage is reflected in the analysis of the comparable sales, which have similar mortgages.

The Market Data Approach is particularly persuasive because Sale Nos. Six and Seven are comparable to the appraised property from a physical as well as an economic standpoint. Sale No. Five is located directly across Cherry Ridge from the subject property. It is not considered to be as persuasive because of the rental of 4,200 square feet of net leasable area on a long-term lease below prevailing market rentals. For this reason, this sale was adjusted upward for condition of sale.

The Income Approach is considered to be extremely persuasive. Only one year's history of income and expenses on the appraised property was available for analysis. However, the historical income and expenses are well supported by an analysis of many comparable properties. The forecast for the next 12-month period is very close to the previous 12-month experience and both are considered to be reasonable and well supported by market evidence. Also, the overall rates and factors derived from an analysis of the comparable sales indicate a tight range and consistent pattern. The value range utilizing market derived rates and direct capitalization is between $1,541,800.00 and $1,566,500.00.

After careful consideration of the values indicated by each of the approaches utilized, it is the considered judgment of your consultant that the Market Value of the fee simple title to The La Plaza Office Building property, subject to existing financing and the limiting conditions herein stated as of the current date, March 1, 1981, was:

ONE MILLION FIVE HUNDRED SIXTY THOUSAND DOLLARS ($1,560,000.00).

VALUE OF THE LEASED FEE ESTATE

According to Chapter 18, what is a leased fee estate?

Rent loss occurs when market rent is greater than contract rent.

See Chapter 18, the section entitled "Partial Interests in Real Property" for discussion and examples of estimating the value of a leased fee estate.

Estimated by Present Value of Rent Losses:

The leases in the subject office building currently vary from one month in duration to 4.59 years. They are at various rents from the current estimated economic rental of $0.80 per square foot per month to as low as a base rental of $0.55 per square foot per month.

By estimating the economic rental or prevailing market rental to increase at the inflationary rate of 7-1/2% per year compounded for the next five years and starting with $0.80 per square foot per month as a prevailing market rental, it is possible to calculate the rent loss as a result of the current leases. It is assumed that each of the office spaces will be rented at the prevailing market rental at the time the leases expire.

The total net rent losses for the first year are calculated to be $28,801.00; for the second year, $22,522.00; for the third year, $17,847.00; for the fourth year, $16,873.00; and for the fifth year, $8,865.00.

Real estate investors interviewed have indicated that they would require at least a 17% return on a short term income stream. If these rental losses are discounted at a 17% annual yield rate, the resulting total present value of the rent losses is $65,260.00, say $65,000.00. At a 20% annual yield rate, the present value of the rent losses is $61,668.00, which is rounded to $62,000.00.

Money market certificates have varied in the past few months from a low of 13-1/2% to a high of approximately 16-1/2% and are currently yielding in the vicinity of 14-1/2% to 15-1/2%. Considering these facts, it is the judgment of your consultant that a reasonable yield rate that an investor would typically expect for capital invested in the subject property is 17% to 20% annually. The calculations pertaining to the rent losses are shown on the following table.

> DISCUSS IN CLASS: Should the rent loss be discounted before or after deducting operating expenses? If so, should fixed or variable expenses be deducted? Are there other expense deductions?

The present value of these rent losses is calculated below:

Year	*Net rent loss*	*17% Present value factor*	*Present value*	*20% Present value factor*	*Present value*
1	$28,801	.8547	$24,616	.8333	$24,000
2	$22,522	.7305	$16,453	.6944	$15,639
3	$17,847	.6244	$11,143	.5787	$10,328
4	$16,873	.5337	$ 9,005	.4823	$ 8,138
5	$ 8,865	.4561	$ 4,043	.4019	$ 3,563
Total rent loss			$65,260		$61,668
rounded to			$65,000		$62,000

This rent loss to the owner is a rent advantage to the various tenants. This tends to indicate the value of the Leased Fee Estate to be as shown on page 474 of this report. A chart showing the calculation of the rent loss is on page 473 of this report.

Gross Rent Loss Calculations as of March 1, 1981

Office Number	*Tenant*	*SF/Area*	*Lease expiration*	*% of year remaining in lease*	*1st year rent loss*	*2nd year rent loss*	*3rd year rent loss*	*4th year rent loss*	*5th year rent loss*
100	Chevron Oil	4,967	1-31-82	.92	$9,870	$0	$0	$0	$0
101	Ray Rendcn Insurance	303	6-30-83	2.33	545	764	324	0	0
103	Texas Medical Foundation	103	12-31-81	.84	52	0	0	0	0
111	Standard Register	296	1-31-82	.92	588	0	0	0	0
120	R.C. Bender & Associates	2,087	12-31-81	.84	1,052	0	0	0	0
123	Associated Beauty	219	4-30-81	.16	63	0	0	0	0
131	Gene Wilson, App.	250	2-1-82	.92	0	0	0	0	0
133–36	Dictaphone Corporation	3,009	6-30-83	2.33	7,583	9,749	3,932	0	0
135F	Neil Johnson	300	3-1-81	0	0	0	0	0	0
202	4-6's, Tim Collins	632.7	mo-to-mo	0	0	0	0	0	0
203	Tribble & Stephens	1,848	5-31-81	.25	832	0	0	0	0
205	Bill Shannon, Inc.	462	5-14-81	.20	166	0	0	0	0
210	W.F. Lackey & Associates	450	mo-to-mo	0	0	0	0	0	0
212	Marriage License Lab	300	5-31-81	.25	135	0	0	0	0
215	Mohawk Data Sciences	1,927	3-31-81	.08	314	0	0	0	0
230	McCarty, Thompson	5,450	9-30-85	4.59	14,061	17,985	21,909	26,487	18,714
219	Ezequiel Garcia, CPA	611	7-31-83	2.42	880	1,320	739	0	0
216	Harvey Olsen	1,000	11-30-82	1.75	1,200	1,440	0	0	0
Total rent losses					$37,341	$31,258	$26,904	$26,487	$18,714

The net rent loss is the difference between the estimated net operating income and the actual net operating income expected to be received.

Net Rent Loss Calculations

Year	*NOI increasing @ 7.5% per year*	*Actual NOI*	*Net rent loss*
1	$148,820	$120,019	$28,801
2	$159,982	$137,460	$22,522
3	$171,980	$154,133	$17,847
4	$184,879	$168,006	$16,873
5	$198,744	$189,879	$ 8,865

Estimated Market Value of the Fee Simple Title	$1,560,000.00
Estimated Rent Advantage of the Various Tenants $62,000.00 to $65,000.00, say	$ 63,500.00
Estimated Market Value of the Leased Fee Estate	$1,496,500.00

> CLASS DISCUSSION: Does the tenant(s) enjoy a leasehold interest when the prevailing rent exceeds the amount of rent specified in the lease, even though subleasing of the leased quarters is prohibited by the lease?

Estimated by Present Value of Lessor's Benefits:

The Leased Fee Estate has the right to collect the contract rents plus the right to reversion of the offices at the end of the lease periods. The longest existing lease is four plus years so at the end of the fifth year, the property will be available to rent for market rental. As the leases terminate, it is assumed that the space will be leased for the prevailing market rental at that time.

Informed investors are keenly aware of the effect of inflation on real property ownership. They are cognizant of the government forecast for this year of an 11% plus inflationary rate. They are also conscious of the current efforts by government to curb this double digit inflationary rate. In this office market, both tenants and owners anticipate increasing rentals as well as operating costs. Local investors are predicting that both rent and expenses will increase at compounded rates of between 6% and 9% annually. Most investors contacted, who recently purchased office building properties, believe an estimate of 7% to 8% inflation rate is reasonable. For purposes of this analysis,

7.5% per year has been forecasted for estimating the operating expenses and the sixth year net operating income.

Because of the risk involved (the uncertainty of the forecast of both future cash flows and value) as well as the availability of alternative investments, most informed investors contacted require the prospects of equity yields to be in the vicinity of 17% to 20%. More liquid, more management and risk-free investments are currently available in the money and capital markets with yields approaching 15% to 17% before taxes. With the forecast of income and expenses increasing at the compounded rate of 7.5% per year, the consensus of the investors contacted was that they would require the anticipation of an equity yield of approximately 17% to 20% to be attracted to the subject property as an investment. For purposes of the analysis made, 17% and 20% have been utilized. A summary of the calculations made follows:

Calculating cash flow to equity:

Year	*Increasing @ 7.5% a year gross market Income*	*Gross rent loss*	*Actual gross income*	*5% management*	*Increasing @ 7.5% other operating expenses*	*Net operating income*	*Annual debt service*	*Equity cash flow*
1	$234,134	$37,341	$196,793	$ 9,840	$66,934	$120,019	$64,248	$ 55,771
2	$251,694	$31,258	$220,436	$11,022	$71,954	$137,460	$64,248	$ 73,212
3	$270,571	$26,904	$243,667	$12,183	$77,351	$154,133	$64,248	$ 89,885
4	$290,864	$26,487	$264,377	$13,219	$83,152	$168,006	$64,248	$103,758
5	$312,679	$18,714	$293,965	$14,698	$89,388	$189,879	$64,248	$125,631

Present value of equity:

Year	*Cash flow to equity*	*17% PVF*	*Present value*	*20% PVF*	*Present value*
1	$ 55,771	.8547	$ 47,668	.8333	$ 46,476
2	$ 73,212	.7305	$ 53,482	.6944	$ 50,842
3	$ 89,885	.6244	$ 56,122	.5787	$ 52,017
4	$103,758	.5337	$ 55,370	.4823	$ 50,038
5	$125,631	.4561	$ 57,302	.4019	$ 50,488
Present value of cash flow to equity			$269,944		$249,861

Reversion:

Gross market rent 6th year (1.075) = FVF 1.4356 × $.80 per S.F. per month × 12 = $13.78 per S.F. × 24,389 S.F. N.L.A. =	$ 336,130
Less vacancy and collection losses 3%	10,084
Effective gross income	$ 326,046
Operating expenses (1.075) = FVF 1.4356 × $78,290 =	112,395
Net Operating Income	$ 213,651
Capitalized @ 0.095 (R_0)	2,248,953
Less mortgage balance at end of 5th year	460,202
Future value of equity reversion	$1,788,751

> Does the 1.4356 FV factor relate to the rent received at the beginning or end of the sixth year?

Present value of reversion:

@ 17% PVF .4561 × $1,788,751		$ 815,869
Present value of cash flow to equity @ 17% yield		269,944
Present value of equity		$1,085,813
Present balance of mortgage		546,700
Present value of leased fee estate		$1,632,513
Discounted @ 17% yield	Rounded to	$1,633,000

Present value of reversion:

@ 20% PVF .4019 × $1,788,751		$ 718,859
Present value of cash flow to equity @ 20% yield		249,861
Present value of equity		$ 968,720
Present balance of mortgage		546,700
Present value of leased fee estate		$1,515,420
Discounted @ 20% yield	Rounded to	$1,515,000

The range in the value of the Leased Fee Estate estimated by discounting the lessor's benefits is $1,515,000.00 to $1,633,000.00 using 17% and 20% equity yield rates. Giving equal weight to the yield rates indicated, it is concluded that the indicated value of the Leased Fee Estate by this technique is $1,575,000.00.

> Explain the relationship between the leased fee and the fee simple value of this property.

Conclusion:

The value of the Leased Fee Estate estimated by the present value of the rent losses is $1,496,500.00. The value of this interest estimated by yield discounting of the lessor's benefits is $1,575,000.00. It is concluded that the estimated Market Value of the Leased Fee Estate as of the current date, March 1, 1981, was:

ONE MILLION FIVE HUNDRED THOUSAND DOLLARS ($1,500,000.00).

Respectfully submitted,

Scruggs Love, Jr., M.A.I.

According to Chapter 19, what is the purpose of the appraiser's certification?

CERTIFICATE

The undersigned does hereby certify that, except as otherwise noted in this appraisal report:

I have no present or contemplated future interest in the real estate that is the subject of this appraisal report.

I have no personal interest or bias with respect to the subject matter of this appraisal report or the parties involved.

To the best of my knowledge and belief the statements of fact contained in this appraisal report, upon which the analyses, opinions and conclusions expressed herein are based, are true and correct.

This appraisal report sets forth all of the limiting conditions (imposed by the terms of my assignment or by the undersigned) affecting the analyses, opinions and conclusions contained in this report.

This appraisal report has been made in conformity with and is subject to the requirements of the Code of Professional Ethics and Standards of Professional Conduct of the American Institute of Real Estate Appraisers of the National Association of Real Estate Boards.

No one other than the undersigned prepared the analyses, conclusions and opinions concerning real estate that are set forth in this appraisal report.

> Why would the appraiser include this paragraph that restricts the dissemination of the contents of the report?

Neither all nor any part of the contents of this report (especially any conclusions as to value, the identity of the appraiser or the firm with which he is connected, or any reference to the American Institute of Real Estate Appraisers or to the M.A.I. or R.M. designation) shall be disseminated to thc public through advertising media, public relations media, news media, sales media or any other public means of communication without the prior written consent and approval of the undersigned.

The American Institute of Real Estate Appraisers conducts a voluntary program of continuing education for its designated members. M.A.I.'s and R.M.'s who meet the minimum standards of this program are awarded periodic educational certification. Scruggs Love, Jr. is certified under this program through December 31, 1983.

____

San Antonio, Texas

> The purpose of this section is to show the client that the appraiser is qualified through education and experience to handle the appraisal assignment. It is recommended that a sample of the different classes of clients be included, as well as a summary of offices held in professional appraisal organizations. There is no justification for including positions held or honors received that have no bearing on the appraiser's professional competence.

QUALIFICATIONS OF ALBERT SCRUGGS LOVE, JR.

Presently, and since 1960, Albert Scruggs Love, Jr., is engaged in the general real estate consulting and appraisal practice. He is a partner in the firm of Love and Dugger, Real Estate Consultants and Appraisers, 802 Main Plaza Building, San Antonio, Texas 78205.

Appraisal assignments executed by him have been for banks, corporations, individuals, insurance companies, law firms, lending institutions and Realtors. During the time of his employment with the Texas Highway Department in Corpus Christi (1958–1960), his time was divided between reviewing, supervising and appraising real estate. Since that time, he has been exclusively engaged in the general practice of real estate appraising. His practice includes the appraisal of virtually all types of real property. Some of his clients include the following:

Alamo National Bank
Alamo Savings & Loan
Bexar County
City of San Antonio
City Public Service Board of San Antonio
Connecticut General Life Insurance Company
Corpus Christi National Bank
D. Ansley Company
Department of the Navy
Equitable Relocation
First International Bank in San Antonio
First National Bank of San Antonio
Frost National Bank
General Services Administration
Gill Companies
Gulf Oil Corporation
Internal Revenue Service
International Business Machines Corporation
Jefferson Standard Life Insurance Company
Merrill Lynch Relocation Management, Inc.
Mortgage Bankers of San Antonio
Mortgage Investment Corporation
Ramada Inns of America
Ray Ellison Industries
Rouse & Company
San Antonio Bank & Trust
San Antonio Conservation Society
San Antonio Development Agency
Southwestern Bell Telephone Company
Texas Savings and Loan Association
Texaco, Inc.
Texas Highway Departments: San Antonio, Pharr, Corpus Christi & San Antonio Districts
Trinity University
U.S. Postal Service
United Savings & Loan, Corpus Christi, Texas
Volkswagen Company of America
Western Electric Company
World Savings
Xerox Corporation

Generally, his trade includes South Texas including the San Antonio area, the Corpus Christi area and the lower Rio Grande Valley of Texas. Other appraisals have been made in West Texas, Arizona, New Mexico and Georgia.

His specified teaching experience includes "Real Estate Appraisal Principles," "Basic Valuation Procedures" and "Capitalization Theory & Techniques Part I, II and III" for the American Institute of Real Estate Appraisers. Other courses taught include Courses 101 and 201 for the Society of Real Estate Appraisers. Other teaching assignments include numerous workshops, seminars and courses for the Texas Association of Realtors.

His educational background includes Texas A & M University, College Station, Texas, from June, 1951 through May, 1952; Texas A & I University, Kingsville, Texas, BBA Degree, September, 1952 through May, 1955; and the University of Texas, Graduate School of Commerce, Austin, Texas with a major in Real Estate, September, 1957 through February, 1958.

Technical training in Real Estate includes Course I, American Institute of Real Estate Appraisers, 1958, Course II, American Institute of Real Estate Appraisers, 1959; Texas Highway Department, Course III, 1961; and Course IV, American Institute of Real Estate Appraisers, 1963 and Course VI, American Institute of Real Estate Appraisers, 1974.

Offices of nationally recognized professional appraisal associations include the following:

President, Chapter No. 65, Society of Real Estate Appraisers, 1968.
President, Chapter No. 29, American Institute of Real Estate Appraisers, 1974.

National Committee Assignments, American Institute of Real Estate Appraisers: Vice Chairman, Division of Curriculum, 1979, 1980 and 1981.

Elected member of the Governing Council, American Institute of Real Estate Appraisers, 1980, 1981, and 1982.

Professional Recognition Award, American Institute of Real Estate Appraisers.

Professional Affiliations include the following organizations:

Member, American Institute of Real Estate Appraisers, Certificate No. 3699
Senior Real Property Appraisers, Society of Real Estate Appraisers
Senior Member, American Society of Appraisers
Active Member, San Antonio Board of Realtors
Member, American Right-of-Way Association

CONTINGENT AND LIMITING CONDITIONS
(Unless Stated Otherwise in this Report)

The estimate of value for the property analyzed in the attached report is subject to the following limiting conditions:

The legal description furnished the appraisers is assumed to be correct. No responsibility is assumed for matters legal in character, nor is any opinion rendered as to title. Liens and encumbrances have been considered in the value reported and the property has been appraised on the basis of responsible ownership and competent management.

The boundaries of the land and the dimensions and size thereof as indicated to the appraisers are assumed to be correct, no provision having been made for a special survey of the property. Valuation is reported without regard to questions of encroachments.

The information contained in this report and identified as having been furnished by others is believed to be reliable, but no responsibility is assumed for its accuracy.

No responsibility is assumed, nor is any guarantee made as to the structural soundness of the improvements. The property is assumed to be free of insect infestation and dry rot.

Possession of this report or a copy thereof does not carry with it the right of publication, nor may it be used for any other purpose by any but the applicant without the previous written consent of the appraisers.

The appraisers, by reason of this report, are not required to give testimony or attendance in court or at any other hearing with reference to the property in question unless arrangements therefore have been previously made.

The distribution of the total valuation in this report between the land and the improvements applies only under the existing program of utilization. The separate valuations for land and improvements should not be used in conjunction with any other appraisal and are invalid if so used.*

The appraisers have no present or contemplated future interest in the property which is not specifically disclosed in this report. Neither their employment for making this analysis nor the fee to be received therefor are contingent upon the valuation placed on the property.

*The value reported in this report includes the value of the real property and the value of the existing favorable financing.

Did the appraiser disregard all liens and encumbrances in appraising this property? If not, explain the effect of these liens and encumbrances on the value of the property.

Would you have included any other limiting conditions in this appraisal? Explain.

ADDENDUM

PHOTOGRAPHS OF THE APPRAISED PROPERTY

Looking north from Cherry Ridge showing parking lot and front of La Plaza building

Looking northwest at the southwest side (rear) view of La Plaza building

View of east (rear) parking lot of appraised property looking northwest

Looking northeast across Cherry Ridge at the front of the La Plaza building

Looking southeast; taken from intersection of Cherry Ridge and Vantage looking at the northwest corner of the La Plaza building

Typical interior hall scene showing first floor corrider

Looking out of main entrance of La Plaza to the front parking lot. Stairway to second story on the right of photograph

A sales location map should be included in an appraisal report. It should show the location of the subject property and the comparable sale properties. The map can be made to look more professional by using dry transfer symbols rather than hand-drawn symbols.

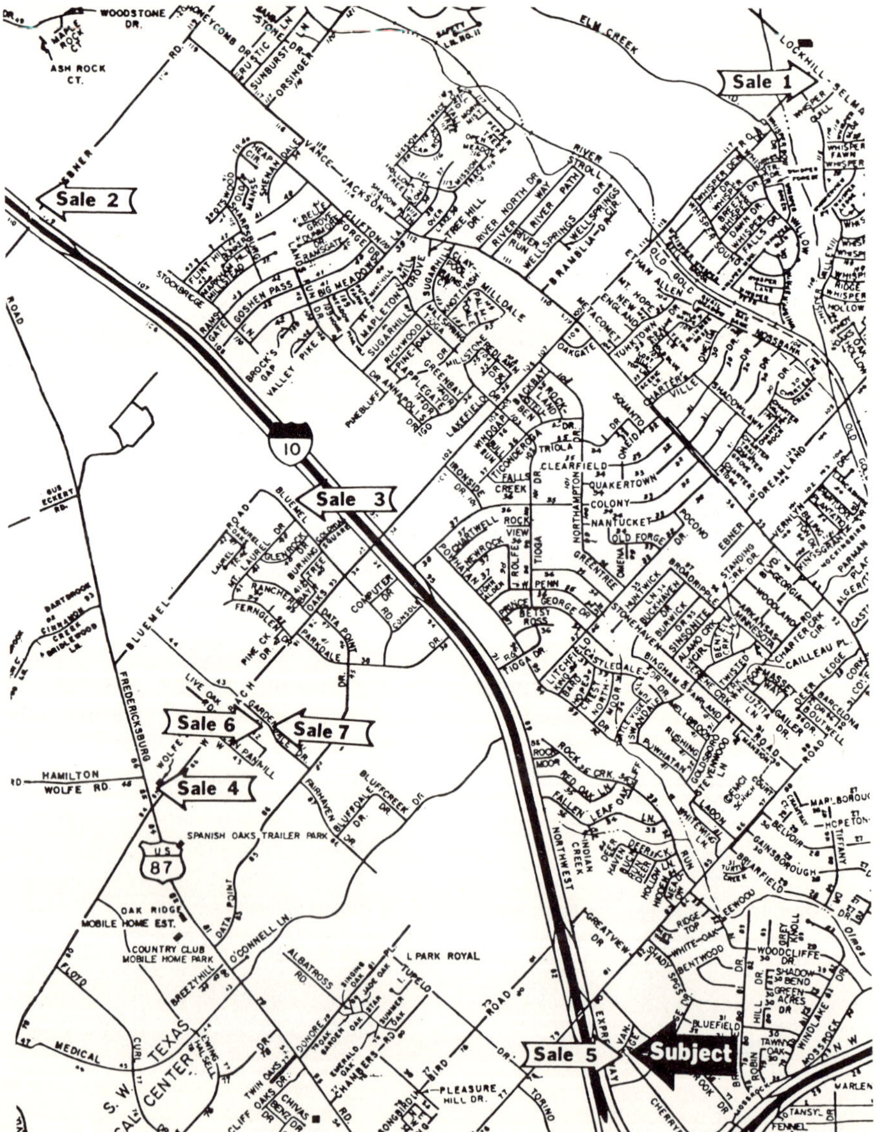

INDEX